The Kiss Sacred and Profane

Caressing Lovers. Codex Manesse. The large Heidelberg MS. Universitätsbibliothek, Heidelberg, Cod. pal. germ. 848, fol. 249ᵛ.

The Kiss
Sacred and
Profane

NICOLAS JAMES PERELLA

An Interpretative History of

Kiss Symbolism

and Related

Religio-Erotic Themes

UNIVERSITY OF CALIFORNIA PRESS

Berkeley and Los Angeles 1969

University of California Press, Berkeley and Los Angeles, California
University of California Press, Ltd., London, England
Copyright © 1969 by The Regents of the University of California
Library of Congress Catalog Card Number: 75–83292
Designed by Dave Comstock
Printed in the United States of America
SBN 520–01392–1

For Vivian

Acknowledgments

n part the research for this study was made possible by grants from the American Philosophical Society and The John Simon Guggenheim Memorial Foundation.

My thanks go out to all those who have contributed to this study in one way or another. They include Professors Louise G. Clubb, Gustavo Costa, John Polt, and Ruggero Stefanini. A particular sense of gratitude and obligation is felt toward Professors Charles S. Singleton, who first brought me to experience the richness of Dante and the Middle Ages, Arnolfo B. Ferruolo, who first brought the Italian Renaissance to life for me, Catherine Fehrer, who first introduced me to French literature, and Enrico de' Negri, who, after reading the first draft of my work, made suggestions which I consider invaluable.

I am pleased to acknowledge a debt to Mrs. Margaret D. Uridge and Mrs. Jeannot H. Nyles of the Interlibrary Borrowing Service of the University of California in Berkeley. A special thanks must go to Miss Karin Gerstung who carried out—with unfailing good humor—the seemingly impossible task of producing a typescript from my manuscript, to Mrs. Muriel Kittel for her able assistance in preparing the translations and index and in proofreading, and to Mrs. Diane Beck of the University Press for her many kindnesses during the editorial process. My greatest debt is to my wife, to whom this book is dedicated.

Contents

Illustrations follow page 116

Just so may love, although 'tis understood
The mere commingling of passionate breath,
Produce more than our searching witnesseth:
What I know not: but who, of men, can tell
That flowers would bloom, or that green fruit would swell
To melting pulp, that fish would have bright mail,
The earth its dower of river, wood, and vale,
The meadows runnels, runnels pebblestones,
The seed its harvest, or the lute its tones,
Tones ravishment, or ravishment its sweet,
If human souls did never kiss and greet.

John Keats, *Endymion*, I, 832–842

Introduction

ove's wealthy croppe of kisses" (to borrow a line from Ben Jonson) is far too great to be harvested and winnowed by a single toiler in that rich field. Hence the present work is not a treatise on the varieties of the genus *kiss* through the ages and in different climes, but rather an essay on some aspects of the use of the kiss as a religio-erotic symbol in the West.[1] But even this limited purpose requires that at the outset we at least touch on the difficult question of origins. Anthropologists, physiologists, and psychologists who have concerned themselves with the problem have put forth the theory that the kiss may very well be a vestigial remainder or a carry-over of a primitive habit of eating and thereby assimilating into the self any object felt to be "good" or desirable. If this is so, then it is all the more curious and significant that the labial kiss, which is so much taken for granted in Western societies, is not at all a universally practiced custom, for it was unknown to the majority of primitive peoples as well as to large segments of Asiatic cultures until introduced into them by Westerners. In 1897 the French anthropologist Paul d'Enjoy pointed out that the Chinese felt a kind of horror, as at some cannibalistic act, when confronted with the Western custom of mouth-to-mouth kissing. It was d'Enjoy's view that the basic elements or activities connected with the European kiss are biting and sucking.[2] This relationship seems to have occurred to Sigmund Freud, who apparently, however, did not suspect its full anthropophagous implications. Discussing the preliminary and excitatory sexual activities, he wrote: "The kiss between the mucous membrane of the lips of two people is held in high esteem among many nations, *in spite of the fact* that the parts of the body involved do not form part of the sexual apparatus but constitute the entrance to the digestive tract."[3] From such an observation one is inclined to think that Freud himself found the erotic kiss somewhat distasteful.

Without doubt the senses that are brought into active play during the kiss point to a connection with eating. When Havelock Ellis noted that "manifestations resembling the kiss, whether with the object of expressing affection or sexual emotion, are found among various ani-

1

mals much lower than man" (from snails to birds and dogs), he affirmed that "as practiced by man, the kiss involves mainly either the sense of touch or that of smell."[4] On the link between the tactile kiss and eating, Ellis quoted the Italian psychologist Mantegazza to the effect that "the affectionate child not only applies inanimate objects to its lips or tongue, but of its own impulse licks the people it likes." But it is not possible to accept his view that "there seems little evidence to show that the kiss contains any gustatory element in the strict sense." For one thing, such an assertion betrays an utter disregard for or skepticism toward the testimony of love poetry since the time of the Song of Songs and earlier. The innumerable references of poets to taste imagery (the most common allusion is to honey, which is both sweet and nutritious) in the matter of their ladies' kisses constitute an eloquent proof, even after we have made allowances for poetic fancy and the fact that the tactile sensations involved in lovers' kisses are sometimes overwhelming in themselves. Where the gustatory sensations are more apt to be in evidence is in the passionate buccolingual kiss in which the tongue plays an active part. In the Song of Songs (4:11) we read: "Thy lips drip as the honeycomb, my spouse: / Honey and milk are under thy tongue."

Long before the Song, in a Babylonian hymn (c. 1600 B.C.) inviting devotees to join in the praise of Ishtar, there occurs the theme of honey or sweetness on the lips, and, of even more significance, the idea that life itself resides in the mouth of this most august of goddesses, who is referred to also as the queen of heaven or of the gods:

> Praise the goddess, the most awesome of the goddesses.
>
> .   .   .   .
>
> Ishtar is clothed with pleasure and love.
> She is laden with vitality, charm, and voluptuousness.
> In lips she is sweet; life is in her mouth.[5]

The deep-rooted biological association between the kiss and eating was confirmed by Robert Briffault. In his monumental work *The Mothers*, he observes that "among the ancient Egyptians the word which is translated by Egyptologists as 'to kiss' meant 'to eat,'" and he suggests that "the desire expressed by lovers to 'eat' the object of their affection probably contains more sinister biological reminiscences than they are aware."[6] Corroboration of the ideas of d'Enjoy and Briffault is to be found in the observations made by Bronislaw Malinowski concerning the natives of North-Western Melanesia. Malinow-ski notes that although the kiss (European style) is not used in Tro-briand lovemaking as preliminary erotic play, there is very active mouth play. Besides nose-rubbing there is mouth-rubbing. "Gradually the caress becomes more passionate, and then the mouth is predomin-ately active; the tongue is sucked, and tongue is rubbed against tongue; they [the lovers] suck each other's lower lips, and the lips will be bitten till blood comes; the saliva is allowed to flow from mouth to mouth. . . . In the formulae of love magic, which here as elsewhere abound in over-graphic exaggeration, the expressions, 'drink my blood' and 'pull my hair' are frequently used."[7]

Support for the views of the anthropologists can be had from what may at first seem an unlikely or rather a surprising source. In the sev-enteenth century, the influential French bishop of Meaux, Jacques Bénigne Bossuet, writing of the Eucharistic communion in which the Christian believer "eats" of the Body of Jesus Christ, went as far as one can go in equating the act of loving, sexually or spiritually, with the desire to eat and incorporate the beloved:

> In the ecstasy of human love, who is unaware that we eat and devour each other, that we long to become part of each other in every way, and, as the poet said, to carry off even with our teeth the thing we love in order to possess it, feed upon it, become one with it, live on it? That which is frenzy, that which is impotence in corporeal love is truth, is wisdom in the love of Jesus: "Take, eat, this is my body": devour, swallow up not a part, not a piece but the whole.[8]

The fact that Bossuet maintains that the effort of human lovers to effect a corporeal assimilation of one another is hopeless does not keep him from considering that their desire to do so is real.

But the poet referred to by Bossuet is, if I am not mistaken, Lucretius; and it is worthwhile to recall the passage to which the French bishop seems to have been alluding. In his *De rerum natura* (IV, 1073–1120) where the Roman poet vividly depicted the rage of lovers during copulation, he first noted that in eating, one takes in and assimilates a desired object, an act which brings appeasement. In the sexual embrace, on the other hand, lovers can only make a grotesque and vain effort at such incorporation. The striving, interlaced bodies and the joining of mouths, the furious mixture of saliva and the biting of lips, all this is as futile as it is indecorous.[9] Yet it is a fact that what Lucretius declared to be an impossibility and a madness, many lovers have claimed to know by experience and have praised as the highest bliss—the sensation of a union or merging of two into one, a subject of which this study will have much to say.

Perhaps the view that contrasts most dramatically with Lucretius' picture is to be found in the blissful calm of the enlaced and kissing *mithuna* couples of Indian temples. Concerning such *mithunas* of the temples of Khajuraho and Konaraka, Radhakamal Mukerjee writes as follows: "In the most ardent kiss there are not only mutual psychological rapport and exchange which Vatsyayana [author of the Kamasutra] commended as the soul and art of love, but there are also detachment and poise symbolised by the closure of eye-lids or the omission of eye-balls and the serene inflection of the intertwined bodies of the lovers."[10] The lovers of these Indian sculptures are often meant to recall and sometimes to represent directly the archetypal gods Shiva and Shakti, the separated male and female principles of an original primordial Absolute and Unity; their embrace and kiss indicate the need and the effecting of their reintegration. A famous relief of an embracing and kissing couple of the rock-cut temple of Kailasa at Elura (eighth century A.D.) depicts just such a reintegration or conjunction of opposites in the figures of Shiva and Shakti (Fig. 1).

We may also note here that there is in the mystical Sahajîjâ cult a ritual in which, at the stage of mystic meditation (*dhyana*), the disciple kisses a woman sitting on his left, "in such a way that the spirit is inbreathed," as the text says, according to Mircea Eliade.[11] (The disciple, of course, must seek to reunite the principles of opposites in himself.) The concept of breath plays a great part in Indian philosophy, and given the fact that among the contrasting pairs that have to be reintegrated are the two "breaths" *prana* and *apana*, the kiss that Shiva and Shakti exchange (as in the Elura temple which embodies Tantric Hinduism) is of cosmic and "spiritual" import.

Thus the kiss—especially when, as in much Indian iconography, it implies the intermingling of breaths—is at the same time more than "the mere commingling of passionate breath"; it is indeed a dramatic symbol of a reintegration, of a transcending of dualism. Its principal effect or felt value is then fusional. It is true that this idea of a fusion or union of two in one is also symbolized or even ritualized by sexual union, as is suggested even in Genesis 2:24 and reaffirmed by Jesus in Matthew 19:5 ("And the two will become one flesh"). The kiss, however, has the advantage—whatever its origins—of expressing the concept with or without erotic overtones and, in either case, of doing so *spiritually*. This is owing to the unique value associated with the idea of breath. Without doubt, water, wine, blood, and the phallus (with its seed) are great and pervasive symbols of the life force which is felt as deriving ultimately from the deity. But equally, if not more, basic and pervasive than these is the idea of breath or spirit (*pneuma*), which is the reality most immediately connected with the idea of biological and "spiritual" life. It is also the notion that lends itself most readily to the concept of the possibility of communion and union between two human creatures as well as between man and the source of life. Perhaps more than any of the other great symbols and realities of life, it has figured prominently not only in purely religious thought and ceremony, but in philosophical speculation as well. Besides the importance of breath in Indian speculation, one need only think of the Stoic concept of the World Soul, *anima mundi*, and of the Holy Breath that is one of the Persons and *trait d'union*, the very osculant, as we shall see, of the Christian Triune God. Here we may also recall the biblical narration (Gen. 2:7) of the creation of man by a God who *infused* the *spirit of life* into his creature by breathing into him. A twelfth century mosaic in the splendid cathedral at Monreale—some five miles from the heart of Palermo—portrays the Creator infusing the life-spirit into man by way of the mouth. Though the figures are not touching one another, the line indicating the transmitting of the spirit goes from mouth to mouth (Fig. 3).[12] Or we may think of the passage from Virgil's *Aeneid* (VI, 11 ff.) where it is said of the sibyl that the god Apollo "breathed into her a great mind and soul." And in the *Symposium* (179) Plato speaks of "that courage which, as Homer says, the god breathes into the souls of some heroes, Love of his own nature infuses into the lover." At this point, then, we are led to consider with sympathy that theory which holds that the kiss has its origins in the magical idea of the infusion of a power or the exchange or union of "spirits" or "souls" carried by or even identified with breath and, sometimes, with saliva. This theory would fit both the mouth-to-mouth kiss and the "nose-kiss" (or "sniff-kiss"), if we may be allowed to speak of the latter as a kiss. Such a theory does not necessarily exclude all anthropophagous associations.

Long ago the German experimental psychologist Wilhelm Wundt made the connection between the ceremony of the bond of brotherhood through the mingling of two men's blood, and that of a kiss by which spittle or breath, as transmitters of the life-force or the blood-soul, is exchanged and mixed. At the same time Wundt suggested that the kiss between man and woman might have its origin in the idea that an exchange or mixture of breath (i.e., breath-soul) played a role in the act of procreation.[13] In support of this theory, he pointed to a pre-Columbian Mexican picture illustrating the copulation of a pair of deities or the first human couple. The two figures, facing one another, are kneeling each on one leg with the other leg extended so that contact is made by their feet. Each holds one arm akimbo while the one holds the other's second arm by the wrist. But the most striking feature of the scene is the way the couple is joined mouth to mouth by what is evidently a breath symbol which is red-colored, perhaps in token of the old idea of the blood-soul. This is clearly indicative of a "kiss" by which the pair intermingle their life-forces or souls (Fig. 2).[14] Something similar may be observed in a fragment of a Phoenician clay tablet in Madrid. Here a human couple stand facing one another in what is surely a copulation scene despite the fact that the two are covered from the waist down. The sperm of the man issues in a spiral as an extension of the penis and makes contact with the woman. It is shown being nourished by the milk spurting from the woman's uncovered bosom. As in the pre-Columbian picture, here too a breath symbol (though saliva could be intended) joins the couple mouth to mouth, suggesting the intermingling of the pair in a kiss that figures also as part of the procreational process.[15]

When, in his study *The Belief in Immortality and the Worship of the Dead*, James Frazer adduced proof for the idea of the soul as a breath among the Maoris of New Zealand, he drew upon an early nineteenth century account of a French traveler who sought an explanation for the Maori form of salutation of rubbing noses together. "The French traveller," wrote Frazer, "was told that the real intention of this salute was to mingle the breath and thereby the souls of the persons who gave each other this token of friendship."[16] At the turn of the present century, this same French traveler was referred to by Christopher Nyrop, who made the following comment in connection with the "nose-kiss" as practiced among the natives of Madagascar: "It always excites the merriment of Europeans, and yet it has its origin in an extremely refined idea. The invisible air which is continually being breathed through the lips is to savages, not only, as with us, a sign of life, but it is also an emanation of the soul—its perfume, as they themselves say—and, when they mingle and suck in each other's breath and odour, they think they are actually mingling their souls."[17] It is curious, I think, that Nyrop should have thought this to be an idea peculiar to savages, although he recognized it to be a "refined idea," for the idea that souls can migrate or mingle in a kiss has a long and distinguished history in the literature of the West. Indeed, to judge from its antiquity and its popularity down to our own times, the erotic conceit of the soul-in-the-kiss, or the fusion of two in one in a kiss, must be considered one of the greatest commonplaces of amatory literature. Like so many of the philosophico-literary and religio-erotic conceits in our culture, this too may be found in that fountainhead of Western civilization, Plato, although it would be sought for in vain among his philosophical writings. Rather it occurs in a distich, attributed to the philosopher, that has come down to us in the *Greek Anthology* (V, 78) and in Diogenes Laertius' *Lives*. It goes like this:

> My soul was on my lips as I was kissing Agathon.
> Poor soul! she came hoping to cross over to him.[18]

This engaging image has not gone completely unnoticed by scholars. In 1924 it was taken up by Stephen Gaselee, an eminent student of classical literature, in a short article which traced its fortune well in pagan antiquity, but beyond that became sketchy and failed to see the true extent and importance of the conceit.[19] Although Gaselee's study dispenses us from tracing the soul-in-the-kiss conceit in pagan antiquity (chiefly Greek), it will be well to record here the chief examples that figure in his article. Following the Platonic epigram, the earliest and perhaps one of the most significant uses of the conceit occurs in Bion's *Lament for Adonis* (I, 45). Gaselee's own version reads:

> Adonis, wake and give
> Me one last kiss
> Long as a kiss may live,
> Until in this
> Kissing, thy spirit do
> From body part,
> And breathed be unto
> My lips and heart.

This I think one of the most important early examples of the image because it was to be echoed by Renaissance poets in similar scenes.

7

Another interesting feature of it is that, despite its erotic overtones, the conceit as it appears here seems related to a primitive idea that it is possible for a survivor to catch up the departing life-spirit or soul of a dying relative by a kiss. This custom was known to the Romans.[20]

To return to Gaselee's examples of the kiss conceit, worth quoting is the one by Dio Chrysostom's pupil, the philosopher Favorinus of Arles (c. A.D. 85–150). The source is a fragment reproduced by the grammarian Stobaeus: "At what else does that touching of lips aim but at a junction of souls? They would out-pass the body, if they could, and, as it is, they seem to strain earnestly at the bodily barrier as at a door." Here, I believe, one can catch a Lucretian echo. Gaselee's other references to Greek writers are to Meleager of Gadara (first century B.C.) in the *Anthologia Palatina*, V, 171; Achilles Tatius (end of the third century A.D.); and Aristaenetus (fourth century A.D.). Examples from Latin literature, namely, Petronius and Aulus Gellius, will be given later in the course of this study. Of the twenty-five examples given by Gaselee in all, only seven are from the Renaissance period: a brief epigram by Robert Herrick in imitation of the original Platonic distich; a fleeting reminiscence of the conceit in John Donne's verse epistle "To Sir Henry Wotton, Knight"; the famous exclamation of Christopher Marlowe's Faustus to the vision of Helen; two Latin poems by the fifteenth century poet-humanists Giovanni Pontano and Angelo Poliziano; and a poem by Voiture. The seventh, for which no source is given, is a Latin quote said by Gaselee to be by the "famous Renaissance physician Balthasar Castilio [sic]": "Animus conjungitur et spiritus etiam noster per osculum effluit; alternatim se in utriusque corpus infundentes commiscent: animae potius quam corporis connexio."[a] Gaselee's attribution represents a curious error indeed, for this passage is nothing less than a Latin translation or paraphrase of a part of a famous page from one of the best-known works of the Renaissance, Baldassare Castiglione's *Book of the Courtier*. The passage appears, exactly as Gaselee quoted it, in the marginal notes of another famous Renaissance work, Robert Burton's *The Anatomy of Melancholy*, where Castiglione's name is indeed written as Balthasar Castilio.[21] The ten or so modern examples of the image supplied by Gaselee are randomly culled and range from Shelley's imitation of Plato's epi-

---

[a] "The breath is joined and even our spirit flows out through the kiss; they mingle together, pouring into one another's bodies in turn: it is a joining more of the soul than of the body."

gram to a passage from the novelist John Galsworthy. In short, Gaselee's article was meant as a series of marginal annotations on the Platonic distich, so that E. R. Curtius' statement that it traces the influence and the imitations of Plato's epigram through world literature is somewhat misleading.[22]

Besides Gaselee's brief study, the only other significant notice given to the Platonic epigram as such, as far as I know, is to be found in two scholarly books by James Hutton dealing with the influence of the *Greek Anthology* in France and Italy down to the year 1800.[23] But even Hutton's listings of examples of the image, which are themselves quite limited, include several cases of mere mention or translation of the original epigram or one of its early imitations; they do not give a just or critical appraisal of the scope and significance of the conceit in European literature. Here it should be pointed out that the Platonic epigram did not come to play an important role in the diffusion of the soul-kiss image until the Renaissance period. Until then the image, as we will be tracing it through the centuries, owed nothing to Plato's distich, which, for all its importance and antiquity, cannot be referred to as the ultimate source of the soul-in-the-kiss conceit. Hence, the chief shortcoming of the studies by Gaselee and Hutton, from our point of view, is the total absence of any mention whatsoever of early and medieval Christian literature as well as of the medieval romance and lyric; but even more surprising is their failure to note the image in the writings of the Renaissance Neoplatonists. Yet it is in these areas (and in the Renaissance poets) that the richest development—the "history," we may say—of the image is to be noted. A major, though not the sole, purpose of the present study is to follow the employment of the image from early Christianity through the Renaissance writers, giving attention to the contexts—sacred and profane—in which the conceit is used, the function it is made to serve, and the modifications it undergoes. I have given some consideration to a few other amatory conceits which tended to accompany and sometimes even derive from the kiss conceit. The most important of these are the migration and exchange of the souls or hearts of lovers; the union and transformation of lovers into one another; the metaphorical "death" and subsequent resuscitation (or "new life") of lovers in the beloved; the oneness of lovers unto and beyond the grave, that is, the love-death. In both the sacred and the profane traditions such themes are most often found separately, each having its own particular and noteworthy history.

Here, however, I am concerned with them primarily insofar as they illuminate or are directly associated with the central image of the soul kiss.

Because the present study is a history—the history of a number of religio-erotic themes—it has something of an encyclopedic range. But I trust it will become clear that my effort has not been to compile a cold academic catalogue. The soul kiss and other amatory *topoi* that are dealt with herein have served as much as anything to supply me with a key to essay explanations on topics that vary from theological exegesis and mystical allegory to the love lyric of the troubadours, the great love legends of the Middle Ages, and Dante; from the Renaissance concept of Platonic love to a number of Renaissance-Baroque poets. In this sense I have sought, in the presentation of the large amount of material, to build up a meaningful process of stratification, as it were, leading to a step-by-step, concrete interpretation of texts. Hopefully, this process functions to create progressively a cultural context within which each successive passage studied finds its place and is illuminated. For example, in my reading of Dante, what is set forth as the summarizing and definitive word on the medieval attitude to the various amatory conceits and the concept of love they imply presupposes much if not all that precedes it as an historico-cultural perspective.

There remains the question of the specific context of the works from which I have drawn my passages. Obviously it could not be my intention to deal with all aspects of those works nor even to attempt a full treatment of the love doctrines they expound overtly or covertly. Some time ago a writer on the story of the evolution of love, in a brief but nonetheless ecstatic excursus on the kiss, exclaimed: "Wonderful pilgrimage of this old Proteus! Through all heavens and through all hells. Through all loves! The whole history of human love-life could be demonstrated by the kiss alone; it is like a colossal knot therein, and if this knot alone were undone, all the strands in human love would be shown at the same time."[24] But that is almost all that Wilhelm Bölsche had to say about the kiss in the 1124 pages of a tome bearing the title *Love-Life in Nature*. I trust I have not given cause to be charged with the opposite excess, that is, of having paid so much attention to kisses as to forget love. Yet I have certainly not aimed at giving a total history of love *sub specie osculi*. Bölsche's call is alluring, but to heed it absolutely would most certainly prove fatal; hence I am glad it came to me only after I had finished my own book. Needless to say, in wishing to trace a history of the significance and variations of religio-erotic symbolism, particularly of the kiss, I was aware that I could not avoid doctrines of love. Accordingly, I have dealt with them, at times even at length, but chiefly as contextual background to my main themes. In doing so, I have tried to maintain a balance suitable to my scope. Within this perspective, the amatory symbolism I have investigated may be expected to tell us, if not all, at least something of importance concerning certain love doctrines, sacred and profane.

1. The Early Christian Centuries

mong many peoples the kiss has been known as an expression of passionate love and as a salutation—without erotic significance—denoting affection or respect. This was true of the ancient Hebrews. The Old Testament, which has references to both usages, records the kiss primarily as a sign of affection given between relatives at farewells or welcomes, but also as a mark of reconciliation, as when Jacob was reconciled with Esau. However, there are also instances of the kiss exchanged between friends, of which the most striking example is the kiss of affection between Jonathan and David.[1] The only clear mention of the kiss being given on the mouth is connected with the passionate love of the Song of Songs: "Let him kiss me with the kisses of his mouth" (1:1); "Thy lips drip as the honeycomb, my spouse: / Honey and milk are under thy tongue" (4:11). Given the number of kisses in the Old Testament, it is noteworthy that the kiss seems not to have been used by the early Jews in any specifically ritualistic way. This contrasts with what we find in the Christian tradition, where the kiss apparently had an important ritualistic and sacramental function from the beginning. Nonetheless, that Christianity owes something of its earliest kiss symbolism to Judaism is hardly to be denied. The references to the kiss in the life of Jesus have all the marks of authentic reports of customs prevailing among the Palestinian Jews of New Testament times. This is the impression one gets from a passage in Luke where we read that Christ reproached the Pharisee Simon for not greeting him with a kiss after inviting and receiving him into his house (Luke 7:45). Even the betrayal of Jesus with a kiss reveals at least that among some groups of Jews the kiss was given to a leader or master as an act of reverence and homage, the sign of a special bond.[2] Such a usage was to be quite common among the Jews through the centuries.

Of capital importance in the development of the kiss as a symbol of union in the Christian tradition are the exhortations, made four times by Paul and once by Peter, that the brethren salute one another with a holy kiss, or with a kiss of love.[3] The repeated use of this formula and the contexts in which it occurs suggest that the kiss was

12

quickly institutionalized in the young Christian community as a mystic symbol both in liturgical and non-liturgical ceremony. Here, in any case, is the origin of what was to become known as the kiss of peace and the Christian kiss of friendship. It will be well therefore to look at the New Testament texts for the connection to be found between the kiss and the ideas of peace, union, and love.

The New Testament Kiss of Peace

Because the idea of peace was one of the key notions associated with Jewish Messianism, its importance in Christianity was assured. Few words have been so fundamental to the Christian vocabulary as the word peace, *pax*. For the Christian, the Prince of Peace spoken of in Isaiah 9:6 is another name for Jesus Christ. Speaking of the new faith as open to both Jew and Gentile, Paul avers that "He is our bond of peace; he has made the two nations one" (Eph. 2:14). As we know, one of the chief concerns of the apostle was that there be no want of unity in the body, that is, the Church, for "all of us have been baptized into a single body by the power of a single Spirit" (I Cor. 12:25; 12:13). These last remarks are made to the brethren at Corinth among whom Paul was endeavoring to restore order. The epistle carries with it the plea that they exchange the holy kiss among themselves (I Cor. 16:20). In his second Epistle to the Corinthians, shortly after reminding them that Christ Jesus lives in them (II Cor. 13:5), Paul again urges them to kiss one another, this time in a context that even more closely associates the kiss with the ideas of unity, peace, and love: "Perfect your lives, listen to the appeal we make, think the same thoughts, keep peace among yourselves, and the God of love and peace will be with you. Greet one another with the kiss of saints" (II Cor. 13:11–12). The kiss is here an invitation to reconciliation and the unity of spirit that Paul wants to see prevail among his coreligionists. It is true that concord was a matter of vital practical necessity for the survival of the new faith, but more than that, for Paul, it was a condition and sign of the mystical reality of the Church as the body of Christ, an idea that is predicated by his concept of the indwelling of the Spirit or of Christ Jesus in those who embrace the faith. In insisting on the need for concord and peace among the Church's members, Paul was consciously being the apostle of Jesus' command that men love one another. That there may be no disunity in the body, he says, the "more excellent way" is love. The great lesson on love in I Corinthians 13:1–13 is made precisely in connection with the problem of preserving the unity of the members of the one body of Christ. It is love that knits the many into one. The kiss is an expression of love and a symbol of union. The holy kiss that Paul urges the brethren to give one another is a unitive kiss of love.[4]

In the second Epistle to the Corinthians, the invitation to kiss is immediately followed by a reference to the fellowship or communion of the Holy Spirit: "the imparting of the Holy Spirit be with you all." It is well known that Paul uses apparently with the same mystical significance such expressions as "in Christ" and "in the Spirit," or "Christ in us" and "the Spirit in us." There also occurs the expression "the Lord is the Spirit" (II Cor. 3:17), suggesting that wherever the Spirit is, there too is Christ. Such texts reveal that in Paul (as in some of the earliest Church Fathers after him) the identification of the Son with the Spirit was not uncommon.

Of the many texts that have bearing on our discussion, a few are of such importance that they may assist us in determining the particular mystical significance of the New Testament *holy kiss*. In Romans—another of the Epistles in which the kiss is urged upon the faithful—we find a fundamental Pauline concept in the words "a man cannot belong to Christ unless he has the Spirit of Christ" (8:9–10). Collectively those who are to exchange the kiss are the body of Christ, but individually each would be expected to have the Spirit of Christ within him. It is in this sense, in fact, that Paul repeatedly applies one of his most magnificent and far-reaching metaphors: the bodies of the faithful are the temples of the living God. The principal texts occur precisely in the Epistles that speak of the kiss: "Do you not understand that you are God's temple, and that God's Spirit has his dwelling in you? If anyone desecrates the temple of God, God will bring him to ruin. It is a holy thing this temple which is nothing other than yourselves" (I Cor. 3:16–17). "Surely you know that your bodies are the shrines of the Holy Spirit, who dwells in you" (I Cor. 6:19). "And you are the temple of the living God" (II Cor. 6:16).[5] By that Spirit (which is the force of Love or Charity) dwelling in the individual members (bodies) the many are made to coinhere in a spiritual corporate oneness that is the one mystical body whose head is Christ. The Spirit is, as it were, the Soul of this collective body which is the Church, an idea that we shall find explicitly stated by St. Augustine. But this is already Paul's great principle of unity, and we can understand why he admonishes the brethren to preserve the unity of the Spirit in the bond of peace; for they are, he says, "one body, with a single Spirit" (Eph. 4:2–5). "We too, all of us, have been baptized into a single body by the power of a single Spirit . . . , we have all been given drink at a single source, the one Spirit" (I Cor. 12:13). When the individual bodies kiss, they give evidence of being knit together by virtue of the Spirit they have in common. It may be said that they kiss one another with that Spirit.

Thus although the New Testament holy kiss is, in one sense, a continuation of the Jewish custom of a kiss accompanied by a wish for peace, when seen, as it must be seen, in the context of Paul's pneumatology, it is revealed as a mystic symbol that goes far beyond anything for which Judaism could have been responsible. That the kiss could be made to acquire such extraordinary significance was not only because it was the expression of love and reconciliation and effected a union of spirits (breaths), but also because the very spirit (breath) that was emitted or exchanged in the real kiss could figure as a symbolic vehicle for the immaterial Spirit (Breath) indwelling in the spiritualized bodies of the brethren.

The question arises as to what, if any, other influences were operative in the New Testament *holy kiss* or in the subsequent Christian ritualistic use of the kiss of peace. That the kiss as a mark of reconciliation and union following discord was well known and in practice in Paul's time is made clear not only by earlier Old Testament references, but also by its metaphorical employment in two passages of Philo Judaeus' *Questions on Exodus*, a work whose Greek original exists only in fragments but which was preserved in an early Armenian translation. In both passages the kiss is used to indicate matters of a cosmic nature. The first (Bk. II, 78) speaks of the meeting of the things of creation in an embrace and kiss of concord. The second (Bk. II, 118) is even more suggestive, for it comes in connection with Philo's discussion of the divine Logos as the mediator and bond of all things, weaving together all parts of the universe, including contrarieties. It is this Logos that exercises a compelling force (love) that causes things that are apparently inimical to each other and irreconcilable by nature to unite by way of a communion, an embrace and kiss of love.[6] These passages led an outstanding scholar of Philo and Christianity more than seventy years ago to maintain that the kiss of peace was perhaps a formal and ceremonial institution of the Jewish Synagogue.[7] Unfortunately this supposition remains unwarranted, inasmuch as there is no documentary evidence supporting it. It is enough for us, however, that Philo should have used the kiss in the metaphorical way he did. Jew though he was, and fundamentally true to the faith of his fathers, Philo was nonetheless steeped in Hellenistic learning and ever ready to make use of the erotic symbolism of the Greeks.[8] It is tempting to think that his application of the kiss image to a philosophico-religious context owes something to a Greek source or habit of expression, that beyond the Old Testament references to the kiss of reconciliation, he was familiar with the ritualistic kiss of some Hellenistic-Oriental mystery cult. Nor can we entirely exclude the possibility of an esoteric Jewish tradition contemporaneous with Philo in which Jewish customs concerning the kiss were merged with Hellenistic usage. But again, on such questions we can only conjecture. Now the same questions necessarily arise in the case of Paul because the Hellenistic and Palestinian Jewish communities mutually influenced one another.

The problem of determining the degree of acquaintance Paul had with Greek philosophy and the Hellenistic mysteries is a vexed question in which we need not become involved, except to say that it does not seem reasonable to deny that the Apostle must have had some acquaintance with them. It is certainly true that already with Paul Christianity was appropriating to itself something of the language of the mystery religions. Nonetheless, even allowing that the kiss itself might have had a special symbolical function in some of the initiation rites of the mysteries, there is no record that it was used with the kind of significance Paul seems to give to it.[9] However, mention should be made here of a custom that existed among the Pythagoreans or Neo-Pythagoreans. Notice of it comes from Plutarch when, in his essay on brotherly love, he says that "We should pattern ourselves after the Pythagoreans, who, though related not at all by birth, yet sharing a common discipline, if ever they were led by anger into recrimination, never let the sun go down before they joined right hands, embraced each other, and were reconciled."[10] It is not unlikely that this ceremony included a kiss as a natural part of the reconciliatory embrace. The interesting point here is that there is a passage in Paul that is strikingly like what we have just read. Because we are members of one another in one body, Paul says, let not the sun go down upon your anger (Eph. 4:25–26). Still, this is perhaps too tenuous a link to authorize a view that Paul's *holy kiss* was influenced by a Neo-Pythagorean practice.

The repetition of the exhortation to kiss found in the New Testament, we have said, strongly suggests that from the earliest times the kiss was a well-known ceremonial practice in the Christian community. The manner and context in which it is recommended would seem to presuppose a familiarity with it as a mystical symbol and as a liturgical observance. If this were not so, Paul's references to it would not make much sense. Whether Paul was himself the originator of the liturgical kiss is a moot question. His allusions to it in the Epistles to the Corinthians and Thessalonians are made to Christian communities founded by him, but he also mentions it to the Roman assembly. Besides this there is the reference to it in the Epistle attributed to Peter. Whatever the extent of its practice then was, it is certain that the kiss continued to be used in a mystical sense in Christian ceremony. In view of its subsequent development this can be affirmed, even though there is no mention of it in post-scriptural literature until about A.D. 150, when we find Justin Martyr noting simply that the kiss is exchanged by the brethren following the prayers that are part of the Eucharistic service.[11]

Following the passing but important reference in Justin Martyr, mention of the kiss continues for some time to be scarce, though significant enough to assure us of the extraordinary consequence attached to it in the earliest Christian centuries. Its use outside the context of a specific liturgical ceremony is attested by the *Acts of Perpetua* (VI, 4) which describe the martyrdom of the African martyrs Perpetua and Felicitas in A.D. 202. This document is generally accepted as being by a contemporary of those martyrs. It is very likely, as Dom Anselm Stolz has pointed out, that there is no martyrdom without mysticism.[12] In the *Acta* the martyrs are portrayed not only as having mystic visions, but also as welcoming death out of great love. It is after they have been mangled by the beasts and are about to be put to the sword that we read of these martyrs that "they first kissed one another, that they might consummate their martyrdom with the kiss of peace."[13] This is as sublime a testimony as one can hope to find of the mystic nature of the Christian holy kiss. There are other notices, however, that reveal more about its meaning in the broader context of Christian spirituality.

A case in point occurs in the writings of Hippolytus at the beginning of the third century. From this source we learn that a newly consecrated bishop received the kiss from all the members of his

17

church before officiating as bishop for the first time in the offering of the Eucharist. A more significant detail is the role the kiss had in the rites accompanying the initiation of a neophyte into the Christian community. Following his baptism, he was confirmed by the bishop, who then gave him the kiss along with the chrism denoting the gift of the Spirit. Before this solemn moment in which the neophyte received the bishop's kiss and the chrism, he was not allowed to exchange the kiss of peace with any of the brethren.[14] Besides the Pauline pneumatology and *holy kiss* that evidently inspire this particular kiss symbolism, one can perhaps observe in it the influence of another New Testament episode. In the Johannine Gospel it is said that when Jesus appeared to the Apostles for the first time after his resurrection, he breathed the Holy Spirit into or upon them. Significantly, this act was immediately preceded by the offering of peace: "He therefore said to them again, 'Peace be to you! As the Father has sent me, I also send you.' When he had said this, he breathed upon them, and said to them, 'Receive the Holy Spirit'" (John 20:21–22). Such a passage, it seems, is at least in part behind the ceremony of the bishop's kiss to the neophyte. This idea receives support when we remember that the bishop is a vicar of Christ (*repraesentatio Christi*) and that in the Johannine passage just quoted, the reference to Christ's "breathing" the Holy Spirit upon (but also, one may say, *into*) the Apostles was easily capable of being understood as a kiss, especially by Christians who were so conscious of the mystic kiss symbolism.

The Kiss that Transmits the Holy Spirit

Thus when St. Augustine commented on this particular text, he noted its meaning to be that the Lord somehow put his mouth to the mouth of the disciples [i.e., the Church] in order to transmit his Spirit. "Concerning that same Spirit the Apostle says: 'Now if any man have not the Spirit of Christ he is none of his' (Rom. 8:9). It was also the same Spirit that the Lord gave his disciples when he breathed [*insufflavit*] on them and said 'Receive the Holy Spirit.' For he in some way placed his mouth to their mouth when he gave them the Spirit by breathing on them" [Os enim quodam modo super os posuit, quando insufflando Spiritum dedit].[15] This statement is a precious confirmation of what one would surmise to have been the case, that is, that scriptural and other references to the inbreathing or infusion of spirit spontaneously evoked in the minds of Christians the image of the kiss as the vehicle for transmitting that spirit. In the same way even the Genesis (2:7) account, which relates that the Lord God, having created or formed man from the dust of the ground, "breathed" or infused the vital spirit into him, allowed Christians to figure the scene by the kiss metaphor. Here in fact were the two great "kisses" of life in the history of man, both of them involving the concept of a divine insufflation: the one, coming before the Fall, gave man the spirit of life and, as some theologians held, a rational soul; the other, after the redemptive Passion and Resurrection of Jesus Christ, gave man (through the Church) new life in the Holy Spirit.[16] Hippolytus' description of the Christian initiatory ceremony—that the neophyte was excluded from exchanging the kiss of peace with the brethren until he had himself received the bishop's kiss—was evidently based on the idea that until then he had not been fully infused with Spirit and so was not yet a whole member of the body of Christ, that is, of the Church.

A similar ritualistic employment of the kiss, although not in the context of a specific ceremony, was recorded by Clement of Alexandria. It has been preserved for us in *The Ecclesiastical History* (II, 9, 2) of Eusebius who, after recounting how Herod had killed James, the brother of John, goes on to say: "Concerning this James, Clement adds in the seventh book of the *Hypotyposes* a story worth mentioning, apparently from the tradition of his predecessors, to the effect that he who brought him to the court was so moved at seeing him testify as to confess that he also was himself a Christian. 'So they were both led away together,' he [Clement] says, 'and on the way he asked for forgiveness for himself from James. And James looked at him for a moment and said, *Peace be to you*, and kissed him. So both were beheaded at the same time.' "[17] While this kiss recalls the exchange of the kiss of peace before martyrdom, such as we have observed it in the *Acts of Perpetua*, it also has very much the same character of the kiss bestowed by the bishop upon the neophyte of Hippolytus' passage, and like the latter, it suggests a connection with the text from John 20:21–22. The James that is understood here is the very brother of John and hence one of the original disciples of Jesus who had received the peace greeting and the Spirit from the resurrected Master. According to the Johannine text, when Jesus breathed on the disciples and spoke first the greeting of peace and then the words "Receive the Holy Spirit," he did so in apprising them of the mission that was to be theirs,

19

saying to them: "Whose sins you shall forgive, they are forgiven them; and whose sins you shall retain, they are retained" (John 20:23). The passage from Clement (by way of Eusebius who, it is worth noting, says Clement had it from the tradition of his predecessors) shows us the disciple James transmitting the Spirit by the kiss and remitting the sins of one who had asked forgiveness from him.

We are aided in assessing the extent of the implementation of the kiss symbolism in the early centuries of Christendom by some remarkable examples in the writings of Christian Gnosticism, especially that variety known as Valentinianism. In the Odes of Solomon (28:6–7), for example, as the author exults in the firm faith that sustains him, he exclaims joyously:

> And deathless life embraced me
> And kissed me.
> And from that is the Spirit within me;
> And it cannot die, for it lives.[18]

Here the theological concept of the pneumatization of the believer by the Spirit is accommodated to the image of an infusion and impregnation effected by a kiss, and the text may in fact allude to some such rite as we have seen described in Hippolytus. At any rate, with it before us, we may turn, for an even more extraordinary text, to the Gospel of Philip, which scholarship has convincingly shown is Valentinian.[19] Among the "sayings" (31) of this Gnostic compilation we find the following, which is defective in the first three lines but intact and clear in the last five:

> . . . . out of the mouth
> . . . . the logos came forth thence
> He would nourish . . . . . . from the mouth
> And become perfect. For the perfect
> Conceive through a kiss and give birth. Because of this
> We also kiss one another.
> We receive conception from the grace which is
> Among us.[20]

Again spiritual impregnation and fecundation are figured or rather effected by a kiss which transmits the Spirit. The "perfect" are the practitioners, that is, the Gnostics who, like the Christians in general of that early period, exchange the kiss. Here, however, the suggestion is very strong that the kiss was used in an even more central way in a mystery rite. The passage is best seen in conjunction with another that occurs a little later in the Gospel, a startling "saying" (55) that describes Mary Magdalene as the consort of Christ receiving many kisses from him:

> . . . . And the
> Consort of [Christ is] Mary Magdalene.
> [The Lord loved Mary]
> More than [all] the disciples, and
> Kissed her on her [mouth]
> Often. The others too . . . . . .
> . . . . they said to him
> "Why do you love her more than all of us?"[21]

Mary Magdalene thus may be said to have become a spiritually pregnant "perfect" by receiving grace (or the Spirit) and *gnosis* directly from the Lord's (real) kisses, more so than all the disciples. Here one is tempted to bring to bear once again the passage from John 20:21–22.

On the basis of these two kiss passages, H. M. Schenke has argued that the fundamental mystery of Philip is the kiss that the initiate receives from the mystagogue. Moreover, by connecting the references in Philip with what Irenaeus of Lyons says about the cult practice and formulae of the Valentinian teacher Mark, Schenke has also suggested that a kiss was the basic mystery of the Valentinians in general.[22] Irenaeus' scornful description is relevant enough to our purpose to be quoted here:

> For he busies himself most about women, those especially who are elegantly clad, and wear purple, and are most wealthy: and often, trying to mislead them, he says to them flatteringly, "I desire to impart to thee of my grace, inasmuch as the Father of all sees continually thine Angel before His face. Now the place of thy Greatness is in us: it is meet for us to become one. Receive first from me and through me the grace. Prepare thyself, as a bride awaiting her spouse, that thou mayest be what I am and I what thou art. Settle in thy bridal chamber the seed of the light. Receive from me the bridegroom, and comprehend [contain] him and be comprehended [contained] in him. Behold the grace is come down upon thee."[23]

Whatever may have been the true nature of the hierogamotic rite alluded to here, it seems reasonable enough to say that at its core was a mystico-magical kiss by which grace or spirit is bestowed or transmitted.

21

There is a non-Christian parallel to Irenaeus' account of Mark which is the more fascinating and worthy of being noted here because it dates from the same period, the second half of the second century A.D. In one of his most entertaining and satirical essays, the skeptical Lucian describes the mystery religion improvised by the charlatan Alexander on the model of the famous Eleusinian mysteries. This Alexander passed as a miraculous mystagogue and hierophant, and at the culmination of the central mystery would embrace and kiss the mystes. Lucian goes on to describe him and his cultists in the following way: "He made it a rule not to greet anyone over eighteen years with his lips, or to embrace and kiss him; he kissed only the young, extending his hand to the others to be kissed by them. They were called 'those within the kiss' . . . It was a great thing that everyone coveted if he simply cast his eyes upon a man's wife; if, however, he deemed her worthy of a kiss, each husband thought that good fortune would flood his house."[24] The similarity to the kiss symbolism of Christian and Gnostic ritual is at the very least striking. But rather than speak of an influence of Christian practice on Alexander, it is safer to assume that the kiss also held an important role in the initiatory rites of other mystery religions of the first centuries. If we return now to the passage quoted first from Irenaeus, the formula "Receive first from me and through me the grace" again brings to mind the divine insufflation of John 20:22. In addition to this, there may be an echo of the Song of Songs, not only in the use of nuptial symbolism as such (the importance of which, as of the Song, we must soon consider), but in the idea "that thou mayest be what I am and I what thou art." In this there already is the idea of a psychic exchange or identity of two in one for which the formula in the Song is "I am unto my beloved and my beloved is unto me" (6:2, and cf. 2:16). But it is the specific concept of a union of two in one ("it is meet for us to become one") to be effected by a kiss that we would consider now.

In this connection we are able to draw on still another Gnostic text, the group of writings known as *Pistis Sophia*. Not the least significant factor here is that this example involves a biblical passage which itself employs the kiss image metaphorically. It is said that when Mary, in compliance with her Son's request, interpreted the words "Justice and Peace have kissed" (Psalm 84:11), she did so by recounting an episode from that time of the childhood of Jesus when the Spirit had not yet come upon him. One day there appeared to her a figure in the exact likeness of Jesus, asking for the latter as for his brother. Thinking him to be an evil phantasm intent on deceiving her, Mary bound him; when hearing of it, Jesus demanded to be taken to him. When the figure was loosened, Mary reminded her Son, "He kissed you and you kissed him, and you two became but one." Now the figure that so merged with Jesus in the kiss was no one less than the Holy Spirit, who had come down from the height of the First Mystery or God manifest of which Jesus is the Incarnation.[25] This then would seem to be a variation on the theme of the Gnostic syzygy between Christ and the Pneuma to make for the Christ-Pneuma.

A similar example of this particular kiss motif occurs in a sixth century Bohairic text which gives an account of the assumption of the Virgin. It is said there that when Mary died, Jesus, who had come down again to earth, took her soul and brought it into Heaven, where he presented it to the Father and the Holy Spirit. After two hundred and six days from the Virgin's death, Jesus once more descended with Mary's soul [in the semblance of her physical likeness] seated in his bosom. At the tomb he bade Mary's body come forth, whereupon, the document says, the body arose and "embraced [kissed] its own soul, even as two brothers who are come from a strange country, and they were united with one another."[26] It is significant that at this point of the narration the writer cites the words from Psalm 84:11: "Mercy and Truth have met; Justice and Peace have kissed."

Our examples of the kiss image in Gnostic writings are really in keeping with and help throw light on other notices of the kiss in more "orthodox" contexts; whenever the kiss image appears having Christian symbolic value, Christ *and* the Spirit are present.

What the Lips Do

The fact that the kiss is mentioned in almost all the primitive liturgies indicates that its importance as a mystic symbol had never been brought into serious doubt. Here the only question was to be about the particular moment that it was to be exchanged.[27] It is in connection with the liturgy that we see the kiss definitely becoming known as the *kiss of peace*. When the Church Fathers speak of the kiss, whether in reference to the liturgy or not, they invariably recognize it to be a sign of peace in which the hearts and souls of the faithful are brought together. Thus the most significant idea attached to the kiss continued to be its unitive function. This was expressed quite explicitly, for example, by St. Cyril of Jerusalem, in whose words there is the suggestion that the kiss exchanged by the brethren is more than just a symbol, for his words incidentally inform us that the kiss between ordinary friends was common even among non-Christians; hence, he insists on the uniquely mystic quality and holiness of the Christians' kiss:

> Think not that this kiss ranks with those given in public by common friends. It is not such: this kiss blends souls one with another, and solicits for them entire forgiveness. Therefore this kiss is the sign that our souls are mingled together, and have banished all wrongs. . . . The kiss therefore is reconciliation, and for this reason holy: as the blessed Paul has in his Epistles urged: Greet ye one another with a holy kiss; and Peter, with a kiss of charity.[28]

St. Augustine has similar references to the kiss. It is he, for example, who informs us that following the consecration of the Eucharist the priest speaks the words "Pax vobiscum," whereupon the members kiss one another. What the lips do, says Augustine, the hearts of those who kiss should do, that is, join with the lips and heart of the one who is kissed: "After this is said: 'peace be with you'; and Christians kiss one another with a holy kiss. It is the sign of peace; as the lips make it known so let it be in our minds. That is to say, as your lips approach the lips of your brother let not your heart withdraw from his."[29] This passage is of great interest for at least two reasons. For one thing, it seems to make clear that the kiss was made mouth to mouth, a matter, as we shall later see, of no small consequence. In addition to this, it establishes or points to a vital connection between the kiss of peace and the Eucharistic communion of the Mass. It was to be the Roman rite in particular that most closely and firmly linked the kiss with actual communion, for which sacrament it came to be considered a necessary preliminary. This was to remain the case throughout the Middle Ages.

Now the Eucharist itself is a sign of love and union, and it effects an incorporation of the partaker in Christ. Here the relationship between Christ and peace again becomes pertinent. Christ is the Incarnate Peace that is intended in the formula *Pax vobiscum* and that is about to be assimilated by the communicants. Moreover, it can even be said that Christ is himself the very Kiss of Peace. Paul had said that Jesus as the Incarnation of Peace united the two nations [Jews and

Gentiles] in himself and that he laid himself as the Cornerstone of the foundation for the building of the Church (Eph. 2:14–20). In a sermon on the Epiphany, Augustine went on to equate Paul's image of the Cornerstone with the kiss of peace, for "what is a corner but the joining of two walls coming from different directions, which then, as it were, exchange the kiss of peace?"[30] Hence, it is with good reason that in yet another context, when referring to the formula *Pax vobiscum* at the Eucharistic service, Augustine exclaims that the kiss of peace is a great mystery or sacrament: "Pax vobiscum. Magnum sacramentum osculum pacis."[31] Before partaking of the most mystic of sacraments, the brethren manifest their own unity of spirit by the exchange of the kiss of peace which is made in Christ's name and in his Spirit, a sign that they are one by that Spirit. Only then are they ready to receive the Host, that is, the Eucharistic Body of Christ by which their mystical incorporation in Christ is effected. It is then that they *are* the Body of Christ [i.e., the Church] breathing with and animated by his Spirit. In a Whitsun sermon (267, 4) Augustine noted that "What the soul is in the body of a man, that is the Holy Spirit in the body of Christ, which is the Church; what the soul works in the several members of a single body, that the Holy Spirit works in the whole of the Church."[32] This is perhaps a good place to recall the significant fact that the word *Pax*, which came to be used by itself to refer to the kiss of peace (*osculum pacis*), was also the term used in the early Latin Christian centuries to refer to the *unity* of the *ecclesia*.

Another significant statement concerning the relationship between the liturgical kiss and the notion of an indispensable unity comes from the Pseudo-Dionysius, a writer whose works (by way of a ninth century translation by Scotus Erigena) were to exercise an immense influence on medieval spirituality in Western Christianity. Dionysius also speaks of the kiss of peace as a sacred mystery preparing for the Eucharistic communion. Communion is a mystic participation in the One, but that participation cannot be effected as long as the believer is divided in himself or separated from others. The kiss of peace, he says, is a call to the life of unity, first of all to the unification of the self, for this is the principle of union that permits a union of many individuals and allows us to unite with God, who as the source of all unity makes possible the assimilation into the One.[33] There are Neoplatonic echoes in Dionysius, but here they are secondary to a fundamental Christian tenet that would be looked for in vain in Neoplatonism. For Dionysius, not only is love the compelling force of unity; love comes from and is the One, and, unlike the abstract essence of the Neoplatonists, that One is a personal God. In the context of the sacrament of the Eucharist, it is Christ.

Among the Greek Fathers it is St. John Chrysostom who most often refers to the kiss as a way for souls to unite. In a passage that recalls Augustine's words, he tells us that when we exchange the kiss as a symbol of love with our neighbors the Lord wants our souls to kiss and our hearts to embrace.[34] And, like Dionysius, he explains that the kiss the brethren are to exchange just before Communion is a call to the life of unity that is necessary before they can receive the kiss directly from the Master (such is how Chrysostom refers to the Eucharist). That kiss, according to him, effects a real meeting and union of souls, thereby resulting in the creation of a unique corporate body of many members having one heart and soul such as existed when, according to Acts 4:31–32, the Apostles were all filled with the Holy Spirit: "When we are about to participate in the sacred Table [the Eucharist], we are also instructed to offer a holy greeting [kiss]. Why? . . . We join souls with one another on that occasion by means of the kiss, so that our gathering becomes like the gathering of the apostles when, because all believed, there was one heart and one soul. Bound together in this fashion, we ought to approach the sacred mysteries."[35] Closely connected with the idea expressed in this passage is one we read of in Chrysostom's explication of Paul's invitation to the brethren that they greet one another with a kiss in I Corinthians 16:20. After explaining that Paul brought harmony among certain of the brethren who had been at variance, Chrysostom says that the great Apostle then naturally bade them exchange the holy kiss, "because this unites and makes one body."[36] It goes without saying that the reference here to the union in one body, said to be produced by the kiss, is again to be understood in the sense of the mystical body of Christ, that is, the Church whereby the members are made one. This is the body that has "one heart and one soul."

Over and over we see that insofar as the kiss is recognized as a way of joining bodies and spirits (or, indeed, breath-souls), it lends itself to Christian spirituality as a symbol in the truest sense of the word: it is itself what it signifies—a fusional or unifying action. Now the symbolic value of the kiss because of this "inherent" characteristic is further enhanced when we remember that the kiss is also felt to be a natural expression of love, and that the union Christianity envisions depends entirely on an act of love. The Petran Epistle, we remember, speaks of a "kiss of love." So, too, when Chrysostom comments on II Corinthians 13:12, he says that "the kiss is to be given as a fuel to love, that it may generate affection." And again the Greek Father notes that the kiss is a mingling of souls: "In this way our souls are bound unto one another. Thus when we have returned from a journey we kiss each other, our souls moving towards a mutual intercourse."[37]

Such expressions as this and, indeed, all others where a union of souls or spirits is understood, plainly indicate that whatever form the Christian holy kiss was taking—for example, an embrace and a light cheek-to-cheek press—the notion behind it implied a mouth-to-mouth contact. As for Chrysostom, there is no doubt that he is speaking of the kiss on the mouth. In fact, to explain why souls move to meet in the kiss, he says that the mouth "is the organ which most effectively declares the working of the soul." But an even more explicit statement that a mouth kiss is intended occurs when Chrysostom adds another mystic dimension to the meaning of the Christian kiss. Precisely in reference to the kiss, he twice recalls Paul's idea that our bodies are the temples of the Lord. Thus immediately after the above-quoted words he observes: "Something more may be said about this holy kiss. Wherefore? We are the Temple of Christ; thus when we kiss each other we kiss the vestibule and the entrance of the Temple. . . . Through these gates and doors [the mouths of the faithful] Christ has entered and enters when we partake of communion."[38] And elsewhere the same thought appears with a clearer reference to the Spirit: "The Holy Spirit has made us temples of Christ. Therefore when we kiss each other's mouths, we are kissing the entrance of the temple."[39] Thus we see why the Christian kiss of peace is indeed so sacramental an act. We will not overstrain Chrysostom's thought if we say that it strongly suggests that in kissing one another Christians are also kissing Christ. When, at the celebration of the Mass, the priest kisses the altar, he is kissing Christ of whom the altar is a symbol. And every Christian who has the Spirit within him is another Christ.

The Kiss of Betrayal

That the love which binds the brethren into one body must not be feigned goes without saying. References to the kiss of peace sometimes include warnings that it be given without dissemblance. The fourth century *Constitutions of the Apostles*, speaking of the kiss in the liturgy to be given before the Eucharist, makes the following admonishment: "Let no one have any quarrel against another; let no one come to it [to the Host] in hypocrisy. Then let the men give the men, and the women give the women, the Lord's kiss. But let no one do it with a deceit, as Judas betrayed the Lord with a kiss."[40] In all such warnings against deceit the example of Judas is implied or explicitly evoked. We observe it in St. Augustine, who regards the kiss of Judas as the prototype of a lack of correspondence between the lips and the heart, hence of treachery. Because the kiss of peace is a holy mystery, one should kiss so as to inspire love. Be not like Judas, Augustine warns us. The traitor Judas kissed Christ with his mouth, but in his heart he was betraying him.[41] The implication here is that Judas did not have a kiss in that true or spiritual sense whereby it is the symbolic vehicle for the uniting of hearts or souls in a bond of peace and love.

This idea, in fact, was expressly enunciated before Augustine by his great forerunner, St. Ambrose. Discussing the Christian message of the Advent of the Messiah and the peace that he brings to those who acknowledge him, Ambrose writes:

> A kiss is the sign of love. What kiss could the Jew have, seeing that he has not known peace, has not received peace from Christ, who said: "My peace I leave with you." . . . So the Pharisee had no kiss, except perhaps the kiss of the traitor Judas. But Judas had no kiss either; and that was why, when he wanted to show the Jews the Kiss he had promised them as the sign of betrayal, the Lord said to him: "Judas, betrayest thou the Son of man with a kiss?" He meant, do you offer a kiss when you have not the love which goes with a kiss, do you offer a kiss when you know not the mystery of the kiss? It is not the kiss of the lips which is required, but the kiss of heart and mind [soul]. . . . A kiss conveys the force of love, and where there is no love, no faith, no affection, what sweetness can there be in kisses?[42]

That Judas betrayed his master with a kiss was accounted by Christians a betrayal of the kiss itself as well as of the Lord. Precisely because the kiss was so sacred and sacramental a sign of the love, peace, and unity that should reign among men, especially among the brethren, the kiss of Judas has struck Christians as an act of unspeakable perversion. Once again Ambrose supplies us with an early and forceful text. It is a sign of the profound impression the act had upon him that he recalls it in the context of a eulogy of man's body, in particular of the mouth, which is praised as the instrument of speech, but even more as the organ for the kiss by which man gives expression to peace and love: "Hence the Lord, condemning His betrayer as a species of monstrosity, says: 'Judas, dost thou betray the Son of Man with a kiss?' That is to say, changing the emblem of love into a sign of betrayal and a revelation of unfaithfulness, are you employing this pledge of peace for the purpose of cruelty? And thus by the oracular voice of God reproof is given to him who by a bestial conjunction of lips bestows a sentence of death rather than a covenant of love."[43]

The most eloquent testimony to the extraordinary place the great betrayal has had in the minds of men is to be found in Christian iconography, which has over and over depicted the scene in a way that accentuates the sense of abhorrence and the idea of division caused by that kiss. Its definitive treatment is perhaps in the justly celebrated fresco by Giotto (Fig. 5). As Judas carries out his embrace and kiss, the folds of his cloak are being wrapped around Christ so that the two figures seem to be merging into one. But at the same time, the painter has made Judas appear as the very species of monstrosity that Ambrose spoke of, "who by a bestial conjunction of lips" belies the union which is suggested by his embrace and is normally signified by the kiss. It is worth noting that the Church omits the kiss of peace from the Mass on Holy Thursday as an expression of its horror and sorrow at the kiss of betrayal.

The Impure Kiss

The use of the kiss in Christendom was evidently not without its perils. Christians themselves were alert to the sensual dangers that lurked in kisses, and the entreaties to keep the kiss holy sometimes referred to more than keeping it free from hypocrisy and deceit. In his *Plea Regarding Christians* (c. A.D. 176), Athenagoras warned against the abuse and perversion of this religious salutation: "We thus feel it a matter of great importance that those, whom we thus think of as brothers and sisters and so on, should keep their bodies undefiled and uncorrupted. For the Scripture says again, *If anyone kisses a second time because he found it enjoyable.* . . . Thus the kiss, or rather the religious salutation, should be very carefully guarded. For if it is defiled by the slightest evil thought, it excludes us from eternal life."[44] The

29

source Athenagoras had in mind when he attributed this thought to Scripture is unauthenticated, and the phrase is broken off in his own original text. The point he is making, however, is clear enough.

Some scathing remarks by Clement of Alexandria also give us a picture of the abuse of the kiss among some of the early Christians. Clement's vehement denunciation makes it clear that the Christians provoked scandal by promiscuous osculation. While recognizing Paul's authority and the existence of a "mystic" kiss, he is so outraged by the deceit and secret lust of many that he comes close to denying the necessity of the kiss as a sign of true Christian love. At the very least we have an eloquent contrast between the kiss of charity and the kiss of lust:

> Love is not proved by a kiss, but by kindly feeling. But there are those that do nothing but make the churches resound with a kiss, not having love itself within. For this very thing, the shameless use of a kiss, which ought to be mystic, occasions foul suspicions and evil reports. The apostle calls the kiss holy. When the kingdom is worthily tested, we dispense the affection of the soul by a chaste and closed mouth, by which chiefly gentle manners are expressed. But there is another, unholy, kiss, full of poison, counterfeiting sanctity. Do you not know that spiders, merely by touching the mouth, afflict men with pain? And often kisses inject the poison of licentiousness. It is then very manifest to us, that a kiss is not love. "And this is the love of God," says John, "that we keep His commandments" (I John, 3); not that we stroke each other on the mouth.[45]

In connection with such admonishments, it is relevant to recall a somewhat striking page from the second century religious "novel," *The Shepherd of Hermas*, one of the most widely read books in Christendom during the early centuries. In this work, which teaches a strict Christian morality, there is a moment when the narrator Hermas recounts a curious episode. That we have to do with a vision takes nothing away from its piquancy. Having been left alone by the shepherd in the company of a band of virgins, Hermas is invited not only to take shelter among them but also to sleep with them "as a brother, not as a husband." Hermas blushes with shame, but his reticence is dispelled when he is kissed first by their leader and then by the others who now frolic with him. In the evening, inside the house, the virgins disrobe and Hermas is made to lie in their midst. But throughout the night the virgins did nought but pray, and Hermas along with them, so that they were glad for it.[46] It is clear that this interlude (for such it is in the "story") is an adaptation of an erotic pagan theme. The Christian element would then be in the abstinence of Hermas in the midst of temptations and the rejoicing of the virgins on account of it. It may be, as modern criticism says, that the episode reflects a dangerous experiment of some early Christian groups, that of living as brothers and sisters in a sort of communal life.[47] But if this is so, then it must still be said that Hermas is put through a kind of trial, for the kisses that are bestowed upon him are blandishments; though they occur after he is called "brother," they are meant to coax him. Thus one is tempted to say that those kisses cannot be understood as the Christian spiritual kiss of peace or friendship. It is interesting to note that just prior to his own escapade with the virgins, Hermas was observing their activity as the guardians of a tower that was being constructed. When the Master of the tower arrived to inspect its progress, the virgins ran toward him and greeted him with a kiss. Now this Master, it turns out, is Christ, portrayed as taller than the tower, which, we learn, is nothing less than the Church. Thus it is the same virgins who kiss Christ who also kiss and entice Hermas. The difficulty in accommodating the two kisses may derive as much from our own remoteness from the spirit and literary devices of this early Christian work as from an infelicitous appropriation by its author of the pagan erotic theme.[48]

The Kiss Between Creature and Creator

The liturgical kiss of peace and the holy kiss of salutation or friendship have already a deep mystic significance inasmuch as they indicate the union of the souls of the faithful in Christ. It is to be noted that these kisses, which are real, refer to a relationship between creatures and are not colored by the erotic language of human passion. But that the image of the kiss and the embrace was used early to depict the blessed union between the creature and God is evidenced by a passage from St. Cyprian in the middle of the third century: "Holding to this faith, and meditating thereon day and night, let us too aspire to God with all our heart, disdaining the present and thinking only on the things that are to be, the fruition of the eternal kingdom, the embrace and the kiss of the Lord, the vision of God."[49]

It is clear that these words are spoken as much from an eschatological as from a strictly mystical point of view; St. Cyprian is address-

31

ing those who were facing martyrdom for their faith, and he encourages them to remain firm and to think of the blessed union that awaits them when their earthly travail is over. Since nuptial symbolism is not present in the context from which this passage comes, one cannot be sure whether the kiss is here paternal or conjugal. In its efforts to express the intimate, personal relationship between God and man, Christianity has developed a twofold symbolism according to which the soul is thought of as the bride or daughter of God. There is another early example of the eschatological kiss which would seem to suggest the Father-child relationship obtaining between God and the soul, although we cannot be absolutely sure even here. This is found in the *Acts* or Passion of Perpetua to which we have already referred. Among the visions the martyrs have in that little treatise, there is one had by Saturus which describes how he and the others (including Perpetua), having been martyred, were received into Paradise by angels who brought them into the chamber of the Most Holy. The seated figure of the Deity is there seen as a hoary, white-haired man but with a youthful face: "vidimus in eodem loco sedentem quasi hominem canum, niveos habentem capillos, et vultu iuvenili." The martyrs, being raised by the angels to the throne, kiss the Lord: "et quattuor angeli sublevaverunt nos: et osculati sumus illum."[50] However fascinating this example is, we are not helped by it in determining the quality of the kiss in St. Cyprian. But although Cyprian has not specified its character, the fact that his kiss is accompanied by the embrace makes it more likely than not that it is conjugal. At the time Cyprian wrote, the Song of Songs, as we shall soon see, was beginning to influence spiritual writing with its sensual imagery. Meanwhile our opinion may receive support from the consideration of a curious but revealing feature of early Christian funerary symbolism which is much to our purpose.

In the early centuries it was the practice of Christian iconography to borrow motifs from well-established and still current pagan myths. Especially in the case of sarcophagi designs, this was partly because the artisans upon whom the Christians depended for services were very likely pagans and therefore accustomed to reproducing certain common motifs without difficulty. Besides this, Christians could use such motifs on their own funerary monuments without arousing too much suspicion or adverse comment. Understandably, they would look for those myths that could, while retaining a pagan semblance, be interpreted in a Christian key. Among the motifs applicable in this way were those connected with the myth of Psyche and Eros; and of the various aspects of this myth the one clearly favored by the Christians of Rome was that which showed the pair embracing and kissing. In his study on the myth of Psyche in Greek and Roman art, Maxime Collignon listed seven Christian sarcophagi, dating from the second to the fourth centuries, that bear representations of this group.[51] That the same group appears frequently on pagan funerary monuments of the same period is itself a fact of the greatest significance. Collignon notes that in the second and third centuries of the Christian Era at Rome, few subjects are as frequently represented on sarcophagi as the group Eros and Psyche united in a divine embrace and kiss.[52] Psyche, of course, is the human soul of the departed, and Eros—even when represented as a *putto* or as a youth—is always a powerful god of love. Although usually awkwardly executed on the sarcophagi, the amatory couple is invariably represented in the manner of the beautiful and famous statue (fourth century B.C.) in the Capitoline Museum in Rome (Fig. 6). It is Eros who bestows the kiss with all the suggestion that he is infusing the spirit of new life into Psyche. Thus the adoption of the myth by Christians is easily accounted for. On pagan and Christian funerary monuments alike, the motif indicates a belief or a hope in an afterlife in which the soul enjoys the eternal bliss vouchsafed it by Love.

The kissing couple may very well depict a wedding union in heaven. Particularly suggestive of this is the depiction of the motif on the bottom of a painted vase found in the Priscilla catacombs (Fig. 7). Here too Psyche and Eros kiss in the fashion of the Capitoline group, but in addition there is an inscription which reads: *Anima dulcis fruamur nos sine bile. Zeses* (Sweet soul, let us enjoy this bliss without misgivings. Live). From this motto and other elements in the scene, Filippo Buonarotti, who first published this fragment in 1716, deduced the significance to be a convivial invitation such as was made at weddings by the groom to the bride.[53] In this representation, like those on the Christian sarcophagi, pagan Eros is an allegory of the Christian God who is Love wedding the soul unto himself eternally. The scene may be perfectly glossed with the words quoted earlier from St. Cyprian, or by these of the same writer: "Fully blessed are they, who among you, having walked by this path of glory, have departed from the world and . . . have already attained the embrace and the kiss of the Lord."[54]

In passing from such representations of the eschatological union of the soul and God to a consideration of the image of the kiss and embrace in the description of the mystical union between God and the soul of the still living creature (or the Church as the embodiment of all the individual members of the faith), the first thing to be said is that here the language of human passion is employed unabashedly. Indeed, the eroticism in the language of the mystics increases in ratio to the intensity of the spirituality of their experience. Of course, between divine love and carnal love there can be no confusion, because the two are incommensurable by virtue of their different objects of desire. And yet the history of Western spirituality shows that the most adequate language mystics have fashioned in order to describe their experience of union reverts to the imagery of bold human love and intense carnal pleasure. The justification for this usage can depend only on a principle of analogy.

The mystic's path to God is primarily a way of love because it is felt that love is that which best implements a union between lover and beloved. Needless to say, the conception of love as a unifying force is older than Christianity, being common in the love literature and philosophy of the ancients. There can be no doubt, for example, that in the West one of the most far-reaching and influential statements concerning love was made by Plato in the *Symposium* when he illustrated by way of the androgyne myth the idea that love is the desire for the whole. What every lover wants, says the interlocutor Aristophanes, is "that he should melt into his beloved, and that henceforth they should be one being instead of two. The reason is that this was our primitive condition when we were wholes, and love is simply the name for the desire and pursuit of the whole."[55] Or we may recall that Lucretius began his philosophical poem with an invocation to the great force that, coursing throughout nature, brings male and female into union, though it is significant that later (Bk. IV) he was careful to show that the desire and efforts of passionate lovers to fuse into one another was a madness worthy only of ridicule.

Now it is a fact that the Judeo-Christian tradition had within it one of the richest possible sources for the idea of the fusional or unitive character of love in reference to the human couple. Genesis spoke of marriage as a cleaving of man and woman to one another by which they become one body or flesh (Gen. 2:24). The thought attributed to Christ in Matthew 19:4–6, and the remarkable Pauline text from Ephesians (5:29 ff.), which we are soon to consider, echo this view of the unitive function of marriage and, it should be noted, have nothing to say about a procreative end. It is well known, however, that subsequently Christian writers, perhaps needing to overcorrect sexual laxity, established a priority in marriage which gave to procreation such prominence that the unitive function was greatly underplayed, though it would be wrong to think that this aspect did not continue to impress itself in the imaginations of the faithful and of the theologians in particular, the same who could have little to say openly on behalf of earthly marriage. At any rate, it is a fact that with the triumph of Christianity, the idea of the unifying motivation and function of love simply became more and more the greatest single truth concerning love, one that was to be repeated down the centuries by spiritual and carnal lover alike. Hence, in his classic definition, St. Augustine did not fail to note that both kinds of love—spiritual and physical—have this copulative and unifying effect as their chief characteristic and function: "What then is love but a kind of life somehow uniting or seeking to unite two [beings], that is, the lover and his beloved? And this is also the case in external physical loves."[56] Love is so much a matter of desiring to become one with the beloved that the intense pleasure of lovers is to be explained by the fact that their bodies have become one: "What is all love? Does it not desire to be made one with what it loves and if it touches it, become one with it? That pleasure gives such strong delight for no other reason than that bodies loving one another are made into one."[57]

As for the Greeks, though they had a complete theory about love as a unifying power—in physical love, friendship, and political concord —they did not apply it to a definition of the Deity. Even for Neoplatonism, love is a way for man to seek after and climb to God, but it is not itself of the nature of Deity. The Christians, of course, find love to be at the very core of God and deriving from him; hence love between God and man is a mutual affair. Nor will this metaphysics or, if one prefers, psychology of love be seriously disputed by most readers; for indeed it is the chief premise guiding the investigations into the nature of love being made by modern psychologists, whether these be Christian believers or not.[58]

Thus it is essential to keep in mind this fundamental truth regarding love as understood by Christians: the principle or, indeed, the source of love is *one* regardless of the direction it may take in an individual. This idea, which is implicit in Augustine's words quoted above, was worked out by the saint in his famous and influential conception of the contrast or tension between charity and cupidity. The medieval writers were to keep fairly well within the Augustinian terms in their own discussions of love, although this did not exclude personal and original insights. In the twelfth century, Hugh of Saint-Victor reminded his audience that love is the ultimate source of all good and all evil because "a single fount of love, surging up within us, gushes out into two streams: one is the love of the world, cupidity; the other the love of God, charity."[59] The heart of man is the theatre where the drama of tension takes place. Love is a movement of the heart (*motus cordis*), single and one by nature, but divided in its act according to whether it is ordinate or inordinate.[60] For the Christian the whole problem of love is one of setting charity in order.

Nuptial Symbolism

That the source or principle of love is one and the same regardless of the object desired and loved is at least a partial explanation for the use mystic lovers make of the language of human passion. Most often the erotic imagery employed by Christian writers is contained within the broader symbolism of spiritual nuptials wherein the relationship between God and the Church or the individual soul is regarded as a conjugal bond of love uniting two in one. For the use of the marriage metaphor Christians had before them not only the New Testament's references to Christ as a Bridegroom, but more particularly the great authority of the Pauline text which made of the conjugal union of man and wife a symbol for the spiritual union between Christ and the Church:

> The man is the head to which the woman's body is united, just as Christ is the head of the Church; . . . and women must owe obedience at all points to their husbands, as the Church does to Christ. . . . And that is how husband ought to love wife, as if she were his own body; in loving his wife, a man is but loving himself. It is unheard of, that a man should bear ill-will to his own flesh and blood; no, he keeps it fed and warmed; and so it is with Christ and his Church, we are limbs

of his body; flesh and bone, we belong to him. That is why a man will leave his father and mother and will cling to his wife, and the two will become one flesh. Yes, those words are a high mystery, and I am applying them here to Christ and the Church (Eph. 5:23–33).[61]

Elsewhere Paul writes to the brethren that he has wed them to a single and unique bridegroom, Christ, so that he alone may have them as a virgin without stain (II Cor. 11:2). We must observe here that in the Pauline texts the mystical application of the nuptial idea is restricted to Christ and a collective body of persons, that is, the Church; hence, although there are passages in Paul that show his belief in a personal mystical union with Christ, his nuptial symbolism cannot be said to justify the subsequent Christian extension of the idea to a marriage between God and the individual soul. In seeking the source of this idea (which was to appear clearly in a Christian writer for the first time with Origen), one is brought to think of the Greek and Oriental mysteries and of early Neoplatonism. According to Evelyn Underhill, "The symbolism of the spiritual marriage between God and the soul goes back to the Orphic Mysteries and thence via the Neoplatonists into the stream of Christian tradition."[62] This is quite likely, because although the nuptial idea is present in the Old Testament, the bride there, as in Paul, is a collective body; indeed, the idea of the individual soul as the bride has never been congenial to normative Judaism.[63] Nonetheless, as important as may have been the Neoplatonic influence and such passages as those we find in Paul, of themselves these would hardly have led to the truly extraordinary development of nuptial symbolism and, in particular, to the high degree of eroticism associated with it in the Christian tradition. What really made that possible was the presence of the Song of Songs in the Jewish and Christian biblical canon.

Whatever the origins of the Song may be (such as secular love poems, or liturgical poems of the Adonis-Tammuz fertility cult), Christians were very naturally led to read it as a spiritual epithalamium in which the Bridegroom was God and the bride was the Church. The Christian retention of the Song stems from the fact that it was already one of the cherished books of the Jews, who understood it to be the expression of a special and intimate bond between Yahweh and the community of Israel. If, as seems likely, such an allegorical interpretation was current among the Rabbis in Paul's time, it is almost certain that the great convert's own appropriation of the nuptial idea to the Christian context owes something to it. But the most important point is that, from the time of the first Christian commentaries on the Song, we find the exegetes extending the symbolism of the bride from the Church to the individual soul athirst for the love union with the Bridegroom and desirous of being fructified by him.[64]

It is clear that the joy proclaimed by the Shulamite could hardly be tolerated if referred to a real bride, because marriage did not in itself justify such desires and pleasures.[65] Nor could the yearning of the bride be accepted as a longing for a human bridegroom, since the only proper and salutary yearning of the creature is that which is directed toward the Creator. But what had to be denied to the flesh and human love (even within the marriage bond) could be allowed, in fact, was necessary, in the courtship and love existing between the soul and God. Or rather, since there is no question of an equivalence between the two kinds of betrothals and no doubt about the nature of divine love, the "sinful" pleasures of human passion could be applied as metaphors to the legitimate and holy longing of the enamoured soul seeking union with God; within such a context they become laudable virtues. In this connection, it is worthy of note that the Song of Songs, which supplied the mystics with most of their erotic imagery, was almost unanimously considered by the Christian exegetes to be pure allegory; that is, no literal or profane meaning was to be attributed to its text. Here the cleavage between the letter and the spirit is absolute and everything is accommodated to the latter. Gregory of Nyssa may be cited here in order to indicate with what sureness Christians could appropriate the Song's language of passionate love, and in order also to exemplify the principle of analogy that we have already suggested was operative in the employment of erotic imagery by the writers of divine love. The great wisdom of Solomon (the "author" of the Song of Songs), Gregory says, is manifested by the fact that he knew how to use words to signify the opposite of what their literal sense seems to indicate. In this way the senses and the passions are made to purify themselves.[66] The Song is addressed not to the outer man and the external senses, but to the inner man and the spiritual senses; it teaches us then that we have two orders of senses: the one physical, the other spiritual. Kissing, Gregory writes, is effected by the sense of touch; in the kiss two pairs of lips meet and touch. But there is also a higher order or spiritual sense of touch—hence, a spiritual kiss also—by which one comes into contact with the Word.[67]

In the final analysis, it is this concept of an order of spiritual senses, based on the principle that the activities of the soul (or the spirit) are analogous but superior to the activities of the body, that makes tolerable the application of amatory imagery to the description of spiritual or divine love.

It was Origen of Alexandria who had first given some sort of systematic expression to the doctrine of the spiritual senses, and although he betrays Neoplatonic influences, his statement of it is grounded in the Pauline opposition between the natural and the spiritual man and in scattered references and images in the Scriptures. Among the most suggestive of such biblical images is one that exhorts man to *taste* and so see (i.e., know) how *sweet* the Lord is (Ps. 34:9). The spiritual writers frequently connect this text with the image of the kiss and, in particular, with the kisses of honey and myrrh of the Song of Songs (4:11; 5:13). Especially significant here is the fact that as the spiritual senses are made (in Gregory of Nyssa, for example) to correspond to various degrees of a mystical nearness or ascent to God, there is an inversion in the traditional (Platonic) hierarchy of the senses which placed sight far above all. In the spiritual senses, sight and hearing are lowest (though not scorned), whereas smell and, even more, taste and touch are the most exalted. This was a development whose importance was to be second to none in the history of Western mysticism. And with the sense of touch the kiss was the supreme expression.[68]

Thus while it is true that in their descriptions of divine love the religious writers borrowed heavily from the language of passionate human love, it is equally true that what may at first seem like the most dangerous sexual imagery loses all suggestion of a profane and sensual love in the context of their discussions. As we have seen in the case of Gregory of Nyssa, the mystics and mystical theologians themselves, as though anticipating the puzzlement or unholy titillation their method might cause in less wary readers, invariably call attention to this basic fact. Centuries after Gregory, for example, Richard of Saint-Victor notes that the four degrees of violent love are different "according to whether we speak of divine sentiments or human sentiments, for they are not the same in spiritual and carnal desires. In spiritual desires, the greater the love the better it is; in carnal desires, the greater the love the worse it is."[69] What makes the difference is not the psychology of love but the specification of the beloved or desired object. The language used in describing the two loves is the same, but curiously (because borrowed from human love), it is more appropriate in the description of spiritual love. Clearly, then, there is something about the intimate and intense nature of the mystical experience that is best conveyed by that language which pertains first to sexual love.[70]

The language of the Song of Songs is indeed daring, and if it is asked how far the Church Fathers and medieval mystics could go in adopting it in their symbolism of the conjugal relationship between the soul and God, the answer must be that they could go even beyond the amatory expressions of the Song, for we should note that almost invariably what begins as an exegetical treatment becomes a description of experiential knowledge or affective mysticism in which the Song serves as a stepping-stone and point of reference. In the writings of the Christians, then, we find the bridal chamber and the embrace (*spiritalis amplexus*) and, indeed, the kiss. But spiritual union and even conception are considered to be the effect not only or primarily of the embrace, but rather of the kiss. At the very beginning of the Song of Songs, the mystics and theologians found they had to contend with the bride's bold request for kisses: "Let him kiss me with the kisses of his mouth." Even so, the mystics, unlike ordinary lovers, tend to make of the kiss not merely a preliminary of the love relationship, but love's very terminus.

The Kiss in Marriage Ceremonies

Given the importance of the nuptial idea as the chief though not the only metaphor within which the theme of the mystic kiss was to be employed, it will be well, before proceeding further, to consider briefly the role of the kiss in the betrothal and marriage ceremonies of the first Christian centuries. The earliest Christian notice of it is by Tertullian who, in a passing reference to the betrothal of pagan women, speaks of their becoming mingled with a male both in body and spirit by way of the kiss and the clasp of the right hands: "Si autem ad desponsationem velantur (virgenes), quia et corpore et spiritu masculo mixtae sunt per osculum et dexteras. . . ."[71] Tertullian is here referring to a Roman practice, but although he does not say whether it was at that time a custom kept by Christians, there is every reason to suppose that this was the case. A little later, for example,

St. Ambrose supplies evidence that it was so when, on one of the many occasions in which he refers to the Church as the bride of Christ, he notes that unlike the Synagogue the Church has kisses, "for the kiss is, as it were, the pledge of marriage and the privilege of wedlock."[72] But another important testimony to its use in Christian betrothal or marriage ceremonies is found in the funerary motif of Psyche and Eros kissing, used as a symbolical representation of the union and wedding of the soul and God in Paradise. Such a motif, borrowed, as we have seen, from paganism, could have been acceptable and meaningful to Christians only if it reflected a custom that they also shared.

Under Roman law of the Empire, the kiss bestowed by the male at betrothal gave important juridical rights to the woman, who thereby became a *quasi uxor*; thus failure to follow with marriage carried severe sanctions. So, too, the kiss determined the legality of the disposition of betrothal gifts and other property in the event one of the partners died before marriage.[73] It is obvious that the symbolic value of this kiss depends upon the deeply rooted idea of the kiss as a vehicle for the transference or exchange of power or "souls." The fact that the kiss was what solemnized the promise to wed indicates that on such occasions it must have been felt to effect a psychophysical union of two in one. Whether Tertullian approved of the practice or not, his words show clearly enough that in his time it was thought of in this way. To be sure, this feeling could be weakened in time, making the betrothal kiss appear more or less a formality in the rite and therefore in need of the support of the law. But this is also a proof that at the time of the law the kiss must have yet retained some quasi-magical or even religious value, for otherwise the law would have been totally unrealistic. In any case, for Christians under the Empire, the sense of a psychophysical value attached to the betrothal or wedding kiss must have been enhanced, if anything, in the light of the place the *holy kiss* had in their religious life and St. Paul's idea that human marriage is a union of two in one flesh and a symbol of the mystical union between Christ and the Church.

In Christianity the kiss eventually became part of the wedding ceremony because as the betrothal ceremony was more and more neglected some of its ritual (such as the kiss, the joining of hands, the exchange of rings—which originally was a single giving of the ring by the man to the woman) was incorporated into the actual marriage rite.[74] The exchange of the wedding kiss by the newly married couple at the Nuptial Mass persisted throughout the Middle Ages although it was often transformed into the liturgical kiss of peace, partly perhaps under the influence of changing notions of propriety, but also because of the desire to impress upon the minds of the married couple the idea of the sanctity of the union.[75]

The Kiss Symbolism of Origen and St. Ambrose

In the history of Christian spirituality, Origen occupies a place of first importance, not because he was the first Christian mystic, an honor belonging to St. Paul, but because he gave the first important impetus to a systematization of the Christian mystic experience, a feat he accomplished in his Commentary to the Song of Songs. According to Origen, perfect knowledge or perfect unity is the subject of the Song of Songs. Origen was not the first Christian to explicate the Song, but he was the first to interpret it allegorically not only as the union between the Church and Christ, but as the union of the individual soul and the Word as well.[76] Although he insists upon the necessity of love as a motive force in the soul's quest for union, for him the mystic way is fundamentally an intellectual process rather than an affective experience such as we find, say, in St. Bernard of Clairvaux. Thus the request for the Bridegroom's kiss made by the soul-bride, "Let him kiss me with the kisses of his Mouth," is the prayer of the soul for an illuminating grace. Specifically, the theme of the Song in the individual interpretation is that of the soul desiring to penetrate into the mysteries of the Word; but these mysteries which are contained within the sacred writings are not easily perceived. Reason, free will, and natural law, which are the bride's betrothal gifts, do not suffice. Nor is the teaching of masters enough to bring her to the full satisfaction of her desire for understanding. Thus she prays for the direct visitation of the Word of God that she may be fully illuminated. This is to enter into the Bridegroom's chamber and to be kissed. Therefore, when her mind (*mens*) is filled with divine perception and understanding obtained without the ministration of men or angels, then she may be sure she has received the kisses of the Word of God. For this reason, for the sake of these kisses, let the soul praying to God say: *Osculetur me ab osculo oris sui.*[77]

The image of the kiss as a symbol of the culminating moment of a process which, its mystical quality notwithstanding, is intellectually orientated, has allowed Origen to introduce into his discussion the suggestion of a direct experiential contact between soul and God (as the Word) within a personal relationship. At the same time, the affective side of the experience is also enhanced as Origen goes on to elucidate the meaning of the "mouth" of the Bridegroom. To be noted here is the fact that the Bridegroom is the *Word*. The connection between word and mouth is one that comes naturally, and in a spiritual or mystic sense, the *Word* too would have a Mouth: "By the mouth of the Bridegroom we understand the power of God by which He enlightens her mind and, as *by some word or other of love spoken to her* (if she be worthy of bearing the presence of so great a power), makes clear to her whatever is unknown and obscure. This is that truer, closer and holier kiss which is said to be offered by the Bridegroom— the Word of God—to the bride, that is, to the pure and perfect soul. It is of this circumstance that the kiss we exchange with each other in church at the time of the mysteries is a figure."[78] It is most interesting to see Origen pointing to a connection between his allegorized kiss of the Song and the liturgical kiss of peace in a way that suggests the latter to be a figure (*imago*) of the former; the kiss the brethren give one another at the time of the liturgical celebration of the mysteries is, as it were, a copy or symbol of the greater kiss (union) between God and the soul. This manner of thinking is in keeping with Paul's statement that the conjugal union of man and wife is a figure of the greater mystical union between Christ and the Church.

Of equal importance in Origen's exegesis is the fact that his application of the kiss image to figure the fundamental Christian concept of illumination as an infusion of grace serves to put into clear focus the idea that knowledge of divine things is intimately associated with love. The Christian view of Spirit (*Pneuma*) is one which, like that of Philo and the Gnostics, sees it also as a divine light granted to man for the purpose of revealing to him truths he could never perceive by means of his own limited powers.[79] Now grace of any kind is always understood by the theologians to signify the presence of the Spirit by an infusion of God's love (*infusio caritatis*). Hence we see the appropriateness of the kiss image here. The kiss is the symbolic vehicle for the infusion of that breath of love which, in mystical theology, is the Breath (Spirit) of the Deity.

St. Ambrose is a pivotal figure in the development of Christian kiss symbolism. Since it was he who introduced the ideas of Origen (whose works he knew in the Greek) into Western Christianity, we are not surprised to see that the kiss appears in his writings as a symbol of the infusion of an illuminating grace into the purified and enamored soul. For Ambrose, too, the kiss signifies the knowledge of divine things and the presence of the Word in the soul. But what is especially noteworthy is that with him the kiss image takes on an even greater erotic character than it has in Origen. The soul is depicted as being lovesick and in yearning, impatient for the Beloved's visit and kisses. Nor can it be satisfied with one kiss; it is like a woman in love who implores many kisses and with each kiss abandons herself more and more completely to her love.[80] By means of such an allegorization, Ambrose translates a matter of orthodox theology into the language of passionate human love.

For our consideration, a most significant point is the fact that Ambrose justifies the image of the allegorical kiss of union on the grounds that in the real corporeal kiss itself lovers join and mingle spirits. In kissing, he says, lovers adhere to one another and enjoy the sweetness of an interior grace. By just such a kiss the soul cleaves to and unites with the Word, whose Breath passes into it. Ambrose goes so nonchalantly from the kiss of earthly lovers to the kiss between the soul and God that we are under the impression that he is talking about a real kiss. The kiss between the soul and God is again compared to that given by lovers who, being unsatisfied with the mere enjoyment of the lips, kiss so deeply as to interchange their spirits with one another:

> Osculum est enim quo invicem amantes sibi adhaerent, et velut gratiae interioris suavitate potiuntur. Per hoc osculum adhaeret anima Deo Verbo, per quod sibi transfunditur spiritus osculantis: sicut etiam ii qui se osculantur, non sunt labiorum praelibatione contenti, sed spiritum suum sibi invicem videntur infundere.[a]

Of course, we know that the human lovers in Ambrose's passage are mingling breaths with one another. The parallel made between their kiss and the allegorical mystic kiss depends upon the pluralistic

[a] "For a kiss is that by which lovers mutually adhere to one another and take possession [of each other] as if by the sweetness of an interior grace. By this kiss the soul adheres to God the Word, by this kiss the breath-spirit of him who kisses is transfused into it [the soul]; just as those who kiss one another are not content with the tasting of their lips but seem to pour their spirits into one another." PL 14, 531–532.

meaning of the words spirit and soul. In Latin both words—*spiritus* and *anima*—carry an earlier meaning of breath but also the significance of the immaterial stuff of spirit and soul. But beyond this, yet connected with it, is the fact that here Ambrose brings us directly into the heart of Pauline pneumatology. Paul taught that a union between the soul and God could take place on the level of the transcendent Spirit, but only insofar as a man has been pneumatized, impregnated by the divine Spirit. Only he who "receives the Spirit of God" may attain to union and divine knowledge, because only the Spirit reaches into the deepest things of God (I Cor. 2:10–16). Ambrose's description of the mystic kiss of the Song is built upon such Pauline concepts. Thus we find at the very core of his description one of Paul's most deeply and radically mystical utterances, a text of incalculable importance in the development of Christian spirituality: "He who clings unto the Lord is one spirit with him" (I Cor. 6:17). (The Vulgate has "Qui autem adhaeret Domino, unus spiritus est.") Ambrose, however, has brought the text into conjunction with the Song of Songs so that Paul's already extraordinary thought is now fully eroticized. It is by way of a kiss that the soul cleaves to and unites with God—*per hoc osculum adhaeret anima Deo Verbo*—for that is the way lovers (such are God and the soul) effect their transforming union.

In another context, Ambrose clearly states that to be infused with a special grace, or—what comes to the same thing—to receive the Spirit, is to kiss Christ, an interpretation which, curiously, is applied to Psalm 118:131: "Concerning the same infusion of special grace Scripture teaches you that he who receives the Spirit kisses Christ, as the holy Prophet says: *I opened my mouth and drew in the Spirit.*"[81]

The Kiss and the Eucharistic Banquet

Earlier we noted that the liturgical kiss of peace was exchanged by the brethren as a preparation to Eucharistic communion. A text from Ambrose will show also that Christians could think of this holiest of sacraments as itself being a kiss. Communion, we know, is thought of as continuing the process begun by baptism of the incorporation and transformation of the faithful into Christ, but it is at the same time a coming of Christ into the communicant. It is this sacramental union that Ambrose refers to as a kiss when he states that the words "Let him kiss me with the kisses of his mouth" may be understood either as an invitation made by Christ to the communicant or as a just request made by the communicant to Christ:

> You have approached the altar, and the Lord Jesus now calls you (both you and the Church) and says: "Let him kiss me with the kisses of his mouth." Would you apply that to Christ? Nothing is more pleasing. To your soul? Nothing is sweeter. "Let him kiss me." He sees that you are pure of all sin, for your wrongs have been cleansed away. Thus he holds you worthy of the heavenly sacraments and invites you to the heavenly banquet: "Let him kiss me with the kisses of his mouth." And yet because of what follows, your soul or the Church seeing that it is purified of all sins and worthy enough to come to the altar—for the altar, in fact, is the form or figure of the body of Christ—and seeing the wonderful sacraments, says: "May Christ impress a kiss upon me."[82]

This particular accommodation of the kiss symbolism to the Eucharistic communion is even more erotically drawn by the fifth century bishop of Cyrrhus, Theodoret, who explicitly fits it into the context of the idea of spiritual nuptials. The passage, in fact, occurs in Theodoret's own Commentary on the Song of Songs when he is explicating and justifying the use of the kiss as a religious symbol: "Should anyone whose thoughts are base be troubled by the term *kiss*, let him consider that at the moment of the sacrament when we receive the members of the Spouse, we kiss and embrace him . . . and we imagine a kind of nuptial embrace; we consider that we unite ourselves to him by embracing and kissing him, for as the Scriptures say, love casts out fear."[83]

Thus we see that in the minds of authoritative Christians there was a connection between the rite of communion and the idea of spiritual nuptials. Insofar as this is true, one may speak of the sacred rite as being felt to be a kind of *hieros gamos*, effected, however, by a direct union with the Deity, not through an intermediary agent as in the ancient fertility cults of the Near East and in the Hellenistic mysteries.[84]

St. Augustine and Divine Love

In turning to St. Augustine one must express some wonder that the great saint—in whose writings the kiss of peace, nuptial symbolism, and references to the Song of Songs figure prominently—does not once quote or comment directly on the first verse of the Song.[85]

It is hardly to be thought that Augustine refrained from commenting directly on the bride's kisses because of a reticence to apply the language of human love to spiritual matters, for he is, in fact, one of the richest Christian sources for this tendency. Indeed, there is in his writings an extraordinary passage in which he makes use of the most daring imagery of erotic love outside the area of nuptial symbolism. In the page in question Christ is feminized into the personified figure of Truth, or better, Sophia, and the relations of men with this Lady Wisdom are described in terms of chaste love embraces:

> In truth or wisdom, then, we possess that which we can all enjoy in common. There is no lack or defect in her. She receives all her suitors (*amatores*) without arousing jealousy in them; she is shared by all, and with each she is chaste. No one says to another: get back so I may approach, take your hands away that I may embrace her. All cling to her, all hold her at the same time. Hers is a food that is in no way divided; you drink nothing from her that I cannot drink. When you partake of her, nothing becomes your exclusive possession, for what you take of her remains entirely for me too. I do not wait for you to return what she has breathed into you in order to be inspired in turn.[86]

Here then Sophia appears as an inexhaustible life-giving source— one may even say goddess—to all who would love her. Since she belongs to all and loses none of her infinite breath in the intercourse she has with any individual, there is no jealousy among her suitors. Now although there is no direct mention of a kiss in Augustine's words, the sense of the passage seems to require it. In addition to the fact that the embrace of lovers naturally suggests an accompanying kiss, the reference to Sophia's breathing into her lovers—during an embrace!—makes it clear that we have to do once again with a case of the infusion of spirit (the "Spirit" of Wisdom) by way of a kiss: "Quod te inspirat non exspecto ut reddatur abs te, et sic ego inspirer ex eo."

Such a representation of Wisdom is not an isolated example in Augustine's writings. A similar account occurs in the *Soliloquia*, where it is said that the lover of Wisdom desires to see and embrace her in her beautiful nakedness. Of course, hers is a chaste beauty, and she grants her favors only to those who are devoted to her alone.[87] In these passages Augustine is drawing on the sapiential books of the Bible. For example, for a moment in the Book of Proverbs, Wisdom figures as a goddess when she is made to say "I will pour out my spirit upon you" (1:23), and in the Book of Wisdom (6:13–21) she is shown as a woman hastening to meet those that seek her. As we have suggested, however, Augustine's Sophia is both a divine hypostasis and an allegory of Christ; and this is in keeping with Paul's identification of Christ with Wisdom (I Cor. 1:23–24). This being so, we can say that in Augustine's passages we do have an allegorical representation of the amatory relationship between the Deity and the individual soul which is not unlike that described in the mystical exegeses of the Song of Songs.[88] An interesting difference would seem to be that in Augustine's words the Christian soul figures as a male principle and wooer, for Sophia, after all, is feminine—in fact, the very she-soul of Christianity. Though his figure of Sophia has some of the earmarks of the great Mother-Goddess who is Divine Harlot and yet perpetually chaste, such as is found in the earliest religions of the Near East and in some Gnostic sects of the early Christian centuries, it is also true that in these encounters it is Augustine (or the soul as he has represented it) who needs and yearns for fulfillment in the kiss, much in the same way as does the bride-soul in the Christian exegetical treatment of the Song. In this description of the *hieros gamos* the vital spiritual force is given by Sophia-Christ. In relation to its Creator, the Christian soul has a feminine psyche, a fact which is preeminently true of Augustine, who, it is worth remembering, in the field of apologetics is a model of virile and combative Christianity.

But there is yet another text which shows Augustine in the guise of the yearning bride-soul burning with desire for the divine kiss, although again, as in the passages we have just studied, the kiss image is not immediately obvious to modern readers. And yet it is one of the best-known and most lyrical passages in the entire corpus of the saint's writings: the magnificent "Sero te amavi" from the *Confessions* (X, 27) in which Augustine tells of his anxious search and finding out of God.

> Too late did I love Thee, O Fairness, so ancient and yet so new! Too late did I love Thee! For behold Thou wert within, and I without, and there did I seek Thee; I unlovely, rushed heedlessly among the things of beauty Thou madest. Thou wert with me, but I was not with Thee. Those things kept me far from Thee, which unless they were in Thee, were not. Thou calledst, and criedst aloud, and forcedst open my deafness. Thou didst gleam and shine, and chase away my blindness.

48

Thou didst exhale odors, and I drew in my breath and do pant after Thee. I tasted, and do hunger and thirst. Thou didst touch me, and I burned for Thy peace (*tetigisti me et exarsi in pacem tuam*).[89]

It cannot escape the reader that this text is a superb example of the doctrine of the spiritual senses and the inner as opposed to the outer man. The last part of the passage describes a progressive march toward God or, if one prefers, God's conquest of the saint's soul and, in doing so, employs an ascensive hierarchy of the five senses by which the Deity is seen to invade the inner man. The order is hearing, sight, smell, taste, and finally, touch, in which sense the experience culminates. At the same time, the intense spiritual experience is accommodated to the sensuous imagery and vocabulary of the love passion, and here the echoes of the Song, which revels in the amoristic delights of the several senses, are surely heard. The voice, the beauty (visible to the "eye"), the fragrance, and the sweetness of the beloved are in Augustine's passage as they are in the Song. And so, too, I believe, is the kiss, or better, the embrace and the kiss. What perhaps keeps us from seeing this is the absence of the word *kiss*. Augustine, however, has used a "synonym" for it in the word *peace*. The formulae *Pax tecum* and *Pax vobiscum* were signals for the exchange of the liturgical kiss of peace, and the *osculum pacis* was itself known simply by the word *Pax*; from this it was not a great step to referring to a kiss in general by the same term. The word for kiss in Gaelic, for example, is from the *Pax*. But it is specifically the connection between the theological concept of peace and the kiss of lovers that is relevant here. We earlier noted that Origen had related the liturgical kiss of peace to the kiss yearned for by the bride. The bride of the Song pleads for the kiss and embrace that would quiet her desires: that is, for the peace that is union and blessed fulfillment. This is the peace or kiss that Augustine burned for after being touched by the Deity. And he burns for it yet, as is suggested by the phrase *in pacem* (*in* plus the accusative). That is because he has already experienced something of it. Just as Augustine inhaled the fragrance exhaled by the Deity and *now* pants after that divine odor, and just as he tasted and *now* hungers and thirsts after the sweetness of the Lord, so too he was *touched* by the Lord and *now* burns for the fulfillment of that touch: "Tetigisti me et exarsi in pacem tuam." We saw earlier that when Gregory of Nyssa, one of the first theologians of the divine sweetness, contrasted the two orders of senses, he exemplified the sense of touch by the kiss. On the other hand, when, shortly before the passage under discussion, Augustine introduced the doctrine of the spiritual senses and the inner man, he associated the sense of touch more specifically with an *embrace*, though this could indeed include a kiss: "amo Deum meum . . . amplexum interioris hominis mei."[90] At any rate, if we wish to keep the correspondence between that passage and the present one, then we must allow that here too the "touch" signifies an embrace. Let us not forget that it is a lover, and one who would be loved in return, that speaks, and also that love, as the spiritual writers were fond of noting, casts out fear. Then we too may without fear suggest the following to be the meaning of Augustine's climactic prayer and ecstatic vision: "Thou didst embrace me and inflame me; and I burn for (the peace of) thy kiss."

2. Medieval Mystics

ollowing the period of the Church Fathers, there is no conspicuous use of kiss symbolism until the twelfth century, which age can be said to mark an apogee in its development. The reason for this is not difficult to ascertain. The twelfth century is one of the decisive periods in the evolution of Western man's psychological life, especially in the awakening to the life of the sentiments. The century abounds in treatises that seek to explain the complex stirrings and movements of the heart, and the passionate investigation into the psyche of man tends to be focused on the phenomenon of love precisely because the center of the inner life of man is recognized to be love. "The heart's life," says Hugh of Saint-Victor, "is love, hence it is wholly impossible that there be a heart wishing to live without love."[1] Accordingly, love is studied in all its aspects from brute carnal appetite to spiritual love of friend and God. As is well known, to the plethora of religiously inspired writings on love there is an important secular counterpart in the poetry and romances of the age. But even if one were interested only in the human side of the question, as much is to be learned about the nature of love and its psychological or psychophysical repercussions in the lover from the churchmen of the twelfth century as from their secular brethren.

As studied by the spiritual authors, the psychological life of man is naturally considered in relation to man's position vis-à-vis God as the supreme object and subject of love. It is therefore a psychology that cannot be understood without taking into account what is, after all, its *terminus ad quem*, the experience and notion of ecstasy.[2] One might say that in their descriptions of divine love the mystics at least are interested primarily in recording an experiential knowledge of God and only secondarily in the psychological life of man. The point is, however, that they excel in portraying the latter because they are talking about an *experience*; in the matter of affective mysticism, speculation and experience are one. The affective mysticism which reaches its zenith in the twelfth century is connected with the Song of Songs either by way of direct exegeses of that book or by the bor-

51

rowing of its imagery for other kinds of mystical writings. In the application of the metaphor of spiritual nuptials few have been as impassioned and coherent as St. Bernard of Clairvaux; in the use of kiss symbolism no one has approached him. For this reason, even within the limited area of our concern, he must occupy a large place.

The Kiss Symbolism of St. Bernard

Two of the most religiously charged terms in the Christian vocabulary are *peace* and *love*. The connection between the kiss and the notion of peace is never forgotten by the mystics. For this reason they always see a tie between the mystical kiss of the bride-soul and the liturgical kiss of peace. Thus, although it may come as no surprise, it is nonetheless significant that almost at the outset of his Sermons on the Song, Bernard calls attention to the theme of peace in relation to the kiss motif that opens the Canticle. Commenting on the very title of the book, which, he says, is *The Beginning of Solomon's Canticle of Canticles*, Bernard writes: "Observe first how proper it is that the name of the Peaceful One, which is what Solomon means, is at the head of a book that has its beginning in a sign of peace, that is, in a kiss."[3] For the Christian, as Origen long before had noted, Solomon, the Peaceful One, was a type of Christ.[4] This idea is carried on in the second Sermon where Bernard identifies the kiss of the Song with the Incarnate God, Jesus Christ, the Prince of Peace. It is here that the saint introduces a subtle distinction between the kiss of the Mouth and the kiss of the Kiss. The Mouth is the eternal Word, to be kissed by whom was the unique prerogative of the *assumptus homo*. The Word assuming is the *os osculans* (the Mouth that kisses), the flesh assumed is the *osculatum* (the mouth that is kissed); the Kiss in which the two meet and become one—for such is the function of a kiss—is the *persona* compacted of the two. Bernard then says that the most one can aspire to is to be kissed by this Kiss which is the Incarnate Word, Christ Jesus, the mediator between God and man. This Kiss, which is the Incarnation, is an extraordinary act of love and condescension to mankind, the meaning of which is explicated in terms of the fulfillment of the biblical promise of peace when Bernard introduces two texts of Paul. The joining of lips expresses the embrace of souls or hearts; but this Kiss unites the divine and human nature thereby *making peace between the things of earth and heaven, for He is our*

Peace who has made one out of both.[5] The rest of the second Sermon goes on to illustrate that the kiss of the Song refers to the *Princeps pacis*, who has finally come to quiet the querulous voices of those who were sorely lamenting that the promised peace and the Messiah prophesied by the prophets had not yet arrived.[6]

The second Sermon, then, interprets the kiss of the Song as the hypostatic union in Christ. Important as this is, it is not the most characteristic feature of Bernard's kiss symbolism. In the sermons that follow, the kiss is considered principally within the context of the betrothal of the soul and the Word or Christ.[7] Here Bernard leaves the realm of strict exegesis for that of experimental mysticism. In this context Christ is no longer the kiss itself, although it is he who gives it to the bride-soul. That is, the role of Mediator remains uniquely his.

In Bernard's discussion of the mystic itinerary, each of the three major stages is signified by a particular kiss image: the purgative stage is figured by the kissing of Christ's feet, the illuminative stage by the kiss of Christ's hands, and, finally, the moment of union itself is indicated by the kiss of Christ's mouth. Since these kisses are progressive, the soul must have attained the first two before being ready to receive the unitive kiss. Only then, says Bernard tremblingly, "We perhaps may dare to reach to that glorious Mouth, not solely to contemplate it, but even to kiss it; for Christ the Lord is a Spirit before our face, with whom, and by whose grace, we will be made one Spirit by cleaving to him in a holy kiss."[8] As in the passage from St. Ambrose, so here we note that the kiss image is built upon Paul's great mystical utterance, thereby heightening the idea that spiritual union with Christ is an act of love.

For Bernard, however, the bride-soul cannot or should not aspire to kiss the Mouth proper (*osculum ab ore*). Just as in Sermon II the kiss of the Mouth proper was reserved to the *assumptus homo*, the Christ-man, here it is a kiss reserved to the Father and the Son, with the Father as *osculans* and the Son as *osculatus*. To be kissed by the Mouth would be to know God in essence, that is, in the same way that the Father and the Son know one another. Hence the bride's request is more modest: to be kissed with the Bridegroom's Kiss, not with his Mouth. But this is no mean desire inasmuch as the Kiss is nothing less than the Third Person of the Trinity—the Holy Spirit: "If it is so that the Father is the one that kisses, and the Son is the one that is kissed, it will not be wrong to understand the Kiss itself as the

Holy Spirit, the most tranquil peace of the Father and Son, their indissoluble bond, their single love and indivisible unity."[9] It is no wonder, then, that St. Bernard says that the supreme gift the bride may receive —to be kissed "with the Kiss" of the Bridegroom (Christ)—signifies "to receive the infusion of the Holy Spirit."[10] The request for the kiss is the prayer to be infused with the Spirit. We see by this that with Bernard the symbolism of the kiss is brought into the very heart of Trinitarian mysticism. The kiss between the soul and Christ is modeled on and made possible by a participation in that infinitely greater Kiss that pertains to the Trinity in a consubstantial way. The Holy Spirit (Breath) as the unifying principle of love and knowledge by which the Father and the Son are One is rightly called a Kiss, for the kiss is by nature, as it were, the perfect affective image of the union in spirit. God, of course, is Spirit; and the Kiss of the Father and the Son is the expression of their mutual love and their unity of Spirit.

The same Kiss which is common to the Father and Son is also the effective agent that draws the human soul into a union with the Triune God. Yet, Bernard's mysticism is without doubt chiefly Christocentric. Christ's role is essential in bringing the soul to the Father. Hence, Christ gives the Kiss to the soul. The importance of this is heightened in the light of the fact that Bernard bases the image and the concept upon the Latin Church's doctrine that the Holy Spirit proceeds from the Son as well as from the Father. Thus it is worth noting how Bernard adduces scriptural evidence for the idea of the transmitting of the Spirit by way of the Son. Commenting on John 20:22, where it is said that Jesus breathed upon the Apostles with the words "Receive the Holy Spirit," he observes that this was a kiss that the Lord gave the Apostles, that is, the primitive Church. Not the material breath of Jesus was the kiss but the invisible Spirit which was conveyed by it:

> Behold a young bride receiving the new kiss, not from the Mouth, but from the kiss of the Mouth. "He breathed on them," it is said (John 20:22), that is, Jesus on the Apostles, the Primitive Church; and he said, "Receive the Holy Spirit." That was indeed a kiss he gave. What? Was it the corporeal breath (*flatus*)? No, rather the invisible Breath (*Spiritus*) which was given by way of the Lord's breathing, so that we would understand that he proceeds from him (the Son) equally as from the Father, like a true kiss that is common to the one who kisses and to the one who is kissed.[11]

The Holy Spirit, then, is the Kiss of the Mouth of the Father and of the Son; and so, "it is enough for the bride [Bernard is again speaking of the soul] to be kissed with the Kiss of the Bridegroom, even if not by his Mouth." In this Kiss the Father and the Son are made known to the bride in a privileged but participatory way. The bride asks this boon of the Son, for it belongs to the Son to reveal the Father to whomsoever he will. In revealing himself, the Son also reveals the Father. "Without doubt, the Son reveals this by way of a Kiss, that is, by the Holy Spirit."[12] No creature may claim of its relationship to God what is true of the relationship between the Father and the Son who kiss one another as equals. The creature's union with God is not consubstantial; the kiss is given to it as a privilege. Thus not even the great Paul, when he was rapt to the third heaven, received the kiss of the Mouth, but only the kiss of the Kiss. Great as he was, Paul could not raise his lips to those of the Most High. A kiss had to be sent down to him from above.[13]

It is significant that Paul's mystic rapture is translated by Bernard into the language of kiss symbolism. Again we see how the kiss image brings into relief the affective nature of a saint's relationship to God. For Christian spirituality, Paul and Moses are understandably the great examples of souls privileged to have had a special encounter and union with God. Both are spoken of as great lovers of the Lord, and just as Bernard could speak of Paul's rapture as a kiss, so too the face-to-face meeting of Moses and God could become a kiss of union.[14]

Bernard himself explains why the image of the kiss is proper in the description of abtruse theological questions when he makes the connection between knowledge and love: "That is true knowledge which is given by means of a kiss, and is received with love, for the kiss is a token of love."[15] The soul, moreover, not only accepts the kiss with love, but yearns for and solicits it from the Bridegroom. It is within the context of this *motus* of the soul's desire that Bernard's kiss symbolism takes on erotic coloring. The soul can never merit the kiss unless it desires it as a lover who craves with an all-consuming passion and will be satisfied with nothing less than the unifying kiss itself:

"Let Him kiss me with the kiss of His Mouth." Who speaks thus? The bride. Who is this bride? It is the soul thirsting for God . . . She that solicits a kiss is in love. Of all the natural sentiments that of love is the most excellent, especially when it returns to its source which is

> God . . . The bride-soul in love asks for a kiss. She does not ask for liberty, nor for a reward (*mercedem*), nor for an inheritance, not even for learning, but for the kiss.[16]

Such is the soul's yearning that it becomes unabashed and unrestrained in its cry for the unitive kiss. It is grateful but not appeased by the privilege of kissing the Feet and the Hands: "I can have no rest until he kisses me with the kiss of his Mouth . . . I am not ungrateful, but I love. I admit I have received beyond my merit, but it is too little for my desire. I am carried by my desire, not by reason" (*Desiderio feror, non ratione*).[17]

While it is true that in such passages as these love seems to take precedence over knowledge in the soul's way to God, such passionate protestations must not keep us from seeing that Bernard does not always exclude reason from the experience of mystical union. On the contrary, for the saint the soul's spiritual apprehension of God at the apex of contemplation necessitates an active participation of both the will and the intelligence. Even this important idea is translated into the language of kiss symbolism. Both those who think they know truth without loving it and those who claim to love it without understanding are incapable and unworthy of receiving the holy Kiss which admits of neither error nor tepidity. The bride (i.e., soul) who would receive it must give herself completely; she must offer both of her lips, that is, both reason and will.[18] The bond between love and knowledge could not be closer.

Before leaving Bernard, there is another aspect of his kiss symbolism to be considered. As he follows through the symbolism of mystical marriage between the soul and God, the saint does not hesitate to speak of the bride's impregnation and fecundity. The bride conceives and her breasts grow full with the milk that will be fed to the children she is to bear. (The spiritual children she is to bear are the good works born of and carried out in Charity.)[19] Now although the image of the mystical embrace is common in Bernard, here in the description of spiritual conception it is the infusion of the Spirit into the soul by a kiss that effectuates the impregnation of the bride:

> While the bride is speaking of her Bridegroom, suddenly, as I have said, he is present; he grants her desire, gives her the kiss. Proof of this is the filling of her breasts. Such is the efficacy of this kiss that as soon as she receives it the bride conceives, witness the swelling of her breasts and the overflow of their milk . . . Wherefore the Bridegroom

may say: "My bride, you have what you pleaded for and the proof of it for you is that your breasts have become better than wine. Your evidence of having received the kiss is that you feel you have conceived."[20]

The idea of spiritual union and fruition could hardly find a more seemly and efficacious image by which to commend itself, for anything beyond it more suggestive of a sexual union would not convey so accurately the concept of the unitive relationship as the mystics *experience* it. Along with the sense of self-fulfillment it brings, that relationship is felt as a reciprocal love and mutual indwelling. The image of the intermingling of the breath-soul of the creature with the Breath (Spirit) of the Creator in a kiss best tells us something of the experiential nature of the mystic union.[21] Our next religious also attests to this.

William of Saint-Thierry and the Song of Songs

Bernard's fellow Cistercian, William of Saint-Thierry, is the author of an *Exposition on the Song of Songs* which, for its beauty and richness of mystical theology, is second only to Bernard's own sermons on the canticle. Its chief interest for us is in some passages where the use of kiss symbolism is conciously grounded in the physiology of the real kiss. From the outset, William makes it clear that, in his explication, the bride and Bridegroom of the Song are to be understood as the soul and Christ.[22] The request the bride makes for the kiss of the Bridegroom is an expression of the soul's desire for direct contact and union with Christ. Here William gives a definition of the real kiss that is meant to explain its appropriateness as a symbol for the mystic union: "The kiss is an affectionate external union of bodies and a sign of and spur to an inner union. By the ministry of the mouth, it seeks not so much a union of bodies as of spirits (souls) through a mutual exchange." Although this passage is clearly influenced by that of Ambrose which we have already analyzed, it seems to me to be more remarkable for its greater suggestion that in the real kiss it is *souls* (or at least a psychic substance) that are seeking to mingle. Certainly something more than mere breath is to be understood by *spiritus* in this context, for we note that in carrying out the analogy in the mystic kiss, William says that when Christ kisses the bride, he draws her "spirit" into himself and in turn infuses his own "spirit" into her so that by this mutual indwelling the two are made one spirit: "spiritum ejus sibi attrahens, et suum infundens ei, ut invicem unus spiritus sint."[23]

For William, as for Bernard, although Christ is the Bridegroom, the area in which the soul meets with the Deity is the Holy Spirit. Here too we find the kiss symbolism used in a description of Trinitarian mysticism. The kiss of union experienced by the soul is itself the Holy Spirit, which is the same Kiss that joins the Father and the Son in their most intimate and consubstantial unity. Caught up, as it were, in the unifying Kiss of the Father and the Son, the soul is rapt into the very heart of the Trinity and even begins to know as she is known.[24] At the height of this rhapsodic passage, in describing the unitive kiss received by the soul, William reverts once again to the analogy of the real kiss. Now, however, rather than Christ, it is said to be the Creator-Spirit with whom the soul as created spirit seeks its union: "And like lovers who in their kisses transfuse their souls (spirits) into one another in a sweet and mutual exchange, so the created spirit pours itself entirely into the Spirit that creates it for this very reason; and into it the Creator-Spirit infuses itself as it wishes, and man is made one spirit with God."[25]

The description emphasizes the infusion of the Spirit into the soul and the soul's surrender and immersion into the Spirit. It is the most ecstatic moment, the climax of the unitive life as described by William, and now, in making the parallel to the real kiss, he speaks of the latter more explicitly as being a kiss of lovers who in their ecstacy are made one by the interfusion of their breath-souls. Thus it is no wonder that the bride-soul cannot be satisfied with any consolation short of the embrace and that kiss which is the sweetness of a mutual union.[26] The kiss, William notes, is the most daring and yet necessary symbolic vehicle by which the soul, in its supreme yearning and drive, entertains the clarity of God's visage.[27]

St. Aelred of Rievaulx and the Kiss of Friendship

St. Aelred of Rievaulx, a younger contemporary and disciple of St. Bernard, holds a place of great importance not only in the history of the Church in England, but in the development of the idea of Christian friendship as well. In his treatise *De spirituali amicitia* he applies a trichotomous symbolism of the kiss to three stages of Christian friendship. In introducing the mystic kiss as a symbol of union between friends, Aelred is in part inspired by, though he goes beyond, the liturgical kiss of peace.

Christian friendship between two human beings is an act by which man carries out on a smaller scale the friendship God offers to man. Friendship is thus a way of becoming God's friend, and in it Christ is both the real beginning and the end. It is because God is *Amicitia* and because all friendship derives from him that a man may reach him by way of love and friendship with a fellow creature. Ultimately a friend is loved because of what we perceive to be divine in him. It is the spiritual climb of the soul to God by way of friendship that Aelred speaks of in terms of the threefold kiss: physical, spiritual, and intellectual. When friend unites with friend, says Aelred, the two become as one heart and one soul rising by love to attain the friendship of Christ and to become one spirit with him in a kiss.[28] In its desire for this unitive kiss, the soul cries out "Osculetur me osculo oris sui." Like love, friendship is felt to be an ecstatic and unifying experience, and, for Aelred, in this spiritual experience the kiss offers itself as a natural symbol because of the unifying nature of the real physical kiss. Following a traditional Christian expository method of passing from the natural to the spiritual, Aelred considers, with a kind of scientific realism, the corporeal kiss to be a real means by which "spirits" meet and intermingle:

> Let us consider the nature of the carnal kiss in order to pass afterwards from carnal to spiritual things and from the human to the divine. Our life is sustained by two sustenances: food and air. Now without food we may yet survive for a time, but without air we cannot live even for an hour. Consequently, in order to live we breathe in air with the mouth and then exhale it. *It is precisely what is exhaled or inhaled that has been given the name of spirit. Wherefore in the kiss two spirits meet and mingle and are joined.* And from such kisses, there arises a certain sweetness of the mind that guides and controls the affection of those who kiss. Thus there exist the physical kiss, the spiritual kiss, and the intellectual kiss [*Est igitur osculum corporale, osculum spiritale osculum intellectuale*].[29]

Aelred recognizes that the physical kiss is too easily abused and profaned by the wicked, who indulge in it for the intrinsic sensual pleasure it gives. When exchanged by the pure, however, it is a natural and true sign of peace, as it is for the faithful about to partake in communion at the Mass. It is also proper when given as a sign of affection between man and wife, or even between friends reunited after a long absence. And it is also a sign of the concord and unity of Christians, who kiss their guests when receiving them. Nonetheless, in the context of his discussion of friendship, it is not such symbolical usage of the real kiss that Aelred has in mind when he speaks of the spiritual kiss between friends. In describing the physical kiss, Aelred used the word *spirit* in its sense of breath. Now for the "spiritual" kiss, he draws exclusively on the word in its meaning of non-corporeal spirit—soul or mind (*osculum spiritale conjunctione animorum*). This kiss then is not made by the contact of mouths, but by the affection of the mind; it is effected not by the joining of lips but by the mingling of souls (or spirits).[30]

The same idea occurs with the same terms—but more lyrically —in a passage of the *Speculum Charitatis* where Aelred is mourning the death of his fellow monk and friend, Simon. Recalling the sweetness of that friendship, Aelred says he used to embrace and kiss Simon, not, however, by bodily contact and with the lips, but with the heart and the affection of the mind (i.e., love).[31] As is readily seen, Aelred's "spiritual kiss" of friendship is a pure metaphor just as is the mystic kiss between the soul and God, but its truly unique feature is that, unlike the latter, it is adapted to a relationship between two human beings. In this respect, it anticipates the marriage of minds and the disembodied kiss of souls that were to be exalted by many a Renaissance writer.

Aelred's discussion of friendship is meant as a Christian adaptation of Cicero's treatise on friendship, and certainly the Roman's thoughts are strewn throughout the Christian writer's work. But there is, of course, a fundamental difference between the two. That Christ, the Word made flesh, is the way and terminus of friendship is something Cicero could not know. For Aelred, on the other hand, the presence of Christ is so essential to the spiritual union of friends that this union may be said to be the very kiss of Christ. The thought is developed in a beautiful image when Aelred says that in the spiritual kiss between friends, it is really Christ who is kissed or kisses, not with his own mouth, however, but with the mouth (metaphorically) of the creature. It is Christ kissing because it is he who inspires that holy affection in the two friends whereby they feel as one soul in two bodies. From this Christ-inspired spiritual kiss the lover-friend climbs quite naturally to a desire for the direct unitive kiss of Christ's own mouth.

This is the *osculum intellectuale*, which is understood as the infusion of the grace needed for full union:

> Then the mind [mens], familiar and sated with this spiritual kiss, and knowing that the sweetness comes from Christ, thinks to itself: "Oh, if he himself would only come"; and yearning for that intellectual kiss, it calls out with boundless desire, "*Let him kiss me with the kiss of his mouth.*" Thus all earthly affections being put to slumber, and all worldly desires and thoughts silenced, it takes its joy only in the kiss of Christ and rests in his embrace, exulting and saying: "*His left hand is under my head, and his right hand shall embrace me.*"[32]

At the height of the soul's ascent, when soul and God meet directly, the experience of orthodox Christian mysticism is verified by Aelred, for although the soul has made its ascent by way of fellow creatures, all earthly connections and human affections have been finally and completely put aside; or, we may say, the friendship between creatures is totally subsumed under the friendship between creature and Christ. But whereas, in speaking of the unitive relationship between friends, Aelred tended to attenuate the amatory connotation of the kiss, when he comes to the union between God and creature it is the erotic language of human love—inspired, as usual, by the Song of Songs—that is used to describe the theopathetic experience.

Friendship and the Two-in-One Sentiment

Given the complementary concern of the present study for the two-in-one motif, we must add another word here about the friendship theme that Aelred has led us into. Within the context of Aelred's Christian friendship, the joining of souls refers to the harmony and love that prevail between two friends who are attracted by a principle of affinity. The friends are as one, each wishing the perfection and blessedness of the other as though for himself. The sentiment of two in one is as important in the history of friendship as it is in the history of love. For that matter, it is not always easy to distinguish between the two sentiments. Plato knew that where there is no reciprocity there is no friendship (*Lysis* 212 D). From Aristotle to Cicero and beyond, thinkers were to say that a friend is another self. Cicero also notes that in the search for a true friend, one seeks out another "whose soul he may so mingle with his own as almost to make one out of two" (et alterum anquirit, cuius animum ita cum suo misceat, ut efficiat

paene unum ex duobus. *De amicitia*, xxi, 81). St. Ambrose has a Cice-
ronian passage on friendship at the close of his *De officiis* (III, 22) in
which he too asserts that a friend is a partner in love, with whom one
can join spirits in an intermingling whereby the two become one; a
friend is someone to whom one is joined as to another self.[33] And like
Aristotle, Cicero, and Ambrose, St. Augustine tells us that the mark of
true friendship is reached when there is but one soul in two bodies.
One of the most striking pages of the *Confessions* (IV, 6)—Augustine
was later to retract it—develops this idea when the Bishop recalls his
grief at the death of his friend: "I was astonished that other mortals
lived, since he whom I loved, as if he would never die, was dead; and
I wondered still more that I, who was to him a second self, could live
when he was dead. Well did one say of his friend, 'Thou half of my
soul,' for I felt that my soul and his soul were but one soul in two
bodies; and, consequently, my life was a horror to me, because I would
not live in half."[34] It was, in all probability, from Augustine that
Aelred derived something of his own lament (or its language) for the
loss of Simon; his words (too many to record here) echo those of
Augustine. The same is true of a part of Bernard's extraordinary
threnody—perhaps unsurpassed even in the literature of profane love
—raised by the saint on the occasion of the death of Gerard, his
brother in the flesh and the spirit. At one point Bernard writes: "My
soul cleaved [*adhesit*] to his soul, and the two of us were made one
not so much by the tie of consanguinity as by the oneness of our feelings . . . , by the conformity and harmony of our wills."[35] And Bernard
even appropriated to this friendship (but we may call it love) the great
theme of Acts 4:32 ("There was one heart and soul in all the company of believers") in saying that he and Gerard formed "one heart
and one soul," so that death cut through their common soul, dividing
it in two, sending the better part to heaven while laying the lesser
part low in the quagmire of the earth.

The concept of a special bond between *two* friends creates a slight
problem in a Christian context precisely because, ideally, friendship
should reach out to embrace the entire Christian community. But the
Cistercians could point to Scriptures for justification of the idea of a
unique bond and more intimate relationship between two men. David
and Jonathan, of course, were a conspicuous example of such friendship, and we may recall that these biblical friends are shown to have
kissed. But Aelred argues for an even more exemplary friendship by

pointing to Christ's special affection for "the beloved disciple" John. Though Christ loved all equally, says Aelred, he nonetheless had a particular love for John. The thought occurs in the *Speculum Charitatis* (Lib. III, cap. xxxix) where Aelred speaks of a friend's spiritual kisses as healing the sickness of our worried hearts.[36] We will have occasion, in the next chapter, to speak of friendship in connection with medieval love poetry, and again later in discussing the erotic imagery of Marsilio Ficino's otherwise rigidly correct intellectual masculine friendship.[37]

Love and Death: Death by the Kiss

A matter of the profoundest significance is the association between the kiss as a symbol of the fulfillment of love's desire and the theme of death. The medieval proverb holding that "to die of love is to love too much" is a thought that belongs to the "popular" mind of the Middle Ages.[38] The lovers of God, as Christians from the time of the first martyrs knew, could never love the Beloved enough.[39] Hence they account it the greatest happiness to be able to die for him. It is with good cause that the Church has always regarded the martyrs as its saints par excellence. As examples of the willingness to die for love, the martyrs are themselves loved and revered as the true imitators of Christ. Their death is a surrender of the self accompanied by a transport. But if it is true that there is no martyrdom without mysticism, it is equally true that there is no mysticism without martyrdom. In this sense the medieval mystics see themselves as following the path of the martyrs, and their mystical dying as patterned on the mystico-literal death of the martyrs. The same principle of ecstatic love operates in the two groups as they seek death, secure in the words of St. Paul, "Where then, Death, is thy sting?" (I Cor. 15:55), and anxious to return the love of Christ by an act of self-immolation. In choosing love, the mystic, like the martyr, chooses to die.

Both know, in the words of the Song of Songs, that "love is strong as death" (8:6), a theme found over and over in the writings of the mystics. It is from this motif that Hugh of Saint-Victor derived the inspiration for his short but ecstatic paean to Love, *De laude Caritatis*, which is so important for its treatment of love in connection with the idea and theology of martyrdom. Hugh notes that the martyrs went to their torments unflinchingly, and that their flesh scorned their external wounds to the degree that love had wounded them within. Martyrs and mystics (we are at that point where the titles are equivalent) desire and glory in the wound caused by love. There are many, says Hugh, who carry love's piercing arrows in their hearts, longing for them to be driven in deeper.[40]. And Gilbert of Hoy, who continued St. Bernard's sermons on the Song, exulted at the thought that love not only wounds, but kills outright since it is as strong as death: "Non modo vulnerat, sed etiam necat; Fortis est enim ut mors dilectio."[41]

Thus one of the most accepted truths about the *unio mystica* is that it necessitates or effects a death. For Orphic, Christian, and Sufi lovers, the need to die is axiomatic.[42] If the full realization of the Christian's hope of union with God entails a definitive earthly death, the *unio mystica*, which is a preview of that eschatological state of blessedness, involves an anticipation of death. Whatever one may think about the mystery of the bodily resurrection in the afterlife, Christian thinking has been overwhelmingly of the opinion that in the mystic union the body can have no share.

As concrete examples by which to study the nature of the mystic union, Christian writers most frequently and most naturally turned to Moses and Paul. Whether one thought of Paul's rapture as being a real apprehension of the Divine Essence or merely a foretaste of the beatitude to be known only after final corporeal death, it was plain that the experience was such that it could not be had without a kind of death here and now. Commenting on Paul's words "Whether in the body or out of the body," St. Augustine, for example, held that suspension of the ordinary mental activity during rapture is a state that must be considered not merely a sleep but a death; and in his account of Moses' wish to behold the Essence of God, he explained that the words of the Deity, "Man shall not see my face and live," speak of the necessity of a death to this life.[43] In a less strictly mystical vein but in an intensely spiritual sense, Augustine himself yearned for the death that would bring him to see God's face: "Tell me . . . even for thy mercy's sake, O Lord my God, what thou art unto me. Say unto my soul, 'I am thy salvation,' but say it so that I may hear thee. . . .I will run after the sound of that voice and thereby lay hold on thee. Hide not thou thy face from me; let me die, that I may see it, lest otherwise I die because I see it not" (*Confessions*, I, v).[44]

For Christians the fundamental text concerning the ecstasy of death in a mystical sense is Paul's exalted cry: "I am crucified with Christ. Yet I live; nay, not I, but it is Christ that lives in me" (Gal.

2:19–20). When the Pseudo-Dionysius wished to demonstrate that the nature of scriptural love (*agape*) was ecstatic (hence inclusive of the concept of *eros*), he cited Paul's words, saying that the great Apostle thereby proved himself to be a true ecstatic lover who had gone out of himself into the Beloved and now possessed not his own life but that of the One for whom he yearned.[45]

The equating of the soul's love ecstasy with death in this mystic sense was made by St. Bernard, for whom the bride's repose in the embrace of the Beloved is a deathlike sleep. "Therefore," he writes, "I am not to be thought absurd if I call the bride's ecstasy a death" (*Proinde et ego non absurde sponsae exstasim dixerim mortem*).[46] Bernard too aspires to this death which is a transcendence of corporeal sensations and impressions that endanger the soul's true life. Thus it is a good death which, instead of depriving one of life, transmutes one's life into something infinitely better; it is a death which does not make the body fall but rather causes the soul to be elevated: "Bona mors, quae vitam non aufert, sed transfert in melius; bona, qua corpus non cadit, sed anima sublevatur."[47]

In William of Saint-Thierry this mystic death is more closely associated with the image of the kiss itself. When the bride first tastes the sweetness of the Bridegroom's kiss, she is experiencing but a foretaste of the full bliss that is to be known; but her appetite having been whetted, she desires even now the plenitude of the kiss. Thus, accompanying the mystic kiss or resulting from it is the desire to die the real definitive bodily death: "She wished to die [*Dissolvi volebat*] and be with Christ, since having tasted the supreme Good, she did not deem it necessary to remain in the flesh."[48] Behind this too is St. Paul. In all such cases of dying, death is a gain, and that gain is union with Christ, who first loved and who, because of that love, first died for man. It is no accident that what I have called the fundamental Christian text connected with the mystic's death-ecstasy speaks of being with Christ on the Cross.

For the Christian, then, the sting of death was removed by Christ's death on the Cross. Franciscan spirituality in particular insisted on the devotion to and contemplation of the Cross (the supreme symbol of self-sacrifice and death as love's choice) as a way of sharing in the death by which new life in union with Christ is gained.[49] In carrying forward a trend of Bernardine piety, this movement also contributed to the erotization of the Cross itself. Thus in a passage inviting us to the love and contemplation of the Cross, St. Bonaventura attributes to St. Bernard the description of the crucified Christ in the attitude of a lover: "Behold, Bernard says, Christ's head leaning down to kiss us, his arms extended to embrace us, his hands pierced to make us a gift, his side open for the sake of loving, his whole body disposed to a giving."[50] We see then that the picture of the suffering and sacrificial Christ nailed to the Cross did not exclude the idea of Christ as both Lover and Beloved. On the contrary, inasmuch as the Crucifixion signified the greatest act of love, Christ appears on the Cross as the very apotheosis and *form* of Love, the Supreme Martyr. But this eroticism of the Cross and death is not unique to Bernardine and Franciscan devotional ardor. It occurs early in Christian speculation and, as one ought perhaps to expect, in a way that connects the Cross with the marriage metaphor. Like Christ's death, the consummation of marriage involves a sacrificial act.

One of the most remarkable pronouncements in the area of nuptial Christology was made by St. Augustine when he interpreted Christ's real death on the Cross as the consummation of his marriage with the bride. In consenting to impregnation by the Holy Spirit, Mary won the eternal gratitude of mankind. Her faith gave access to the Divinity, for in her womb, as in a nuptial chamber, God prepared the marriage of the Son. But if the birth of Christ from the Virgin Mary betokened the wedding of the Word and Humanity (i.e., the Church), the marriage was not consummated until Calvary:

> Like a bridegroom, Christ came forth from his chamber, and with a presage of his nuptials he went into the field of the world. He bounded like a giant exulting on his way; he reached the marriage-couch of the Cross, mounting it, and there he consummated his marriage. When he heard the sighs of the creature, by a compassionate exchange he surrendered himself to the torment in place of his bride. Like a ruby he offered up the carbuncle, and thereby forever joined the woman to himself. "I have betrothed you to one spouse," the apostle says, "that I might present you to Christ as a chaste virgin" (II Cor. 11:2). Behold now how she who was once ugly is now beautiful . . . Therefore, oh brethren, let us rejoice in this union of God and man, of Bridegroom and bride, of Christ and the Church, of the Saviour and the Virgin.[51]

As is indicated by the reference to II Corinthians 11:2, the marriage metaphor as applied here to the Cross depends ultimately on

St. Paul's view of the relation between Christ and Church as a mystic marriage. In this respect the more significant reference is the great passage from Ephesians which sets up that mystic marriage as the archetype for the marriage of the human couple. There it is stated that Christ suffered and died for the sake of the bride (the Church): "Husbands, love your wives, just as Christ also loved the Church, and delivered himself up for her, that he might sanctify her, cleansing her in the bath of water by means of the word; in order that he might present to himself the Church in all her glory, not having spot or wrinkle" (5:25–27). The Cross, then, is the true epiphany of love. In Augustine's text the self-immolation of Christ appears as the mystical enactment of a redemptive and salvific *hieros gamos*.

The Crucifixion revealed the intensity of the Bridegroom's love; the bride—collectively and individually—must love in return with equal ardor. In the thirteenth century, the Franciscan affective mysticism that centered its life in the reenactment of this hierogamotic death received its most dramatic accents in the vernacular poetry of the Umbrian poet and mystic, Jacopone da Todi. The following single stanza contains the more important religio-erotic conceits that we have been tracing in the present work:

> Amor, amor, Iesù desideroso,
> Amor, voglio morire te abbracciando,
> Amor, amor, Iesù, dolce mio sposo,
> Amor, amor, la morte t'ademando;
> Amor, amor, Iesù si delettoso,
> Tu me t'arrendi en te me trasformando.[a]

This is a passionate appeal for that mystic kiss (as usual, the image of a lovers' embrace indicates a kiss) by which the lover dies into union with Christ; it is the yearning of the lover for the transformation of the self into the beloved. This very transformation and surrender of the self the lover knows to be possession: "Tu me t'arrendi en te me trasformando."[52]

Before leaving Jacopone it will be worthwhile to observe how this theme of the transformation or mystic conversion of lovers is dealt

---

[a] "Love, love, longed for Jesus; love, I yearn to die embracing thee; love, love, Jesus, my sweet bridegroom; love, love, I implore thee for death; love, love, Jesus so beloved, thou givest thyself to me by transforming me into thee." *Laudi, trattato e detti*, ed. Franca Ageno (Florence, 1953), p. 378.

with by him in a poem about St. Francis. In keeping with Bonaventura's account of the life of Francis, Jacopone understands the stigmatization of the saint as a transformation into Christ:

> L'amore ha quest'ufficio, unir dui en una forma:
> Francesco nel supplicio de Cristo lo transforma;
> Emprese quella norma de Cristo ch'avea en core,
> La mustra fe' l'amore vestuto d'un vergato.
> L'amor divino altissimo con Cristo l'abbracciao:
> L'affetto suo ardentissimo sì lo ce 'ncorporao
> Lo cor li stemperao como cera a segello:
> Empremettece quello ov'era trasformato.[b]

Here, in typical Franciscan fashion, it is love through contemplation of the Cross that works the miracle of binding two into one form, and there is a remarkable insistence on the concept of incorporation or indeed of a corporeal transformation. The word *form* in Jacopone's text is particularly laden with mystical significance. It is a Pauline echo, for indeed it was Paul who first spoke of a *forming* of Christ in the faithful: "My little children, again I am in travail of you, until Christ be formed in you" (Gal. 4:19). And, as we have seen, it was Paul who preached the need of dying with Christ, of patterning one's life on the model of Christ's life and death.

Much of what we have said about human souls in their mystical life as brides of Christ can be most naturally applied to those virgin sisters who formally wed themselves to him, thereby renouncing any claims to an earthly spouse. Besides the formal nuptial vows that have been taken by countless nuns, the number of those who have had visions in which mystical marriage with Jesus is experienced is itself large. It goes without saying that in the descriptions of such visions, the language is at times exceedingly erotic.[53] For the most part, the references to kisses and embraces add nothing new to what we have already found. There is a case or two, however, of particular relevance to our present subject inasmuch as they offer us the most dramatic examples of the association between the mystic kiss and death.

---

[b] "Love has this function of uniting two forms into one; it transforms Francis into the suffering Christ. He took that model of Christ that he had in his heart, and love, dressed in folly's cloak, showed the way. Divine love, most high, embraced him with Christ; his deeply burning passion so incorporated him into him [Christ], it softened his heart like wax for the seal, and impressed on it that one [Christ] into whom he was transformed." *Laudi*, pp. 248–249.

In the thirteenth century *Exercises* of St. Gertrude the Great, the request for the kiss that consumes and unites is made with all the fervor that is found in the Song of Songs and the most erotically charged commentaries of the preceding century. The prayer at the end of the fourth exercise has the following invocation: "Come, O Love, my King and my God, O Jesus my dearly Beloved . . . Unto Thyself, in the delightsome breathing of Thy sweet-flowing Spirit, attract me, draw me, and consume me. There in the joy of eternal attainment of Thee, in the kiss of perfect union, immerse me."[54] But it is the Prefatory Instruction to the evening of the fifth exercise that contains a passage where the kiss, cleaving, death, and passing over to become one spirit with the Beloved are part of one psychic and mystic process: "In the evening thou shalt long and faint with anticipation of enjoying the eternal vision of the glorious face of God and of the Lamb; and thou shalt cast thyself into the embrace of Jesus, the Bridegroom and the Lover, like a busy bee, clinging with thy soul's kiss unto His loving Heart. *Thou shalt ask of Him the heavenly kiss that will make thee die unto thyself, that by this death thou mayest pass over into God and become one spirit with Him.*"[55] These words reveal plainly the image that was latent in some of our previous examples of the mystic kiss: the death of the lover on or by a kiss.

Finally, we may consider a moving and remarkable document drawn up shortly after the death, at seventy years of age, of St. Juliana Falconieri (d.1341). In this account of the last moments of the saint, we learn that because she was unable to assimilate food of any kind, she was not allowed to receive the Host before her death. Then her desire to kiss Jesus (the Host) was refused her as unseemly. At last she obtained the wish that the Host be put on a veil and placed over her breast. The Host no sooner touched this loving breast than it disappeared, miraculously penetrating into Juliana's heart. The account concludes with these words: "And when the Host had vanished, Juliana, with a mild and happy face, as if she were rapt in ecstasy, died in the kiss of her Lord [*in osculo Domini moritur*], to the astonishment and admiration of those present."[56] The singularity of this example is that in it the kiss image is connected with an actual corporeal death which occurs during an ecstatic rapture. That is, here the mystic death and real death are one; St. Juliana died in an ecstasy, or, in the remarkable words of our document, she died in the kiss of the Lord.

Some three hundred years later the English Catholic poet Richard

Crashawe was to envision the death of St. Theresa of Avila as just such a kiss by which God ravished her soul unto himself:

> O thou undaunted daughter of desires!
>
> . . . .
>
> By the full kingdome of that finall kisse
> That seiz'd thy parting Soul, and seal'd thee his.

Crashawe's use of the image may derive not only from a Catholic tradition but from a Jewish one as well. In fact, the image and the expression "to die in (or *by*) the kiss of the Lord" must lead us into a discussion of the kiss image in Jewish religious writings, for a similar thought which was there elaborated was to become well known to Christian writers in the Renaissance period as the *mors osculi*. Before turning to it, however, it will be well to conclude our consideration of the kiss in medieval Christianity by some observations regarding the kiss and the Virgin Mary.[57]

The Kiss and the Virgin Mary

In Bernard we saw the kiss figure as the symbol of a fructifying union between the soul and the Deity whereby the soul is fecundated and will bring forth spiritual children, that is, good works. We may here recall that in the matter of both spiritual and physical impregnation the Breath or Spirit of God had always been thought of as the great fecundating principle and life-giving source, from the hovering of the Spirit over the waters and the breathing of the spirit of life into man by God to the fructification of the Virgin by the Holy Spirit. The Middle Ages did in fact picture the impregnation of the Virgin by the Spirit as accomplished by a kiss. An eleventh century liturgical *tropus* (*De beata Maria Vergine*) offers a charming case in point:

> Pater per secula
> sponsam ad osculum
> invitat virginem.
> Adulescentula,
> confestim credula
> gignit propaginem.[c]

[c] "The Father from eternity invites the virgin bride to the kiss. The young maiden, instantly believing, bears his child." In *Florilège de la poésie sacrée*, ed. Jean-Pierre Foucher (Paris, 1961), p. 210.

Here we see that the Annunciation episode is interpreted in conjunction with the Song of Songs. The Virgin is the bride, and it is significant that the kiss (the Spirit) is given to the Virgin-bride by the Father. Jesus, of course, is the fruit of this unique mystic union.

In point of fact, in the Catholic exegetical tradition of the Song of Songs, a third major current is that which holds the bride to be the Virgin. Although there is no systematic or comprehensive application of this interpretation in the early Christian centuries, Ambrose does appear to be the first Western Church Father to have explicated some verses of the Song in a Marian sense.[58] Of particular interest in this respect is the fact that in one place he interpreted the kiss of the first verse of the Song as referring to the infusion of the Holy Spirit in the Virgin at the Annunciation: *"He shall kiss me with the kisses of his mouth* means the grace of the Holy Spirit coming upon her, as the angel said to Mary, *The Holy Spirit will come upon thee. . . ."*[59] Such a pronouncement from the great bishop of Milan was to count for much among medieval exegetes. Now in all three of its main interpretations, the Song is certainly a paean to the Incarnation, but it is in the ecclesiastical and Marian exegeses that this is foremost or most obvious. Even a modern theologian writes of the Song: "Its intention is to celebrate the first union of the Word with human nature in the womb of Our Lady—the first kiss of the Word which is the pledge of the final union."[60] However, just as the Incarnation is understood to be the love union—the Kiss, as indeed we have heard Bernard refer to it—which joins the divine and the human natures into one, the Incarnation as it is effectuated in the womb of Mary may be thought of as the extraordinary fruit of the love union, of the kiss exchanged between God and the Virgin.

It may be deemed strange that Bernard, the saint so closely associated with the advancement of the cult of the Virgin, nowhere in his Sermons on the Song suggests a Marian interpretation.[61] And yet, although there are occasional indications of a Marian exegesis in patristic literature, it was in the twelfth century that this interpretation became truly popular and widespread. Note here that in the context of nuptial symbolism as applied to the Virgin, Mary, of course, becomes the bride of God, but there is no unanimity among Marian exegetes as to which Person of the Trinity is the Bridegroom. The angel's announcement to Mary was "The Holy Spirit will come upon thee" (*Spiritus sanctus superveniet in te*), and there was no question

71

about the impregnation being made by way of the Spirit. But the Bride-groom could be any one of the three Persons. To be sure, this role could be assumed by the Trinity. This, for example, was the view of Gilbert Foliot, whose explication of the kiss of the Song is a long and intricate tour de force of multifold applications of meanings to the bride and Bridegroom.[62] And Godfrey of Admont speaks of the three Persons of the Trinity as the lovers (*amatores*) of Mary.[63] For the most part, however, exegetes chose one of the divine Persons for the role of Lover and Bridegroom. In the eleventh century *tropus* we quoted above, it is the Father. This is true also for Rupert de Deutz, one of the first to apply a comprehensive Marian interpretation to the Song of Songs. At the beginning of Rupert's commentary it is the Virgin-bride, exalted by the love announced to her by the angelic messenger, who calls for the kiss of the Father. By their kiss of love the Holy Spirit enters and impregnates the Virgin, who gives birth to the God-man.[64] On the other hand, Amadeus, a twelfth century bishop of Lausanne, saw the Holy Spirit as the Bridegroom. In one of his eight homilies in praise of the Virgin, he has the Holy Spirit address the Song's invitation to Mary: "Arise, hasten, my love, my dove, my fair one, and come."[65] In yet another place Amadeus' language becomes even more realistically erotic as he himself renews the invitation to the Virgin, urging her to hasten to the prepared nuptial bed where her Bridegroom, the Holy Spirit, will come to her. Then she will be kissed with the kiss of the mouth and enfolded in a blissful embrace. Your Creator, says Amadeus to the Virgin, has become your Spouse. By this celestial kiss and embrace of union, the Virgin will be fecundated.[66] What is said here of the Virgin is much like what Bernard says of the fecundation of the human soul by the divine kiss, although the fruit of the Virgin's womb is incomparably greater than anything the human soul can bring forth.

The most curious application of Marian nuptial symbolism would seem to occur when the Virgin is said to be the Bride of her Son—*Sponsa Christi*.[67] In one sense, there is nothing unusual in this, for the soul of any of the faithful is a *Sponsa Christi*. The uniqueness of Mary is that she is both Bride and Mother of the Son. We find this particular relationship brought out by Aelred of Rievaulx, who goes so far in carrying out the nuptial symbolism as to talk of the Annunciation as a marriage between the Son and the Virgin with the angel as best man (*paranymphus*). The Son, says Aelred, is the Bridegroom; the Mother is the Bride. The Deity incarnated comes forth from Mary's womb as a Bridegroom from the nuptial chamber.[68]

But the most unrestrained eroticism in connection with our present subject is to be found in Philip of Harvengt, for whom the Song of Songs is a dramatic dialogue between the Virgin and the Word. Mary is chosen to be the Mother because she is beautiful. But Mary is not only the Mother that embraces her Son, she is also a Bride tenderly embracing her Bridegroom. The embraces are enjoyed by both when the Son, resting sweetly between her breasts, kisses her, and the kiss is truly consummated when it is given mouth to mouth and is accompanied by an embrace breast to breast. The mouth-to mouth-kiss is not complete without confirmation by such an embrace. Thus the Virgin is right when she says that their tender love is proved by the glue of their embrace.[69] The Virgin as Bride asks for the kiss—the Spirit—from the Son. By this kiss Mary, the creature and child of God, conceives and brings forth her Son.[70] Mary is thus Daughter, Bride, and Mother of God, a theme which was not restricted to the writings of theologians[71]

A late medieval legend proclaimed the Virgin herself to have been conceived not *ex coito* but by the way of a kiss—*ex osculo*. This legend is connected with the development of the idea (now Catholic dogma) of the Immaculate Conception, that is, the conception of the Virgin herself, privileged to be born without the stain of original sin. The salient features of the legend may be briefly stated. After twenty years of marriage, Joachim and Anne are still childless. When his offering is refused by the high priest, Joachim retires in shame into solitude with his shepherds. However, an angel (Gabriel) announces first to him and then to Anne, who has remained in Jerusalem, that they are to have a child. Hastening homeward, Joachim meets Anne at the Golden Gate of Jerusalem, and there the two greet one another with a kiss. By that kiss the spotless Virgin was conceived.

The Kiss in Medieval Art

In the West the legend of the kiss at the Golden Gate was depicted in art for the first time by Giotto in a scene which is no less remarkable than his *Kiss of Judas*. As in the latter, so in the *Meeting of Anne and Joachim* the two figures coming together in a kiss are seen to fuse into one compact mass. The scene is unusual also for the fact that it portrays the kiss between a man and a woman—that Giotto's couple is old matters not—so unequivocally as a mouth-to-mouth contact. Such a depiction is not common in the Middle Ages, and not even in medieval art dealing with profane love does one meet with it very easily. Raimond Van Marle notes that there are very few illustrators of love scenes who have dared to represent the kiss, evidently because the latter had a much more intimate meaning in the Middle Ages than it does today; and this is probably the reason why, in the literature of love of that period, it is a subject infrequently mentioned.[72]

That the references to kisses in medieval amatory literature are scarce is certainly far from the truth. It may also be said that the kiss is represented in medieval art with more frequency than Van Marle suggests. What is true is that rather than a clear labial kiss of lovers, one often finds something like a cheek-to-cheek representation and, sometimes, a hand of the male caressing the face of the woman. Partly, however, the reason for this seems to have been the desire to portray the faces in a full or three-quarters view. This may be observed in the many scenes, both in sculptured relief and painting, depicting the kiss of Judas or the theme of the Visitation, where again there is no question that a real kiss is intended, although in order to show as much of the faces as possible actual labial contact is hardly shown. Concerning the depiction of the Visitation, some theologians considered the text from Psalm 84:11 ("Mercy and Truth are met together; Justice and Peace have kissed") to have been a prophecy or anticipation of that event, and the artists followed them in this by portraying the Visitation scene as an embrace and a kiss between Mary and Elizabeth, just as the text of the Psalm was itself depicted allegorically by two feminine figures (Justice and Peace) kissing. So too there are medieval representations of the meetings of Saints Peter and Paul that show them embraced while exchanging the kiss of peace. It will be remembered that the New Testament references to the holy kiss and the kiss of love are made by these two Apostles. One even finds the kiss in miniatures introducing the text of the Song in medieval Bibles. (See Figs. 8, 9, 10, 11.)

A fourteenth-century miniature that shows secular lovers kissing (Fig. 12) is noteworthy because of the impression it creates of a merging of the lovers into one, an impression that is heightened by the fact that they wear the same or similar style of costume and the same (red) color. Even more extraordinary in this respect is an earlier

74

art object (c. 1150–1250), the handle of a bronze-cast mirror depicting a couple fully merged as one figure from the waist down and, from the waist up, clasped in an embrace and a kiss. (See Fig. 13 and pp. 115–116.) But another point to be made here is that medieval iconography commonly uses the representation of a kissing couple as an illustration of the vice of luxury. (See Fig. 16 and p. 154.)

The Kiss in Jewish Mysticism

Although the kiss was an ancient practice among Jews, a truly unique symbolism does not seem to be attached to it in Jewish writings until relatively late.[73] Medieval Judaism, however, produced a notable kiss symbolism. We may observe first the concept of a death by the divine kiss, remarking in passing that it was from the Jewish tradition that this beautiful image was to pass into the writings of Renaissance authors albeit somewhat transformed from its original meaning and not without some idea of Christian meaning attached to it.

Interpreting the scriptural words "and Miriam died there" (Num. 20:1), Rashi says: "She too [as Moses and Aaron] died by a [Divine] Kiss."[74] And in the Midrash on the Song of Songs we read that "the souls of these [the righteous] will be taken away with a kiss." It is Moses who most frequently serves as the great example of the death by a kiss. By this expression, however, the rabbinical exegetes do not have in mind anything like the Christian mystic kiss in the sense of a dying to the present life during an *excessus* which brings union with God. Nor do they refer to a real death accompanied by a mystical ecstasy as in the case of St. Juliana Falconieri. For them it indicates rather the real but absolutely peaceful death of the righteous, free from all anxiety or suffering. Originally, then, it is a metaphor referring to a privileged death that God bestows on his saints; as such it was very likely connected with the texts of Psalm 115:15 ("Precious in the eyes of the Lord is the death of his righteous ones") and Numbers 23:10 ("May I die the death of the just"). Eventually, however, this metaphor does come to be applied in a way that has a significance similar to that which is given to the kiss in Christian symbolism. This transition is clearly marked in the twelfth century by a passage from *The Guide of the Perplexed* (III, 51) of Moses Maimonides, the greatest Jewish thinker of the Middle Ages.

When a man's thought is free from distractions and entirely given over in contemplation to the apprehension of God, says Maimonides, that man can be visited by no evil, for "he is with God and God is with him."[75] The body, especially in youth, is a serious impediment to the attainment of that pure thought which leads to a "passionate" love and perception of God. But as the faculties of the body weaken and their desires are quieted, then the intellect is strengthened and perception is purified. Thus it is when a man given over to the life of contemplation has reached old age and nears death that "this apprehension increases very powerfully, joy over this apprehension and a great love for the object of apprehension become stronger, until the soul is separated from the body at that moment in this state of pleasure" (p. 627). This, it seems to me, must be considered a rapture; and to it Maimonides applies the rabbinical image of death by a kiss:

> Because of this the Sages have indicated with reference to the deaths of Moses, Aaron, and Miriam that the three of them died by a kiss. They said that the dictum [of Scripture], *And Moses the servant of the Lord died there in the land of Moab by the mouth of the Lord* indicates that he died by a kiss. Similarly it is said of Aaron: *By the mouth of the Lord, and died there.* And they said of Miriam in the same way: *She also died by a kiss.* But with regard to her it is not said, *by the mouth of the Lord*; because she was a woman, the use of the figurative expression was not suitable with regard to her. Their purpose was to indicate that the three of them died in the pleasure of this apprehension due to the intensity of passionate love. In this dictum the Sages, may their memory be blessed, followed the generally accepted poetical way of expression that calls the apprehension that is achieved in a state of intense and passionate love for Him, may He be exalted, *a kiss,* in accordance with its dictum: *Let him kiss me with the kisses of his mouth* (pp. 627–628).

This way of dying which, Maimonides says, is in reality a "salvation from death," is still the death of God's great saints, but accompanied now by a true *excessus.* Moreover, in explaining this image, the Jewish thinker has suggested that the kiss as a symbol is used in cases other than the real death of such saints. He seems to say, in fact, that the "Sages" applied to the particular scriptural texts referring to the deaths of Moses, Aaron, and Miriam an image—the kiss—which was already well established as a poetical metaphor expressing the attainment of a superior degree of perception or apprehension of the Deity by way of an intense love. It may be doubted that this was the order of happening in the Jewish tradition, but the fact that Maimonides puts it this way leads us to assume that by his time—the second half of the twelfth century—as in Christian so in Jewish thinking, the kiss was familiar as a symbol of the highest stage of contemplation. Moreover, as the Jewish thinker's words show, it was the kiss of the Song of Songs that was being interpreted in this way, that is, not merely within the context of a marriage between God and the collective community of Israel (the traditional Jewish allegorical reading of the Song), but as the culmination of an amatory relationship between God and the individual. Maimonides does not have the collective community of Israel in mind in his discussion of love of God. In fact, as for the Jewish tradition, the allegorization of the Song in terms of the individual rather than of the community of Israel may owe most to Maimonides himself, for his application of the Song in the overall context of the passage we have quoted is really to a philosophic question on the relationship of the rational soul to the Active Intellect.

Following Maimonides, for some three centuries, philosophizing Jews were to adopt and elaborate some such form of philisophical allegory, seeing in the Song the story of the mutual desire for union between the rational soul and the Active Intellect.[76] The Shulamite's kisses, when referred to, would signify the realization of that union. Understandably, a certain amount of eroticism attaches to the kiss in such an interpretation, although it is not heightened beyond the terms of the Song itself. But it would be improper to infer from this that anything like the Christian *unio mystica* was involved. Maimonides, of course, was the intransigent Jewish rationalist, opposed to anything even remotely suggestive of pantheism. In the description that he has given us of the kiss, it is an intellectual perception that is had, and this is accompanied by an abundance of joy and love. However, by the use of the kiss image, the link between knowledge and love is clearly and persuasively established. As for the principal image of Maimonides' discussion, the "death by a kiss," death is closely associated with if not actually said to be caused by an *accès* of love. The soul has been kissed (rapt) up by God.

The eroticism of the rabbinical death-by-a-kiss is minimal if we can refer to it as such at all. Even Maimonides duly noted that though it was said of Miriam that she died by a kiss, it was not said that she died *by the mouth of the Lord*, for inasmuch as she was a woman, such an expression in regard to her was not seemly.[77] But as in Christianity so too in Judaism, when the kiss image was employed in a full-fledged mystical doctrine, it was capable of acquiring all the erotic coloring that can be attached to it. In the esoteric kabbalistic tradition sex becomes an integral part of and the very key to a grandiose system of interpretation of God, the universe, and man's destiny; and here the kiss becomes a major symbol of mystic and cosmic significance. This is evidenced above all by the Zohar, the principal work of Jewish theosophy, written or compiled mostly in the late thirteenth century.[78] The Zohar, of course, is a work that defies any attempt at a brief summary; hence, we must renounce any wish to give a fair idea of the scope of its doctrine and its complicated symbolism; at best, we can only touch on some of the more important points.

In the Zohar, as in Judaism in general, the concept of loving God cannot be thought of outside the schema of the love between God and Israel. Membership in the community of Israel is a condition necessary to salvation. Nonetheless, such membership is not in itself a guarantee of salvation, so that responsibility for salvation remains an individual matter as does the matter of loving God, of "adhering" to him. The soul of a man is a particle of the Divinity, which it seeks to know in such a way as to be reunited with it. Yet for all its emphasis on the yearning of the soul toward God, the Zohar does not characterize it as a passion of lovers but rather within the terms of a father and child relationship. Thus there is an eschatological description which tells of the righteous and pure soul that has made its way after death into the Palace of Love of the King. In this palace, where "all His love-kisses are," the King himself appears and then *Jacob kisses Rachel* (Gen. 29:2), that is, the Lord discovers each holy soul, and takes each in turn up unto himself, "fondling and caressing her ... even as a father treats his beloved daughter."[79] Here then the kiss symbolizes the union or reunion of the soul with the very source from which it issued forth, but without any erotic intimation.

But if the relationship between the individual soul and God is kept on the plane of a father and daughter kinship, the zoharic conception of the love obtaining between God and Israel finds expression within the passionate language of the Song. It is in connection with this love that the Zohar applies the kiss image to a spiritual context on the principle of a cleaving and union of spirits (breaths) that the real kiss as an expression of love is felt to effect:

It is the Community of Israel who says this [to God]. Why does she say "Let Him kiss me" instead of "Let Him love me?" Because, we have been taught, kissing expresses the cleaving of spirit to spirit; therefore the mouth is the medium of kissing, for it is the organ of the spirit [breath]. Hence he who dies by the kiss of God is so united with another Spirit, with a Spirit which never separates from him. Therefore the Community of Israel prays: "Let Him kiss me with the kisses of His mouth," that His Spirit may be united with mine and never separate from it.[80]

In the Zohar such an application of the kiss of the Song to the description of the mutual love of God and Israel has more mystical significance than is immediately apparent from this one isolated passage. To appreciate this fact, one must have in mind the all-important kabbalistic concern for the unity of God and the central place that the mystery or law of sex has in its theosophy. Kabbalism, as G. Scholem has noted, sought for the mystery of sex in God himself.[81] At one time, the paradisiacal time, everything was as one, but the fall of Adam caused a division or dualism between the upper world and the lower world, a division reaching into God, as it were, or rather into the life and action of the Divinity. This was a break in the perfect harmony and union that existed between God and his creation. Stated in another way, God as transcendent in the "upper world" and God as immanent in the "lower world" became separated. God as immanent has the name of Shekhinah, which, while by no means a new concept in Judaism, acquired a peculiar and unique character in kabbalism by being very distinctly conceived of as the feminine principle of the Divinity, differentiated from, if not quite opposed to, the masculine principle. After the Fall, the Shekhinah is in exile but dwells among the community of Israel. Moreover, there is a mystical equivalence between the Shekhinah and Israel, whereby the latter becomes a mystical hypostasis of the Divinity. The true Shekhinah and God are not so divided that there is no union at all between them, but it is no longer a continuous union as before Adam's fall. Yet only in this union of God and the Shekhinah lies the true unity of God. Together they constitute God as the *One*; but insofar as they are separate, there is no *One*.[82] The mystery of their union (and similarly the mystery of the union between God and Israel) is figured at times by a frank and full sexual symbolism.[83] The ultimate and definitive union of the Shekhinah and God by which the dualism of male and female that characterizes all aspects, great and small, of the universe is to be transcended can take place only by a restoration of the original harmony. Man has an essential role to play in this restoration, by creating the conditions necessary to it. Man, that is, participates in the work of redemption and reintegration by living the true religious life. In a way, then, the salvation of the world and the unity of God himself depend upon man, although it is understood that man accomplishes this only by obedience and conformity to the commands and will of God.

Now for the kabbalist, even more than for the orthodox Jews, the religious life includes marriage and procreation as a sacred responsibility. No less than for the Jewish Christian St. Paul, marriage is for the kabbalist a sacred and profound mystery. And as human marriage was for Paul a symbol of the mystic union between Christ and the Church, so it was for kabbalism a symbol of the union between God and the Shekhinah (as well as of the union of God and Israel). But unlike Paul's and many another early Christian's praise of celibacy and begrudging approval of marriage (and unlike Hasidic Judaism), the kabbalists were more likely to consider celibacy (as distinct from chastity) defective, and marriage a sacred duty; for besides the idea that procreation was felt to increase the force of God, there was the deep-rooted conviction that, like God, man was not one until he was male and female.[84] For the kabbalist the supreme law is reintegration, that is, the transcendence of the dualism of male and female contrarieties that make up all aspects of the universe. The union of the masculine with the female principle takes place among human beings by way of sexual union within marriage, and this union both symbolizes and helps to satisfy the fundamental yearning for unity that courses throughout the universe. That is, sexual union between man and wife has cosmic redemptive value; not only does it reflect the union between God and Israel, between God and the Shekhinah, but it actually works toward the definitive supernal union of God and the Shekhinah, of the upper and the lower worlds, hence for the reintegration into the primordial unity. By so participating in the restoral of unity, man brings down blessings from the upper world.[85] Now within the context of this mystery and law of sex, kabbalism under the influence of the Song has considered the kiss to be a superior form or expression of the love union, so that not only must a man kiss and embrace his wife before sexual intercourse, but even during coition kissing should be engaged in as effecting union. The kiss, which is so important an act in the life of man, is also the way of communication for intellectual beings. The kisses of the *Song* are understood as referring to the metaphysical and cosmic kiss of the En-Sof (i.e., God in himself, infinite, non-knowable) and the first Sephireth (the first of the ten emanations of the En-Sof which form the way of approach to God). This supernal kiss is the ultimate principle of all life and all union.[86]

The extraordinary role which is thus accorded to the kiss depends, as we have already seen in the last quoted passage from the Zohar, upon the notion of a union in spirit. But it has been necessary to sketch something of the kabbalistic notion of the mystery of sex in order better to understand still another passage, which is among the most rhapsodic and remarkable descriptions of the nature and effects of the kiss that we are likely to find in all the literature of kissing. In the Song of Songs, says the Zohar, Solomon sang a hymn that surpasses all others, a paean "in honor of the Supernal King who is the lord of all peace and harmony"; by it Solomon brought about the perfect love union between the celestial Bridegroom and the bride, a union between the upper and the lower world.

> Another interpretation of "Let him kiss me with the kisses of his mouth" is as follows. What prompted King Solomon, when recording words of love between the Upper and the Lower world, to begin with the words, "Let him kiss me"? The reason is, as has been laid down, that no other love is like unto the ecstasy of the moment when spirit [*ruah*-breath] cleaves to spirit in a kiss, more especially a kiss on the mouth, which is the well of spirit [breath] and its medium. When mouth meets mouth, spirits unite the one with the other, and become one—one love.[87]

Thus far there is nothing that we have not met with already in Christian symbolism except for the notion of the upper and lower worlds. But as for the kiss image itself, what is said here reminds us of writers like Ambrose, Aelred of Rievaulx, and others. As with them, Jewish mysticism here speaks of a spiritual or supernal union in terms of a symbolic kiss and justifies this usage by extolling the real kiss as a mark of the highest physical bliss wherein two become as one by the mutual cleaving or mingling of breath-spirits. As in the case of the Latin word *spiritus*, so here in the word *ruah* there is the semantic ambiguity that allows for the dual meaning of breath and spirit. But the zoharic description goes on to recount how the two spirits that unite in the kiss to become one are also four spirits, evidently because in another sense each one of the kissing partners now has two spirits, his own and that of the other. At this point the subject is brought into conjunction with the recondite mysticism of letters and names that plays such a great part in kabbalism:

> In the Book of the first R. Humnuna the Ancient it is said of this sentence, "the kiss of love expands in four directions [*ruhoth*], and these are unified in one, and this is part of the secret of Faith." The four spirits ascend in four letters, these being the letters from which depends the Holy Name, and with it all things that are, both above and below. Also the hymning of the Song of Songs derives its meaning therefrom. And what are these four letters? *A H B H* [Love], which form a supernal chariot.[88]

In the Zohar the "secret of Faith," which we find mentioned here, is invariably understood as the mystery of the law of sex or the union of the male and female principles. Love—*A H B H*—forming a supernal chariot means that Love is or produces a manifestation of the Divinity.[89] All things of the upper and lower worlds depend upon Love, a tetragram that is evidently another name here for the Tetragrammaton *Y H V H*; for as the text goes on to say, the four letters *A H B H* constitute "the linking of all things into a perfect whole," and this, like the idea that all things of the universe (the upper and lower worlds) depend upon the four letters of the Holy Name, is a concept generally referring to the Ineffable Name of the Tetragrammaton. Hence, to say that it is Love that holds things in harmony and works for the full reintegration, is to say that love is God's activity in man and throughout the universe. Now the two who kiss form a unity by which they become one and four, and this suggests a reintegration of an original androgynous type and a consequent restoral of likeness to the Tetragrammaton, hence, also an "adhesion" to God: "These four letters are the four directions [spirits] of the love and joy of all the limbs of the Body without any sadness at all. Four directions [spirits] are there in the kiss, each one fulfilling itself in union with the other. And when two spirits thus become mutually interlocked they form two which are as one, and thus the four form one perfect whole."[90] It is the one "offspring" spirit of the two-four spirits, born of the kiss of love, that makes a mystic journey to the "Palace of Love" where all love is centered. But now it is not an eschatological vision or kiss that we have. What is described here occurs whenever two lovers join and become one spirit in love:

> When that love spirit enters the Palace of Love the love-yearning for the supernal kisses is aroused, those concerning which it is written: "And Jacob kissed Rachel" (Gen. 29:2), so that the kisses of the supernal love are duly brought forth, and they are the beginning of the awakening of all supernal love, attachment and union. For this reason the Hymn begins with the words: "Let him kiss me with the kisses of his mouth." Now who is "he"? He who is hidden within the supernal concealment. Can, then, the Most Recondite be the fount of kisses, and kiss that which is below?[91]

Throughout this passage, the author is alluding to the supernal kiss or union of the upper and lower worlds; at the same time, however, while explicating the principle of such a "spiritual" or metaphysical union in terms of the kiss, he has woven into the whole the idea of the participatory role of human love in furthering the cosmic union. Under the proper circumstances, the effect of a kiss between human lovers is to produce an amatory response from the Deity (the Most Recondite) who "kisses" or moves to unite with the lower world. In keeping with his idea of an esoteric causal relationship between macrocosm and microcosm, the kabbalist conceives of the kiss of the human couple as a theurgic ritual that promotes a mystico-cosmic kiss of reconciliation.

3. The Medieval Love Lyric

ontemporary with the rich flourishing of speculation on divine love in the twelfth century, there was an extraordinary development of the literature of secular love. As is well known, the first important body of love lyrics in a vernacular tongue presents a conception of love between the sexes that was hitherto relatively unknown or unexpressed in the West. Although it cannot be the purpose of this study to inquire into the many problems concerning the origins and complicated nature of what is commonly known as courtly or troubadour love, we must say at least a brief word on the matter in order better to understand the presence in that phenomenon of some fundamental amatory conceits that do interest us—among them the image of the kiss, which has so conspicuous and even peculiar a place in medieval love poetry.

The theories regarding the origins, nature, and development of troubadour love have been many: from that stressing Ovid's influence to that linking courtly love to the Catharist heresy in southern France in the eleventh and twelfth centuries; from the claim that Arabic poetry and Sufism are at the source to the idea that Christian liturgical tropes or St. Bernard of Clairvaux are the truest influences. It would seem that several or all of the factors implied in these theories and others as well had a role in the evolvement of troubadour love, for they by no means exclude one another as influences. Surely no one of them taken by itself can do justice to the complex question. One of the striking things about the twelfth century is, after all, the confluence of various currents into the mainstream of its culture. But although several factors may have operated in the development of courtly love, it is hardly possible that the part Christianity had in it should have been anything but of paramount importance.[1] And yet, because this love is directed not to God but to a creature (and sometimes seems to exalt not only the creature but carnal love itself), there are those who would deny that it bears anything more than a surface resemblance to Christian divine love. At first sight, one finds this opinion difficult to reject; it can, however, be stated too dogmatically. One of the most persistent and able critics holding to this view was Father A. J. Denomy.

Pursuing some arguments that had been set forth by Etienne Gilson, Father Denomy writes that "No one will deny that mysticism, whether Cluniac or otherwise, did influence the form and the language of the courtly lyric in general as well as those of the poems of Marcabru in particular. But as regards 'the ideological content of early troubadour poetry,' there are fundamental differences between the troubadour conception of love and the love of God or charity that preclude the possibility of their identification or *even of the influence of divine love on the origin or formation of that conception.*"[2]

It would be foolhardy, of course, to speak of an identification of the two loves, but that divine love did more than influence just the language of the troubadour love lyric and had a bearing on the very formation of the conception of troubadour love is entirely possible. It may even be argued that in a very real way Christian divine love determined something of the nature of troubadour love. By Denomy's own admission, "for the troubadours, love is not a complacency, a quiescence in attainment of the beloved, but rather a ceaseless desire, a yearning that is unappeased."[3] Nothing, I think, is truer than what is said here concerning troubadour love or at least of that side of it that is of chief interest to this study. But, surely, one need not go outside the Christian tradition to look for the determining influences. (In Appendix II the reader will find remarks on some of the more important studies dealing with Christian elements in the troubadours, followed by more detailed comments on the views of those few critics who have made significant mention of the kiss motif in connection with courtly-love poetry.)

Love as a Yearning

The whole matter of yearning for the beloved, the restless longing for something superior to and beyond the immediate grasp of mortality, accompanied by the belief that it would, if possessed, bring an untold bliss and solace—this is at the very heart of troubadour love poetry; but all this was first at the very heart of Christian spirituality. If everything else about troubadour or courtly love consisted of nothing but heretical accretions, this, its central element, would suffice to indicate that the troubadour love lyric is rooted in a Christian soil. If one argues against the specific influence of Bernardine mysticism on the grounds that it was contemporary with and not prior to the troubadour love lyric, the answer is simply that the tradition of Christian spirituality had long before then taught men that the nature of love was to desire without cease. Here the figure that immediately comes to mind is St. Augustine, for it was he, in the final analysis, who had the greatest impact on Latin Christianity throughout the Middle Ages, and it was he who remained the great educator of the psychological life of man, even for the writers of profane love. From the meeting of his own intense personality and Christianity there emerged a profound awareness and a dramatic recording of the depth and complexity of the soul in love. In this respect, the influence of the great saint goes beyond the orientation he gave to Christian theology in the West and reaches into the area of the human psyche itself.

Augustine's words frequently give poignant utterance to that *desiderium* which is the core of his religion but which is also the underlying psychological and spiritual principle of affective mysticism. For Augustine this *desiderium* was so central to the Christian life that he conceived of it as a part of God's working in man whereby the soul is prepared and made capacious enough to receive its fulfillment: "The entire life of a good Christian consists of a holy yearning. Now what you yearn for you do not yet see . . . By withholding himself, God extends our yearning; through yearning he extends our soul; by extending it he enlarges the room in it. So then, brethren, let us yearn, since we are to be filled . . . This is our life, that we be exercised by yearning."[4] Thus in order that desire may increase and not die, full possession is withheld deliberately, as it were. The Christian life is here envisioned as a kind of schooling in desire, and love is considered a yearning for union that forever draws the soul in a journey to God. The Christian is not only forever a pilgrim, *homo viator*, but also forever a lover: "Give me one who loves, and he will feel what I say. Give me one who yearns, who hungers, who in feeling himself a pilgrim in this desert is athirst, one who sighs for the fountain of his eternal homeland. Give me such a one and he will know whereof I speak. But if I speak to one who is cold, he will not understand what I say."[5] As we have seen in our analysis of the majestic "Sero te amavi" passage from the *Confessions*, Augustine was just such a lover-*viator*. (See close of chapter 1.)

In the case of Gregory of Nyssa this psychology (and metaphysics) of love as yearning informs a context that is even more specifically mystical. Commenting upon Moses' request to see God after their face-to-face meeting as though the patriarch had not seen him, Gregory pictures Moses as a passionate lover longing for a fuller vision of the supernal archetype of beauty. He explains that the yearning which Moses experienced for the Supreme Good filled his soul and that he was asking to see God not merely in a participatory way, but in essence. But God would not have revealed himself at all if the vision were meant to have the effect of ending Moses' longing. For it is in this that the true vision of God consists, in the fact that he who raises his eyes up to God never ceases to desire him.[6] Given the transcendence and infinity of the Deity, the lover's desire must be endless. Any apparent vision of God is no resting place, but a springboard for another move toward him. Here is the real significance of seeing God—never to have desire appeased.[7] Desire and love urge man ever onward in a restless and endless search for knowledge of God. Because God is infinite, Moses' quest has no end.

This dynamism of unsatisfied desire acquires erotic coloring in Gregory's commentary on the Song of Songs. Here the soul-bride is first seen as attaining its heart's desire and an apparent transforming union with the Bridegroom. "The two are united: God comes to the soul, and the soul in turn unites itself with God. For she says: *My beloved to me, and I to him who feedeth among the lilies.*" But this is a momentary illusion rather than a reality, for the soul is quickly undeceived and informed that "far from attaining perfection, she has not even begun to attain it."[8] Later, elucidating the words of the Song (5:7), "The keepers that go about the city found me: they struck me: and wounded me: the keepers of the walls took away my veil from me," Gregory writes the following of the soul-bride that has been drawn by the voice of the Beloved:

> The soul, having gone out at the word of her Beloved, looks for Him but does not find Him. She calls on Him, though He cannot be reached by any verbal symbol, and she is told by the watchman that she is in love with the unattainable, and that the object of her longing cannot be apprehended. In this way she is, in a certain sense, wounded and beaten because of the frustration of what she desires, now that she thinks that her yearning for the Other cannot be fulfilled or satisfied. But the veil of her grief is removed when she learns that the true satisfaction of her desire consists in constantly going on with her quest and never ceasing in her ascent, seeing that every fulfilment of her desire continually generates a further desire for the Transcendent.[9]

This is as clear a statement as one can expect to have of a psychology of love which places the true joy of the lover in the quest. But we should remember that the frustration of nonpossession is always balanced by the hope of fuller possession. Indeed, the truly religious and mystical aspect of this dynamism of love is that to seek does not mean to be completely without that which one desires.

Centuries after Augustine and Gregory of Nyssa, Bernard was repeating essentially the same ideas. In one of the last of his sermons on the Song, commenting on the words "In the night, as I lay abed, I searched for my heart's love, and searched in vain" (3:1), he wrote:

> My brethren, to seek God is a great good which I esteem to be second to no other of the goods of the soul. . . . What virtue can be ascribed to one who does not seek God, and who would put a limit to the search for God? *Seek his Face evermore*, it says [Ps. 104:4], wherefore it is implied that even after one has found God, one must not stop seeking him. God is not sought by means of our bodily movement but by way of our desires. And the happy attainment [of God] does not extinguish this holy yearning, but rather increases it. How can it be that the consummation of joy be the end of desire? Rather it serves as oil to desire which is like a flame. And so it is. The happiness is made perfect; yet there is no end to the desire, and hence there is no end to the seeking.[10]

Inasmuch as there is always something of God that yet remains to be known or experienced by the Christian lover-pilgrim, the words of Augustine are implicit in Bernard's pronouncements also: "What you yearn for you do not yet see." This is the metaphysics and psychology of love behind the apparent paradox (but mysticism is constrained to speak in paradoxes, which is one way of making human language and natural images say more than they can normally express) we find in those mystics who claim that attainment of the final stage of the mystic ascent is equivalent to a state of insatiability or indeed of emptiness. St. Paul, it is true, said that though we *now* see dimly, as in a mirror, we will see *then* face to face. But even this thought occurs in a passage which opens with the ringing words that "Love never ends" (I Cor. 13:8). The theme is echoed over and over by the spiritual writers.[11]

Thus at the very time Christianity was teaching its adherents how to be cleansed of earthly attachments and passions, it was schooling them in the most exquisite of sentiments. In so educating men how to love the Deity, Christians adapted to their nature that which in the pagan classical mind was usually thought to be characteristic of the feminine psyche. It is not so much of a loss of self that Christian spirituality speaks, but rather of the hope for the self's fulfillment by a union with the beloved that alone can satisfy it. In the classical attitude, it was the woman who depended upon the male for such fulfillment. Love as an involvement of the whole person, as *passio amoris* in which one yearns and is sick with desire, was deemed an unmanly emotion leading to the derangement of the faculties.[12] It was characteristic of woman. The Song of Songs and the greater part of the Jewish tradition show that the same ideas prevailed among the Hebrews. Likewise among Christians, who, after all, but continued and accentuated the classical and Jewish outlook in this matter, the relationship between the sexes was governed by the patriarchal attitude of the male's "natural" superiority. It is worthy of note that in the Latin Vulgate version of the Bible the word *amor* is found in very few places, and that in the Song of Songs, where it is most conspicuous (2:5; 5:8), it is used by the Shulamite in the expression *amore langueo*, "I am sick with love." But in his relationship to God, the Christian aspired to be a bride, individually (the soul) and collectively (humanity or the Church). Henry Osborne Taylor has a succinct and eloquent statement on the feminine psyche of St. Augustine that can serve us here: "His is the woman-nature turned toward God, poured out at his feet, bathing them with its flood; the repentant woman-nature, grateful, devoted, surrendered, and abased, utterly filled with love of Him, and the woman-nature which is not narrowed by love's devotion, but is broadened through it to include tender consideration of whatever needs love's sympathy."[13] These words may be applied to the greater part of the writers of Christian spirituality in general, but especially to affective mystics. But they may also, and without much violence, be used to characterize the attitude or relationship of the poet-lover to his lady in the tradition of courtly love.

If there can be no question of an equivalence between the divine love of Christian spirituality and the conception of love in the troubadours, that is certainly because the object of love is so different in the two. And yet, to a significant degree, troubadour love is both a derivation and a deviation from Christian divine love. It represents, if not the first, perhaps the boldest moment in the history of the secularization or, better, the profanation of Christian love by the fact that it transferred not only the language but something of the very sentiments of love, as taught by Christianity, from God to woman, thereby leading to a pseudodivinization of the latter. Leaving aside the question of the specific object of love, it is clear that essential elements of the psychology of love are the same in Christian and troubadour lovers. Both place great stress on the value of the beloved and on the act of loving itself. In both there is often an emphasis on the distance separating the lover from the beloved and on the desire and need to bridge that distance. And for both this is the mainspring for a conception of love as an ecstatic experience in the sense that it takes the lover out of himself in a quest for union with the beloved. From this groundwork there emerge in Western literature such important amatory conceits as the migration of the lover's spirit or heart to where the beloved is, the lover's heart dwelling in or by the beloved, and the exchange of souls or hearts. Such themes depend then upon the notion of love as a movement and a cleaving of the self to the object of desire.

Love as a Migration and a Cleaving

Love, we have seen, is a driving force (*motus animi*) or motive weight that carries the lover to where he loves: *Pondus meum amor meus; eo feror, quocumque feror* (*Conf.*, XIII, 9), "My weight is my love; I am borne by it, whithersoever I am borne." Of course, this is a journey or migration made not by the body but by the soul or spirit, or, indeed, by the heart: *Imus non ambulando, sed amando*, "We go not by walking, but by loving," as Augustine has it (*Ep.* 155, 4). Love is also a cleaving. One of Augustine's favorite and characteristic texts is, in the words of the Psalm (72:28), "It is good for me to cling [*adhaerere*] to God," just as for Bernard and other medieval spiritual writers a key text is Paul's mystic utterance: "He who clings unto the Lord is one spirit with him." In Augustine's description of divine love some of the most important words are *haerere, adhaerere, cohaerere*, "adhere, cling to, cleave to." But it is especially noteworthy that he could apply the image of the *cleaving heart* to a description of profane love as well. Thus in telling of his mistress's forced separation from him he writes: "My mistress being torn from my side as an impediment to my marriage, my heart, which clung to her [*cor, ubi adhaerebat*], was racked, and wounded, and bleeding."[14] The heart was the seat of the affective life and in this sense was to win a place beside soul and spirit in the description of love, especially among the secular poets.

If Augustine appears as the most dramatic and authoritative voice of such sentiments and imagery, it is nonetheless true that these are the common heritage of Christian spirituality. The particular conceit of the migration of the amorous soul, for example, is stated succinctly in the fifth century by Diadochus, bishop of Photice, who defined hope as "an emigration of the mind under the force of love toward the object hoped for."[15]

In similar fashion, Gregory of Nyssa spoke of the biblical account of Abraham's departure from his native land (Gen. 12:1–4) in a spiritual sense as a migration of the soul. Like Moses, Abraham is thought of as a lover drawn by the divine attraction and yearning to gaze on Beauty bare. No physical migration could bring one to a knowledge of the divine Beauty, but only a migration of the soul from its present habitat, which is to say, out of the self and the world of senses toward a spiritual apprehension of God in an élan of love, faith, and hope.[16]

Later, in the Latin Middle Ages, we find the same ideas crystallized into a widespread formula of Christian ecstatic love—the saying that the soul (or spirit, or heart) is more where it loves or yearns than in the body it animates. In explicating two passages from St. Paul— "Conversatio nostra in coelis est" (Phil. 3:20), and "Quamdiu sumus in corpore, peregrinamur a Domino" (II Cor. 5:6)—St. Bernard offered an explanation within the context of Christian Charity: "Neque enim praesentior spiritus noster est ubi animat, quam ubi amat"—For our spirit is not more present where it animates than where it loves. In the following century St. Bonaventura recalled Bernard's maxim, and by replacing *spiritus* with *anima*, he rephrased it into a formula that was to be even more popular: "Puto, anima mia, quod verius es ubi amas quam ubi animas"—I think, my soul, that you are more truly where you love than where you animate.[17] In the meantime, Aelred of Rievaulx, in one of the great twelfth century treatises on Christian love, was noting that once we have chosen an object, love fills the soul with a desire that carries it toward that object. It is this movement of desire, says Aelred, that is known as love. (*Speculum Caritatis*, III, 8). For the Christian, then, as such remarks remind us over and over, love is ecstatic by definition. In this connection we should not forget to mention a fundamental New Testament text—it is specifically quoted by Bernard in support of his own statement—the passage from the Sermon on the Mount in which Jesus says that our heart is where our treasure is: "Ubi est thesaurus tuus, ibi est et cor tuum" (Matt. 6:21).

For the sake of exactitude and because of the importance of the subject, it is necessary to point out that I do not mean to imply that these concepts originate in any absolute sense with Christianity. In Judaism the yearning for the Messiah was at times extraordinarily intense. But even more interesting, from our present point of view, is the situation in the West. In the brilliant pages in which he studied the Greek awakening to new or unmapped areas of the psyche—in the archaic lyric writers, significantly enough—Bruno Snell shows how, with Sappho, longing bridges the distance between herself and the beloved by stimulating memory to an activity that in part conquers separation. Writing of the extant part of a poem by Sappho (98) Snell states: "Literally the first sentence says: 'Often she has her mind here from the direction of Sardes.' This is the sort of formulation which for Homer would have been impossible. For Sappho, the mind is capable of dissociating itself from its place, and so a community of thought and feeling is entirely feasible. These concepts have become common coin in our world, but Homer does not yet have them."[18] It is in this sense that human beings—they are, in Sappho's context, lovers—are united, despite spatial separation, by a nonphysical quality, "by something that lies in the realm of the soul."

Without doubt the importance of this achievement is not to be underrated, but it must be pointed out that what is involved is a communion made by the reciprocal *memory* of actual sensuous moments lived together. Despite some variations and further refinements, including at times the Platonic concept of *anamnesis*, this was to remain the case through most of the classical period of the West. Of course, the Platonic epigram on kissing Agathon, and some early imitations of it (see the Introduction) where movement of the soul or union of souls is suggested, bring us closer to what we are presently concerned with. But here too it is the sensuous ground of reality that determines the quality of the emotion. Within such a context we are still a long way from the concept of an experiential migration of the soul (influenced, to be sure, by a Platonistic philosophical current) or the experiential union, be it among friends or between the soul and God, that Christian spirituality bespeaks.

Even so, as the examples of Augustine and others have already revealed to us, the theologians knew full well that the conception of love as a migration and an adhering of the soul or heart to the beloved was true of both *caritas* and *cupiditas*. Nonetheless, because of the particular orientation and purpose of their speculation, we may, when speaking of it in connection with such authors, refer to it as a religious conception of love. Now the truly secularized counterpart—again in terms of orientation and context—of this view of love is found in most troubadour poets, but perhaps nowhere more tellingly than in Jaufré Rudel. It is not without significance that the best-known and best-loved of the biographies of the troubadours has always been that of Jaufré, depicting as it does both the migration of the lovesick poet to the far-off land where the beloved (heard of but not yet seen) resides and the expiration (on a kiss in some versions) of the lover upon reaching the object of his search. In his verse we find the poet writing:

> De dezir mos cors no fina
> Vas selha ren qu'ieu pus am.[a]

But not only does the poet's heart yearn toward the beloved; under the motive power of that desire it leaps the distance and cleaves to the beloved. Even at night when the poet is asleep, his spirit (in dreams) is with her:

> Lai es mos cors si totz c'alhors
> Non a ni sima ni raïtz
> Et en dormen sotz cobertors
> Es lai ab lieis mos esperitz.[b]

Because it has gone to the lady, the heart no longer has its place (*ni sima ni raïtz*) in its normal body. The same ecstatic phenomenon appears in the following lines by Bernart Marti:

> Qe en dormen e en veillan,
> Qant si desvest dal seu mantel
> M'est vis qe mos cors s'i sejorn.[c]

[a] "My heart does not cease from yearning toward the object I love most." From "Quan lo rius de la fontana," in *Les chansons de Jaufré Rudel*, ed. A. Jeanroy (Paris, 1924), p. 5.

[b] "There [where the beloved is] is my heart so completely that elsewhere it has neither top nor root; and when I sleep under the covers, my spirit is there with her." From "Pro ai del chan essenhadors," in *Les chansons de Jaufré Rudel*, pp. 7–8.

[c] "While I am asleep or when I am awake, when she removes her cloak it seems that my heart dwells with her." From "Quant la pluei' e.l vens e.l tempiers," in *Les poésies de Bernart Marti*, ed. E. Hoepffner (Paris, 1929), p. 29.

The motif is expressed as a kind of victory over separation in the following exclamation by Guilhem de Cabestanh:

> Partis? Non me, nei ja ni me partria,
> Anz es mos cors ab leis e noit e dia.[d]

But we are reminded that the troubadours are sometimes anxious for more than such spiritual union by the fact that Arnaut Daniel wishes he were with his lady in body as well as in soul:

> Del cors li fos, non de l'arma
> E cossentis m'a celat dinz sa cambra.[e]

The troubadours were fond of playing on the words *heart* and *body* (*cor(s), cors*) and on the image of the heart drawn or migrating from the body. In the verses just quoted Arnaut wishes that his body (*cors*) would be where his soul is, with the lady in her chamber. Soon after, in the same poem, he tells us that his *cors* clings to the beloved at all times, wherever she may be. Now, however, the poet means his heart. Force is lent to the concept of the heart's cleaving by the image of the fingernail and the bark:

> On q'ill estei, fors en plaz', o dins cambra,
> Mos cors no'is part de lieis tant cum tan l'ongla.
> C'aissi s'empren e s'enongla
> Mos cors en lei cum l'escorss' en la verga.[f]

Once the heart's migration to the beloved under an ecstatic impulse of desire appeared as an amatory conceit, it was inevitable that it should lead to the idea of the heart as messenger, either to plead the lover's cause with the lady or to recall to the poet the charms of the beloved. Or the poet sent his heart to serve his lady, who sometimes, however, held it as a prisoner. Italian poetry in particular was to create a surfeit of such images. But the subsequent development of the conceit of the heart's migration need not detain us here. For the moment my purpose has been to point to its psychological and historical

---

[d] "Leave her? Not I indeed, for never will I go from her; on the contrary, my heart is with her night and day." From "Mout m'alegra douza vos per boscaje," in *Les chansons de Guilhem de Cabestanh,* ed. A. Langfers (Paris, 1924), p. 23.

[e] Would I were hers with body, not only with soul, and that she would take me secretly into her chamber." From "Lo ferm voler q'el cor m'intra," in *Canzoni,* ed. Gianluigi Toja (Florence, 1960), p. 376.

[f] "Wherever she may be, out in the square or in her chamber, my heart does not separate from her the space of a fingernail. For thus my heart adheres and becomes like a nail to her as the bark to a twig." *Ibid.,* p. 377.

foundations, which lie at the very core of Christian spirituality. None-theless, by way of one last example, the following treatment by the thirteenth century poet Rustico di Filippo gives some indication of how widespread the motif had become:

I' aggio inteso che sanza lo core
Non po' l'om viver né durar neiente,
Ed io vivo sanz'esso, e lo colore
Però non perdo né saver né mente:

Ma solo per la forza del segnore
Che 'l n'ha portato, ch'è tanto potente:
Lo dipartì dal corpo, ciò fue Amore,
E l'ha miso in balìa de l'avvenente.

Lo cor, quando dal corpo si partìo,
Disse ad Amor: — Segnore, in qual parte
Mi meni? — E quel rispose: — Al tuo disio.

In tale loco è, che già mai non parte.
Insieme sta il meo core e 'l desir meo:
Così fosse il corpo in terza parte![g]

Besides the idea of the heart's migration under the force of love (per-sonified here), we find again the play on the heart-body (*cor-corpo*) theme and the poet's wish that his body were there where his heart and desire (the beloved) are. But particularly noteworthy is the line that speaks of the heart being with the poet's desire: "insieme sta il meo core e 'l desir meo." One is struck by the very closeness of the ex-pression to the religious formula of ecstatic love.

Love as a Psychic Union

Related to the conceit of the heart's migration is the theme of an exchange or union of hearts or spirits. This too, as we have seen, is of the very essence of Christian spiritual love, whether among the

[g] "I have heard that man cannot live nor endure at all without his heart; but I live without it, and yet I do not lose my color nor my knowledge nor thought. But solely through the might of that lord who has taken it from me, and who is so powerful. That is, it was Love who separated it from my body and put it into the fair one's power. The heart, when it was separated from the body, said to Love: 'Lord, whither do you lead me?' And he replied: 'To your desire.' It is in a place that it will never leave. My heart and desire remain together. Would that my body were likewise there, as a third party." *Rimatori comico-realistici del Due e Trecento*, I, ed. M. Vitale (Turin, 1956), 169–170.

faithful in Christ or between the soul and God. However sensuous the love poetry of the troubadours could become, it did include a conception of *fin' amors* or true love which held that love consists in the union of hearts and in the contemplation of the mind. In the following verses Bernart de Ventadorn invites his lady to exchange spirits with him. In that way they will be part of each other and "know" each other thoroughly; and their two hearts will be as one:

> Domna, s'eu fos de vos auzitz
> Si charamen com volh mostrar,
> Al prim de nostr' enamorar
> Feiram chambis dels esperitz!
>
> Azautz sens m'i fora cobitz,
> C'adonc saubr'eu lo vostr' afar
> E vos lo meu, tot par a par,
> E foram de dos cors unitz.[h]

For human lovers, then, no less than for divine lovers, love seeks to unite two hearts in one or to bring about a mutual transformation of the lover and the beloved. Medieval poets of different lands knew this motif well. The idea of two lovers joined in one heart or sustained by one same heart is spelled out carefully in the following verses from a thirteenth century French poem in which the poet begins by asking the lady to allow his heart to find a place in her:

> Or vous voudrai proier et par amors moustrer
> Que vous lessiez mon cuer avoec vous reposer,
> Le mieu cuer et le vostre vueil ensamble atorner.
> Certes dui vrai amant doivent I cuer porter
> Et leur II cuers en I ajoindre et bien fermer.[i]

We can point to a witty treatment of the motif to illustrate how widespread the mystical amatory conceit had become. In an example

[h] "Lady, if I were but heard by you as earnestly as I wish to show you, at the start of our love we would exchange our spirits. Thereby a clever wit would be bestowed upon me; for then I would know your affairs and you mine, equally, and we would from two hearts be made one." From "Can lo boschatges es floritz e vei lo tems renovelar," in Bernart de Ventadorn, *Seine Lieder*, ed. Carl Appel (Halle a S., 1915), p. 227.

[i] "Now I would like to beg of you, and to prove for love's sake that you should let my heart dwell with you; I wish my heart and yours to move together. For indeed two true lovers should bear one heart, and their two hearts should unite in one and hold fast." Quoted in *Les saluts d'amour du troubadour Arnaud de Mareuil*, ed. P. Bec (Toulouse, 1961), p. 51.

in German from the thirteenth century poet Ulrich of Liechtenstein, the lover proposes a psychic exchange and merging of persons into one; the lady, however, declines, preferring that their identities remain separate:

> Vrouwe, dâ soltû mich meinen
> Herzenlîchen als ich dich,
> Unser zweien sô vereinen,
> Daz wir beidiu sîn ein ich.
> Wis du mîn, sô bin ich dîn!
> "Herre, das mac niht gesîn.
> Sît ir iuwer, ich bin mîn."[j]

Here one detects the influence of the Song of Songs and perhaps that of its exegetes. In the Song the Shulamite twice exults that her true love is hers and she all his (2:16; 6:2). In the Middle Ages both the secular and the religious love lyric were borrowing freely from the imagery of the Song. Thus alongside the verses of Ulrich of Liechtenstein we may place the following that speak of the soul's desire for Christ:

> Verwundet ist das hertze min,
> Da hastu, lieb, geschossen in . . .
> O herr, du bist min, so bin ich din,[k]

or these which refer to the union between Christ and the cloistered nun:

> Ich du, du ich, wir zwei sin ein,
> Also wirt ein von uns zwein.[l]

Returning to the profane tradition, we note that one of the earliest love lyrics in German (second half of the twelfth century) is a brief anonymous strophe whose first line is: "Dû bist mîn, ich bin dîn"— Thou are mine, I am thine.[19]

---

[j] "Lady, then should you love me as cordially as I do you, and so unite the two of us that we both become one only. Do you be mine, as I am yours! 'Sir, that may not be. Do you stay yours, I am mine.' " Ulrich von Liechtenstein, *Frauendienst*, II, ed. Reinhold Bechstein (Leipzig, 1888), 157–158.

[k] "My heart is wounded, since thou, love, hast shot at it . . . Oh Lord, as thou art mine, I am thine. . . ."

[l] "I thou, thou I, we two are one, and so is one made from us twain." Quoted in Arnold Oppel, *Das Hohelied Salomonis und die deutsche religiöse Liebeslyrik: Abhandlungen zur Mittleren und Neueren Geschichte*, Heft 32 (Berlin and Leipzig, 1911), pp. 28–29.

Here it is not without interest to note that the play on the heart-body theme and the "mysticalness" implied in the idea of the migration or exchange of hearts in the description of human love was very early such as to provoke no less a writer than Chrétien de Troyes, in the latter part of the twelfth century, to devote a brief discussion on the matter in an attempt to reduce these amorous *topoi* to a realistic psychology. In *Cligès*—which has with good cause been referred to as an *Anti-Tristan*, the *Tristan* legend being replete with an erotic mysticism—when Chrétien describes the enamorment scene between the young lovers, he says that as Fénice has placed her eyes and heart in Cligès, so the latter has promised his heart to her. Nay, not promised, but surely given. Truly given? No. For in actual fact nobody can really give his heart. In order to clarify the question, Chrétien presents an account that effectively explains the image as a kind of poetic license. His position may be summarized thus: it cannot be said that two hearts unite in one body, because it is simply not true that two hearts can exist in one same body. On the other hand, it can be said that two hearts behave in unison without *materially* joining with one another. They behave in unison only when the will of each passes to the other, in the sense that they agree in willing the same things; and it is precisely because they have a unity of desire that there are those who say that each of them has two hearts. One sole heart, however, is not in two places. The will, on the other hand, can be one and the same, even if each person conserves his own heart, just as diverse persons can sing in unison a song or a *vers*. Thus it is evident that one body cannot be said to contain two hearts merely because each knows all that the other loves and hates, just as the various voices that unite in such a way as to seem one same thing cannot belong to one alone. The triumphant conclusion of this reasoning is that one body can have only one heart—"Ne peut cors avoir cuer que un."[20]

Now this reasoning is irreproachable from both a realistically psychological and a theological point of view. Even the ecstatic Bernard of Clairvaux, like many, indeed most theologians, when he wishes to explain in orthodox fashion and accordingly accommodate experience to the language of reason, speaks of love—even love between the soul and the Deity—as a conformity of wills, which is just Chrétien's point. Bernard's Sermon 71 on the Song, for example, explains the difference between the unity within the Trinity and the union between the soul of an individual and God by noting that in the Trinity there is truly but *one* Will, whereas the union between God and the human soul consists of a union of two distinct and separate wills. So too, as we have seen in chapter 2, the sense of spiritual oneness with his brother Gerard, to the point of saying they were one soul, is also explained as a conformity and harmony of their two wills. But just as Bernard very often found such unimpeachable language insufficient to describe the experience of divine love, so too Chrétien's aridly rational explanation would seem unsatisfactory to those poets of his age and after who sought to express the nature of an experiential mystic love between creatures.

It would be a mistake, however, to see in the examples of this section a transposition pure and simple from the language of divine love to that of human love. The two-in-one motif acquired vast proportions in the literature of the Middle Ages, and because it will be occupying our attention again, we may observe now that its presence in medieval love-literature is connected not only with the description of Christian divine love but also with the idea of friendship as described by classical and Christian writers, and even with certain ritual ceremonies by which friendship or blood-brotherhood was effected between two males. The role of this latter phenomenon as an influence in the development of the relationship between man and woman in medieval courtly love has recently been studied at great length by René Nelli.[21] But while there is an important element of truth in the connection Nelli makes between the "primitive" rites of male friendship and certain conventions and myths of love in the Middle Ages, the sophisticated language of the poets is such that at least where they (the poets) are concerned we can more safely speak of a borrowing of the vocabulary (and, to some degree, of the sentiment) of the classico-Christian ideal of friendship in their songs of heterosexual love. We need not embark on a long discussion of this matter here. For our purposes it is enough to remember that the most significant psychological or even mystical aspect of friendship from Aristotle and Cicero to Augustine, Bernard, and Aelred of Rievaulx is contained in the idea that a friend is another self and in the concomitant image of *one soul in two bodies*. (See chapter 2, at the end of the discussion on Aelred.) Certainly it is not always easy to determine whether a poet making use of the two-in-one or the "one soul (or heart) in two bodies" motif is drawing upon the mystics' description of divine love or upon the language of friendship. Very likely both are alternately or simultaneously at work in some poets, and it may even be said that the two have much in common. In a Christian context, of course, it would be difficult to keep a sharp distinction between love and friendship; at the very least, the first is the foundation of the second.

Without doubt the examples we have noted in this section, and even more those we shall later consider from medieval romances, bespeak an affection which partakes of both love and friendship: a sentiment that is *amor-amicitia*. Such a sentiment implies a relation that lifts woman to a plane on which she is the equal of man and in every way worthy of being his "friend." But one of the most well-known yet nonetheless remarkable things about medieval love poetry is the amount of it which places the lady in a position of superiority vis-à-vis the male, although this does not rule out the motif of friendship. Most of the lyric poetry that suggests love to be something more than the desire for physical possession of the female by the male keeps this relationship, and a small but significant part of it employs the kiss motif in making its point.

The Kiss: Prelude or Terminus?

The most famous pronouncement concerning the courtly conception of love as a union of hearts and a contemplation of the mind was made by the "codifier" of courtly love, Andreas Capellanus. Its fame rests on Andreas's curious notion that the practitioners of the highest form of heterosexual love are allowed the physical delights of kissing, embracing, and a judicious contact in the nude. The final solace of sexual intercourse is not to be indulged in, for then love would die, whereas "pure love" (such is Andreas's name for it) continues to increase indefinitely and leads the lover to moral excellence:

> And pure love is that which joins the hearts of two lovers together with a complete feeling of delight. Moreover, this [love] consists in the contemplation of the mind and the affection of the heart; it even goes as far as the kiss of the mouth and the embrace of the arm and the modest contact of the nude mistress except for the final solace; for those who wish to love purely are not allowed to practice that. This is the love which anyone who is resolved to love should embrace with all his power. For this love knows increase without end, and we have learned that no one has repented its practice; and the more one takes from it the more one desires to have. This love is distinguished by

being of such great power (virtue) that from it comes the source of complete integrity.[22]

We will not here press a comparison between Augustine's "withholding of the vision" and Andreas's withholding of the final solace except to say that both seem to function to exercise man in desire, to increase desire. Equally striking is the resemblance between Andreas's idea of the pure lover going as far as the kiss and chaste embrace of the beloved in the nude and Augustine's description of the spiritual lover hoping to behold and embrace—chastely—the beloved Sophia in her beautiful nakedness (see p. 47). But whatever may be the ultimate reason for, or sense of, this *amor interruptus* in Andreas's passage, it is clear that the kiss and embrace are established as a terminal rather than a preludious bliss. The same attitude is boasted in a thirteenth century *lai* in which the poet claims that he is unlike other lovers because he seeks no solace beyond the kiss and the embrace:

> Ce font il, mais je nel fas
> Ni li quier autre solas
> Fors de baisier et de bras.[m]

Of course, any reader of medieval literature knows that this is not the only, nor even the dominant, attitude of lovers in the Middle Ages. Medieval literature is replete with kisses and embraces, most often as a sign or hope of something more to come. In fact, this is the case in that "mixed" love that Andreas distinguishes from "pure" love by saying it includes the final solace. The attitude toward mixed love, however, is somewhat ambiguous. The first thing to note is that the casuistry concerning the two loves occurs in that section of Andreas's book that treats of the amorous relationship between men (including clerics) and women of the highest caste. Although Andreas (or the interlocutor) says that even mixed love leads to virtue, it is at best approved conditionally; and in the context of the dialectic between the two loves, it is explicitly declared to be inferior, not only because it is more offensive to God and leads to serious consequences, but also because of its brief duration (*parvo tempore durat*). The practitioner of pure love, on the other hand, is not even to think of coitus as his due. Insofar as the intimacies allowed are concerned, the mixed love

[m] "This they do but I do not do it, nor do I seek other solace beyond the kiss and the embrace." "Lai des Pucelles," vss. 67–69. In P. Abelard, I *'Planctus,'* ed. G. Vecchi (Modena, 1951), p. 112. The *lai* is found in a thirteenth century manuscript, Bibliothèque Nat., Paris, fr. 12.615.

spoken of here is not different from what is said earlier in Andreas's treatise where the talk is about love between commoners. There love is said to have been ordered from antiquity into four distinct and successive stages: the first consists in the granting of hope, the second in the granting of the kiss, the third in the enjoyment of the embrace, and the fourth culminates in the yielding of the entire person.[23]

The position granted to the kiss in this particular progression to love's fulfillment in coitus is inferior to its position within the more common *topos* of the five "points" of love. In the latter amatory schema, which has been briefly traced from antiquity into the Renaissance by E. R. Curtius, the kiss figures as the penultimate step following sight, conversation, and touching (i.e., the embrace and caressing).[24]

The kiss as a promise or stimulant of a further physical intimacy is indeed ancient, as even Andreas indicated, and it continued to be thought of as an Ovidian preliminary by many (perhaps most) poets, the troubadours among them. Peire Vidal, for example, after stealing a kiss from his lady, claims he will die if he cannot have the rest:

> Intrei dins sa maizo
> E·lh baizei a lairo
> La boca e·l mento.
> So n'ai agut e no mas re,
> E sui tot mortz, si·l plus rete.[n]

And Bernart de Ventadorn, whom we will soon call upon to illustrate an opposite tendency, shows himself in one poem to be among those poets who are incited by the kiss to ask for *del plus*:

> E car vos plac que·m fezetz tan d'onor
> Lo jorn que·m detz en baizan vostr'amor,
> Del plus, si·us platz, prendetz esgardamen.[o]

Among medieval French works we find in the *Roman de la Rose* that when Amant requests permission to kiss the rose, Bel Aceuil explains that Chastity forbids him to allow anyone that privilege because

---

[n] "I entered into her room and stole a kiss from her on the mouth and chin. That is all that I had. I am dead if she withholds the rest." From "Ajostar e lassar," in *Les poésies de Peire Vidal*, ed. J. Anglade (Paris, 1923), pp. 62–63.

[o] "And since it pleased you to do me so high an honor that day when you gave me your love with a kiss, take heed now, I beg you, to grant the rest." From "Be.m cuidei de chantar sofrir," in Bernart de Ventadorn, *Seine Lieder*, ed. C. Appel (Halle a S., 1915), p. 76.

whoever manages to kiss the beloved is not able to rest content but aspires to "the rest":

> Car qui au baisier puet ataindre
> A poine puet atant remaindre;
> E sachiez bien cui l'en otroie
> Le baisier, il a de la proie
> Le miauz e la plus avenant
> Si a erres dou remenant.[p]
>
> (3404–3408)

And in *Le Chastiement des Dames*, a versified manual for the behavior of ladies, Robert de Blois warned of the perils that lurk in the kisses of men other than one's husband, although his words might well have created more of a titillating curiosity than a distaste for the "sorplus" that such kisses inevitably lead to:

> Li baisiers autre chose atrait,
> Et quant il a la fome plait
> Qu'ele le veut et le desirre,
> Du sorplus n'i a aul que dire;
> S'ensi n'est que li leus lor faille,
> Le sorplus vuet ele sanz faille.[q]
>
> (129–134)

It is the same warning and understanding of woman's frailty that was spoken of by Chrétien de Troyes in the *Perceval* when an outraged lover explains that although his beloved claims she had only been kissed, and against her will at that, by a fair stranger, there can be little doubt that things went beyond that; for any woman who surrenders her lips will easily and anxiously offer up the "sorplus":

> Et s'il le baisa mal gre suen
> Ne fist il aprés tot son buen?
> Oïl, ce ne querroit ja nus
> Qu'il le baisast sanz faire plus,
> Que l'une chose l'autre atrait.
> Qui baise feme et plus n'i fait,

---

[p] "For whoever can achieve the kiss can scarcely remain at that stage; and know indeed that whoever is granted the kiss has the best and most pleasant part of the prize, for thus he has the pledge of the remainder."

[q] "The kiss leads to other things, and when it so pleases a woman that she wants and desires it, there is no doubt about the rest; indeed it is only the place that they lack, for she will have the rest without fail." In John Howard Fox, *Robert de Blois, son oeuvre didactique et narrative* (Paris, 1950), pp. 136–137.

> Des qu'il sont sol a sol andui,
> Dont quit je qu'il remaint en lui.
> Feme qui se bouche abandone
> Le sorplus molt de legier done.[r]

But the kiss itself can be evoked as an image suggesting the full extent of the physical intimacies of sensual love. In the work of the very first troubadour, Guillaume IX, there is a reference to a kiss that stands out because of its boldness and setting. Here the lover will die if he does not receive the kiss:

> Si·m breu non ai ajutori,
> Cum ma bona dompna m'am,
> Morrai, pel cap sanh Gregori,
> Si no·m bayz'en cambr'o sotz ram.[s]

The image of receiving the kiss *en cambr'o sotz ram* is perhaps another borrowing from the Song of Songs, which opens with the passionate request for kisses and later speaks both of the beloved's dwelling and of the trysting place under an apple tree: "Sub arbore malo suscitavi te" (8:5). In Guillaume's verses the kiss is deemed necessary to keep the poet in life, but there is no doubt about the brutally sensual nature of the love involved. Indeed here one can almost read the term *kiss* as a euphemism for coitus. In any case the quality of the love and kiss of such passages is not essentially different from what we find in the Latin love lyrics of the "goliardic" poets, who were the contemporaries of Guillaume and the other early troubadours. It will be useful to consider them at this point.

The Latin Love Lyric of the Goliards

The thirteenth century manuscript of Benedictbeuren contains a body of twelfth century love lyrics (the *Carmina Burana*) particularly

---

[r] "And even if he did kiss her against her will, didn't he go on afterwards to do as he wished? Indeed, one cannot believe that he kissed her without doing anything more, for the one thing [i.e., the kiss] leads to the other. If a man kisses a woman and does not urge for more when they are alone, I believe it is the man who shows restraint. For a woman who surrenders her mouth easily gives up the rest" (3855–3864). *Le roman de Perceval ou le conte du graal*, ed. William Roach (Geneva and Paris, 1959), p. 113.

[s] "If shortly I do not have assistance from the love of my good lady, I will die, by St. Gregory's head! unless she kisses me in her room or under a tree." From "Farai chansoneta nueva," in *Les chansons de Guillaume IX*, ed. A. Jeanroy (Paris, 1927), p. 20.

notable for references to kisses whose Ovidian character betrays a totally secular application of the Song of Songs. Thus we find the lover desiring to embrace and kiss the object of his desire beneath a leafy tree:

> Si tenerem quam cupio
> In nemore sub folio,
> Oscularer cum gaudio.
> Dulcis amor!^t

Another lover invites kind Phyllis to give him that peace which comes from the love embrace and kiss:

> Ergo fac, benigna Phyllis,
> Ut iocundar in tranquillis,
> Dum os ori iungitur
> Et pectora mamillis.^u

In the intensity of desire still another goliard lover envisions his felicity as surpassing that of Jove if he could but lie with and kiss his lady; his happiness would be such that he could die upon that kiss:

> Si me dignetur quam desidero,
> Felicitate Iovem supero.
> Nocte cum illa si dormiero
> Si sua labra semel suxero,
> Mortem subire,
> Placenter obire,
> Vitamque finire
> Libens potero,
> Hei potero, hei potero, hei potero
> Tanta si gaudia recepero.^v

---

^t "If I might hold whom I desire in the grove beneath the leaves I would kiss [her] with joy. O sweet love!" "Veris dulcis in tempore . . . ," *Carmina Burana: Lateinische und deutsche Lieder und Gedichte einer Handschrift des XIII Jahrhunderts aus Benedictbeuern.* Bibliothek des literarischen Vereins in Stuttgart, XVI (Stuttgart, 1847), p. 195.

^u "Therefore do this, kind Phyllis, that I may rejoice in peace while mouth is joined to mouth and chest to breast." "Salve ver optatum . . . ," *Carmina Burana*, p. 194.

^v "If she whom I desire should think me worthy, in happiness I'll outstrip Jove. If by night I might sleep with her, if once I might kiss her lips, [then] to suffer death, to die willingly, and to end my life, I shall do gladly. Ha ha! I shall do, shall do, shall do, [for] such immense delight I shall have had." "Sic mea fata canendo solor . . . ," *Carmina Burana*, pp. 229–230.

Besides this motif of expiring upon a kiss, that is, from an excess of contentment in fulfillment, there is the equally significant theme of the lover suffering cruelly and dying from the love wound, though certain that he could be restored by a kiss from his lady:

> Amare crucior, morior
> Vulnere, quo glorior.
> Eia, si me sanare
> Uno vellet osculo,
> Que cor felici iaculo
> Gaudet vulnerare!ʷ

Like Guillaume's rabid outcry, these are all expressions of a love that not only is carnal in desire but exults in the expectation of the joy of full physical possession. At the same time, however, the reader of these various poems of the *Carmina Burana* cannot but be struck by the implementation of Christian sentiments and vocabulary. We need not dwell on the transference of Christian *gaudium* to the joy of sensual abandonment which seems obvious enough. Associated with this motif but more specifically to our purpose here is the theme of the martyr who dies for love. For the Christian, martyrdom, as Clement of Alexandria had said, is the perfect work of love. Particularly in the last group of verses we have quoted we find a sacrilegious application of the intensely Christian mystic theme of a death by way of a love-wound that glorifies the martyr. In a recent discussion of the secularization of religious sentiments of love in the *Carmina Burana*, James J. Wilhelm remarked on the first two lines: "Glory in death: this is the new Christian dimension that is utterly lacking in Ovid, Catullus, and Sappho, where death is always a disaster. We must go to Prudentius' hymns to the saints or to the *Acta Martyrorum* for this tonality."[25]

Indeed, that the death of the martyrs is a glorious victory—or, we may say, a victory that brings the martyr to *glory* in the eschatological sense of assurance of participation in the divine glory of God— is an idea found regularly in early Christian writings. Moreover, the expression usually employed to indicate the martyr's death is *gloriosa mors*, and one also thinks of the fortune of *gloria passionis*.[26] The word *gloria*, of course, continued to be used throughout the Christian

---

ʷ "Loving torments me, I die from the wound in which I glory. Ah! if she would cure me by a single kiss, how my heart would rejoice to be wounded by such a happy dart!" "Estas in exilium . . . ," *Carmina Burana*, p. 132.

centuries in its profane sense, and the Christian writers were fond of contrasting the religious ideal of glory with the secular ideal. Where martyrdom was concerned, it was only in Christ's passion that a Christian could glory. Again a text from St. Paul served as the model: "Mihi absit gloriari nisi in cruce Domini nostri" (Gal. 6:14), "Far be it from me to glory in anything but the cross of our Lord." Now it is something of the Christianized value of the word that the *Burana* poet has adapted to a profane love. Despite the incommensurability between divine and human love, here a Christian sentiment has been transposed to a human passion, charging the latter with a certain piquancy and a new intensity.

Nonetheless, Wilhelm's characterization perhaps goes too far. The "tonality" (to use his word) of the two verses in question cannot be easily equated (but this may not be Wilhelm's intention) with that of the *Acta Martyrorum* or the Christian hymns. The total context of the *Burana* poem lends a different value to the religio-erotic image employed by the secular poet. This is to be noted especially in the development of the love-wound and balm motif in the verses following, in which the poet calls for the restorative power of the maiden's kiss, an appeal that for Wilhelm signals a fall from a height of idealism if not of spirituality: "Suddenly, however, the wings of the poet droop. He thinks about a remedy for his love-sickness: a kiss to repair the wound created in his heart by the shaft of love. In Christian hymns, the loving Christ is the only remedy for the sickly soul. . . . The lady's kiss shows us that we are once again in the realm of the sensible."[27] But as far as this poem is concerned, we are in the realm of the sensible from beginning to end. The verses "Amare crucior, morior/Vulnere, quo glorior" come as the cry of pain and triumph confirming what the poet has said up to that point, that is, that although spring and summer (the usual "seasons" of love) have gone, even in the cold of winter he suffers the heat of passion. This poet was on no heights from which to fall, for his lovesickness was still Ovidian and in no way Platonic or Christian. In asking for the salutary kiss, he is really on the same plane as when he proclaims himself a martyr *of* love; but he is not, after all, as the Christian martyr is, a martyr *for* love. It is the plane of sensual love and religious parody that he moves on all along, and it is curious that Wilhelm does not see that the hope for balm in the kiss, coming as it does directly upon the poet's reference to his martyrdom, is a continuation of the religious travesty.

After making the request for the restorative kiss, the *Burana* poet dwells on the thought of the lady's sensual lips and sweet kisses, the taste of which, he now exclaims, lifts him above the state of mere mortality: "Ut me mortalem negem aliquando." The beloved's kiss can, according to the poet's hyperbole, conquer death. Such is the meaning here and in the following verses from another poem of the *Carmina Burana*, which also repeats the lover's exultation in the love-wound inflicted by that one or unique lady-beloved:

> Unam quidem postulo
> Tamen michi dari,
> Cuius quidem osculo
> Potest mors vitari.
> Huic amoris vinculo
> Cupio ligari.
> Dulce est hoc iaculo
> Velle vulnerari.[x]

Here are kisses that infuse a "grace" that sends the lover into a state of rapture. As in the case of the other *Burana* poet who would die upon his lady's lips (see above) these are kisses that derive, somewhat ostentatiously and willfully, I believe, from the lovesickness and the kiss of the Song of Songs even as it was being explicated by Christian exegetes. Thus in the context of these poems of sensual love which are charged with a religiously inspired language, the kiss can be seen to figure prominently in the profanation of a mystic motif. In a way, the secular poets have succeeded in reclaiming the kiss of the Song, although one cannot help feeling that something of the mysticalness that it had acquired as a religious symbol has been carried over with it in the process. Nonetheless, as in the case of the troubadour Guillaume, these kisses, along with the poems in which we read of them, cannot without serious reservations be equated with the kisses and songs of troubadour *fin' amors* or courtly love. I do not find it possible to accept the view of those critics who, like Peter Dronke, are of the opinion that "a substantial proportion of twelfth- and thirteenth-century Latin love-lyrics can truly be called songs of *amour courtois*."[28]

This is not to say that the *Burana* love poems are never anything more than paeans to sensual passion. The medieval Latin poet also may

---

[x] "One lady indeed I ask to be given me, by whose kiss indeed death can be avoided. With this love's bonds I wish to be bound. It is sweet to desire to be wounded by this dart." "Tempus transit horridum," *Carmina Burana*, p. 180.

voice a desire for an amatory relationship that looks beyond physical pleasure without necessarily excluding it. The verses that follow show us a poet speaking of his love captivity, then dreaming of the sweet labor of kissing his lady mouth to mouth, only to conclude—contrary to the usual pattern that finds the poet achieving solace and fulfillment in the kiss or hopeful of more to come—that the meeting of lips will not cure him until their two hearts and wills have become one heart and one will:

> Illius captus sum amore,
> Cuius flos adhuc est in flore.
> Dulcis fit labor in hoc labore,
> Osculum si sumat os ab ore.
> Non tactu sanabor labiorum,
> Nisi cor unum fiat duorum
> Et idem velle. Vale, flos florum![y]

It is strange that neither Wilhelm nor Dronke discuss these verses, which seem to be pregnant with the concept of *amor-amicitia* that is at the heart of some of the highest moments of the spirituality of courtly love, just as it is at the core of the classico-Christian ideal of friendship: *Idem nolle et velle*! But it is possible, I suppose, to read the ending of the above strophe in a less idealistic key, in which case its author would have to be classified among those more cynical and sensual lovers for whom the kiss is not enough, and who hope that the lady will share their desire for *del plus*.

The Wound of Love

The theme of the *vulnus amoris* merits special attention, the more so for us in the light of the theme of the restorative or salutary kiss,

[y] "I am captive to her love whose flower is now in flower. Sweet becomes labor in this toil when mouth takes kiss from mouth. I shall not be healed by the touch of lips, unless one heart is made of two and desires the same. Farewell, flower of flowers!" "Anni novi rediit novitas . . . ," *Carmina Burana*, p. 145. The Ciceronian-Augustinian tradition of friendship is to be noted in the following verses of Bernart de Ventadorn as the poet tells us that love between two true lovers consists in a mutual desire to please one another; true lovers share the same desire and love cannot be said to be worthy unless the lovers' wills are equal:

> En agradar et en voler
> Es l'amors de dos fis amans.
> Nula res no i pot pro tener,
> Si'lh voluntatz non es egaus.

From "Chantars no pot gaire valer," in *Seine Lieder*, ed. C. Appel (Halle a S., 1915), p. 86.

of which we will have yet more to say. Although the "wound of love" by which the poet says he dies and is glorified, "Amare crucior, morior / Vulnere, quo glorior," is a *topos* of classical literature, medieval poets, as Renaissance poets later, derive it also from the religious sphere, and in their application of it one hears again the echoes of the Song of Songs and Christian writers. The Vulgate translation of the Song has the verses (4:9):

> Vulnerasti cor meum, soror mea sponsa,
> Vulnerasti cor meum in uno oculorum tuorum,
> Et in uno crine colli tui.

It is to be noted that at 2:5 and 5:8 of the Song the Vulgate has the famous words "quia amore langueo"—"for I am sick with love." On the other hand, the Septuagint Greek speaks of being wounded by love, and this is just what we find in Rufinus' translation of Origen's Commentary on the Song: "Quia vulnerata caritatis ego sum." It was Origen, in fact, who first, and quite consciously, transposed the theme of the wound caused by love's darts from pagan Eros to the Christian God. In the Prologue to his Commentary we find the phrase *vulnus amoris* and the idea that the soul "suffers" this wound happily, knowing it to be salvific and inflicted by the Word of God. Likewise in the Second Homily on the Song, which was preserved in St. Jerome's translation, Origen uses the phrase "quia vulnerata caritatis ego" and goes on to explain that it is beautiful and praiseworthy to receive the wounds of love.[29] I find the phrase used by St. Jerome himself in his letter [LXV, 12] to the virgin Principia, where it is connected with the Song. Jerome writes to her that now that she is pierced by the Lord's dart, she can, like the bride of the Song, exult that she is wounded by love: "Quae iaculo Domini vulnerata cum sponsa in Cantico canis: *vulnerata caritatis ego*." One of the better-known expressions of the motif is in Augustine's *Confessions* (IX, 2, 3): "Sagittaveras tu cor nostrum caritate tua et gestabamus verba tua transfixa visceribus"—"Thou hadst pierced our hearts with thy love, and we bore thy words fixed in our bowels."

Coming down to the twelfth century, we note Hugo of Saint-Victor's idea that there are many who carry Love's piercing arrows in their hearts, longing for them to be driven in deeper, for wounds caused by Love are sweet.[30]

The One who was wounded by love first was Christ on the cross. Commenting on the verse "Vulnerata cor meum, soror, mea sponsa," Honorius of Autun explains that it was for love of the Church that Christ was wounded, for he wanted the bride to share in his glory. Here, it is as though being scourged and being crucified were love torments. It is the theme of Christ as the supreme Martyr for love.[31] At the outset of his *De IV gradibus violentae caritatis*, Richard of Saint-Victor twice employs the expression "vulnerata caritate ego sum" in place of the Vulgate's "quia amore langueo," although the latter phrase is also employed by him in the same work.[32] Perhaps the most intense descriptions of the *vulnus amoris* in a religious context were to come a few centuries later in St. Francis of Sales (*Traité de l'amour de Dieu*, IV, 9) and in the Spanish Carmelites St. John of the Cross and St. Theresa of Avila. The most justly celebrated artistic representation of this erotico-religious motif is Bernini's sculpture of the transverberation of St. Theresa's heart, in the church of Santa Maria della Vittoria at Rome.

The Kiss as Goal or Reward

Returning to the love lyric in the vernacular, let us note first that in the work of the poets of the generation immediately following Guillaume, there are references to the desire for kisses that are not susceptible to the same extreme sensual interpretation that we were able to apply to the "first" of the troubadours. At the same time, while they have seemingly a resemblance to the examples from our medieval Latin poems, there is really less abandonment here than in the goliards. While intending real, even sensual kisses, they do not represent the kiss as a preludious bliss or as a promise of further favors to come, but rather as their ultimate goal or reward. This attitude is not found in all the love poetry of these same troubadours but usually only where the love is said to be that special kind that the poets call *fin' amors* as opposed to a concept of false love. This is very much what Andreas, writing after some of these poets, called pure love. The difference, however, is that the poets do not speak of refraining from sexual intercourse as a renunciation of a final solace or consolation. Nor do they conceive of the kiss and the embrace in the nude as a fanning of desire as Denomy believed.[33] The fact is that the troubadours have desire enough, which does not need to be fanned by kissing and embracing. Rather, in a number of cases, they conceive of these intimacies as the very terminus of their true love; that is, the conferring of the kiss and, sometimes, the nude embrace represent for them the solace and quietude so greatly yearned for.

The poet Cercamon, for example, like so many other troubadours, feels he will die if he is not granted the kiss and embrace of his lady:

> Messatges, vai, si Deus ti guar,
> E sapchas ab mi donz furmir,
> Qu'eu non puesc lonjamen estar
> De sai vius ni de lai guerir,
> Si josta mi despoliada
> Non la puesc baizar e tenir
> Dins cambra encortinada.[z]

Despite the apparent similarity to Guillaume's kiss allusion (the kiss in the room), the tone here is somewhat different although the expression of great desire is not less intense. But not only does Cercamon not suggest that anything beyond this is desired; in another poem he makes it quite clear that his desires would be fully satisfied if he could but have a kiss from his lady:

> Toz mos talenz m'aemplira
> Ma domna, sol d'un bais m'aizis.[a]

A similar expression of the marvelous efficacy of the kiss can be noted in some verses by Jaufré Rudel. Again the lovesick poet can be restored by a kiss alone:

> Per so m'en creis plus ma dolors
> Car non ai lieis en luecs aizitz,
> Que tan no fau sospirs e plors
> Qu'us sols baizars per excaritz
> Lo cors no'm tengues san e sau.[b]

[z] "Go, messenger, and God be with you. And seek to communicate with my lady [*donz*]. For I cannot long endure and live nor be cured if I cannot kiss and hold her nude in a curtained room." From "Ab lo temps qe fai refreschar," in *Les poésies de Cercamon*, ed. A. Jeanroy (Paris, 1922), p. 7.

[a] "I would be satisfied in all my desires, my lady, if you would only grant me a kiss." From "Per fin' Amor m'esjauzira," *Les poésies de Cercamon*, p. 28.

[b] Therefore my pain is yet increased because I do not have her in suitable places. For my sighs and tears are not such but that one kiss alone would make my heart whole and saved." From "Pro ai del chan essenhadors," in *Les chansons de Jaufré Rudel*, ed. A. Jeanroy (Paris, 1924), pp. 8–9.

112

Even allowing that Jaufré Rudel "has no expectation of possessing his beloved," that his is "a love which does not wish to possess but to exult in that state of non-possession," the fact remains that within his conception of distant and good love, the kiss is thought of as that boon which would bring salvation and fulfillment were it but granted.[34]

The same can be said for Bernart de Ventadorn, in whose work appear several allusions to kisses and embraces as the ultimate reward or solace for which the poet longs:

> Bo son tuih li mal que 'm dona;
> Mas per Deu li quer un do:
> Que ma bocha, que jeona,
> D'un douz baizar dejeo.[c]

Like the first example from Cercamon, this seems to be rather close to Guillaume's kiss. But in a different vein, Bernart has other verses in which he says that his lady's kiss has the power to pierce him to the heart; by this sweet kiss he is made the receiver of that true love which transforms him from a state of deadly sullenness to one of unequaled bliss:

> Domna, per cui chan e demor,
> Per la bocha 'm feretz al cor
> D'un doutz baizar de fin' amor coral,
> Que 'm torn en joi e'm get d'ira mortal.[d]

The poet Arnaut Daniel has need of a kiss as the only balm that can cool his burning heart, for the winter season and the snow on the ground have no effect on his desire:

> C'ab tot lo nei
> M'agr' ops us bais al chaut
> Cor refrezir,
> Que no'i val autra goma.[e]

[c] "Good and dear to me are all the ills she gives me, but, in God's name, I ask one gift of her: that she break the fasting of my mouth with a kiss." From "Bel m'es can eu vei la brolha," in Bernart de Ventadorn, *Seine Lieder*, ed. C. Appel (Halle a S., 1915), p. 56.

[d] "Lady, for whose sake I sing and remain [true], you wound me to the heart through the mouth with a sweet kiss of pure heartfelt love that restores me to joy and releases me from deadly grief." From "Can par la flors josta.l vert folh," in Bernart de Ventadorn, *Seine Lieder*, p. 236.

[e] "Despite all the snow, I need a kiss to cool my ardent heart. No other balm will avail." From "L'aur'amara," in *Canzoni*, ed. G. Toja (Florence, 1960), p. 256. In a *tenso* between Marcabru and Ugo Catola the latter seeks to explain that when he is weary and melancholy his lady's kiss restores him wholly:

One may assume that in the matter of kisses a lover does not need the advice of others; but in the case of poets who seek to give expression to their amorous sentiments and sensations, the influence of literary and other traditions is seldom if ever lacking. As in the goliard poets, so too in the troubadours the dual influence of Ovid and the Song of Songs is considerable. As for the Song, moreover, it may very well be that not only the biblical text but contemporary theological implementation of its erotic imagery in the context of affective mysticism also exercised its fascination on the poets. We have seen how important the image of the kiss was as a symbol of union or fulfillment and as the symbolic vehicle for the infusion or bestowal of a supernatural grace. We shall not repeat what has been amply demonstrated in earlier pages, but it will be worthwhile to quote some verses from Landri of Waben's twelfth century French allegorical paraphrase of the Song to indicate, at the very least, the remarkable similarity between the religious and profane traditions in the choice of the kiss as the mark of a unique blessing necessary to the well-being of the lover:

> Port moi le baiser de sa boche,
>   Cest co ki plus al cuer ma toche.
> Ja mais naurai ne bien ne aise,
>   Se ses baisers ne me repaise.[f]

We also read that if the soul *loves* and *serves* God well (cf. the language and concept of love service of the courtly lover), it becomes one spirit with him (the Pauline echo). Then one will have overcome all trials and tribulations. It is the kiss that brings (or signifies) this union in one spirit; hence it is the kiss to which the lover of God aspires, the kiss for which the amorous soul cries and sighs:

> A soi me ioigne par esperit.
>   Kar co ai io trove escrit,
> Ki par amor a deu saert,
>   Ki tresbien laime e bien le sert,

Marcabrun, quant sui las e.m duoill,
E ma bon'amia m'acuoill
Ab un baisar, quant me despuoill,
M'en vau sans e saus e garitz.

The severe Marcabru repudiates this love in the poem. In *Poésies complètes du Troubadour Marcabru*, ed. J. M. L. Dejeanne (Toulouse, 1909), p. 26.

[f] "Let him bring me the kiss of his mouth; it is that which touches my heart the most. I shall never have well-being or ease unless his kisses give me peace."

> Uns esperiz est avec lui.
> Co vaint tot mal e tot ennui,
> Cest li baisiers o io aspir,
> Por cui tant pleur e tant sospir.[g]

The mutual influence exerted by the religious and secular traditions of amatory literature on one another in the Middle Ages was such that if there are no specific references to the object of love or devotion, passages of poems and even entire poems may be read in either key. This, of course, is true of the Song of Songs itself, for it is a secular epithalamium celebrating human love until it is subjected to an allegorical reading in which it becomes a song of divine love.[35] So too the most famous medieval Latin love lyric combining Ovidian (or classical) and Solomonic (i.e., the Song) echoes is the *Iam dulcis amica* which, perhaps with slight variants, was "sung as a sacred conductus at Saint-Martial or Saint-Martin in the same decades [or slightly later] as it was performed as a sophisticated love-song."[36]

While we are on this important topic—and still with the kiss and two-in-one motifs—it should be remarked again that the same ambiguity exists in the figurative arts, especially in objects of medieval handicraft. In chapter 1 we had occasion to observe the Christian implementation in funerary art of the kiss of Eros and Psyche. In the Middle Ages, too, a seemingly profane content often bore a Christian significance or allegory. Hanns Swarzenski writes that "Wearing apparel, such as buckles and containers for cosmetics are decorated with scenes which often leave one in doubt as to whether they represent biblical subjects like David and Abisaig, or Solomon and the Queen of Sheba, or secular love scenes such as that of Tristan and Iseult."[37] Now one such example of this uncertainty has to do with a truly remarkable bronze-cast mirror from Bussen (Suabia). The handle of the mirror is shaped in such a way as to indicate a couple so closely

---

[g] "Let him join me to himself in spirit. For I have found it written; whoever through love would serve God, whoever loves him well and serves him well, is one spirit with him. This conquers all evil and all trouble; it is his kiss to which I aspire, for which I cry and sigh so greatly." The verses are as quoted in F. Ohly's *Hohelied-Studien: Grundzüge einer Geschichte der Hoheliedauslegung des Abendlandes bis um 1200.* Schriften der Wissenschaftlichen Gesellschaft an der Johann Wolfgang Goethe-Universität Frankfurt am Main, Geisteswissenschaftliche Reihe Nr. 1 (Wiesbaden, 1958), pp. 289–290. Landri of Waben's poem, circa 3000 verses, was written between 1176 and 1181 and paraphrases the Song up to V, 14. It is preserved in Le Mans: Bibliothèque publique, MS 173, fol. 33ᵛ–112ʳ. See Jean Bonnard, *Les traductions de la Bible en vers français au moyen âge* (Paris, 1884), p. 154.

embraced that they appear to be a single figure from the waist down, while from the waist up the fused two-in-one figure divides only slightly enough to distinguish the two lovers in the act of kissing. (Fig. 13.) The man's right arm is crooked in a V-shape with the hand caressing the face of the woman, while the heads are nestled into each other. The identification of the couple is no easy matter, and the disagreement on the part of art critics illustrates our point. Swarzenski, for example, holding the mirror to be the work of the thirteenth century, suggests the figures are Tristan and Iseult, whose story became popular in Germany only at that time through the version of Gottfried of Strassbourg. But this interpretation has been rejected by Heinrich Kohlhaussen, who dates the piece around the middle of the twelfth century (the argument does not seem totally convincing to me) and holds that the figures may represent the Bridegroom (*Christus Sponsus*) and the bride (*sponsa ecclesia*) of the Song.[38]

The Kiss Bestows a Grace

In the context of true love or *fin' amors*, the troubadours' insistence upon the marvelous and quieting (not inflammatory) effects of the kiss strongly suggests that they attributed to it something of a mysto-magical value. To be kissed by the beloved was to receive an unparalleled grace. We note, in fact, that in a poem by Bernart Marti the kiss is clearly connected with the important courtly love theme of the ennoblement of the lover. That Love or Charity ennobles or makes one more virtuous and worthy is, of course, an important concept in Christianity. In particular, the infusion of grace (which is a gift of the Divine Love) elevates man to a supernatural sphere of activity and allows him to perform salutary acts. The troubadours, however, attributed analogous ennobling power to the love and kiss of a lady. Our poet, claiming to be a perfect lover of an excellent and pure lady, speaks of receiving from her kiss the gift that ennobles him:

> Pero ges ieu no'm n'esmai
> Del ben qu'm n'avenha.
> Gen baizen m'estrena
> De que m'asenhora.[h]

[h] "Wherefore I am not worried about the good that may come to me from her. In sweetly kissing me, she offers me that gift whereby I am ennobled." From "Amar dei," in *Les poésies de Bernart Marti*, ed. E. Hoepffner (Paris, 1929), p. 3.

1. *The Kiss*. Rock-hewn.
A.D. 600–850 In the
Kailasa Temple, Elura.

2. *The Kiss and Copulation
of Two Gods*. Pre-Columbian
(Aztec) Mexican pictograph
in the Codex Borgia.

3. *God "Kissing" Man.* The infusion of the spirit of life in man (Gen. 2:7). Mosaic in the cathedral at Monreale.

4. *The Kiss*. Iberian stone relief discovered at Osuna (Spain), now in the Madrid National Archaeological Museum. Fourth to second century B.C.

5. Detail from Giotto's *Kiss of Judas*, in the Scrovegni Chapel, Padua.

6. *Eros and Psyche.* The Capitoline Museum, Rome.

7. *Eros and Psyche Wedded in Heaven* (Christianized). From a painted vase found in the Priscilla catacombs.

8. *The Visitation.* Detail from the altar-front from Lluça. In the Episcopal Museum, Vich.

9. *Justice and Peace Have Kissed* (Psalm 84:11). Detail from a miniature in a late fifteenth century manuscript of the *Golden Legend*. Paris, Bibliothèque Nationale, ms. franc. 244, fol. 107.

10. *The Kiss of Peace* exchanged by Saints Peter and Paul. Mosaic in the Palatin Chapel, Palermo.

11. *The Kiss of the Bride and Bridegroom.* "Osculetur me osculo oris sui." Miniature illustrating the opening of the Song of Songs. In the Bible said to have been Saint Bernard's. First half of the twelfth century. Bibliothèque de Troyes, ms. 458².

12. *Secular Lovers Kissing and Fusing into One.* Miniature from a fourteenth century Venetian manuscript containing Cecco d'Ascoli's *Acerba*. Biblioteca Mediceo-Laurenziana, ms. Plut. 40, 52.

13. *Two in One*. Bronze-cast mirror from Bussen (Suabia). Date uncertain, c. 1150–1250. Frankfurt a. M. Museum für Kunsthandwerk.

14. *Paolo and Francesca, with the Whirlwind of Lovers.* Engraving by the poet-mystic William Blake, 1826.

15. *The First Kiss of Lancelot and Guinevere.* From *Lancelot du Lac* (M. 805), c. 1310. The Pierpont Morgan Library, Lewis Cass Ledyard Fund, 1938.

16. *Luxuria.* Relief representation of the vice on the Cathedral at Amiens, France. Date c. 1225.

17. *The Kiss*, by A. Rodin. Marble, the Musée de Luxembourg, Paris.

18. *The Kiss*. Marble relief, Greek. First century B.C. Museo Archeologico, Venice.

20. *Enlaced Couple*. From the Cave of
Ain Sakhri. Wilderness of Judah. Natufi
art. Sixth–Seventh millenium B.C.

19. *The Kiss*, by C. Brancusi. Formed from
a single block of stone. In the Montparnasse
cemetery, Paris.

21. *Face to Face to Be*. Cover of an Etruscan Sarcophagus from Vulci. Fourth century B.C. The Boston Museum of Fine Arts.

22. *The Throne of Grace.* Vertical anthropo-zoomorphic Trinity. Miniature from a Missal of the twelfth century. Cambrai: Bibliothèque Municipale, ms. 234, fol. 2.

23. "Dixit Dominus Domino meo: sede a dextris meis"
(Psalm 109). Horizontal anthropo-zoomorphic Trinity.
From the fourteenth century *Petites Heures* of Jean, Duke
of Berry. Paris, Bibliothèque Nationale, lat. 18014, fol. 137ᵛ.

24. *Poliphilus Kissed Back to Life by Polia.* Woodcut from the *Dream
of Poliphilus (Hypnerotomachia Poliphili)*, printed at Venice by Aldus
in 1499.

As in Christian divine love, so too in *fin' amors* the kiss symbolizes the consummation of the poet's love, whereby long-suffering
desire is rewarded with a nonpareil beatitude. The very thought of
obtaining this gift from his lady is enough to ecstasize the true lover:

> De martir pogra for cofes
> Midons, ab un bays solamens;
> Et ieu fora'n totztemps jauzens
> S'a lieys plagues que lo'm dones,
> Qu'adoncs agr'ieu complitz totz mos demans;
> Que, quan m'albir qui suy ni qals seria,
> De sol l'albir suy quays cum s'ieu l'avia.[i]

This extraordinary role and the unique symbolic value attributed
to the kiss in the troubadour lyric are evidenced also (though less
frequently) in the lyrics of the Minnesänger despite the opinion that
"kisses are somewhat out of place in the rarified atmosphere of
hôhe minne."[39] Friedrich von Husen, who has been "wounded" with
love, claims that the kiss of his lady's mouth would profit an emperor;
and Heinrich von Morungen, likewise "wounded," is confident that
if he could but steal a kiss from his lady's lips he would be healed.[40]
But it is the greatest of the Minnesänger, Walter von de Vogelweide,
who best exemplifies the motif. His deeply wounded heart can be restored to health only if he is kissed by his Hiltegunde:

> Mines herzen tiefu wunde
> Diu muoz iemer offen sten,
> Si enküsse mich mit friundes munde.
> Mines herzen tiefu wunde
> Diu muoz iemer offen sten,
> Si enheiles uf und uz von grunde.
> Mines herzen tiefu wunde
> Diu muoz iemer offen sten,
> Sin werde heit von Hiltegunde.[j]

[i] "My lady can change me from a martyr into a blessed man just by a kiss. And
I would be forever in joy, if it but pleased her to grant it to me. Then all my
desires would be fulfilled. For when I think of what I am and what I would then
be, by this thought alone I am filled with joy as if I already had it." From "Ja
tant no cugey que'm trigues," in *Guilhem Peire de Cazals, Troubadour du XII*
siecle, ed. Jean Mouzat (Paris, 1954), p. 43.

[j] "My heart's deep wound, you must stay open always so that she may kiss me
with friendly mouth. My heart's deep wound, you must stay open always so that
you may be cured completely. My heart's deep wound, you must stay open always
to be healed by Hildegund." From the lyric beginning "Die mir in dem winter
fröide hant benomen." In *Die Lieder Walthers von der Vogelweide*, II (*Die Liebe-*
slieder), ed. Friedrich Maurer (Tübingen, 1962), p. 132.

And in another lyric, Walter avows that if he could have but one kiss from his lady's red mouth, he would be forever consoled:

> Wurde mir ein kus noch zeiner stunde
> Von ir roten munde,
> So waer ich an fröiden wol genesen.[k]

It is a fact of some consequence that in the successors to the troubadours, the Italian poets of the manner known as *il dolce stil novo*, it is difficult if not impossible to find allusions to the kiss and other such intimacies, at least as far as their poetry in the sweet new style is concerned. The poets of this current etherealized love of *donna* beyond anything dreamed of by the troubadours, and we will find Dante as the culminating point of this tradition in the *Vita Nuova* making it clear that the most he hoped for and what he thrived on was not a kiss from his lady but her greetings (See chapter 4, n. 9). Thus it is interesting, to say the least, that in a poem outside this vein, Guido Guinizelli expressed a desire for a kiss which is bluntly satyric:

> Ah, prender lei a forza, oltra su' grato,
> E baciarli la bocca e 'l bel visaggio
> E li occhi suoi, ch'èn due fiamme di foco![l]

Perhaps one should not be too surprised to find that the very "father" of the sweet new style could sound like the troubadour-prince Guillaume. For the better poets of the Middle Ages, like those of any age, were as much influenced by, as they were influencers of, literary conventions. So it is that in a *pastourelle*, which genre commonly regarded love's consummation as a full physical possession, another *still novo* poet, Guido Cavalcanti, in a twist that is particularly relevant

---

[k] "Could I have a kiss one more time from your red mouth, so would I be fully saved [restored] by joy." From the lyric "Mueste ich noch geleben daz ich die rosen." *Die Lieder*, II, p. 64. At this point we may insert some German verses of a more popular tone that contain the motif: the second strophe of the poem "Chume, chume geselle min" (*Carmina Burana*, 136a). Here it is the maid who calls out to her lover to "cure" her with his sweet red mouth:

> Süezer rosenvarwer munt,
> Chum und mache miche gesunt;
> Chum und mache miche gesunt,
> Süezer rosenvarwer munt.

In *Anthologie du Minnesang*, ed. André Moret (Paris, 1949), 95.

[l] "Oh, to take her by force against her will and kiss her mouth and lovely face and her eyes that are two flames of fire!" From the sonnet "Chi vedesse a Lucia un var cappuzzo," in *I Rimatori del dolce stil novo*, ed. G. R. Ceriello (Milano, 1950), p. 36.

to our discussion, sounds rather like the poet of the *lai des pucelles* quoted earlier when he states that the extreme solace and favor (or grace), that he asked of his obliging shepherdess was her consent to be kissed and embraced:

> Merzé le chiesi *sol* che di baciare
> E d'abbracciare le fosse 'n volere.[m]

And this was evidently enough, as the end of the poem has it, to send the poet into an ecstasy wherein he beheld the god of love.

With these examples now before us, it may be instructive here to note the presence of the kiss motif in a context that has ties with neither Christian mysticism nor the troubadour love lyric. In the *Greek Anthology*, which is replete with kisses, there is an epigram by a certain Rufinus, of whom all that can be said is that he lived sometime between the second and sixth centuries A.D.: "Thou hast Hera's eyes, Melite, and Athena's hands, the breasts of Aphrodite, and the feet of Thetis. Blessed is he who looks on thee, thrice blessed he who hears thee talk, *a demigod he who kisses thee, and a god [immortal] he who takes thee to wife.*" (V, 94).[41] The basic idea behind this is that posession of the beloved can raise one to a condition that is above the ordinary. To kiss the beloved is to become divine. But what, then, one may well ask, is the difference between Rufinus' hyperbole expressing rapture and the hyperbolizing of the troubadours? The answer, I think, has to do with the Christian heritage of the latter. The kiss Rufinus speaks of is much like that found in Cavalcanti's *pastourelle*, a purely sensual bliss, but it is unlike those aspired to in the poems of *fin' amors*. When the various moments of osculation referred to herein are seen in their historical and psychosexual contexts, it may not be excessive to say that in troubadour *fin' amors* the kiss has much the same role as in the mystics' description of Christian divine love. The Christian mystic kiss signified the gift of the Holy Spirit whereby the soul is "ennobled" and made worthy of the union with God. At the same time, the kiss is itself the symbol of that union. It is true, of course, that the *fin' amors* of the troubadours is a love of creatures, but it is now generally agreed that the practitioner of true love desired something more than a momentary gratification of a physical desire. Professor Valency has neatly stated what we may call the "mystic" character of *fin' amors*: "What in general, the True Lover expected of

[m] "Grace [or reward] I asked of her, that she but wish to kiss and embrace."

his beloved was not a temporary physical appeasement; it was a perpetual benediction; he looked to his lady not for satisfaction, but for blessedness. This blessedness proceeded from the unique psychic exchange which love brings about, that mutual acceptance which makes two hearts beat as one, puts two souls in one breast, and conjures up all the other psychophysical miracles of the romantic genre."[42] To this we may add that the blessedness and, eventually, the psychophysical miracles of which Valency speaks were often intimately connected with the kiss, by which means they were to be effected as by a sacramental rite.

The Heart's Migration in the Kiss

Given the presence in the medieval love lyric of the motifs of the migration and exchange of hearts or souls (or the lover's *self*) one would expect to find the kiss motif used in connection with one or the other of these metaphors of ecstatic love. It is somewhat curious, I think, that this connection seems not to have been made by the earliest troubadours, although it may be implicit in their allusions to the kiss in the examples we have recorded. There are, however, some striking examples in the vernacular lyric of the late twelfth and the thirteenth centuries which reveal that by then such a conceit as the loss or surrender of the lover's heart through a kiss was familiar enough, for it occurs not only in Provençal but in French and Italian poets as well.[43] We may observe its appearance first in the troubadour Folquet de Romans, who begins one of his poems with the memory of a kiss by which his lady drew his heart from his body. (We see here also the play on *cor-cors*):

> Ma bella domna, per vos dei esser gais,
> C'al departir me dones un dolz bais,
> Tan dolzamen, lo cor del cors me trais
> Lo cor avez, domna, qu'eu lo vos lais.[n]

Two further things to be noted here because of their frequent recurrence in subsequent examples of the conceit are that it is a kiss given

---

[n] "My beautiful lady, I should be gay through you, for when we departed you gave me a sweet kiss, so sweetly, you drew my heart from my body. You now have my heart, lady, for I left it with you." From "Ma bella domna, per vos dei esser gais," in *Die gedichte des Folquet von Romans*, ed. R. Zenker (Halle, 1896), p. 45.

at parting and that the heart is drawn by an irresistible sweetness. The poet's heart, moreover, is left with the lady.

I find two cases of the conceit in the most famous of the twelfth century French *trouvères*, Gace Brulé. In the first we again see that it is the sweetness of the kiss that has enraptured the poet's heart:

> Uns douz besiers me fu si savorez
> Que je ne sai se mes cuers m'est enblez,
> Mes contre moi s'en est en li entrez.[o]

The poet's heart has entered the breast of the lady, but the poet asks for its return by way of another kiss, a theme that later was to be especially popular with the Renaissance poets:

> Douce dame, por vostre signorie,
> Por vostre prix et por vostre valor,
> Se vos ameis ne pou ne bien ma vie,
> Vers vo bouche m'estuet reprendre un tour:
> Einsi vos pri ke mon cuer me rendeis.[p]

The same conceit of the heart stolen or enraptured by the kiss and left to dwell with the lady appears in another poem by Gace Brulé, where the poet lingers even more on the motif of the sweet drawing of his heart in a kiss, thus accentuating the sensual element of the image:

> En besant mon cuer me ravi
> Ma douce dame gente;
> Trop fu fous quant il me guerpi
> Pour li qui me tourmente!
> Las! ain nel senti,
> Quant de moi parti:
> Tant doucement le me toli
> Qu'en sospirant le trest a li.[q]

[o] "A sweet kiss was of such sweetness to me that I know not whether my heart was stolen from me. But to my detriment, it has left me and entered into her." From "Ne puis faillir a bone chançon fere," in *Trouvères et Minnesänger: Receuil de Textes,* ed. Istvan Frank (Saarbrücken, 1952), p. 111.

[p] "Sweet lady, by your command, by your worth and merit, if you at all care for my life, allow me to approach your mouth again. And I beg you to return my heart to me." *Trouvères et Minnesänger,* p. 182. These verses are found in only one of the seven manuscripts containing the poem. They are given by Frank among the notes.

[q] "In kissing me, my sweet and gentle lady bereft me of my heart; too foolish was it to leave me for that one who torments me! Alas, I did not feel it when it went from me, so sweetly did she take it from me drawing it to herself in a sigh." From "Les oisillons de mon pais," in Carla Cremonesi, *Lirica francese del medioevo* (Milan, 1955), p. 115.

The next example of the conceit is from one of the better Italian poets of the Sicilian School, Rinaldo d'Aquino. In the lyric "Amorosa donna fina," the poet complains to his lady that, for all his service, he has never received any reward other than a single kiss, and this has proved a disastrous boon inasmuch as his heart was thereby uprooted from his body and given to the beloved, leaving the poor lover in doubt as to how he is to live without a heart:

> Gioco e riso mi levate
> Membrando tutta stagione
> Che d'amor vi fui servente
> Nè de la vostra amistate
> Non ebb'io anche guiderdone
> Se no un bacio solamente.
> E quel bascio mi 'nfiammao,
> Chè dal corpo mi levao
> Lo core e dedilo a vui.
> Degiateci provedere:
> Che vita pò l'omo avere
> Se lo cor non è con lui?[r]

One of the most singular uses of the conceit occurs in a poem by the troubadour Raimbaut d'Orange. Though enamoured of the poet's lady, God restrains himself by not abducting her to himself by a kiss:

> Gran esfort fai Dieus, qar sofer
> C'ab si no la 'npueja baizan!
> Mas no·m vol tolre ni tort far.[s]

This somewhat surprising and daring implementation of the image recalls the medieval mystic idea of a death by the kiss of the Lord, in particular the Jewish conception of the death of the righteous by the mouth (kiss) of God, but it is not possible to ascertain whether

---

[r] "Joy and laughter you take from me when I remember all the time that I have been your servant for love's sake; from your friendship I have had no reward except one kiss only. And that kiss inflamed me, so much that it took my heart from my body and gave it to you. You ought to make some provision for me in this case: what life can a man have if his heart is not with him?" From "Amorosa donna fina," in *Le rime della scuola siciliana*, I, ed. Bruno Panvini (Florence, 1962), pp. 111–112.

[s] "God shows great strength, because He restrains himself from raising her, kissing, up to him! But He does not wish to take her from me or do me wrong." From the poem "Ben sai c'a sels seria fer," in Walter T. Pattison, *The Life and Works of the Troubadour Raimbaut d'Orange* (Minneapolis, 1952), p. 143. I have also used Pattison's English translation of the verses.

there is a direct connection between the two. For the rest, we may note that the idea of the beloved desired by God figures in the canzone "Donne ch'avete intelletto d'amore" of Dante's *Vita Nuova*. Only God's compassion for man causes him to allow Beatrice to tarry yet a while on earth.

I have suggested that the specific motif of an actual exchange of hearts which is not merely attested but indeed effected by the kiss is not easy to find in the medieval lyric poets. But again a German lyric of the thirteenth century in which it does occur suggests that the *topos* was, in fact, well known. Here the occasion is a painful parting between a knight and his beloved, and, as the two offer hearts to one another, the author, Ulrich von Winterstetten, states explicitly by way of conclusion that the exchange took place with a kiss:

> Owe und ach! der jamerbaeren scheiden
> Ir beider herze brach,
> Das [da] geschach von den gelieben beiden:
> Daz schuof in ungemach.
> Der ritter sprach 'gehabe dich wol!
> Din lip ist maniger tugende vol:
> Min herze dir belibet hie.'
> Si sprach 'so füere min herze hin.'
> Der wehsel da mit kus ergie.[t]

In the following chapter we will see that the medieval romance was particularly receptive to this motif, which, like other erotic conventions, it enriched by means of a fuller and more elaborate context of a tale of love.

---

[t] "Alas and alack! both their hearts broke because of the painful parting which took place between the beloved couple. That caused them pain. The knight said, 'Take care of yourself. You [your body] are full of virtue. My heart remains here with you.' And she replied: 'Then let my heart go [with you].' The exchange [of hearts] took place with a kiss." From the poem "Bi liebe lac . . . ," in *Poets of the Minnesang*, ed. Olive Sayce (Oxford, 1967), p. 177.

4. Medieval Love Legends

Flamenca

he conceits of ecstatic love that we have been considering within the context of medieval profane love received
one of their most attractive applications in that beautiful work of Provençal literature (and one of the most
charming books of the Middle Ages), the thirteenth century romance *Flamenca*. Here again we meet with the swoon of the ecstasied
lover (Guillem) whose spirit is wafted by love to the room in the tower
where the beloved (Flamenca) is kept prisoner by a jealous husband:

> Fin' amors l'esperit l'en mena
> Lai en la tor on si jasía
> Flamenca . . . .
>   (2147–2149)[a]

But this lover also complains to Love and wishes that his body were
there where his heart is, for without his heart he can scarcely be said
to be alive:

> Mon cor ai lai en celle torre,
> E si-l cors vos non lai metes,
> Sapias que perdut m'aves.
> Ses cor nom pot hom gaire viure.
>   (2690–2693)[b]

And as long as he is alone in loving, he must die and die alone (4597–
4599). Ideally, however, when love is reciprocal, although lovers outwardly seem to be two, inwardly they are one; for love unites the
two in one:

> Mais amors es cais elemens
> Simples e purs, clars e luzens,
> E fai soen de dos cors u,
> Quar si met egal en cascu;

---

[a] "True love led his spirit there in the tower where Flamenca lay." The edition
of *Flamenca* used is that in *Les Troubadours, Jaufré, Flamenca, Barlaam et
Josaphat*, ed. and trans. René Lavaud and René Nelli (Paris, 1960).

[b] "I keep my heart there in that tower, and if you do not place my body there,
know that you have ruined me. Without a heart, man can hardly live."

Us es dedins e dui defors,
Et ab un cor lía dos cors.
(2076–2081)[c]

Such passages as these show that the *Flamenca*, like other medieval romances, is also partially a treatise on love. In this respect, one of the most important sections of the poem (vss. 6658 ff.) is taken up with a discussion of the relative merits and roles of the eyes and the mouth (kiss) in love. The eyes are said to be superior, on the grounds that the sweetness that lovers derive from gazing into each other's eyes is both purer and more complete, or, we may say, more spiritual than that which comes through the lips. The reason for this is that the eyes are themselves the most spiritual of the senses and thus constitute a pure passageway for love; the sweetness that is conveyed by them moves swiftly and directly to the heart. In the kiss, on the other hand, the mouth cannot help retaining some of the sweetness for itself, thereby delaying arrival to the heart. Nonetheless, although the gazing into each other's eyes is judged the more truly perfect joy of love (inasmuch as it permits the lovers to pass into each other's heart), the author allows that the kiss may be a seal or warranty that the lover is experiencing that perfect joy. It is clear that the author is here talking of *fin' amors* as opposed to what Andreas calls mixed love, for he himself tells us that his views will not be shared by those who can kiss and still go right on to other intimacies. The true lover, on the other hand, even during the kiss and embrace, will not forget the joy of love that derives from the eyes. The author is insistent here in claiming that the intimacies of the kiss and embrace are understood by the true lover only in those terms dictated to him by reason, *merci*, and conscience: the eyes are the gateway of true love (*fin' amors*) and the kiss the sign of its joy or fruition. We recall that Andreas had said that pure love "joins together the hearts of two lovers in a perfect delight," and that it consists "in the contemplation of minds and the affection of hearts." It is obvious, I think, that the allusion to the lovers gazing into one another's eyes in the *Flamenca* passage is meant to define love as just such a contemplation of the mind and affection of the heart. Each of the lovers sees his heart in the mirror, that is, in the eyes, of the other. The same passage, moreover, goes on to speak ex-

[c] "Love is an element, as it were, simple and pure, clear and bright, that often makes one heart of two, when it rests equally in each one. Inwardly it is one, outwardly two. And it binds two into one heart."

125

plicitly of *fin' amors* binding the lovers' hearts so intimately together that if one should happen to be absent the other feels itself failing.

Yet, if in this passage the eyes are ultimately considered to be the superior vehicle of love, it is not long before we come across some verses in which the author describes that most mystical or magical of love's miracles, the exchange of hearts, as being effected by the kiss itself. It is significant that in this case where, as with Ulrich von Winterstetten's couple, a complete exchange takes place, the love is reciprocal and the kiss occurs at the parting of the lovers, who find it impossible to separate until Flamenca herself hits upon and explains the rationale of this marvelous expediency:

> Mais Flamenca, coma cortesa,
> Ab son amic dos motz parlet,
> E dis: "Amix," pueis lo baiset,
> "Ab cest baisar mon cor vos liure,
> E prenc lo vostre que-m fai viure."
> Guillems respon: "Domna, eu-l prenc
> Per tal covinent eu-'l retenc
> Ques ieu en luec del mieu lo tenga,
> E prec vos del mieu vos sovenga."
> (6888–6896)[d]

Here the mutual transformation of lover and beloved into one another by way of the kiss is entire. The lovers will be with each other even in separation and absence, each living with the life, that is, the heart, of the other.

The sophisticated love psychology of the *Flamenca* reaches into another area of the kiss theme that has been and will continue to be of interest to us. This has to do with the connection—so important and so pervasive in the early and medieval Christian centuries—between the idea of peace (also *salus*) and the kiss. In the *Flamenca* the religious nature of this liturgical association is made to serve as the context of a pseudodivine economy within which a profane love begins to have its realization.

In order to observe the inaccessible Flamenca, whom he has not yet seen (she is closely guarded by the typical jealous husband of the

[d] "But Flamenca, as a lady of courtesy, spoke yet sweetly to her lover, saying: 'My love,' and here she kissed him, 'by this kiss I deliver my heart to you and take yours by which I may live.' Guillem replied: 'Lady mine, I take it and in accordance with your terms will guard it, to keep in place of my own, and I pray you care for mine.'"

courtly-love tradition), Guillem has stationed himself in the choir of the church in which she attends services. When Flamenca enters and makes her way into her private pew, her face is veiled. But the sun streaming down on her head causes her to appear as a glowing effulgence, and at this point, apparently in accord with the order of the liturgical service, Guillem intones the *signum salutis*, a phrase which, given the situation, is already ambiguous enough to suggest the accent is on an erotic connotation of *salus*. The erotic element, at any rate, becomes quite overt in what follows when the *Pax*, a breviary in this case, is presented by the altar boy to be kissed by Flamenca. Guillem is able to espy the scene only from a distance and only through a hole in the choir screen, behind which he sits. What he sees and what the author focuses on—through the hole—is Flamenca's pretty little red mouth, "sa bella boqueta vermeilla," in the act of kissing the breviary. When the altar boy returns to the choir, Guillem asks at what page he offers the *Pax* and, upon being shown, falls to kissing it ecstatically over and over in a lover's passion that is mistaken for religious piety (vss. 2489–2607).

This contextual ambiguity is further elaborated the second time Guillem sees Flamenca in church. Now, before the altar boy proceeds to offer the *Pax* to Flamenca, Guillem instructs him that the place to be kissed is the verse "Fiat pax in virtute" (Psalm 121:7). Guillem's reason for this choice is that when David completed the Book of Psalms, he enjoined his son Solomon—whose very name, we remember, means peace—to kiss precisely that verse, indeed, that very word *peace* daily; and for as long as Solomon followed that admonishment, his kingdom enjoyed the maximum state of peace (vss. 3155–3170). Here then the traditional equation kiss=peace is to the fore, but the subtle pun involved depends on the situational irony of the scene. As Guillem's explanation would have it, the religious admonishment that peace is to be found in righteousness carries with it the obligation of a ritual act of kissing. In the case of Guillem, who is righteous or, better, "virtuous" in the courtly-love sense, "peace," again in the courtly-love or erotic sense, is to be had in the kisses of Flamenca.[1]

Among the kisses in medieval literature of profane love, few are as clearly mystico-magical as the kiss of parting we find in the *Flamenca* and in Ulrich von Winterstetten. Nonetheless, the medieval romances offer us other such kisses that were then and are now much better known. Our inquiry would be incomplete without reference to three of the most remarkable and popular love legends of the Middle Ages, those dealing with the pairs Lancelot and Guinevere, Tristan and Iseult, and Pyramus and Thisbe, this last of ancient provenance deriving from Ovid. Though chronologically they precede (in their earliest forms) the *Flamenca* and some of the lyric poets we have mentioned, these legends are best dealt with here because of the continued development they underwent and also because they will lead us most naturally to Dante, the poet who must perforce conclude this chapter.

Lancelot and Guinevere

We will later see that the kiss exchanged between Lancelot and Queen Guinevere in the prose *Lancelot* was to have an eternal echo in Dante's *Divine Comedy*, but it must first be recorded here as a classic example of the kiss as a bestowal of an immeasurable boon conferred by the beloved (the lady) in the role of a superior being. This is in keeping with the kiss of the courtly-love tradition which the Lancelot-Guinevere love affair also agrees with in its character of an adulterous relationship. Though he is an intrepid knight who has proven himself a model of valor for love of the queen, Lancelot is exceedingly timid (indeed he trembles) when it comes to declaring his feelings to her. It is his friend Galehaut who arranges for a meeting between the couple and then successfully solicits the queen to kiss Lancelot. Though the queen is glad to comply even to the point of the kiss, she is just circumspect enough to fear being seen by others who are nearby. Again Galehaut supplies the strategy that allows the couple to kiss. He will stay in the company of the lovers and the three will draw close, pretending to be in earnest conversation; then, at an opportune moment, the lovers will kiss, with Galehaut literally between them. Though the heads of Lancelot and Guinevere are inclined toward one another, the knight is still hesitant, so that it is the queen who takes the initiative; holding the hero by the chin, she kisses him long: "Lors se traient tout troi ensemble et font samblant de conseillier. Et la roine voit que li chevaliers nen ose plus faire, si le prent par le menton et le baise devant Galahot asses longement."[e]

[e] "Then they draw together, all three, and pretend to take counsel. And the queen sees that the knight dares not do more, so she takes him by the chin and kisses him in front of Galehaut for quite a long time." *The Vulgate Version of the Arthurian Romances edited from Manuscripts in the British Museum by H. Oskar Sommer, III, Le livre de Lancelot del Lac, Part I* (Washington, 1910), 263.

That Galehaut should be so conspicuously present at this lovers' kiss may well strike us as a strange thing. But it may help to remember that it was he, in fact, who had asked the queen to kiss Lancelot as a pledge of true love and to do so in his (Galehaut's) presence: "Mais ore covient commencement de suerte. . . . Dont le baisies devant moi par commencement damor vraie."[f] These words of Galehaut, incidentally, also make it clear that there never was any real question about Guinevere being the one who was expected to give the kiss after all. The kiss given here figures as a solemnizing if not a sacramental act, much like the one used at the ceremonies of betrothal and of feudal homage where it was given before witnesses.[2] The latter ceremony is perhaps the more pertinent in the present case. Among the rites associated with the contract of vassalage was the *osculum* which sealed the obligations made by lord and vassal. In this ceremony it was the lord who conferred the kiss, especially when it was to be on the mouth. (The vassal might kiss the feet of the lord.)[3] Now it appears that also in the medieval love-service ritual—in which the lady held the position to the lover that in feudal homage the lord held to the vassal—when the lady finally consented to accept the suppliant lover as her faithful man, the act of amatory homage was modeled on the ceremony of the feudal contract of vassalage. The oath of service and homage made by the *drut* (loyal love-servant) was sealed by a kiss from the lady. Most often this was the first and only kiss.[4] Such, however, was not to be the case with Lancelot and Guinevere; and, indeed, even in reference to this their first kiss, which must certainly be considered one of the major documents of the ritual of medieval love-service, nothing of what we have said detracts from its enervatingly sensual character. As the text says, it was a long kiss.

Another point worth noting in connection with this episode is that when Guinevere agrees to accept Lancelot's love and service and to bless him with her own love in return, she expresses the motif of the union or psychic exchange of lovers in language that echoes the leitmotif of the Song of Songs ("I am my beloved's and he is mine"): "Dame, fait Galahos, grans merci, et ie vous pri que vos li [to Lancelot] dones vostre amor et que vous le prenes a vostre chevalier tous iours, et devenes sa loiax dame a tous les iors de vostre vie. Si lavres fait plus riche que se vous li donnies tout le monde. *Ensi fait ele lotroi ie que*

<hr/>

[f] "But this is the time to begin the pledge. . . . And so do you kiss him in front of me as the beginning of true love." *Loc. cit.*

il soit tous miens et ie soie toute siene."[g] The request for the kiss is made immediately following this avowal as though it were to be not merely the symbol, but the very vehicle for effecting the psycho-physical union implied in the queen's words. How greatly the Lancelot-Guinevere kiss impressed the medieval mind is attested by its treatment in the art of the time. It is the subject of one of the most beautiful miniatures inspired by the entire Arthurian literature. (Fig. 15).

Tristan and Iseult

Even more popular than the love story of Lancelot and Guinevere was that of Tristan and Iseult. When the various fragments and versions of the Tristan legend are considered as a composite whole, it may be said to offer a small but extraordinary gallery of medieval uses of the kiss. Before the episode of the fatal love potion, there is a moment when Iseult, having learned that Tristan is the knight who slew her uncle Morhaut, threatens to kill him while he is bathing. But upon being persuaded of the justification of Tristan's action and of his good will to her, she kisses him (with no erotic intent) on the mouth as a sign of reconciliation and peace.[5] This is followed shortly by a scene in which the infuriated barons of Ireland are about to wreak their own vengeance upon Tristan; but they too are immediately appeased when they see their king kiss Tristan upon the mouth. This particular kiss has special interest, for it apparently marked not only a reconciliation but the establishment of something approaching brotherhood or, at the very least, membership in the group or clan, such a ceremonial usage being yet another symbolic and magic implementation of the kiss in the Middle Ages. At any rate, the solemnity attached to this kiss in the Tristan legend is further evidenced by the fact that in kissing Tristan, the king was fulfilling a promise which had been elicited from him by his daughter Iseult. And that promise was absolutely binding because it had itself been sealed by a kiss![6]

There are a number of kisses exchanged by knights that are recorded in the Tristan legend, but it is the lovers that must occupy us

[g] "Lady, said Galehaut, thank you, and I beg you to give him [Lancelot] your love and to take him for your knight for always, and become his loyal lady for all the days of your life. Indeed you have made him richer than if you gave him the whole world. She made [the oath] thus: I accept that he be entirely mine and that I be entirely his." *The Vulgate Version,* p. 263. My italics.

here. The legend records the first kiss of passion between Tristan and Iseult. It occurs, as is to be expected, shortly after they have inadvertently drunk the love-potion that had been meant for Iseult and Tristan's uncle and lord, King Mark. Much has been written about the role of the love-philtre, but it were best not to become entangled in that question here. Even if we allow that the drinking of the magic aphrodisiac symbolizes the ineluctable or fatalistic nature of a passionate and irrational love, we must nonetheless recognize that it also signals the crystallizing and awareness of desire for one another in the unsuspecting couple. The first natural reaction to that mutual awakening and confession is the coming together in a kiss (so different from the couple's earlier kiss of peace) that seals the lovers in a psychic union which is to last until death. Indeed, in the ecstasy of that first lover's kiss and embrace, Tristan even calls for death.[7] But more than a surrender to death, this call is really love's challenge to death, for note, it is Iseult's maid Brangane who, when she sees the couple kiss, warns them that they have drunk both love and death. In response to this the lovers embrace again, and as they are "trembling with desire and life" throughout their bodies, Tristan exclaims, "Let death come then." This is said in the confident spirit of one who feels that love— even as human passion—is as strong as death.

Of such passionate kisses there are many in the legend: one there is, however, that is truly unique for its psychophysical or mystical implications. Most fully recorded in the great German version (c. 1210) of Gottfried von Strassburg, it is, significantly, a kiss given at a painful parting of the lovers in Iseult's orchard. Knowing that he and the queen have been fully discovered in their unlawful love by King Mark, Tristan must flee from the court. Protesting that he will forever carry the queen in his heart, he pleads that she in turn carry him forever in hers. Then he asks for a parting kiss. But before suffering him to leave, Iseult gives him a ring and expounds the principles of the love that has forever bound them into a oneness of heart, body, and life. If Tristan dies, then her own life dies. In watching over her own life she will be caring for Tristan, but their common life is also in Tristan's keeping. Then as she invites him to the kiss, she reminds him that by it they shall evermore be one and the same. This kiss, she says, is a seal upon their union whereby she is his and he is hers, one identity until death:

Ein lîp, ein leben daz sîn wir.

. . . .

Nu gât her unde küsset mich:
Tristan und Îsôt, ir und ich,
Wir zwei sîn iemer beide
Ein ding ân' underscheide
Dirre Kus sol ein insigel sîn,
Daz ich iuwer unde ir mîn
Belîben staete unz an den tôt,
Niwan ein Tristan und ein Îsôt.[h]

(18348, 18355–18362)

Here the transposition of Christian mystical language is plain enough. Besides the two-in-one-flesh motif which the Judeo-Christian tradition applied to a married couple, the Song of Songs and twelfth century mystical exegesis of the Song are at the very heart of Gottfried's passage, not only in the coupling of the kiss image with the theme of "I am my beloved's and my beloved is mine," but also in the motif of *love being as strong as death* (8:6). We may recall that the Song's motif, "My beloved is mine and I am his," was also linked with the first kiss of Lancelot and Guinevere. Actually, the psychic union it implies was already present in the first kiss of Tristan and Iseult, which, we saw, included the idea that love is as strong as death. It would seem, then, that this parting kiss is a solemn confirmation the lovers make of their union unto death. That the kiss is here accompanied by Iseult's donation of a ring to her lover is another sign of the ritualistic and solemn character of the scene. Here, at any rate, we have a clear case of the mystico-magical conversion of lovers into one another by means of the kiss, much like what we have noticed in the *Flamenca*. Indeed the situation in the two episodes is so similar—in both cases the lovers had long since kissed and consummated their love many times over—that it is likely that the Provençal romance derived its analogous kiss scene from the Tristan legend, most probably, however, from a French source. This raises the question of how much of the episode in the German poem was

---

[h] "One body, one life are we. . . . Now come here and kiss me. Tristan and Iseult, you and I, we two are forever one and undivided substance. May this kiss be a seal [confirming] that I remain yours and you mine, constant until death, but one Tristan and one Iseult." *Tristan und Îsolt: A Poem by Gottfried von Strassburg*, ed. August Closs (Oxford, 1947), p. 180. Also in Friedrich Ranke's edition of the poem (Berlin, 1958), p. 230.

132

Gottfried's innovation. Because Gottfried seems to have adhered closely to the Tristan legend as told before him in French verse by Thomas, it is safe to say that the important elements of the scene were already present in Gottfried's predecessor and perhaps were part of the tradition. Unfortunately, the extant fragment of this scene in Thomas's version is broken off at a critical point.[8] Nonetheless, there is enough to suggest that it might have included the idea of the psycho-physical value of the lovers' parting kiss, a supposition strengthened by the fact that the motif of the oneness of the lovers is already very prominent in Thomas's poem. On the other hand, given the influence that the Song of Songs was exerting on medieval German poets (as on poets throughout Europe), and in view of Gottfried's characteristic practice of applying religious language to his love story (though the tendency was hardly peculiar to him alone) we may surmise that the *particular* mystical coloring lent to the episode is chiefly his own doing.

The twelfth century *Tristan* of Thomas offers us a significant example of the motif of the lady's kiss as a restorative balm bringing health. It is associated with the theme of the beneficent effect of the lady's salutation. The Provençal poets, we know, played on the word *la salut* in its pluralistic sense of greeting and health and, by a metaphorical extension, of salvation or beatitude. The theological concept of *salus* has to do with restoring man's fallen or sick nature, with "healing" man, with at-one-ment. When we recall that the love-sick poets frequently protest that they can never be restored to health unless they receive a kiss from the beloved, we see that the very word *salut*—which is given by way of the mouth—could lend itself to a certain ambiguity which allows a kiss to be thought of. (We should not forget that the actual greeting or salutation with a kiss was still practiced.) This ambiguity, I believe, is operative in a passage from Thomas's *Tristan*. Near the end of that poem, when Tristan has been mortally wounded and unsuccessfully treated by doctors, the lover-knight explains to a trusted friend that only Iseult can console and save him. In bidding his friend to hasten to Iseult with this news, he plays upon the word *salu* in its various meanings and upon the analogous terms *santé* and *conforz*:

> Dites li saluz de ma part,
> Que nule en moi senz li n'a part.
> De cuer tanz saluz li emvei

133

Que nule ne remaint od mei.
Mis cuers de salu la salue,
Senz li ne m'ert santé rendue;
Emvei li tute ma salu.
Cumfort ne m'ert jamais rendu,
Salu de vie ne santé,
Se par li ne sunt aporté.
S'ele ma salu ne m'aporte
E par buche ne me conforte,
Ma santé od li dunc remaine,
E jo murrai od ma grant peine;
En fin dites que jo sui morz
Se jo par li n'aie conforz.[1]

The verse "E par buche ne me conforte" not only refers to words of greeting and comfort brought by the beloved in person (from her mouth), but is rather a more or less veiled allusion to the kind of salutary or beatitude-conferring kiss that we found in the Provençal poets and, for that matter, in the religious tradition. This interpretation seems all the more plausible in view of the past history of the lovers and the intricate, somewhat precious playing on the word and concept of *salut*.[9] Moreover, it is further substantiated by the ending of Thomas's own poem, in Iseult's lament over the dead Tristan. In this early version of the legend, Iseult has arrived too late to succour her lover. As she stands before the corpse of Tristan, her thoughts are that he has died for love of her, and that if she had reached him in time she might have healed him with memories of their love and with fresh kisses and embraces. Failing this they might at least have died together.[10]

One of the most impressive and richly significant parts of the Tristan legend is that which deals with the death of the lovers. In truth it is of a piece with the whole, for the presentiment of death accompanies the couple from the inception of their love. From the time of the drinking of the love potion and the first passionate kiss, they

[1] "Give her *greetings* from me, [tell her] that nothing without her has any part in me. I send her so much *health* from my heart that none remains with me. My heart *greets* her with *greetings* [health], without her no well-being will be restored to me; I send her all my *health* [greetings]. Comfort will never be restored to me, nor *health* of life nor well-being, unless they are brought by her. If she does not bring me *health* [greetings] and comfort me with her mouth, my well-being then remains with her, and I shall die of my great hurt; finally tell her that I am dead unless I have comfort from her." Thomas, *Les Fragments du Roman de Tristan,* ed. Bartina H. Wind (Geneva and Paris, 1960), pp. 133–134.

sense that they have drunk both love and death. We cannot forget that the story of this passion is played against the background of a moral and social order which could only condemn and thwart it. Thus for all the stolen moments of joy the lovers have had, the union of the couple could not have its true fulfillment save in death. Here too—indeed, especially here—the kiss has a major role. In the presence of her dead lover, Iseult's grief is beyond endurance; literally unable to live without Tristan, she lies beside him, and while embracing him, presses her lips to his to join herself with her lover and to die upon that kiss:

> Embrace le, si s'estent,
> Baise la buche e la face
> E molt estreit a li l'embrace,
> Cors a cors, buche a buche estent,
> Sun espirit a itant rent,
> E murt dejuste lui issi
> Pur la dolur de sun ami.[j]

Pyramus and Thisbe

We will soon have occasion to touch on the fuller erotic signifi-cance of this death, but for the moment we may say that there is no doubt that the extraordinary popularity of the Tristan legend lies in the fact that it is the perfect tale, indeed, an *exemplum* of a love unto death. In this respect it is significant that the only other legend of pro-fane love to vie in popularity with the Lancelot-Guinevere and the Tristan-Iseult stories was the sorrowful tale of Pyramus and Thisbe

---

[j] "She embraces him, indeed she lies down, kisses his mouth and face and holds him most tightly in her embrace; body to body, mouth to mouth she puts. She surrenders her spirit there and dies beside him out of grief for her lover." *Les Fragments*, p. 162. P. Dronke remembers these verses in connection with a death scene from a secular Latin poem by Marbod in the second half of the eleventh century: "Ad sonitum cithare solitus sum me recreare." And Dronke writes: "A knight, mortally wounded by a spear, is found dead by his beloved, who dies upon his body in a grief which is almost a climax of sexual passion in the same moment as it seems to mock that passion's living fulfilment. It would be tempting to try to catch an echo here of Tristan's death, to see the lines as evoking the same passionate death as Thomas of Britain's lines. But this is mere speculation: There was assuredly more than one tragic romance of such a kind current in France before 1100." *Medieval Latin and the Rise of European Love-Lyric*, I (Ox-ford, 1965), 214–216. As we shall soon see, the model that Thomas may have used for his death-scene was a medieval version of Pyramus and Thisbe or of the Narcissus myth.

which derived from Ovid's *Metamorphoses*. From the twelfth century through the Renaissance period this was the most popular of the legends of love bequeathed by antiquity.[11] Here, to be sure, the relationship is not adulterous, and the lovers are adolescents who have just awakened to love. But again, theirs is a love that is frustrated by the barriers erected by an unsympathetic, class-minded society. More important yet is the fact that it is a love which, like that of Tristan and Iseult, brings the lovers to a common death. Following the story in the anonymous twelfth century French retelling—*Piramus et Thisbé*—we find that the young couple has arranged for a nocturnal tryst; but when Pyramus discovers Thisbe's bloodied veil, he is led to think that his beloved has been slain by a wild beast, whereupon he kills himself with his sword. Thisbe, when she comes upon the dead Pyramus, strikes herself with the same sword and falls upon his body. Like Iseult, Thisbe expires while embracing and kissing her lover. The similarity between the two is such as to suggest that the author of *Tristan* had the French *Piramus et Thisbé* in mind when he wrote the ending of his own poem:

> Le cors acole et si l'embrace,
> Baise les iex, baise la face,
> Baise la bouche par grant cure,
> Tant com sens et vie li dure.
> Tant con li dure sens et vie
> Se demoustre veraie amie.[k]
>
> (925–930)

As with the Tristan legend, the fascination exercised by this tale in the Middle Ages derived from its sympathetic rendering of the theme of a love that leads lovers who are psychically one to one death. When Thisbe is about to imitate the suicide of Pyramus, she calls on Love to give her the strength to strike the blow that will comfort her lover's soul with the thought that they have died one same death. She is herself comforted by the idea that though they have been kept apart in life, they will be united in death:

---

[k] "She lies by his body and so embraces it; she kisses the eyes, she kisses the face, she kisses the mouth with great care, as long as her sense and life last. As long as life and sense last she shows herself his true lover." *Piramus et Thisbé*, introduzione, testo critico, traduzione e note, ed. F. Branciforti (Florence, 1959), p. 208.

Amours, faites ma main si fort
Qu'a un seul cop reçoive mort;
S'en avra s'ame grant confort,
S'andui morromes d'une mort.
    Amis,
Duel et amour vos ont ocis;
Quant assambler ne poons vis,
Mort nos ioindra, ce m'est avis.[1]
        (880–887)

Thisbe's plea to Love for the *strength* that will enable her to die and so be united with her beloved in death brings to mind once again the theme of the Song (8:6)—love is as strong as death. From this it can be seen that in the Middle Ages the Pyramus and Thisbe legend was an *exemplum* not only of a love unto death but of a love *usque ad mortem et ultra.* The same is to be said of the Tristan legend, especially as it developed in the prose romances—in French first, then quickly in Italian—of the thirteenth and fourteenth centuries. In particular, the representation of the death of Tristan and Iseult underwent an important modification that we must now consider.

The Kiss and the Love-Death

In the prose romances dealing with the Tristan legend, the most significant feature of the death scene is the even greater insistence on the two-in-one motif and the ultimate togetherness of the couple. Now Iseult is present at her lover's side while he is still alive though near death; around the death bed are also King Mark and other knights. Feeling his end approaching, Tristan invites Iseult to die with him, for it is inconceivable to him that the one should live without the other, so

---

[1] "Love, make my hand so strong that at a single blow I shall have death; his soul shall have great comfort from it, so we shall both die one death. My lover, grief and love have killed you; since we cannot be united in life, death will join us, this is what I think." *Piramus et Thisbé*, p. 206. The theme of the psychic oneness of the two lovers is conspicuous in a late twelfth century Latin rifacimento of Ovid's tale.

> Sunt duo, nec duo sunt, quia mens est una duorum,
> Una fides, unus spiritus, unus amor. (5–6)
> · · · · · · · · · · · ·
> Sunt duo, sunt unum, sic sunt duo corpore, mente
> Unum sicque duos unicus unit amor. (9–10)

Quoted in *Piramus et Thisbé*, p. 19.

intimately bound are they to one another, like body and soul. Indeed they have been one flesh, one heart, and one soul: "Ce serait honte sé Tristans moroit sans Iseult qui avons esté une char, un cuer et une ame. Et puisqu'il est ainsi, ma douce dame, que morir volés avoec moi, il est mestier que nous muirions amdui ensemble."[m] Here we seem to have a transference of the wish to die with the beloved from Iseult to Tristan. In one of the fragments from Thomas's poem, it is the queen who declares the necessity of dying together at a moment when she feels this "law" is threatened. In that version, of course, Iseult is hastening to Tristan by sea; imperiled by a storm, she fears she is to perish far from her lover. If she could not have healed him, they would have at least died together from one same anguish: "U nus dous murrir d'une anguisse." That the wish is for an identical and simultaneous death is made clear by Iseult's thought that if she is to die by drowning, then Tristan should by the law of their compelling love somehow come to seek her and drown with her at sea.[12]

In the prose version, we have said, it is the dying Tristan who expresses this sentiment and enjoins it upon the queen. The grieving Iseult desires nothing better, but she does not know how to effect it. Here again, that what is understood is *one and the same death* is made manifest by the fact that the queen has in any case already determined to follow Tristan in death by killing herself when he has died. But now it is as though the writer of the prose romance could not be satisfied with having Iseult die from grief *after* Tristan has first expired. The lovers must not merely follow one another in death, they must truly die together. The voluptuous thought that the author entertains is that they might embrace and die a death of luxury.[13] With death now engulfing him, Tristan tells the queen to lie beside him so that he can die in her arms. When Iseult has laid herself upon him and the two are locked in an embrace and a mouth-to-mouth kiss, Tristan squeezes her with all his remaining strength, as in a spasm, so that she dies at the very moment that he himself expires:

Quant Tristans vit apertement qu'il estoit à la mort venus, il regarde entour soi et dist: Seigneur, je muire, je ne puis plus vivre; à Dieu soyés tout commandé. Quant il ot dite ceste parole, il dist à la royne Iseult:

[m] "It would be shameful if Tristan were to die without Iseult when we have been one flesh, one heart and one soul. And since it is true, my dear lady, that you wish to die with me, it is right that we both should die together." In Paulin Paris, *Les Manuscrits françois de la bibliothèque du roi* (Paris, 1836), pp. 206–207.

Amie, or m'accolés, si que je fine entre vos bras. Si, finerai adonc à aise, ce m'est avis. Iseult s'accline sur Tristan, quant ele entent ceste parole; ele s'abaisse seur son pis. Tristan la prent entre ses bras, et quant il la tint seur son pis, il dist si haut que tuit cil de léans l'entendirent: Des ore ne me chaut quant je muire, puis que je ai ma dame avoec moy. Lors estraint la royne de tant de force que il li fist le cuer partir, et il méesmes morut en tel point. Si que bras à bras et bouche à bouche moururent li dui amant, et demourèrent en tele manière embraciés. Mort sont amdui par amour, sans autre comfort.[n]

There is a coherence in this death of Tristan and Iseult. We have already suggested that the social and moral order that the lovers move in could never permit the true fulfillment of their union. It is a most important feature of the legend that despite the awareness the lovers have that they are psychically one, their love is not so disembodied as to permit them to withstand separation or sexual abstinence. On the contrary, whenever they are forcibly kept apart, Tristan and Iseult suffer the cruelest torments. The "mystic" quality of their love involves a complete participation of the flesh as well as a conformity of wills. This mystico-sexual reality informs their real death. In their supreme embrace and kiss the lovers surrender themselves to death, but also, it would seem, to one another in an inviolable union. And because it is love that moves them to die together, the fear of death gives way to the voluptuousness of death; the dying from one same anguish is also a dying in a swell of ecstasy. Here then is the true consummation of love and death, of a love that leads lovers to one death. The passage is truly extraordinary. It is, I think, the first great representation in the vernacular of the equating of death with the sexual act and vice versa.[14] In the Middle Ages this love-death has its parallel only in the religious eroticism of the time; and though, as we shall see in subsequent chapters, Renaissance authors were to pun endlessly on death in this sexual sense, the grandeur and the poignancy of the scene

[n] "When Tristan saw clearly that he was come to death, he looked about him and said: 'I die, my lord, I can live no more; may you be commended to God.' Having spoken these words he said to the Queen Iseult, 'My love, take me now that I may end in your arms. Thus I shall end comfortably, as I think.' Iseult leaned over Tristan when she heard these words; she lowered herself onto his chest. Tristan took her in his arms and when he held her on his chest he said so loudly that everyone there within heard him: 'From now on I do not care when I die because I have my lady with me.' Then he pressed the queen with such force that he made her heart break and he himself died at that moment. Thus embraced and mouth to mouth died the two lovers and stayed embraced in that way. Both died for love with no other solace." P. Paris, *Les Manuscrits*, p. 208.

from the prose *Tristan* were not to be matched in the literature of profane love until the elegiac sensuality of Torquato Tasso's muse created the great love-in-death episodes of the *Gerusalemme liberata*— that is, at the time of the Counter Reformation, another age in which love, precisely because it walked in the shadow of death, seemed the more voluptuous.

Canto V of the Inferno

When all is said and done, medieval literature bequeathed no kiss more justly famous than the one we read of in the fifth canto of Dante's *Inferno*, during the account that Francesca gives of the love that has led her and her lover Paolo to eternal punishment in the circle of carnal sinners. Its greatest relevance to our study is in the fact that that kiss effected and sealed a union of lovers which is to last forever; but it cannot be amiss to examine also, however briefly, that part of Francesca's account which leads up to her reference to the kiss, for the latter comes as the culminating point of her tale. In telling her story, Francesca speaks of love as an ineluctable passion that has bound her and Paolo together in such a way that even now in the afterlife they continue to be united:

> Amor, ch'al cor gentil ratto s'apprende,
> Prese costui della bella persona
> Che mi fu tolta; e 'l modo ancor m'offende.
> Amor, ch'a nullo amato amar perdona,
> Mi prese del costui piacer sì forte,
> Che, come vedi, ancor non m'abbandona.
> Amor condusse noi ad una morte.°
> (100–106)

Since these lovers are in the Inferno, we know that what Francesca is talking about must be bad love. And yet not everything she says about love is to be judged as bad. There is really nothing wrong, for example, with the characteristics of love as they are stated by her in the somewhat parenthetical phrases following the word "Amor" the

---

° "Love, that quickly finds access to the gentle heart, gripped this man [Paolo] with the beautiful form that was wrenched from me; and the way torments me yet. Love, that absolves no loved one from loving in return, gripped me so strongly with his grace [or: with his delight in me], that, as you see, it still has not forsaken me. Love led us to one same death."

first two times she names it. It is not the idea that love kindles quickly in the gentle or noble heart that can stand condemned; that is really a restatement of the poet Guinicelli's idea of the connaturality of love and the *cor gentile*. And that love constrains one who is loved to love in return is a thought as Christian as it is courtly.[15] It is as though Francesca had seized upon some perfectly legitimate principles of love and, by associating them with her story, was seeking to justify her own sinful passion. Those principles guide one safely, however, only when the love is spiritual. What is wrong with the love of Francesca and Paolo is the direction it takes, and this is abundantly indicated in the words following the interpolated observations we have referred to. If we leave those observations out for a moment, we see what it is that really counts: "Amor . . . prese costui della bella persona che mi fu tolta," and "Amor . . . mi prese del costui piacer sì forte, che . . . ancor non m'abbandona." Their love was grounded in the flesh, and it was also, as we know, adulterous. The lovers, after all, are among those who allowed reason to be overthrown by concupiscence ("che la ragion sommettono al talento").

Commentators usually speak of this part of Francesca's tale in connection with the ideals of courtly love that apparently inform the language of Dante's heroine. It seems, however, that we can do better —at least for our purpose—by referring to something much more concrete: the legends of Pyramus and Thisbe and of Tristan and Iseult. These two couples must surely come to mind, for, as with them, the case of Paolo and Francesca is not merely another medieval representation of the victory of Amor over Raison, but also, and above all, an *exemplum* of a love that leads to death. Francesca's line, "Amor condusse noi ad una morte," is the common epitaph of all three couples and, of course, for all other such pairs (for example, Pyramus and Thisbe in the guise of Shakespeare's Romeo and Juliet). Of this Dante was well aware. For all the importance we will shortly be attributing to that other illustrious pair—Lancelot and Guinevere—Francesca and Paolo have their truest ties with Iseult and Tristan and, to some extent, with Thisbe and Pyramus. In contradistinction to the tale of Lancelot and Guinevere, both the Pyramus-Thisbe story and the Tristan-Iseult legend develop the motif of the lovers' one same death and their burial in one tomb as a sign of union in and beyond death.[16] Dante, however, takes the theme to its logical Christian conclusion by showing what the ultimate consequences of such a love really are beyond the tomb.

141

In this way, his handling of the Paolo-Francesca episode proves unique, relative to the tradition it builds on, by being an *exemplum* of a love *usque ad mortem et ultra* in a literal and eschatological sense.[17]

In her words to Dante, Francesca insists upon the fact that she and Paolo are still united by love. There is—for the reader—a kind of irony here, and it lies in the fact that there is so much truth in what she says. That love could join two lovers in an inseparable union was just what the power of love was commonly known to be. Dante himself had written in the *Convivio* to that effect: "Amore, secondo la concordevole sentenza de li savi di lui ragionanti, e secondo quello che per esperienza continuamente vedemo, è che congiunge e unisce l'amante con la persona amata."[p] And, as we earlier saw, one of those "savi," St. Augustine, had said that this unitive function is true of carnal as well as of spiritual love. In truth, when we read Francesca's verse, "Amor condusse noi ad una morte," we cannot avoid the accent there upon the word *una*, hence upon the idea of the oneness of the lovers themselves as well as of their fate in meeting death at the same time, in the same manner, and for the same reason. In this way the line really intensifies and seals the thought immediately preceding it in which Francesca said that their (or her) love was so strong (*Amor ... sì forte*, etc.) that even now in death and in the afterlife she and Paolo are united. Readers of Dante's time would very likely have recognized a biblical echo in her words and in her situation, the same indeed that we found in a passage from the Tristan legend. In some sense they would have accepted as true and applied to the case of these lovers the thought—perhaps the most striking in the entire corpus of amatory literature—that love is as strong as death: "quia fortis est ut mors dilectio" (Song of Songs 8:6). But Francesca and Paolo being in the Inferno, where they are eternally damned and relentlessly punished by a *mal perverso*, the thought must have evoked a sense of awful irony and of divine justice at work. And is it not perhaps another bit of irony that it is Virgil who enumerates the damned carnal lovers (among them Dido, his own great heroine of passion) and who answers Dante's request to be allowed to speak to the pair hurtling through the air together (they are Paolo and Francesca) with the words "e tu allor li prega/Per quell'amor che i mena; e quei verranno" (77–

---

[p] "Love, according to the unanimous opinion of the sages who have discoursed on it, and according to that which we constantly see in our experience, is that which joins and unites the lover with the person loved."

78).[q] The most famous line concerning love to be handed down from classical antiquity is Virgil's "Omnia vincit amor; et nos cedamus amori"—Love conquers all things; and so surrender we to love. Both the Solomonic and the Virgilian phrases were echoed over and over in medieval literature. Here they meet.

It is true that in a way—though an ironic way—Francesca and Paolo have in the afterlife what they wanted on earth, that is, union. But that is no part of a reward. The love that led them to one same death together also led them together to Hell. St. Augustine, to quote again from one of Dante's favorite *savi* on love, offered the following thought: "Sed vis nosse quale amor sit, vide quo ducat" (In *Psalmum* 121, 1).[r] Although it is true that in the word *amor* spiritual and carnal love have one name, in Christian thinking the primary aspect of love is that which is holy; the other is a corruption of a good. Like Augustine long before him, William of Saint-Thierry expressed this idea clearly enough: "O Amor, a quo omnis amor cognominatur, etiam carnalis ac degener"—Oh Love, from whom all love takes its name, even carnal and ignoble love.[18] And in Purgatory (*Purgatorio*, XVIII, 66) Dante was to be reminded by Virgil that man was responsible for choosing between "buoni e rei amori"—between good and wicked loves. The antithesis *caritas-cupiditas* was not to be circumvented. Francesca and Paolo had been united in a bad love, and that they now continue to *cleave* to one another is a part of their torment, a constant and eternal reminder to one another of their guilt. A correspondence is thereby established between the sin and the punishment, a procedure apparent throughout most of the *Inferno*.

Whatever pity Dante the wayfarer may have felt for the lovers, no more mitigation of punishment is to be read into the togetherness of Paolo and Francesca than can be read into the fact that Ulysses and Diomedes are in one flame. Both pairs are punished in Hell for sins committed together in the earthly life.[19] To interpret, as some still do, the union of the lovers as an alleviation of their punishment or as a special concession is to convert the terrible and hopeless finality of Francesca's words ("Amor condusse noi ad una morte") into a triumphant cry of victory over death: "Where then, Death, is thy sting?" (I Cor. 15:55). But to do so is a manifest absurdity, for the sting

[q] ". . . and do you beg them then, by the love that drives them; and they will come."

[r] "But if you wish to know what is the nature of love, look at where it leads."

of death is not removed for those who, like the "martyrs" of profane love, are among the damned. That is simply axiomatic in the *Inferno*, where the unrepentant are living out through eternity their "second death." Paolo and Francesca have not found a *new life* in death; on the contrary, their old life of disordered love is projected into eternity. It is no Elysium for lovers they find themselves in, such as was fancied by Tibullus (I, 3) in the classical age and later on by poets of the Renaissance; rather they are in something like (but much worse than) those "fields of mourning" where Aeneas in his underworld journey beheld the shades of Dido (who had slain herself because of her desperate love for him) and other lovers who had met an untimely or violent end. (*Aeneid*, VI, 440–471.) There too the sufferings of the lovers have not been removed by death: "curae non ipsa in morte relinquunt." And in Dante's poem, Paolo and Francesca belong to Dido's troop—"la schiera ov'è Dido."

Insofar as the pre-Dantean legends of love unto death were intended to have didactic and exemplary value, what they could point to was the pain and untimely death that unchecked passion might lead to. But it was all too easy for readers (and authors) to come away from the story of such ill-fated couples with feelings of pity, considerable indulgence, and even a secret admiration. Moreover, it was not uncommon in the Middle Ages for the same *exemplum* to serve proponents of diametrically opposed points of view. A sentimental reader might take the love-unto-death legends as illustrations of the triumph of love over death rather than vice versa. At any rate, there can be no question of where lay the real sympathy and inspiration of the fashioners of the great legends of profane love.[20] But as a Christian poet—a poet of rectitude!—Dante really had no choice in the stand he was to take concerning the tale of the lovers from Rimini. It is as though Dante were following the words St. Augustine addressed to his pupil, the would-be poet Licentius, when he laid down the procedure to be followed in dealing with just such a story as Dante treated. In the *De ordine*, once he is satisfied that Licentius' zeal for poetry has been tempered to the point that the young man declares a preference for philosophy over poetry, Augustine tells him that poetry can be efficacious in inculcating moral truths. The poem that the master encourages his pupil to return to has as its subject nothing less than the pathetic love story of Pyramus and Thisbe. But in telling the story of the double suicide, Augustine warns his pupil, you will find in the very painful emotion that your poem must communicate a fitting occasion to reveal the execrable nature of that infamous passion and the poison that produced such miserable effects. Then give yourself wholly to the praise of pure and true love by which souls enriched with learning and made beautiful with virtue may unite with the intelligence by means of philosophy, and not only escape from death, but also enjoy the happiest life.[21] There was good reason for the saint to want to offset any possible reading of the Pyramus and Thisbe story as a story of the triumph of love. Augustine, we recall, once wept over the fate of Dido (*Conf.*, I, xiii), and the thought occurs to us that Dante the wayfarer weeping over the fate of Paolo and Francesca was like that Augustine, but as the author of the *Divine Comedy* he was this other Augustine's kind of poet.[22]

Without detracting from the guilt of the lovers, we may consider Francesca and Paolo to be victims of the tradition and the literature of courtly-chivalric love. The last part of Francesca's account of the ill-fated love relates that it was the reading of the love story of Lancelot and Guinevere that undid her and Paolo. The matter of great interest to us here is that it was but one point in the book—the description of the kiss—that led them to take the irrevocable step that effected their illicit union:

> Poi mi rivolsi a loro e parla' io,
> E cominciai: "Francesca, i tuoi martiri
> A lacrimar mi fanno tristo e pio.
> Ma dimmi: al tempo de' dolci sospiri,
> A che e come concedette amore
> Che conosceste i dubbiosi disiri?"
> E quella a me: "Nessun maggior dolore
> Che ricordarsi del tempo felice
> Nella miseria; e ciò sa 'l tuo dottore.
> Ma s'a conoscer la prima radice
> Del nostro amor tu hai cotanto affetto,
> Dirò come colui che piange e dice.
> Noi leggiavamo un giorno per diletto
> Di Lancialotto come amor lo strinse:
> Soli eravamo e sanza alcun sospetto.
> Per più fiate li occhi ci sospinse
> Quella lettura, e scolorocci il viso;

Ma solo un punto fu quel che ci vinse.
Quando leggemmo il disiato riso
Esser baciato da cotanto amante,
Questi, che mai da me non fia diviso,
La bocca mi baciò tutto tremante.
Galeotto fu il libro e chi lo scrisse;
Quel giorno più non leggemmo avante."[s]

(115–138)

It would be wrong to think that the reading episode was what caused the couple to fall in love. The seed of passion was planted and was germinating in the hearts of the lovers before they read the Lancelot romance. Francesca, it is true, gives this part of their story as the "prima radice" of their love, but what she in fact refers to is the precise moment in which she and her lover, having become aware of the full extent of their desire for one another, betokened the recognition of their love with what proved to be a fatal kiss. Francesca, it is to be noted, uses the expression *prima radice* in replying to Dante's request that she explain *how*, "in the time of the sweet sighs" (the phrase, along with the expression *dubbiosi disiri* and Francesca's "ricordarsi del tempo felice" all suggest a period of time in which their love was in progress), she and Paolo came to know their feelings were mutual. The question was not *why* they fell in love. That was already explained by Francesca in the first part of her story. The reading of the romance helped to crystallize their feelings as it gradually brought them to realize and to reveal the reciprocity of their passion by glances and turning pale. They might yet have resisted had it not been for the kiss passage: "Ma solo un punto fu quel che ci vinse." It is here that the love story Francesca and Paolo were reading has its echo in their own

---

[s] "Then I turned to them again and spoke. I began: 'Francesca, your sufferings make me sad and full of pity and cause me to shed tears. But tell me: at the time of sweet sighs, how and by what circumstance did love bring you to awareness of your unconfessed desires?' And she [replied] to me: 'There is no greater sorrow than to remember happiness in a time of wretchedness; and this your teacher knows. But if you have such a great desire to know the first root of our love, I shall tell of it as one who speaks while weeping. One day for pleasure we were reading of Lancelot, and how love bound him; we were alone and unsuspecting [innocent]. Several times that reading made our eyes meet and drained the color from our faces; but it was one point alone that undid us. When we read of the [queen's] longed-for smile [mouth] being kissed by so great a lover, this man here, who may never be parted from me, all trembling, kissed me on the mouth. A Galehaut was that book and he who wrote it; we read no further in it that day.' "

146

love story: the kiss in the fiction serves as a model for their own kiss. In the French romance, Galehaut (Galeotto) was the intermediary who eloquently pleaded Lancelot's case and incited Queen Guinevere to yield a kiss to the knight. For Paolo and Francesca, who had no such intermediary, the book had the same function of inciting to an unlawful sexual passion; but it was the passage on the kiss that had the specific effect of breaking down all remaining reserve in the lovers, whose surrender to love is marked by their own first kiss. Here is the important link with the Lancelot-Guinevere kiss—the breaking down of reserve by a Galehaut: "Galeotto fu il libro e chi lo scrisse." Needless to say, the accusation leveled by Francesca at the book is also a damning judgment by Dante on the kind of love inspired by it.[23]

The kiss of Francesca and Paolo is the *prima radice* of their love in the sense that it was the beginning of their active life in love together. It corresponds to what Galehaut in the prose *Lancelot* said Guinevere's first kiss should be: the "commencement d'amor veraie." But it is significant that though the kiss marked the "beginning" (in an active sense) of the pair's illicit love, it is the last thing we hear of from Francesca. And we note that it is just here in connection with it that she reintroduces the motif of her inseparable union with Paolo: "Questi, che mai da me non fia diviso,/La bocca mi baciò." We are brought back to the first part of Francesca's story, which came to a conclusion with the statements "ancor non m'abbandona" and "Amor condusse noi ad una morte." By leaving the rest of the love story untold, Dante allows the kiss to acquire extraordinary relief and symbolical—better, exemplary—significance. The reader is almost under the impression that the lovers were joined in their fatal union of love and death by that kiss. And in a way this is true. But the effect indeed is so strong that it has been possible for some readers to hold that the lovers did in fact come to their end (murdered together by Francesca's husband) at the moment of the kiss, an opinion shared by the illustrious Dante scholar Bruno Nardi.[24] This, I think, is an unlikely supposition. We need not stop to debate the question save to recall the warnings of medieval moralists that when a woman allows herself to be kissed, the matter of the *sorplus* can be taken for granted (see above p. 103). What is true, however, is that for Francesca and Paolo the kiss is sentimentally and psychologically connected with both the *prima radice* of their love and the *una morte* to which it ultimately led them. As Francesca refers to the kiss in a narration that telescopes the events of her story into its essentials, that kiss is associated in her mind, as in a cause-and-effect relationship, with the death of herself and her lover and with their present but also their eternal union in Hell.

This way of understanding the episode is apparently the underlying inspiration for what is certainly the most remarkable artistic representation ever designed to illustrate the *Inferno V* episode. In William Blake's engraving, as Dante lies prostrate following his swoon from pity, Paolo and Francesca are sucked up by a whirlwind-like flame that will carry them again into the never-ending blast that hurls the numberless carnal sinners (some of them paired and even kissing) through the air in a vortical movement. With marvelous insight Blake has included a self-contained vision of the couple's fatal kiss within a disk of refulgent light in the background above Virgil's head. The lines that radiate outward from the edge of the disk continue into and merge with the infernal scene. (See Figure 14.)

Here then we may surmise that even in the kiss motif, it is not only the kiss of Lancelot and Guinevere that was in Dante's mind when he wrote his unforgettable episode, but also the kisses exchanged between Tristan and Iseult—their first kiss of love and their kiss at parting, at which time the principle of their union in-one-flesh-and-one-spirit was solemnly declared. This matter is sufficiently important to our discussion to merit further analysis.

Inferno V *and the Tristan Legend*

The connection between Dante's Paolo and Francesca episode and the Tristan legend is made by the poet himself. Before Dante singled out the lovers from Rimini as the shades with whom he would speak, Virgil had enumerated a large quantity of the tormented spirits who were being punished for their passionate love. But of these only seven are specifically identified for the reader. Significantly, the last name that we hear before the encounter with Francesca and Paolo is that of Tristan. While it is true that Iseult is not named by the poet, it is doubtful that any reader of Dante's time—as of our own time—could read the name Tristan without mentally coupling it with that of Iseult:

"Vedi Parìs, Tristano;" e più di mille
Ombre mostrommi, e nominommi, a dito
Ch'amor di nostra vita dipartille.[t]

(67–69)

Thus the reader comes to the story of Francesca and Paolo with Tristan (and Iseult) fresh in mind and also with the idea that the spirits Dante beholds are all of persons who died (violently) for or because of love ("ch'amor di nostra vita dipartille"). This latter thought, in fact, is accentuated by a reference to Virgil's heroine, Dido, in what comes close to being an exception to my idea that Tristan is the last specified shade we hear of before Francesca and Paolo appear. However, Dido was first identified by means of a periphrasis as the second of the seven shades singled out by Virgil: "colei che s'ancise amorosa, e ruppe fede al cener di Sicheo" (61–62).[u] Now her name itself figures in a periphrasis when Dante says that Paolo and Francesca separate themselves from the flock where Dido is—*della schiera ov'è Dido* (85)—so as to approach him. But Dido is not meant to be individuated here; rather, in her character of one who died because of a desperate and irrational passion, her name is used to define the species to which Dante's couple belongs.

On the other hand, Paolo and Francesca seem to be unique in this already select group in that they are together as a couple in Hell, evidently because on earth they were united by love both in life and in death. Now there is nothing in the canto that authorizes us to think that other carnal lovers are paired in the afterlife, although it cannot be absolutely stated that it is not so. Dante seems to have been attracted by the couple because they were together and thereby distinguished from the other shades, for, as the story is told, he did not yet know their identity. But the point here is that before Dante presented his "modern" couple to the world, Tristan and Iseult and Pyramus and Thisbe offered the best-known cases of a love that led a couple to a single death. Precisely because Dante knew this, it is of the utmost significance that he does not name Iseult and makes no mention of Ovid's unlucky adolescent lovers in the canto. The absence from Hell

---

[t] " 'See Paris, Tristan;' and he showed me more than a thousand shades, pointing as he named them whom love had torn from our life."

[u] "She who had killed herself for love, and broke faith with the ashes of Sycheus."

(in the sense that they are not specified, for they may well be there) of the latter couple is the more suggestive when we note that Dante twice in other parts of his poem alludes to them and their death.[25] That he avoided reference to them in *Inferno V* as a matter of taste and delicate reserve in view of their tender age is, I think, quite possible, though not the sole reason. But what of Iseult? That Dante placed Tristan's name last in the series of shades named, breaking off the enumeration just there, is due to more than considerations of chronology and meter. Had he placed it anywhere else, he almost would have had to name Iseult. It is as though the poet deliberately withheld her name so as to avoid the necessity of openly declaring either her separateness from or her togetherness with Tristan in Hell. Certainly he could not have sundered them in the minds of his readers.

But for Tristan and Iseult to have been conspicuously present as a pair would have made it difficult if not impossible for Dante to bypass that most illustrious of medieval couples for his lesser-known (at that time) lovers from Rimini. The same would hold true if Pyramus and Thisbe were specified. And, of course, the poet would also have lost his unique opportunity to make his trenchant two-pronged attack on romantic love and romantic literature. If, in the circle of passionate lovers, Dante had not had the unhappy pair from Rimini at hand, he would, I think, have found that Tristan and Iseult were indeed there as *one*, and he would then have chosen to speak and listen to them. As it is, he has given us something of a modernized retelling of their story. It may be observed that Paolo and Francesca are the only "modern" characters Dante notes in the circle of carnal lovers. As for Tristan, the poet very likely thought of him as belonging to a past so remote that he could be considered to be among the ancient ladies and knights that Virgil has pointed out to Dante:

> Poscia ch'io ebbi il mio dottore udito
> Nomar le donne antiche e' cavalieri.[v]

It is then that Dante asks to speak with the couple who turn out to be the lovers from Rimini. Simply to have retold the story of Tristan and Iseult or of Pyramus and Thisbe would have been little to Dante's liking and contrary to his genius. Dante frequently was consciously vying with poets and legends that preceded him, but in doing so, he was also building on them.

[v] "After I had heard my teacher tell the names of the ladies and knights of old."

150

Even the situation in which the fall of Paolo and Francesca takes place has its closest parallel with the circumstances attending the surrender to love of Tristan and Iseult. In 1920 Pio Rajna noted the similarity, pointing out that in both cases the couples are alone and in close contact.[26] Tristan and Iseult aboard ship play at chess; Francesca and Paolo read a book. The reading of the book also corresponds to the famous love-potion, the one and the other causing a precipitation of love passion if not the origin of the passion itself. Dante's "soli eravamo e sanza sospetto"—(we were alone and unsuspecting) echoes the prose romance, which says of the lovers: "Il n'i a nul destourbement, car il sont ensemble seul a seul qu'il n'ont garde de sorvenue,"[w] although this last detail follows the mutual confession of love the lovers make. Still another echo is heard in Francesca's statement that "per più fiate gli occhi ci sospinse/Quella lettura e scolorocci il viso,"[x] which recalls the French author's observation, "Yseus regarde Tristan et Tristans li, et tant s'entresgardent. . . ."[y] Considering this to be the extent of the parallel, Rajna somewhat abruptly and, I think, wrongly judged as fortuitous the connection between Dante's request to learn how the lovers from Rimini were made aware of their feelings and the detail of the French romance that says of the lovers (continuing the last-quoted, broken phrase): "et tant s'entresgardent en tel maniere, que li uns conoist bien la volonté de l'autre et la pensée."[z] On the contrary, this seems to me one of the strongest points of contact between the two episodes.

Rajna's position was determined by the idea that whereas Tristan and Iseult fall in love suddenly, Francesca and Paolo evidently have been harboring a passion for one another for a while before their reading. Because of this, Rajna finds the connection with the Lancelot romance to be the truly important link, for Lancelot, he observes, was in love with Guinevere from his first sight of her, and the queen was early attracted by the knight, so that, as in the case of Dante's lovers, desire came well in advance of the pledging of their love. However, Rajna perhaps interpreted too literally the role of the love-potion in

[w] "There was nothing to disturb them for they were alone together, so that they had no thought of what happened."

[x] "Several times that reading made our eyes meet and drained the color from our faces."

[y] "Iseult looks at Tristan and Tristan at her, and they look at each other for so long . . ."

[z] ". . . and they look at each other for so long and in such a way that each is perfectly aware of the other's will [desire] and thought."

the Tristan legend, claiming that love comes suddenly and inexplicably upon its being drunk, and that without it there is no justification for the passion that consumes the lovers. But even allowing this to be so, the fact is that the French author did take the trouble to show Tristan and Iseult *after* their drink becoming aware of the mutual nature of their desire for one another, an awareness that they are brought to by their looking at one another: "et tant s'entresgardent en tel maniere, que li uns conoist bien la volonté de l'autre et la pensée. Tristans aperçoit et conoist que Yseus l'aime de tout son cuer, et Yseus reconoist bien que Tristans l'aime autresint."[a] Moreover, we do not know in what version, or versions, Dante knew the Tristan legend. Gottfried's poem has many details that the Italian poet could have known of from other sources. Now Gottfried gives a circumstantial account of the thoughts and reaction of Tristan and Iseult between the time of the drinking of the love-potion and the mutual confession of their passion which leads directly to their kiss. A point of particular interest to us here is that Gottfried's account tells us that the lovers exchange furtive glances with one another and that when their eyes meet they change color, either blushing or turning pale. This, says the poet, is because Love was not content to be hidden in the lovers' hearts, but was determined to be revealed on their faces![27] The similarity to the situation of Dante's lovers is certainly striking:

> Noi leggiavamo un giorno per diletto
>
> .   .   .   .
>
> Per più fiate li occhi ci sospinse
> Quella lettura, e scolorocci il viso.[b]

Certain passages of the *Lancelot* romance cause Paolo and Francesca to raise their eyes from the book and to look at each other, a gesture which is accompanied by their turning pale—perhaps causes them to turn pale. As they read of the passion of Lancelot and Guinevere in the book, so they read of their own passion in one another's eyes and in the changed hue of their faces. In this way the lovers are made fully aware of their mutual desire. All it takes for Dante to drive home the full force of this idea is the pause at the end of the verse and the

---

[a] ". . . and they look at each other for so long and in such a way that each is perfectly aware of the other's will [desire] and thought. Tristan perceives and knows that Iseult loves him with all her heart, and Iseult recognizes that Tristan loves her in the same way."

[b] "One day for pleasure we were reading . . . Several times that reading made our eyes meet and drained the color from our faces."

line that follows in which the initial adversative, *Ma*, acquires great dramatic and explicative value: "Ma solo un punto fu quel che ci vinse."[c]

We recall that in the Tristan legend the lovers came together in a kiss as the first natural expression of their love just after they recognized that their desire was mutual. This is also what happens in the episode of Paolo and Francesca. Another important element here is that in Dante's episode it is Paolo who kisses Francesca first. Much has been written in an effort to explain why Dante departed from the *Lancelot* romance (assuming he was following it) when he chose to have the male (Paolo) offer the kiss. In fact, he has Francesca depart from the French romance even in the idea that it was Lancelot who took the initiative in the kiss. May it not be that Dante had the Tristan legend in mind here too and that he merged the figures of Lancelot and Tristan? In that legend it is Tristan who kisses first. One thing is sure; for Dante to have made Francesca take the lead in the act of the kiss would have been so out of keeping with her character as to constitute a major artistic and psychological flaw. As a heroine of romantic love, Francesca has little in common with the blithe figure of Queen Guinevere, whether we think of the latter as receiving or giving the kiss. Of course, Francesca cannot be thought of as an excessively demure maid; she receives but also responds to the kiss. It is plain from her story that she was not really caught by surprise when Paolo kissed her, and one has the impression that Paolo could easily have been repulsed, but that that was far from her mind. But in respect to these points Francesca is closer to Iseult (when the latter was first kissed by Tristan with a lover's kiss) than to Guinevere.

Among the other important points of similarity between Dante's episode and the Tristan legend we may note that Paolo and Francesca are slain by the latter's jealous husband. In the prose *Tristan*, the hero receives his fatal wound from Iseult's jealous husband. There is also an element of incest in both cases. Paolo is the brother of Francesca's husband; Tristan is the nephew of Iseult's husband. Although the Lancelot-Guinevere affair is adulterous, there is no incest involved. Finally, there is the connection between the kiss and the idea of death as its consequence. There is nothing of this in the Lancelot romance, whereas both the Tristan legend and Dante's episode establish a psychological relationship between the fall or the kiss of the lovers and

[c] "But it was one point alone that undid us."

their psychic union unto and even beyond death. How far removed Lancelot and Guinevere are from all this is quickly seen when we remember that in the Lancelot legend, Guinevere died penitent in a convent, and that Dante was of the opinion that Lancelot himself, like Guido da Montefeltro, spent his last years in seclusion, leading an austere religious life (*Convivio*, IV, 28).

At this point, in support of my idea of the exemplary and emblematic character of the kiss in *Inferno V*, medieval Christian iconography may once again stand us in good stead. In the High Middle Ages, the vice of luxury or lust was commonly represented by a couple embracing and kissing. This type is found in the *Luxuria* reliefs of the cathedrals at Chartres and Amiens, that of the latter dating from circa 1225. (See Fig. 16.) In this depiction of lust—as in certain miniatures illustrating the kiss of the Song—it is the man who is shown taking the initiative or the more active role; he is often seen with one hand holding or caressing the face or neck of the woman.[28] The kiss of Paolo and Francesca was just such a one, and, as we know, its end result was to plunge the couple into the infernal circle of the lustful. It may be that also in representing Lancelot as the active partner in the knight's kiss with Guinevere, Dante, speaking through Francesca, was, consciously or unconsciously, following and contributing to this emblematic tradition. Unlike the lovers from Rimini, however, the Arthurian couple had time to repent.[29]

Purgatory and the Kiss of Peace

It often happens in the *Divine Comedy* that an episode in the *Inferno* receives its deeper meaning and fuller symbolic value from another episode later in the poem (in *Purgatory* or *Paradise*) which has some point of resemblance to it. This is the case with the kiss passage we have just examined. In addition to the sensual and sinful kiss of Francesca and Paolo, there is in the *Divine Comedy* an example of the Christian holy kiss of peace and love. Significantly, the latter occurs in that ledge of Purgatory where the souls are cleansing themselves of the sin of lust in a purifying fire. As Dante moves along the rim of that ledge, he sees two groups of shades approaching one another from opposite directions. When these souls meet, they kiss one another and quickly continue on their way:

154

Lì veggio d'ogne parte farsi presta
Ciascun'ombra e baciarsi una con una
Senza restar, contente a brieve festa.[d]
(*Purgatorio*, XXVI, 31–33)

Now Purgatory is an area where Dante frequently insists upon the theme of concord and union, and the salutation by the holy kiss of peace or charity, we know, is a sign of the spiritual union and reconciliation of the faithful. The kiss (i.e., charity) is *concordia*. This then is an indication of the appropriateness of its presence in this part of the poem, where the greeting these souls give one another is called by Dante an "accoglienza amica." Moreover, there is something eminently fitting in the fact that this holy kiss should be given by those who, although now among the saved, had been guilty on earth of unchaste kisses. Here, we cannot help thinking, is where Francesca and Paolo would be had they managed to be repentant before their untimely death. Dante has clearly wished to establish a deliberate contrast with the kiss of lust described by Francesca in the circle of the doomed carnal lovers of the *Inferno*.

There are other elements that help us to see the contrast. One of the surest signs of Francesca's torment is her insistence on the idea of peace. She who is condemned to being hurtled eternally through the air by the infernal blast speaks of peace—*pace*—as a condition she evidently desires but can never have (*Inferno*, V, 91–99). The kiss is the Christian symbol of peace par excellence, but the kiss Francesca exchanged with Paolo brought just the opposite of peace. In *Purgatorio XXVI* Dante addresses the penitents as souls who are sure to come to the blessed state of peace: "O anime sicure / D'aver, quando che sia, di pace stato" (53–54). In the midst of their present but temporal chastisement, the periodic kiss of peace that they exchange presages the eternal peace which will one day be theirs.

There is significant symmetry here as well. The first kiss occurs (or rather is recalled) at the beginning of what may be named Hell proper, for though Limbus is in the first circle of the descent, it is clearly felt to be set off from the rest of the Inferno, even more so than are the sluggards found in the vestibule of Hell. Then at the last ledge of Purgatory in which penalty is assessed occurs the second kiss.

---

[d] "There from both directions I see each shade hurry to kiss one another, without pausing, content with brief but joyous greeting."

At the beginning and at the end of Dante's punitive and purgative system a kiss helps to illustrate the nature of the opposite poles of *cupiditas* and *caritas*, of disordered love and love being set in order. As in so many other things, so too in the matter of the kiss, Dante presents us with a summing-up, and, as it were, the definitive medieval word.

More light is thrown on the kisses of Guinevere and of Francesca when Dante meets with Beatrice in the earthly paradise. What happens there and certain verbal echoes make it clear that Beatrice is contrasted with Francesca (and Guinevere) and that Dante's love for Beatrice is contrasted with that of Paolo and Francesca. When Beatrice appears, her face is veiled. Her handmaidens—the theological virtues—beg her to unveil so that her devotee, Dante, may see not only her eyes but that second and greater beauty which is Beatrice's mouth:

> Per grazia fa noi grazia che disvele
> A lui la bocca tua, sì che discerna
> La seconda bellezza che tu cele.[e]
> *(Purgatorio*, XXXI, 136–138)

We recall that in the *Vita Nuova* Dante says that the eyes are the beginning but the mouth is the end of love (see note 9 of this chapter). In the *Convivio* Dante says that the *smile* is a sign of beatitude, and here in the earthly paradise it is Beatrice's celestial and smiling mouth, "lo santo riso" (XXXII, 5), that causes Dante to be rapt so intensely that he has to be called back to his senses and surroundings by the three handmaidens (XXXI, 139–145, and XXXII, 1–12). Certainly this spiritual splendor of Beatrice's mouth (*bocca* and *santo riso*) is to be contrasted with the seductive but uninnocent passion connected with the mouths of Guinevere (*il disiato riso*) and Francesca (*la bocca mi baciò*). Beatrice's smiling mouth is no less desired by Dante than were Guinevere's by Lancelot and Francesca's by Paolo. But whereas the latter two cases involved ecstatic but illicit kisses by trembling lovers, Dante is ecstasied by contemplation of his lady's mouth. And yet, if not in Florence when Beatrice was a mortal, here in the earthly paradise where we have the transfiguration of Beatrice's mouth, is it possible that in his rapture the poet did not intone—like the mystics, among them Saint Bernard, who was to be Dante's last "guide" in the

---

[e] "For the sake of grace grant us the favor of unveiling your mouth to him so that he may perceive the second beauty that you conceal."

celestial paradise—the first verse of the Song of Songs: "Osculetur me osculo oris sui"? Given the various possible allegorical meanings that attach to Beatrice in the *Divine Comedy* (i.e., Wisdom, Revelation, Theology, the Church), one is tempted to think that he did so—tremblingly.[30]

5. The Renaissance Neoplatonic Phase

s in the Middle Ages, so too in the Renaissance—both Christian and paganizing—the conceits we have been tracing, although frequently found together in a unit, most often appear separately. For the most part, Renaissance writers (especially the poets) thought of these conceits as being Neoplatonic in origin and significance, but they could not have been unaware of their place in the Christian tradition. The *locus classicus* for the concept of the migration and exchange of lovers' souls, or of the transformation of the lover into the beloved, along with the important theme of the death and resuscitation of lovers, as these ideas were employed in amatory literature during the Renaissance, is a section from Marsilio Ficino's Commentary on Plato's *Symposium*. Although Ficino makes no overt osculatory allusions, a close examination may yet reveal that the soul-in-the-kiss conceit was not altogether removed from his thoughts when he composed the passage in question. But even if this proves not to be so, the passage is of paramount interest to us here. Its influence was enormous, and what cannot be doubted is the fact that many subsequent writers—the poets in particular—did not shrink from coupling its amatory concepts psychological and philosophical with the theme of the kiss.

Marsilio Ficino and the Lover's Death and Revival

In exhorting his listeners to love, Ficino urges them not to be dismayed at the idea, said to be Plato's, that the lover dies unto himself and lives in another person: "Neque vos illud deterreat, quod de amante quodam Platonem dixisse ferunt. Ille, inquit, amator animus est proprio in corpore mortuus, in alieno corpore vivens."[a] The source Ficino had in mind when he attributed this thought to Plato has not,

---

[a] "Nor should you be deterred by the saying attributed to Plato concerning a certain lover. 'This lover,' he said, 'is a soul dead to his own body and living in another's.'" *Convivium Platonis sive de amore*: Oratio secunda, caput VIII; in the edition accompanied by a French translation by Raymond Marcel, *Commentaire sur le Banquet de Platon* (Paris, 1956), p. 155. All quotations from Ficino's Commentary are from this edition.

as far as I know, been correctly determined. In his critical edition of Ficino's Latin text, accompanied by a French translation, Raymond Marcel refers the reader to Plato's Phaedrus, 248c; but nothing is to be found there or anywhere else in Plato that corresponds to the passage in question. Touching briefly on the Ficinian allusion, Jean Orcibal suggests that the Italian thinker probably ascribed to Plato a thought that derives from Cato by way of Plutarch's Lives.[1] But, as recorded there, Cato states simply that the lover's soul lives in the body of another. Although this comes close, there is still no talk of the lover being dead unto himself. I find that Plutarch repeats the reference in his own wonderful *Dialogue on Love*, and in a context where he is apparently following the Platonic discussion from *Phaedrus* (252–253) on the connaturality of lovers. Unfortunately, Plutarch's passage is corrupt, there being an obvious lacuna directly after the reference to Cato's saying: "Roman Cato declared that the soul of the lover is ever present in that of the beloved . . . form, character, way of life, and every act."[2] Again the reference is suggestive. But again there is no mention of death. Moreover, in both cases the ascription to Cato is firm, and there is no hint of Plato being behind it. Ficino, on the other hand, introduces his thought as an opinion attributed to Plato by others. (In his own Italian version of his Commentary, Ficino himself was to present the idea simply as Plato's.) This becomes a significant detail if we can find the thought so ascribed to Plato, as indeed we can. And here we are brought back to the Platonic epigram on kissing Agathon:

> My soul was on my lips as I was kissing Agathon.
> Poor soul! she came hoping to cross over to him.

Ficino, of course, knew the distich, for, if in no other place, he read it in Diogenes Laertius, where it is given as the philosopher's.[3] Yet it is doubtful that there is enough in the epigram to have led Ficino to attribute to Plato the thought of the lover's death and subsequent revival in the beloved. There is, I think, a more likely source that was also known to him, one which, while it does in fact ascribe the idea to Plato, spells out the theme of the dying and resuscitation of the lover. This is an expanded Latin version of the original epigram found in Aulus Gellius, an author frequently cited in Ficino's works:

> Cum semihiulco savio
> Meo puellum savior
> Dulcemque florem spiritus

Duco ex aperto tramite,
Anima male aegra et saucia
Cucurrit ad labeas mihi,
Rictumque in oris pervium
Et labra pueri mollia,
Rimata itineri transitus,
Ut transiliret, nititur.
Tum si morae quid plusculae
Fuisset in coetu osculi,
Amoris igni percita
Transisset et me linqueret
Et mira prorsum res foret,
Ut fierem ad me mortuus,
Ad puerum ut intus viverem.[b]

The close parallel between the last two verses and Ficino's words, coupled with the fact that Aulus Gellius first gives the original Greek distich as Plato's, suggests to me that this Latin version had some part in leading Ficino to refer to Plato as the author of the idea that the lover dies unto himself but revives in the beloved. If, as I think, this is so, then it is significant that the Italian philosopher makes no mention of the kiss, and it becomes both necessary and worthwhile to ask why. In order to answer the question, however, we must first examine the rest of Ficino's passage, which has its own inherent relevance to the present study.

Had the few words we have quoted from Ficino been all he wrote on the subject of the lover's death and revival, the idea might not have attracted undue notice in readers and followers. But in fact they serve to introduce a long disquisition on the mystico-magical phenomenology of reciprocal love between true friends, and what Ficino went on to write is one of the most incandescent passages in the literature of Platonic love, perhaps one of the most remarkable pages in the annals of amatory literature.

---

[b] "When with half-open mouth I kiss my young friend and draw the sweet flower of his breath from the opened path, my soul, sick and wounded, rushes to my lips, and seeking passage for its journey through the opening of my friend's mouth and soft lips, it exerts itself to spring across. Then if there were a little longer pause in the union of our kiss, [my soul] urged by love's fire, would cross over and leave me. And it would be altogether wonderful if I became dead to myself and lived within my young friend." *The Attic Nights*, III, ed. and trans. John C. Rolfe (London and New York, 1928), 392. (Bk. XIX, xi.) These same verses are recorded with slight variation in the *Saturnalia* (II, ii) by Macrobius, who evidently got them from Aulus Gellius.

Ficino and Reciprocal Love

Love, Ficino tells his readers, may be simple or reciprocal. In simple love the beloved does not return the affection of the lover, so that the lover may be said to be dead, for, his thoughts and soul having gone out toward the beloved, he does not live in himself, and inasmuch as the unresponsive beloved does not welcome and give a place to the lover's soul, the latter has no dwelling place. Hence the lover is totally dead and without hope of revival unless he be resuscitated by indignation, by which Ficino evidently means that the unrequited lover remains dead as long as he continues to be enamored.[4] In reciprocal love, on the other hand, each partner is both lover and beloved and each lives in the other. That is, the lover's death is compensated by an immediate resuscitation of life; the lover who dies unto himself lives in the beloved and is himself sustained by the soul of the beloved that has come to him. By means of this mutual transformation, the two lovers become one and each becomes two. Such then is that "fortunate death" by which one is resuscitated and acquires a new and double life. This, says Ficino, is love's greatest miracle, for by it there takes place that exchange of lovers' souls resulting in the experience which is the primary aim of lovers—transformation into the beloved.[5]

It is apparent that here we are beyond anything that could have come from the Platonic epigram or from Aulus Gellius's amplification of it. In his glowing purple passage, the Italian philosopher is speaking of love as an ecstasy in a manner that makes us think at once of both the medieval poet and the Christian mystic. Basic to all three is the idea that love is an ecstatic force that seeks to unite lover and beloved (or two *lovers*) by causing an exodus of the deeper self that moves toward its desire. But if Ficino's speculation on the ecstatic nature of love owes something, perhaps much, to the poets, he is ultimately drawing even more, it seems to me, on the tradition of Christian spirituality and mysticism. Especially revealing in this respect is the elaboration of the theme of death and resurrection, the lover dying unto himself but finding new life in the beloved, or living with the life of the beloved. Although he certainly met with such an idea in the poets, Ficino was sure to have been familiar with it in the religious tradition, where it is even more conspicuous. The greatest aspiration

of the Christian is to die unto himself so as to live in the beloved
(Christ) or, what comes to the same thing, to be infused with the
beloved's life (or spirit). The most rapturously mystic utterance in
Christian literature is St. Paul's cry: "With Christ I am nailed to the
Cross. It is now no longer I that live but Christ that lives in me"
(Gal. 2:19–20). Endlessly commented upon by the religious writers
Ficino knew so well, that exalted cry must have been in his mind
when he was writing his own rhapsodic passage. So too, perhaps, were
the following words of an author whose works Ficino and other
Italian Neoplatonists meditated deeply, the Pseudo-Dionysius, who
considered Paul a lover precisely because of his eagerness to die so
that he could be possessed with the life of Christ:

> And the Divine Yearning brings ecstasy, not allowing them that are
> touched thereby to belong unto themselves but only to the objects of
> their affection. . . . Hence the great Paul, constrained by the Divine
> Yearning, and having received a share in its ecstatic power, says with
> inspired utterance, "I live, and yet not I but Christ liveth in me:" true
> sweetheart that he was and (as he says himself) being beside himself
> unto God, and not possessing his own life but possessing and loving
> the life of Him for Whom he yearned.[6]

Now it is possible to see a connection between this and Ficino's
passage. Indeed Ficino, who translated and wrote a close commentary
on Dionysius, noted precisely in connection with these words that
love transports the lover into the beloved: "Wherefore love is said
to cause an ecstasy in the lover, that is, a sort of excess by which he
is carried, as it were, into the beloved."[7] Equally significant is the fact
that in the Commentary on the *Symposium* itself, shortly after his
ecstatic description of reciprocal love, Ficino appealed to Dionysius'
idea that love constrains superior things to move toward lower things
and vice versa, an idea which comes just before the words we have
quoted from the "Areopagite."[8] Hence it is difficult for me to accept
without some qualification the view of Kristeller (adopted by others
on his authority) that in Ficino "the whole technical language of love
which exchanges the Souls of the lovers and transforms them into
each other are evidently taken from poetry and developed into a more
precise system."[9] For the passage we are considering—it is the most
eloquent and far-reaching statement on the question to be found in
Ficino—equally important sources are the writings of Christian
authors. For the latter, we know, love not only wounds but, because it

is as strong as death, kills outright; but in this kind of death, when one dies his life is *hidden* in the beloved. The following quotation from Gilbert of Hoy illustrates this idea by yoking together two key biblical texts:

> Fortunate is he in whom sacred love is a sickness, yet not a suffering . . . O unhealthy, indeed, truly sick heart that does not know it is stricken by this wound! "I am wounded," she says," by love (charity)." Not only does it wound but it kills also; "for love is as strong as death." Finally the Apostle [says]: "You are dead, and your life is hidden with Christ in God."[10]

And later, in the fifteenth century, Jean Gerson recorded the case of a martyr for love, a devout soul who died unto herself and found life in the beloved:

> I am made blessed through my faith—for so I may piously believe—a blessed martyr of love; who could sing no less than this: "I am sick with love, I am love's captive, I love for love's sake, I am wounded by charity, I am even dead from love, dead to myself but alive to my beloved [*vulnerata caritate ego sum, sed et amore mortua, mortua michi et amato viva*]!"[11]

Such passages as these are not meant to be taken as direct sources of Ficino, but rather as examples of the kind of imagery and language which was common to the tradition of Christian spirituality with which the Italian philosopher was familiar. Needless to say, that language was still common in the Christian writers of Ficino's time, and as we shall see, he himself was to employ it in a reasonably orthodox fashion in contexts describing the relationship between God and the soul. Meanwhile, where Ficino would appear to be closer to the poets in this matter is in the fact that the passage from his Commentary is a description of love, not between God and the soul, but between two creatures. Unlike the poets, however, he speaks of a love that is not a heterosexual relationship but rather one between two males, the one a mature man, the other a youth. It is, in fact, intellectual love, or, we may say, spiritual friendship. And now we can understand why the Italian philosopher perhaps deliberately refrained from mentioning the kiss, despite the fact that in wishing to attribute to Plato the ecstatic concept of love as effecting an exchange of souls entailing the death and resuscitation of lovers, he was drawing from a source (or so I believe) in which the kiss as the vehicle of transfer was the dominant

motif. Both the original Platonic epigram and its expanded Latin form
in Aulus Gellius refer to erotic love between a man and a youth. It
appears that in the *Phaedrus* a condescension is made by Plato even
to the noblest lovers, for he allows or tolerates their kissing and embracing.[12] But whatever the actual sexual practices of fifteenth century
Florence were, the mores were not then such as to be openly indulgent
of homosexuality. Since Ficino's own system refers to an intellectual
homosexual relationship whose spirituality must be protected at all
costs, such intimacies as the kiss (even on a metaphorical level) would
have appeared unseemly.

There is another passage later in the Commentary (VII, vi) that
gives us a clue to what I take to have been Ficino's reluctance if not
repugnance to think of the kiss and other sexual intimacies as a means
for effecting or even symbolizing the union or mutual transformation
of Platonic lovers. This occurs where the philosopher, in condemning
pederastic love, tells us that it is the opinion of some that the sexual
embrace between the mature man and a youth is an attempt to effect
the rejuvenation of the older man. Such a thought is based upon the
unhappy belief that a transformation of lovers can be realized by
seminal flow.[13] Ficino acknowledges that though such a practice is
insane, it does confirm the idea that love (even in its carnal expression)
is itself the desire for mutual indwelling. But what is possible of spirits
is not so of bodies, and in illustrating the impossibility of such a conversion of bodies, Ficino cites the "example" of Lucretius ("amantium
omnium infelicissimus"), quoting a part of the famous verses of the
De rerum natura where the Roman poet so vividly describes the rage
of lovers seeking in vain to penetrate into one another and become as
one by means of kisses and the sexual embrace. Hence Ficino had before him a notable literary example illustrating for him the madness
of the idea of the mutual incorporation of bodies.[14]

The fact is that in Ficino's philosophy of love there is simply no
room for carnal contact of any kind, and least of all for the sense of
touch. For him the senses can only keep man earthbound, whereas the
proper and ultimate object of love is the Divinity, who is reflected
among bodies as Beauty. Beauty, however, is a quality that can be
fully appreciated only by the mind assisted in its work of perceiving
and enjoying the divine quality by the sense of sight alone (sometimes
by hearing also), which has an ancillary role by virtue of its relative
incorporeality and its function as an instrument transmitting to the

mind the "splendor" of the deity as found in bodies.[15] It is only right to insist on this point that, for Ficino, the true object of desire, by which the lover is attracted, is the splendor of the Divinity manifesting itself in an earthly creature. Of equal importance, however, is the fact that the lover himself may be unaware of this metaphysics of love. For this reason, Ficino says, lovers are stricken with troubling passions in the presence of the beloved. In this context he refers to and justifies the lover's desire to be transformed into the beloved. In the final analysis, Ficino says, such a desire derives from the wish to exchange one's humanity for divinity, that is, to be transformed into God.[16]

Particularly in view of the latter thought one might wish to see a similarity between Ficino's love philosophy and the notion of Christian friendship as we found it expounded by St. Aelred. But we must hasten to add that there is in Aelred's system an element that is missing from the Ficinian exposition; and it is one that makes for a considerable difference between Christian friendship and the pretensions of Renaissance Neoplatonic lovers (or friends) in general. In Aelred's system, where friendship and union among men are a way of ascending to friendship and union with God, Christ is really always present as Mediator and Terminus. Aelred was able to pass easily, naturally we may say, from the spiritual kiss (union) between friends to the ecstatic intellectual kiss of union between creature and Christ. Of course, it must be allowed that within Ficino's own system friendship, or love between creatures, is intended to be a way of ascension to God, even as the passages we have just examined would seem to indicate, especially where it is said that what the lover desires is the Divinity, of which the particular beauty in the beloved is only a reflection. But we also remember Ficino saying that the lover himself is not aware of what it is he really loves or desires. Now if this be so, then it must be said that in Christian friendship the loving friend begins from a far more advantageous position, which makes the difference. As a Christian, he knows that what he loves in his friends is God, specifically the second person of the Trinity, and better yet, the person of Jesus Christ. Without doubt it would be folly to judge Ficino's overall concept of love and friendship solely on the basis of his Commentary on the *Symposium*.[17] Nevertheless, because it is the work in which his philosophy of love and friendship is most consistently worked out, and because it was the work that inaugurated and then permeated Neoplatonic speculation on love throughout the Renaissance, we may judge it for what it is, that is, a discussion of "Platonic love," not of Christian love or friendship. And this is true despite Ficino's implementation of Christian concepts and his desire to make Plato appear a kind of precursor of Christian truth. The most striking or shocking feature of the work, read from the vantage point of some fifteen centuries (now twenty) of Christianity, is the absence of Christ. Whatever praise one may feel disposed to give to Ficino's Platonic lover as a "Renaissance man" on his own, making his way to the citadel of Truth and Beauty, indeed, to God, it must be said that he makes his way in a groping fashion as no Christian need grope and that he finds himself in a relationship with a God who is far from being a person as the Christian God is a Person.

Quite simply then, Aelred's system of friendship is, as any Christian system of friendship must be, Christocentric. A "Platonic" system, for obvious reasons, cannot be that. Augustine once said that the Platonists would only have to change a few words to be in line with Christian truth, and Ficino quoted the bishop of Hippo on the matter in his own *Theologia Platonica*. But the overwhelming truth of the Incarnation was such that Augustine could not equate Platonism and Christianity. Thus in speaking of man's ability to acquire Wisdom, he once said that there was more than one way to reach it [*Soliloquia*, I, xiii, 23]; but he later retracted that heresy, proclaiming clearly that there was but one way and that it was Jesus Christ: "Ego sum via" [*Retractiones*, I, iv].

Ficino and Divine Love

Although Ficino's exposition of the death, resuscitation, and mutual indwelling of lovers was introduced by a reference which intimated Plato to be at its source, the most significant part of its language, we suggested, perhaps derived from the descriptions of divine love in the tradition of medieval Christian spirituality. It is therefore significant that we find in this writer, who was himself a man of the Church, just such a medieval-like soliloquoy or dialogue between the soul and God which is a more orthodox counterpart to the ecstatical page from his Commentary on Plato's *Symposium*. The value of this short theological dialogue, which occurs in a "letter" to Michele Mercati da San Miniato, is the greater for us in that at its very core we encounter nothing less than the image of insufflation by a kiss. Here the relationship between God and the soul is characterized as one between a father and daughter, and the very first thing the soul wishes for is the certainty that she may have the grace of God *breathed* into her. However, because of the infinite superiority of the Father, she despairs of being able to contain him within herself. God, however, puts the soul's fears to rest by explaining that he is both tiny and immense, that he is the fullness that penetrates all without being penetrated, but that he is in her because she is in him. Following God's reassuring explanations, the "illuminated" soul gives expression to a rapturous hymn. What is this great and tender love that so sweetly dissolves her, that spurs her? What bittersweet feeling [*Quam dulcis amaritudo*] is it that consumes her and, now that she has tasted it, causes her to consider as sweet those things that are bitter? Seized by a holy madness, the soul bursts into the following exclamations, the language and theme of which will seem familiar enough to us:

> Oh, what a living death [*viva mors*] is this! Who would think that that by which I die unto myself makes me live in God; dying unto death I live to life and rejoice in joy [*gaudeo gaudio*]. O pleasure beyond all senses, O happiness surpassing understanding, O joy that transcends the mind! Now indeed I am outside myself [my mind] and yet with mind because above mind. Now I am in a furor; yet I do not descend to low things, for by it I am raised on high. Now I am entirely consumed, and yet I am not diminished, for he who makes me live within him gathers me unto him: God the unity of all unity [*Deus unitas unitatum*]. Therefore rejoice with me you who rejoice in God. Behold, God has come unto me. The God of the universe has embraced me [*Deus universi amplexus est me*]. The God of Gods has entered into my marrow, and now nourishes me. He who begot me now regenerates me. He who created me transforms me into an angel, transforms me into God![18]

I have not hesitated to speak of the kiss image as being at the core of this description. If the father-daughter relationship conveys the idea of a personal God, it is equally clear that the Deity figures also as a cosmic *Spirit*. As in Augustine's embracements with Sophia discussed in an earlier chapter, here too the idea of the infusion or in-breathing (again during an embrace) of a divine Spirit that fills and nourishes leaves little doubt that the kiss as the vehicle of this transfusion is to be understood as an essential part of the picture of this embrace between the soul and God. By this embrace-kiss the soul experiences an ecstatic *enthousiasmos* by which it is transformed into God.[19]

Renaissance Platonic Love and the Hierarchy of the Senses

What we have said of Ficino in regard to Platonic love may also be said of those Neoplatonizing theorists of love contemporary with and after him who insisted on the most spiritual relationship between persons: it would seem that the kiss, whether real or symbolical, could not easily be accommodated to their systems, and such an intimacy and others suggestive of sensual love were ruled out with a conscious and forensic deliberation, at least where love, even human love, was considered in its highest form. It may be useful to pause for a moment on this matter and consider the position of the explicator of a doctrine of Platonic love in Pietro Bembo's *Asolani*. In keeping with Ficino's conception of the hierarchy and function of the senses, Bembo (or rather, the speaker Lavinello) allows sight and hearing to be the only senses by which beauty can be truly known and enjoyed. And as these "spiritual" senses (and man's thought) are exalted, the "material" senses and the pleasures they offer are correspondingly debased:

> Wherefore, if good love, as I have said, is a desire for beauty, and if no part of us and of our senses except our eyes, ears, and mind can lead us to it [i.e., beauty], then all that which is sought by lovers with our other senses—save what is sought for the preservation of life—is not good love but evil. Hence, in the latter case, Gismondo, you would be a lover not of beauty but of disgustful things. For it is foul and beastly to seek those pleasures that lie not in our own control and that cannot be had without seizing and possessing what belongs to another; moreover, such pleasures are inherently disturbing, harmful, terrestrial, and slimy, whereas you are able to have those pleasures of which the enjoyment rests in our power and in enjoying them we do not seize upon anything that belongs exclusively to another, and each one [i.e., each pleasure] is in itself proper, innocent, spiritual, and pure.[20]

It is clear that the condemnation of the "lower" senses is so absolute in the Neoplatonic system of pure love that no room should be found within it for the kiss, since even the chastest kiss brings into operation the two most corporeal senses, taste and touch. This is the rationale that explains the absence, perhaps the deliberate eschewal, of the soul-in-the-kiss conceit in Ficino and Bembo and in other expositors of Platonic love. For the same reason the kiss conceit is not found in some of the more popular treatises on love, such as those by G. Betussi and Tullia d'Aragona. In all these authors love is said to be a desire on the part of lovers for a mutual transformation, but the conviction that bodies cannot be incorporated into one another makes them insist that the transformation can only be achieved as an exchange of souls or hearts whose mode of conveyance must be completely spiritual Tullia d'Aragona gives a neat summary of the "orthodox" position in the following passage:

> Honest love . . . is not born of [physical] desire as the other [sensual love] is, but of reason, and its chief aim is the transformation of the lover in the beloved with the desire that she [the beloved] be transformed into him, in which case from two they become one alone and four; and of this transformation both Francesco Petrarca and the most reverend Cardinal Bembo have discoursed frequently and eloquently. Since this transformation can only be effected spiritually, it follows that in such a love the principal role is occupied by our spiritual senses, that is by sight and hearing, and even more, because it is more spiritual, by our imagination.[21]

And yet, notwithstanding the apparent incompatibility of the kiss with such a system of pure love, during the sixteenth century and after, the kiss was so much associated with Platonic love as to be considered a Neoplatonic sacrament. How this came about, in spite of Ficino, as it were, is a matter to which we may now turn.

Pico della Mirandola and Death by the Kiss

We have seen that the soul-in-the-kiss conceit was at best only latent and perhaps deliberately suppressed in the famous passage from Ficino's Commentary. On the other hand, we have found something like it in his description of the love between God and the soul. But it is in a book by Ficino's brilliant contemporary, Pico della Mirandola, that the image first appears unequivocally in a Renaissance Neoplatonic context, fully developed as to symbolical and mystical significance. In his difficult treatise on love, the *Commento sopra una canzona de amore,* a long excursus on a poem by his friend Girolamo

Benivieni, there is a page where Pico speaks of the experience of the mind's attainment of the highest stages of contemplation. Pico, however, describes this experience within the framework of the Neoplatonic myth of the celestial Venus. The celestial Venus may be seen and kissed (possessed) only when the lover is free from the weight and confinement of the bodily senses. This is the condition of ecstasy or rapture which Pico refers to as a "death" inasmuch as the body can have no share in the experience. Moreover, the author speaks of two kinds or gradations of death, which clearly correspond to the two highest degrees of mystic contemplation, the illuminative and the unitive. It is only with the second death that the lover can go beyond seeing and hearing the goddess to embracing her and uniting his soul with hers in the kiss:

> It is possible then through the first death, which is merely the separation of the soul from the body, and not otherwise, for the lover to see the beloved celestial Venus and, face to face with her, meditating on her divine image, blissfully nourish his purified eyes; but whoever wishes to possess her still more intimately and, not content with seeing and hearing her, to be worthy of her intimate embraces and fervent kisses, must separate himself in total separation from the body through the second death; and then not only will he see and hear the celestial Venus but will be embraced with her in an indissoluble bond, and pouring out their souls one into the other with kisses, they will not exchange their souls so much as perfectly unite together, so that each of them may be said to be two souls and both of them one soul only.[22]

Although Pico's *Commento* is an exposition of divine love in Platonistic coloring, many of its basic principles are closely connected with a well-established tradition of Christian spirituality. In the words just quoted, apart from the concept of the celestial Venus, the character of Pico's presentation is typical of the medieval mystics. There is even the biblical echo of Moses' "face to face" meeting with God (frequently commented upon in the Christian tradition as an example of mystic union) which Pico has used in describing the meeting between the lover and Venus. Like the Christian mystics before him, Pico has employed the language and imagery of carnal love to give an account of a wholly spiritual love. The symbolism of the embrace and, particularly of the kiss by which the "souls" of the lover and the Deity mingle and fuse into one is just what we find in medieval mysticism, and the feminizing of the Deity into the celestial Venus is not unlike Augustine's feminization of Christ into Lady Wisdom (see chapter 1).

Equally striking is the way Pico has employed the metaphor of the lover's two deaths. Christian spirituality always regarded the state of ecstasy or highest contemplation as causing a kind of temporary bodily death. Here Pico almost seems to be following St. Bernard, who had boldly used the metaphor in referring to the soul's rapture: "I am not to be thought absurd if I call the bride's ecstasy a death, not, however, which ends life but one that saves her from the perils of life."[23] Before Pico, Bernard had spoken of the two deaths of the ecstatic mystic, the deaths corresponding to the two highest degrees of mystic contemplation—the illuminative and the unitive.[24] Another important point of similarity is to be noticed in the fact that Bernard referred to the second death as the "death of the angels," an expression used by the saint to indicate that through it man becomes temporarily like an angel, that is to say, pure spirit enjoying the purest vision and experience of the Deity. The same is true of Pico's second death, the description of which comes in the section of his work where he is discussing how man may attain to the life of the angels. The second death, for Pico, as earlier for St. Bernard, indicates that suprarational experience possible only as an act of love which alone can bring one to taste and touch the Divinity, that is, fully *to know* by a possession to which reason cannot attain. To see and to hear, the highest of the physical senses in the Platonic-Christian tradition, refer to the activity of the reason; but in the same tradition they are the least rewarding of the inner or spiritual senses. What are the lowest in the order of the physical senses are the highest in the order of the spiritual senses. Thus the soul must taste and touch the Divinity; it must kiss and embrace. It is clear that for Pico, no less than for the medieval affective mystic, love was, in the final analysis, superior to intellectual knowledge as a way of apprehending and enjoying God, although here (as even with St. Bernard) we must speak of a meeting of love and knowledge.[25]

The union of souls (of lover and the celestial Venus) in a kiss is the most striking image of our passage from Pico, and it is interesting to note that the author was aware of both its boldness and its importance as a mystic symbol. Pico, in fact, continues his reference to it with a gloss in which he justifies his use of the conceit on the grounds that it is the most perfect and most seemly "metaphor" that can be borrowed from carnal love in order to signify the supreme moment of mystic contemplation and union, an attitude which he shares with medieval mystics and the poets of *fin' amors*:

> And take note that the most perfect and intimate union that the lover may have with the celestial beloved is signified by the union of the kiss, because all other coming together or coupling beyond that, as in the case of physical love, is in no way allowed to be used as a metaphor in this holy and most sacred love.

Now, somewhat curiously, in seeking to illustrate this principle Pico does not allude to the medieval Christian mystics but rather to a tradition of Jewish mysticism:

> And because the learned kabbalists maintain that many of the ancient patriarchs died in such an intellectual rapture, you will find in their writings the expression "the death of the *binsica*," which in our tongue means "death by a kiss," which is said of Abraham, Isaac, Jacob, Moses, Aaron, Mary, and some others.[26]

If Pico makes no reference to Christian kiss symbolism, it may be because he was deliberately avoiding specific allusions to Christianity in a work meant to be a Platonistic treatise on divine love. The Jewish mystical tradition could be invoked because it served Pico's syncretistic ambitions. As is well known, Pico looked upon the kabbala primarily as a body of esoteric learning which, going back to Moses, confirmed the deepest truths of Christianity. In the present context the kabbalistic references are to be taken as corroboration of the description of the union between the soul and God, in the conception and description of which Pico is really following a long tradition of medieval mysticism and exegesis of the Song of Songs.

In the writings of the Christian spiritualists, ecstasy or mystic union appears in the metaphors of a death and a kiss, and sometimes as both, that is, as a death by a kiss. This last image, however, had its own development in Judaism, from the rabbinical metaphor of the death of the righteous by a divine kiss (a painless, tranquil death) to the kabbalistic elaboration of it into a metaphor signifying an intellectual ecstasy (see chapter 2). It is to this kabbalistic metaphor that Pico has referred; but in his context the *binsica*, or *mors osculi*, as the Christian kabbalists (and Pico first among them) were to call it, makes for a further eroticizing of death.[27] For, as applied by Pico, the mystic death is associated with the kiss of the celestial Venus. Now it is this mystic kiss of death (or death by a kiss), Pico goes on to say, that Solomon desired in the Song of Songs. This, I need hardly say, will not trouble us. But what must catch us by surprise, if only momentarily, is to find Pico introducing at just this point the Platonic epigram on kissing Agathon as an example of the same desire for the mystic death of the kiss:

> And whoever does not understand our previously stated position will never understand their [the kabbalists] meaning completely; nor will you read more [about it] in their books than that *binsica*, that is, death by a kiss, occurs when the soul unites itself with those things separated from the earth in an intellectual rapture to such a degree that being lifted out of the body it abandons it entirely; but why such a name is appropriate to such a death has not—as far as I have read—been expounded by others until now. This is that kiss which our divine Solomon desires when he exclaims in his Song: "Kiss me with the kisses of thy mouth." [*Baciami co' baci della bocca tua.*] In his first verse Solomon sets forth the whole meaning of the book and the final end of his love. This is what Plato means by the kisses of his Agathon and not what many, seeing Plato as themselves, believe of him. More-over, you will see that neither Solomon, nor Plato, nor anyone else speaking of love, has ever gone further than the kiss when they discoursed on celestial love.[28]

Again we note that Pico refers to the kiss as the extreme metaphor to be used in the description of divine love. That Plato's erotic epigram is here spiritualized into an expression of the desire for the mystic death need not puzzle us for long. Plato is considered by Pico to be a mystic or ecstatic lover. The achievement of mystic union for Pico, as for all mystics and ecstatics, necessitates a death, that is, an egress or deliverance of the soul from the body so that, unobstructed by corporeal contingencies and images, it may attain to knowledge of the true and spiritual order of things. And Plato, like the Christian mystics, not only allowed that such ecstasy or death could be anticipated momentarily while in the earthly life, but even suggested that it should be the most sought-for experience of the wise and spiritual man.[29] Thus, just before the kiss passage, Pico himself had interpreted the Platonic reference (*Symposium*, 179) to the myths of Orpheus and Alcestis as meaning that the philosopher was seeking to show that perfect knowledge, or fruition of intellectual beauty, necessitates a death of the soul to all corporeal images and earthly values.[30] More-over, because the entire process of knowing is also a matter of desiring and loving, it is said that the perfect lover is he who dies for love: "It is therefore Plato's intention to show that we may in no way hope to be able to attain the enjoyment of intellectual beauty unless we first abandon our lower faculties and with them, human life; he does not love perfectly, that is, with perfect love, who does not die for love [*nè ama perfettamente cioè d'amore perfetto, chi per amore non muore*]."[31] Christianity's great lesson to its followers was just the same truth: the perfect lover must die unto the old self and the world for love of the Beloved and in order to be joined with him. In a way, Pico was interpreting Plato as adumbrating the mysteries of Christianity. It is not difficult to see now that in a work that is a Platonistic exposition of doctrines that are felt to be in keeping with Christian truths, Pico should so allegorize the Platonic epigram that the soul seeking to pass out of the body—during a kiss—into the body of the beloved is understood to be the desire for the ecstatic death which brings union and perfect knowledge.

There are two things that may have contributed in encouraging Pico to endorse this particular interpretation. The one is that the name *Agathon* means the *good*. The other is that Pico might very well have believed that the Greek philosopher died during the height of an intellectual ecstasy. In his *Theologia Platonica*, Ficino had already commented on Plato's teaching that the true aim of philosophy was a meditation on death inasmuch as contemplation, or speculative philosophy, is (according to Ficino) a separation of reason from the senses and therefore an anticipatory experience of the ultimate corporeal death, which is a liberation of the soul from the body.[32] But even more striking is Ficino's statement that Plato was given to such supreme contemplation and that he finally died his definitive corporeal death in such a moment: "Since Plato frequently had left the body by long practice of contemplation, he finally withdrew entirely from the bonds of his body in that same [state of] abstraction."[33] Except for the absence of the image of the kiss, this is hardly different from what Pico, following the rabbinico-kabbalist tradition, has to say about the ecstatic death of the ancient patriarchs, of Solomon's death-kiss wish, and of Plato's kissing Agathon.[34] Putting it another way, we can say that Pico speaks of the kisses of Solomon and of Plato in terms that are very much like those in which St. Bernard speaks of the kisses of the bride or of St. Paul.[35]

In interpreting Plato's erotic epigram as an allegory of the mystic lover's desire for union with the Divinity, Pico criticizes those who regard it in any other way: "This is what Plato means by the kisses of his Agathon, and not what many, seeing Plato as themselves, believe of him." This criticism seems to be directed against Marsilio Ficino, whose exposition of Platonic love is challenged more than once by Pico in the *Commento sopra una canzona*, although in this instance he does not cite the particular passage.[36] As we saw earlier, Ficino himself makes no direct reference to the Platonic kiss conceit although he was drawing upon it (in the expanded version found in Aulus Gellius) when he wrote his rhapsodic chapter on the death, resuscitation, transformation, and union of lovers in reciprocal love, and it is to this passage alone, I believe, that Pico could have referred. Now if we ask what it was about Ficino's words that could have so displeased Pico, we may with reason answer that Ficino had applied his description to a love between creatures. Pico, writing from the perspective of a Platonistic-Christian otherworldliness, referred the Platonic kiss to the unitive relationship between man and the Divinity.

Baldassare Castiglione, the Ladder of Love, and the Kiss

Ficino, we saw, had not dared or cared to admit the kiss into his system of Platonic love, not even in a symbolic way, although he waxed eloquent on the themes of death, exchange of souls, and union among lovers. Pico readily adopted the soul-in-the-kiss image, but, like the earlier Christian writers and some medieval Jewish thinkers, only as a mystical symbol of union between man and the Divinity. It was left to Baldassare Castiglione, in the *Libro del Cortegiano* (first published in 1528), to supply the casuistry needed in order to legitimize the kiss within a "Platonic" system of love between creatures. It is not unlikely that Castiglione so dared to relax the rigid spirituality of Platonic love among creatures, as Ficino had not, because the love relationship he speaks of is heterosexual. We must also remember that his book reflects not so much the thinking of the serious or professional philosophers as that of a mundane court society for which it was written. Even so, other popular Platonizing treatises on love, we saw, refused to compromise on such matters—where the purest or highest form of human love was involved. Hence, the function granted to the kiss by Castiglione appears all the more daring and suggestive when seen in its context of the Neoplatonic hierarchy of the senses, for it is during the famous exposition of Platonic love made by the interlocutor Pietro Bembo that we find the kiss passage.[37]

Consistent with the Ficinian theory that the beauty of bodies is but a reflection of the beauty of souls and, ultimately, of God, and that the love most worthy of man is the love of soul or mind, the speaker Bembo holds to the idea that the only senses which should be operative in the love relationship are sight and hearing. Beauty is apprehended and enjoyed, and souls are able to commune with each other through these, the noble senses of man, as they work in harmony with reason, of which they are said to be the ministers. Because they are the senses least contaminated by the necessity of carnal contact, they are worthy of being the alimentary conduits that bring spiritual food to the soul. The beauty in question here is that pertaining to the woman loved:

> And just as we cannot hear with our palate nor smell with our ears, so can we in no way enjoy beauty nor satisfy the desire it arouses in our mind by means of touch, but rather by that sense of which beauty is the real object, namely the faculty of sight. Let us therefore put away the blind judgment of sense, and enjoy with our eyes that resplendence and grace, those scintillations of love, the smiles, gestures and all the other charming ornaments of beauty; in like manner let us enjoy with our hearing the sweetness of voice, the concert of speech, the harmony of her music (if the beloved be a musician); and thus the soul will nourish itself with the sweetest food by means of these two senses which have little to do with corporeal matter and are ministers to reason, and they will do so without passing any unvirtuous appetite because of a desire for the body (IV, 62).[38]

Bembo then speaks of the migration of the beloved's soul to the lover by means of the beauty of voice (sound and harmony) and body. When understood properly, this beauty is seen to be of the soul, if indeed it be not the soul itself. It enters the lover through the eyes and ears, which are said to be the passage (àdito) for the soul: "The lady makes no small sign of love when she grants the lover her beauty, which is such a precious thing, through the channels that are the passage to the soul, namely sight and hearing" (IV, 63). It is shortly after this statement that the speaker distinguishes two kinds of love between man and woman: the one is sensual, the other rational. To the lover of the second kind alone the lady may go so far as to accord a kiss:

> Therefore the beloved, in order to gratify her lover, besides offering him her sweet smiles, her intimate and secret talk, permission to jest and be merry with her and to take her hand, may rightfully and blamelessly go even as far as the kiss, which in sensual love is not allowed; for since the kiss is a joining of the body and the soul, there is a danger that the sensual lover may lean more toward the body than toward the soul, whereas the rational lover knows that although the mouth is a part of the body, it is nonetheless the exit for words which are the interpreters of the soul and for that internal breath which is itself also called the soul [*quello intrinseco anelito che si chiama pur esso ancor anima*]. For this reason [the lover] enjoys fastening his mouth to that of his lady in a kiss, not in order to awaken any unchaste desire, but because he feels that that union is the opening of a passage to their souls [*sente che quello legame è un aprir l'àdito alle anime*], which, drawn to one another by mutual desire, alternately flow into one another's bodies and so mingle together that each of them [i.e., the lovers] has two souls, and one [soul] alone so composed of the two supports two bodies, as it were (IV, 64).

This brings to mind Pico's admonishment that in the description of divine love the kiss is the most extreme yet legitimate image permissible for expressing the concept of union. But because we are now no longer in the realm of metaphor and divine love, we perhaps do better to recall Andreas Capellanus' dictum on pure love, which allowed the lover to go as far as the kiss; or, indeed, *Phaedrus*, where Plato distinguishes different types of lovers and recognizes that even the noblest of them are drawn to kiss and embrace. *Phaedrus*, however, makes no mention of the kiss as a spiritual mingling of souls, which is what we have in the *Cortegiano*, where the mouth figures as a passageway (*àdito*, as in the case of the eyes and ears) for souls, and the kiss is seen as a third vehicle or way for them to migrate and mingle. The souls of the lovers pass from the one body into the other so that at one point each lover has two souls, but when they have fused, it is as though one soul sustains the two bodies, a theme which is a commonplace in the literature of friendship.

One of the most significant and far-reaching points to be made about Castiglione's kiss passage is that it marks the culmination of centuries of effort to raise woman to that status of dignity whereby she is worthy of sharing friendship with man as an equal partner. In the Middle Ages the two-in-one ideal between male and female was effected in a relationship that was grounded in a mystico-physical love passion and was such that the woman was even elevated above the man in worth. It is clear, I think, that this characteristic of the courtly-love tradition also has its part in Castiglione's heterosexual Platonic friendship (or love), for here too it rests in the woman's discretionary power to grant or withhold the blessings intrinsic to the kiss. To be sure, this kiss is said to be the unique reward of rational or pure lovers; but it cannot be forgotten that, as a way for souls to unite, it calls for the active participation of a highly erogenous part of the human body and for the sense of touch which, just a moment before, Bembo had decried as the lowest of man's senses because it was in no way able to enjoy beauty or satisfy the desires of the soul. So too, one might say, does the Christian kiss of peace; and, in truth, we have heard Christian voices raised to denounce the profanation of the liturgical kiss. But the surrounding contexts of the two kisses will not allow for more than surface parallels. Despite the ostensible spirituality of Castiglione's Platonic kiss, it cannot but strike us as being suspect for the simple reason that it does not rise so completely from the earthly as to be solely or chiefly symbolical. In the mundane society of *The Book of the Courtier*, the distinction between Platonic and profane love is a nice one which, especially in the kiss passage, becomes dangerously tenuous. When compared to Pico's more erotically colored but more truly mystical explication, Castiglione's disquisition smacks of sophistry, and one senses that it lends itself readily to abuse.

What we have thus far examined of Castiglione's kiss passage shows a familiarity with the kind of speculation concerning the mouth and the kiss that is found in the medieval mystics: the mouth as the organ for words, which are the expression of the soul, and for the inward vital breath known as soul. On the other hand, the author's concluding remarks betray unmistakable echoes from Pico della Mirandola, especially when the theory of the kiss as a joining of souls is associated with the kisses of the Platonic epigram and the Song of Songs:

Hence the kiss may be described as a joining of souls rather than of bodies, because it has so much power over the soul that it draws the soul toward itelf and separates it from the body; for this reason all chaste lovers long for the kiss as a union of souls; and therefore Plato, divinely enamored [*il divinamente inamorato Platone*], says that in kissing, his soul came to his lips to issue from the body. And because the separation of the soul from things of the senses and its total union with things of the mind can be signified by the kiss, Solomon, in his divine book of the Song, says: "Let him kiss me with the kisses of his mouth," to reveal the desire his soul had to be rapt by divine love to the contemplation of heavenly beauty [*la bellezza celeste*] in such a way that, by intimate union with it, the soul might abandon the body (IV, 64).

Pico had spoken first of Solomon's kiss and then of Plato's (or Agathon's) kisses. Castiglione, we note, has reversed this order. This inverted order is not casual, but rather is demanded by a context and purpose that are quite different form what we find in Pico. If Castiglione has followed Pico in interpreting the kiss of the Song as an expression of the soul's desire for union with the Divinity ("la bellezza celeste"), he departs from him by regarding Plato's kiss as a desire for the union of souls of two creatures. The phrase "il divinamente inamorato Platone" might lead one to assume that in the case of Plato, too, divine love is meant. The fact is, however, that in Castiglione's context Plato's kiss figures not as a metaphor at all but as an illustrious example of the idea that the kiss of chaste but real lovers has the effect of drawing up their souls so that they may unite. That is why, when Plato was kissing (i.e., kissing Agathon, but Castiglione has been careful to leave him unnamed), his soul came to his lips in a desire to issue from his body. Only then does Castiglione tell us that the kiss can also be used as a metaphor or symbol to signify mystical contemplation in which the soul is separated from its body and dwells in the sphere of the suprasensuous or of pure thought. And that, he now says, is why Solomon (but not, as for Pico, Plato also) asked for the kiss in his Song: in order to express the desire that his soul, leaving its body, might be caught up and raised to a union with the Divinity.

Though Castiglione makes no direct mention of kabbalistic lore, the close of his passage, which speaks of the Song and of the kiss as signifying a rapture in which the soul abandons the body, indicates that he had in mind the *mors osculi* or *binsica* as explicated by Pico.

Moreover, this motif is again apparent at the end of the long discussion on love when Bembo raises an impassioned prayer to Love as the vivifying force of all things and asks that the souls of all present be made to know the joy of union with the Divinity:

> Receive our souls, which we offer up to thee as a sacrifice; burn them in that living flame that consumes all material ugliness so that, being wholly separated from our bodies, they may unite with the divine beauty in a perpetual and most sweet bond, and so that we, being outside ourselves, like true lovers may be transformed into the beloved, and rising beyond the earth be admitted to the banquet of the angels where, nourished by immortal ambrosia and nectar, we may finally die that most fortunate and vital death as did long ago those patriarchs whose souls, by the burning power of contemplation, thou didst enrapture from the body and unite with God (IV, 70).

This quotation includes several of the conceits of ecstatic love, among them that of the transformation of the lover into the beloved. The closing image of the death of the ancient patriarchs in an ecstasy of contemplation that joined their souls with God is without doubt an allusion to the mystic death by a kiss. Concerning this image (the medieval phase of which has been dealt with in chapter 2 of the present study), we may here add another word.

Mors Osculi

First introduced to Christian writers by Pico, the theme of the *mors osculi* enjoyed a considerable vogue in the sixteenth century. Edgar Wind has touched on it in connection with the Renaissance interpretation of the mythological scenes of the love between gods and men on Roman sarcophagi. The upshot of Wind's investigations is that Italian Neoplatonists understood the ancients to have conceived of Amor both as a benign god of death and as a god of love; mortal death being an embrace of a god, it meant that "to die was to be loved by a god, and partake through him of eternal bliss."[39] Under the influence and guidance of the Neoplatonizing humanists, Italian artists evidently recreated the erotic scenes in this same mythographic or allegorical key. Hence the popularity of such stories as Leda and the swan, Ganymede and Zeus (or the eagle), or Endymion and Diana, all of which included a representation of kissing as of a sign of copulation and union between the soul and the Deity.[40] Such representations could be regarded as adumbrations of the kabbalistic *mors osculi* and the kiss of the Song (in a kabbalist key) or, for that matter, of St. Paul's more explicit desire to die (be dissolved) in order to be with Christ. This is made evident by the remarks of Celio Agostino Curione quoted by Wind:

> As there are many kinds of death, this one is the most highly approved and commended both by the sages of antiquity and by the authority of the Bible: when those . . . yearning for God and desiring to be conjoined with him (which cannot be achieved in this prison of the flesh) are carried away to heaven and freed from the body by a death which is the profoundest sleep; in which manner Paul desired to die when he said: I long to be dissolved and be with Christ. This kind of death was named the kiss by the symbolic theologians, of which Solomon also appears to have spoken when he said in the Song of Songs: *Osculetur me osculo oris sui*. And this was foreshadowed in the figure of Endymion, whom Diana kissed as he had fallen into the profoundest sleep. . . .[41]

Similar observations on the fable of Diana kissing Endymion were made in an even more influential book, Giulio Camillo's *L'idea del teatro*, which Wind does not mention.[42] It is to be observed that this particular line of speculation departs from Pico (and even from Castiglione) in limiting the concept of the *mors osculi* to a real albeit rapturous death uniting the soul with God in the afterlife. Others, however, such as Leone Ebreo, J. Reuchlin, H. C. Agrippa, and even Giordano Bruno, follow Pico in understanding it both as a real ecstatic death of the saints and as a mystical rapture experienced in the highest stage of divine contemplation during which the soul takes flight, thereby leaving its body inanimate.[43]

The Platonic Kiss: Champions and Skeptics

There is no doubt that the soul-in-the-kiss image received its greatest impetus in the Renaissance through Castiglione's presentation, for no man of letters could be ignorant of the *Book of the Courtier*. Henceforth the conceit was destined to become one of the most abused commonplaces in the literature of love. It was quickly exploited by anyone wishing to praise kisses or—what comes to the same thing— a lady's mouth or lips, even outside any specific Neoplatonic love metaphysics. For example, in a didactic dialogue on the charms of woman (*Dialogo della bellezza*, 1541), Agnolo Firenzuola, while discussing the various parts of the body, gives special attention to the lips and mouth as being a temple consecrated to the religion of love: "Under the nose is set the mouth which has two functions: one is speech, the other is to send food where it is needed; the mouth, split horizontally, was bordered by nature with two lips, as if of finest coral, like the banks of a most fair fountain; these [lips] the ancients dedicated to the fair Venus, because there is the seat of love's kisses which are able to make souls pass from one body to another in mutual exchange."[44] Here the conceit is introduced in order to indicate the exchange of souls as a third and culminating function of the mouth after that of speaking and taking food. We notice also that although the passage is in prose, the conceit has found its way into a context of a madrigalesque preciosity, a phenomenon that will be frequently repeated in the poets of the sixteenth and seventeenth centuries.

A very curious example of the image can be found in one of the most bizarre of Renaissance treatises on woman, Michelangelo Biondo's *Angoscia, Doglia, e Pena* (1546). The author employs it within the context of a nuptial relationship which is not the mystical marriage of the Christian tradition but the marriage here on earth between man and woman: "Oh, sweet mouth, delicious mouth, gentle mouth, pleasing mouth, when we live peacefully in blessed and holy matrimony! because by means of the mouth there enters the spirit [*spirito*] of two bodies, known as 'breath' [*fiato*]. Oh God! How great a mystery of thy majesty this is: to make of two spirits one only, uniform, consonant, harmonious, at peace, and of one same will."[45] One hears the echo of Paul's famous words that speak of man and wife becoming one flesh—words, he said, which are a high mystery and that he applied to Christ and the Church (Eph. 5:31–33). But Biondo has spoken of the two—husband and wife—becoming not one flesh but one spirit. Also worthy of notice is Biondo's awareness that the concept of the joining of spirits in the kiss depends upon the connection between spirit and breath (*fiato*), upon the semantic ambiguity or richness of *spirit*.

In still another curious Renaissance treatise on woman, *Il Convito, overo del peso della moglie* (1554), Giovanni Battista Modio puts the origin of the embrace and the kiss between man and woman in the Platonic androgynous myth: "Now it happened that being in disfavor with the gods for their faults, they were by the powers of Jove and

Apollo each divided into two halves; each of these halves would run to embrace and reunite himself with his other half. Whence was born the embrace and the kiss—and these are the sweetest and most longed-for pledges of love."[46] It is strange, in fact, that there is not more frequent reference to the androgynous myth in the Renaissance employment of the kiss image than we actually find. But that myth must have presented itself to many who thought of the kiss as a desire for union, of a merging of two into one, and we will find other allusions to it.

Of more interest to us in the remainder of the present chapter is the Renaissance speculation on the kiss within broader discussions of love than are found in the treatises on women. In this connection we may say that Neoplatonizing Italians continued to expound the idea that the kiss, when made between chaste or Platonic lovers, was a real means for the mingling or reciprocal transfusion of souls. For example, at the end of the sixteenth century, Annibale Romei, a nobleman of the court of Ferrara, tells us (somewhat like Castiglione before him) that the kiss is allowed as a reward to those who practice "amor casto"—that kind of love in which the partners are moved by each other's human beauty to the contemplation of the "true and essential beauty" with which alone they are content. Romei's chaste lovers desire to kiss only because they wish to mingle souls. And here, once again, the example of Plato's kiss is called upon:

> To this love it appears that the kiss may be granted as a reward, inasmuch as the kiss is more a union of souls than of bodies. For by means of the kiss, in which lovers effect an exceedingly sweet passage of highly lively spirits into one another's heart, the souls of lovers become bound together in so indissoluble a knot of love that from the two one single soul is formed, and thus formed it governs two bodies. For this reason chaste lovers desire to come to the kiss as the true bond of souls. Wherefore the divine Philosopher, enamored with a chaste love, said in his *Symposium* that in kissing, his soul came to his lips in order to fly forth.[47]

Romei has the content of the Platonic epigram right, but his attribution of it to the *Symposium* and to a context of pure love is, of course, incorrect. But the error itself is significant, revealing as it does that the soul-in-the-kiss conceit was felt to be authentically Plato's, a fact that gave it great credit.

Of course, there were always those who openly displayed

skepticism regarding Platonic love itself while defending the necessity and legitimacy of physical love. Already in Castiglione's own *Book of the Courtier*, the realist Morello, with his practical good sense, appears as the advocate of a healthy physical love, although the author evidently meant him to be a foil to Bembo's ethereal conception of love. In response to the idea that the lady's beauty is to be enjoyed outside of any carnal contact in order that it may be engendered in the beauty of the mind, Morello suggests the begetting of real children as a more likely way for beauty to be engendered. It is Bembo, however, who is allowed to have the last word on the matter.

One of the writers to champion the cause of a sober physical love —when sanctioned by wedlock—was Flaminio Nobili, who is of particular interest to us because of the way he brings the matter of the kiss into the controversy. In a *Trattato* (1556), Nobili first criticizes the Neoplatonic theory of the ladder of love, which regards the beauty of the human creature as a way to rise to the contemplation of the Creator. There are the beauties of the heavens, of light, and the general perfection of the universe that are immediately accessible to man and which one may more safely contemplate in desiring to rise to the knowledge of the supreme Beauty that is God. Experience shows, Nobili ironically hints, that too often the would-be lover of the Divine, when beginning with the beauty of the creature, fails to make any progress at all.[48]

Without denying that the union of lovers' souls is one of the aims of love, Nobili suggests that since souls dwell in bodies, they can be expected to unite to the degree that the bodies themselves are joined to one another. That such bodily contact is natural and legitimate is proven by the fact that even children desire to embrace their parents, and brothers and friends desire to embrace one another. There follows the appeal to Plato's androgynous myth, which sets forth the idea that lovers desire to be welded together. Then, as though in pointed opposition to Ficino, who had referred to the famous Lucretian description of the furious sexual embrace of lovers as proof of the impossibility of true union, Nobili avails himself of the same example as one favoring his own opinion that corporeal union is natural and necessary. Finally the author attacks the theorists of Platonic love—"these superstitious writers of love"—on the matter of their allowance and interpretation of the kiss, reminding them that the kiss represents first of all a joining of bodies, and that as such it is common even to animals. As far as he is concerned, however, there is really no need to deny this very corporeal kiss and further carnal union to that honest human love sanctioned by the divine decree that men propagate the human species:

> This is clearly evident in the case of things that are dearest to us, as in our children, brothers, and friends whom by natural instinct we want to touch and embrace. For this reason Aristophanes, according to Plato, had no doubt that lovers would like to find a Vulcan who would fuse them completely with the beloved in order to become one by this welding instead of two as much as possible; and Lucretius, also discoursing on love, said that the lover would like to penetrate with all his body the entire body of his lady. And I see that the kiss is permitted by these superstitious writers on love—and the kiss is after all still the joining of bodies, and common even to animals; so that this joining is not contrary to human love—meaning by human love that which is reasonable and honest—unless followed by the violation of the laws and unless other conditions of moderation are infringed.[49]

One of the most spirited and entertaining attacks on the kiss understood as a sacramental tenet of Platonic love is to be found in the *Dialoghi piacevoli* (1586) of Stefano Guazzo. In the dialogue entitled *Dell'honor delle donne*, as two friends discuss the various types and classes of women and their habits, one of them, Annibale, expatiates with undertones of irony on that particular breed of women who are the *grandes amoureuses* of Platonic love:

> Let us go on to that band of strange women—I mean those who, in order to be thought among the more learned matrons, lend willing ears to Platonic lovers; and while decrying vulgar and lascivious love, turn with joyful countenances to be courted philosophically. Nor are they content to remain in conversation with certain lofty minds and to continue discoursing on how the pleasure that is felt in gazing at a lovely face should be transformed into an inner gazing at a greater beauty, but they graciously agree in the end to three degrees of love: the first is to receive some jewel from their lovers and to give one in return; the second is to allow their hands to be kissed; the third and last is to comfort them with that pure kiss of the mouth, by virtue of which their souls attain mutual marriage [*quell'honesto bacio della bocca, in virtù del quale si vengono a sposar l'anime insieme*], and remain eternally joined by a holy and indissoluble bond. But do not suppose that strength of love, humility of prayers and sighs, tenderness of tears, length of service, liberality of gold and silver, or the whole world

together, would be enough to make them overstep the bounds of these three favors. What do you say now to this Platonic love?[50]

Here then are specific references to Platonic lovers and Platonic love accompanied by the significant allusion to the kiss as a rite by means of which souls are joined in wedlock. The insistence on the kiss as the ultimate intimacy that the lady will grant recalls both Castiglione and Andreas Capellanus. But Guazzo has presented this picture of pure or Platonic love with the intention of ridiculing it as an absurd and even hypocritical convention. Thus in giving his opinion concerning this curious practice, the second interlocutor, Lodovico, wastes no time in discrediting it. Some of his remarks, moreover, are especially acute. This would-be spiritual love is really one that puts the spirit asleep and rouses sensual desire without satisfying it. Besides this, Lodovico complains, there is something dishonest in the way it is carried out, because the women are married and practice their mysteries of love without a word about it to their husbands. This is another point that the practice of Platonic love as described by Guazzo has in common with medieval courtly love. But if they have something in common with the medieval ladies of courtly love, these Renaissance dames also look forward to Molière's *précieuses ridicules*; for, as Annibale says, if they keep their religion of love a secret from their husbands and others, that is because the latter, not having read Plato, might very easily misunderstand the true nature of this love. The remark is obviously ironic, because Annibale summarily concludes the entire discussion with a flat pronouncement that the custom of these ladies may be all very well, but that he for one has no liking for it: "But what more shall I say? Their custom may be fine and good, but it doesn't please me at all."[51]

The case of Guazzo is most instructive, for it is not the kiss as such that he objects to but its abuse—as in hypocritical Platonic lovers. Thus in a different context he provides us with an equally spirited defense of the kiss as a greeting. Protesting against those who would limit osculatory salutations to persons having family ties, Guazzo recognizes that the kiss has become contaminated, but he suggests the possibility of its repristination with an appeal to the philosophers (very likely the Italian Neoplatonists), the kabbalists, the mystical explanation of the Song of Songs, and, failing all this, to the tradition of the kiss of peace which, he says, Christ himself bequeathed to mankind:

186

The wickedness of man has now reached such proportions that in many places the exchange of the kiss between friends in public has been forsaken, and only the kiss between relatives is condoned. But it is meet to remind our overzealous moralists that if they prefer not to lend credence to those philosophers who affirm that in this quite chaste kiss souls unite virtuously, and if they will not believe the kabbalists who maintained that without the kiss we cannot unite with heavenly things nor with God, which kiss, moreover, cannot occur until death dissolves this body of ours that keeps us separated from true union and from the kiss that supernal things would like to give to our souls—which Giulio Camillo holds was signified by Solomon where the latter calls out "Let him kiss me with the kisses of his mouth"—if, I repeat, they are not willing to believe any of this, they at least ought to believe in Christ our Saviour who bequeathed the kiss to us on earth as a sign of peace.[52]

As we shall see, the polemic surrounding the soul kiss and other conventions of Platonic love was engaged in by the poets of the Renaissance-Baroque period in their own inimitable ways. For the moment, however, we may point out another way in which opposition to Platonic love (and its kiss) came not only from realistic or sensual lovers, but from the moralistic voice of the Counter Reformation as well. Toward the end of the sixteenth century the Church authorities called upon one of its scholars, Antonio Ciccarelli, to prepare an edition of the *Book of the Courtier* that would be expurgated of anything not in keeping with strict Catholic morality. In particular, the fourth book was to be annotated wherever Castiglione had written about love in an unorthodox manner, that is, "in those parts in which the author discusses love not according to his own true understanding of it, but in the manner of the Platonic school."[53] Now, interestingly enough, Ciccarelli retained the kiss passage in its entirety, perhaps because it was too well known for him to have done otherwise. His method of attempting to blunt its piquancy was to explain it away as a case of bantering by the author: "He [Castiglione] here jokes about the opinion of the Platonists who maintain that in divine love the kiss is quite in order in its capacity as a sign of the union of minds."[54] But this gloss is as revealing as it is curious. Besides the fact that Castiglione was the first openly to justify the kiss between Platonic lovers (i.e., creatures) and was most likely not jesting, in considering the use of the kiss as a symbol of the union of souls in divine love to be strictly a "Platonic" idea, Ciccarelli was ignoring (wilfully?) the fact that this kiss symbolism had long been in common usage among the most respected and authoritative Christian writers. At any rate, the gloss is yet another indication of how closely associated with Renaissance Neoplatonism the image of the soul-uniting kiss had become.

6. The Renaissance-Baroque Age

From Classical to Neo-Latin Poets

he Neo-Latin poets of the Renaissance occupy an important place in the history of the soul-in-the-kiss conceit, primarily because of the inherent interest of their own poetry, but also because along with the literature of Neoplatonic love their erotic Muse represents a major source for many vernacular poets who subsequently used the image. As found in the earliest of the Neo-Latin poets, toward the end of the fifteenth century, the conceit figures as an amatory image independent of any Neoplatonic influence and very likely derives from an early Greek or Latin example such as those registered by Stephen Gaselee.[1] It was not long, however, before traces of Italian Neoplatonic accretions attached themselves here too, although they did so invariably as refinements of the purely voluptuous pleasures associated with kissing.

As is well known, the love poetry of the Neo-Latin poets was greatly influenced by Catullus and the Latin elegists, Tibullus, Propertius, and Ovid. Under the spell of these ancient masters of sensual love poetry, the Renaissance emulators even created a genre of poetry known as the *basium* in which all the real and imaginary delights of kissing are extolled. Although the soul-in-the-kiss image does not appear in the works of the earlier Roman poets, they nonetheless concern us directly for a very important reason: the bequeathal to their latter-day epigones of the passionate columbine kiss. With the Renaissance Neo-Latin poets, the soul-in-the-kiss image becomes directly related to the kiss in which wanton tongue play is exalted. The connection, moreover, was to prove an enduring one in some quarters. In English, for example, the deep kiss in which lingual stimulation is practiced is known both as "tongue kiss" and "soul kiss," as well as by the more commonly used expression "French kiss."[2]

How well the ancients knew the value of such a kiss as a preludious and sexually excitatory play is demonstrated by Ovid when, in describing how utter was his fiasco in a love combat on one occasion, he tells us that not even the tongue kiss could make him respond:

> Illa quidem nostro subiecit eburnea collo
> Bracchia, sithonia candidiora nive,
> Osculaque inseruit cupidis luctantia linguis,
> Lascivum femori supposuitque femur.[a]

This same lascivious image is evoked again by Ovid when such kisses are said to be *improba* only because they are being given not to him but to someone else:

> Improba tum vero iungentes oscula vidi
> (Illa mihi lingua nexa fuisse liquet):
> Qualia non fratri tulerit germana severo,
> Sed tulerit cupido mollis amica viro.[b]

Such furious lingual combat is also counseled by Tibullus:

> Et dare anhelanti pugnantibus umida linguis
> Oscula et in collo figere dente notas.[c]

Like true epigones, the Renaissance Neo-Latin poets celebrated such kisses with cloying promiscuity. In a few cases, however, the poetic results are not to be scorned, and some of the very best poetry of kissing so lavishly indulged in by these poets is to be found in those instances where the image of the mingling and exchange of spirits or souls is employed. Occasionally, moreover, they couple the image with the erotic conceit of the death of the lover, that is, with the use of the term "death" as a metaphor for the ecstatic sensation experienced at the height of sensual pleasure in kissing or in coition itself. In this connection the following verses of Petronius must have been of some import:

> Qualis nox fuit illa, di deaeque,
> Quam mollis torus. haesimus calentes
> Et transfudimus hinc et hinc labellis

---

[a] "Indeed she threw her ivory arms, whiter than Thracian snow, about my neck, and thrust kisses struggling with passionate tongues, and placed lustful thigh under my thigh." *Amores*, III, vii, 7–10.

[b] "Then indeed I saw them joining shameless kisses (that tongue had belonged to me); such [kisses] that a sister would not have given an austere brother, but that a compliant girl would have given a passionate man." *Amores*, II, v, 24–26.

[c] "And give to the panting [lover] moist kisses with battling tongues and sink marks into the neck with the teeth." I, viii, 37–38.

> Errantes animas. valete, curae
> Mortales. ego sic perire coepi.[d]

Here in a pagan context of antiquity is a clear example of the exchange of lovers' souls in the kiss accompanied by the lover's dying in a sexual sense.[3]

Other pagan examples in Latin of the soul-kiss conceit that could have been known to Renaissance writers are those that occur in the verse of Claudian, a writer of late antiquity (c. A.D. 370–410) who is often called the last poet of classical Rome. It is significant that they appear in the context of epithalamia where it was customary for the poet to invite the bridegroom and bride to the joys of sexual love. Near the end of one such epithalamium it is Venus herself who joins the hands of the young couple and blesses their union with the counsel that they live as one, carrying out the goddess's rites, kissing endlessly, bruising their arms in embraces, and joining their souls at their lips:

> Vivite concordes et nostrum discite munus.
> Oscula mille sonent; livescant brachia nexu;
> Labra ligent animas.[e]

In a similar vein, the following verses from a poem celebrating the marriage of the emperor Honorius urge frequent kisses to be breathed sweetly like those of doves until, the couple's soul-breaths having been united at their lips, sleep may finally quiet their panting:

> Et murmur querula blandius alite
> Linguis absiduo reddite mutuis.
> Et labris animum conciliantibus,
> Alternum rapiat somnus anhelitum.[f]

---

[d] "What a night was that, ye gods and goddesses! How soft the couch! We clung, passionate together and transfused our straying souls back and forth through our lips. Farewell mortal cares! Thus I begin to die." *Satyricon*, 79, 8.

[e] "Live in union and learn our rite: let a thousand kisses resound; let arms turn black and blue in [your] embrace; let lips bind [your] souls." "Epithalamium of Palladius and Celerina," vss. 130–132; in *Claudian with an English Translation by Maurice Platnauer*, I, (Cambridge, Mass., and London, Loeb Classical Library, 1956), 214.

[f] "And to each other's tongues give continually a murmur more soothing than a warbling bird. And while the lips unite the soul, let sleep take each panting breath in turn." "Fescennine Verses in Honour of the Marriage of the Emperor Honorius," IV, vss. 21–24. In *Claudian*, II, 238. Gaselee (see Introduction) mentioned these verses in a note but was of the opinion that they refer not to kisses but only to the low whisperings of lovers!

Between these examples from Claudian and the Renaissance humanist poets may be recalled the verses from the charming "Lydia, bella puella candida," an anonymous poem which has not yet been successfully dated:

> Porrige labia, labra corallina
> Da columbarum mitia basia;
> Sugis amantis partem animi;
> Cor mi penetrant haec tua basia.[g]

As we have said at the outset of the present chapter, this columbine or billing kiss that sucks up the soul-breath was to be particularly appealing to Renaissance poets.

It is also necessary to note that in their osculatory verse the Renaissance poets most certainly kept in mind the lines from Lucretius (*De rerum natura*, IV, 1073–1120) that describe the violent embrace of lovers who, in kissing, intermingle saliva and breath in the vain attempt to interpenetrate one another. But what Lucretius described as an example of the madness and indecorous behavior of men under the dominion of passion, the Renaissance poets exult in as one of life's supreme delights.

The first of the Renaissance Neo-Latin poets to be remembered here is the Neapolitan Giovanni Pontano (1426–1503). If, when kissing his lady, there is no "soul" or "spirit," a coldness and a melancholy come over him. On the other hand, when they exchange passionate, biting kisses in which their souls or spirits mingle, then a languor comes over the poet, and a desire to die. But by those same kisses the poet is in fact kept alive; his mistress's tongue inserted in his mouth keeps the passageway closed so that his soul is prevented from issuing forth and he from dying in her bosom:

> Basia cum strictis offers mihi clausa labellis
>   Deque tuo nullus spiritus ore venit,
> Nescio quid tum triste animum subit ipsaque nostro
>   Frigescunt tacito basia in ore situ.
> At cum rapta sonant mordacibus oscula labris
>   Mixtus et alterno spiritus ore coit,

---

[g] "Offer your lips, your coral lips; give the soft kisses of doves; you suck part of your lover's soul (breath); these kisses of yours pierce my heart." Quoted from *An Anthology of Medieval Latin*, ed. S. Gaselee (London, 1925), pp. 68–69. Gaselee notes that "scholars are not yet agreed whether the pretty little poem is of late imperial days or a medieval Italian production."

Meque color, meque et sensus animusque relinquunt
  Inque tuo iaceo languidus ipse sinu.
At tu, cum dederis mihi suavia, consere linguam
  Inter labra, meo semper et ore fove,
Ne pateant animo egressus, ne frigida lingua
  Torpeat, ipse tuo deficiamque sinu.[h]

In another place Pontano recalls the first kisses of his lady and how, with their lips adhered together, their intermingling spirits passed alternately from one mouth to the other. Also of interest here is the poet's conceit that if death (the *Orcus*) had seized them at that moment, the lovers would have been taken as one soul and one shade, an idea which might just owe something to Dante (see chapter 3):

Illa, uxor, memini nunc, oscula prima fuere:
Nostra tuis, tua labra meis haesere, diuque
Spiritus alterno huc, illuc se miscuit ore.
Tunc Orcus si nos una rapuisset, amantum
Una futura anima, una etiam simul umbra futura.[i]

Among the most admired of the Neo-Latin poets of the Renaissance was the Italianized Greek, Michele Marullo Tarchaniota (1453–1500). One of his best-known pieces develops the soul-in-the-kiss image. When he steals a kiss from his lady, the poet's soul is left on her lips; in vain the poet sends his heart to fetch his soul, for it too remains a captive (but of his lady's eyes). Had it not been for a vital heat that was bestowed by the very kiss in which his soul escaped from him, the poet would surely have died:

Suaviolum invitae rapio dum, casta Neaera,
  Imprudens vestris liqui animam in labiis,

[h] "When you offer me closed kisses with tight lips and from your mouth no breath comes, then an indefinable sadness steals into my mind and our very kisses grow cold in our silent mouths. But when snatched kisses resound on biting lips and mingled breaths unite in each other's mouths, color and soul and sense desert me, and I myself lie fainting on your breast. Now do you, when you have given me kisses, plant your tongue between my lips and keep it ever warm within my mouth, lest passageways are made for the soul, lest the cold tongue stiffen and I myself expire upon your breast." *Carmina*, ed. J. Oeschger (Bari, 1948), p. 423.
[i] "Remember now, my wife, what those first kisses were: my lips clung to yours, yours to mine, and for long the breath mingled together now in that mouth, now in the other. Had Orcus taken us together then, there would have been one soul of lovers, and at the same time one shade." *Carmina*, II, ed. B. Soldati (Florence, 1902), 7. Again, but even more sensually, the conceit appears in connection with the tongue kiss in a lyric generally entitled "Ad Alfonsum Ducem Calabriae": In *Carmina* (Bari, 1948), p. 294.

Exanimusque diu, cum nec per se ipsa rediret
  Et mora lethalis quantulacunque foret,
Misi cor quaesitum animam; sed cor quoque blandis
  Captum oculis nunquam deinde mihi rediit.
Quod nisi suaviolo flammam quoque, casta Neaera,
  Hausissem, quae me sustinet exanimum,
Ille dies misero, mihi crede, supremus amanti
  Luxisset, rapui cum tibi suaviolum.[j]

Marullo's delightful poem was much admired and imitated by vernacular poets; but where the conceits that interest us are concerned, the most important and influential of the Neo-Latin poets was the short-lived sixteenth century Dutchman, Johannes Secundus (1511–1535). Although his amatory *Elegiae* and his extraordinary cycle of nineteen *Basia* frequently reveal that his masters were Catullus, the Latin elegists, and the early Italian Neo-Latin poets, in particular Pontano and Sannazzaro, Secundus has no equal in the sensual use of the soul-in-the-kiss conceit.[4] *Basium X*, for example, after enumerating the various kisses that may be given (upon the eyes, cheeks, neck, and shoulders), speaks of the mouth and tongue kiss as surpassing all others in its marvelous effects of first mingling and then bringing about an exchange of souls. During such a kiss the lovers experience the deathlike swoon of love's ecstasy:

Seu labris querulis titubantem sugere linguam,
  Et miscere duas juncta per ora animas,
Inque peregrinum diffundere corpus utramque,
  Languet in extremo cum moribundus amor.[k]

Secundus was writing after the publication of the *Book of the Courtier*, and Castiglione's idea that during the kiss each body has two

---

[j] "While I stole a sweet kiss from you against your will, chaste Neaera, I, unaware, left my soul upon your lips, and for long soul-less—since it did not come back by itself and even a small delay might be fatal—I sent my heart to seek my soul; but my heart, captured in turn by your lovely eyes, has never returned from there. Wherefore, chaste Neaera, if from that sweet kiss I had not derived a flame that sustains me without my soul, the final day would have dawned for your unhappy lover, believe me, when I stole that kiss from you."

[k] "Or sucking the trembling tongue with plaintively desiring lips and mingling two souls through united mouths, and diffusing each soul into the other's body, love, while dying, grows faint at last." *The Love Poems of Johannes Secundus, A Revised Latin Text with an English Verse Translation*, ed. and trans. F. A. Wright (London, 1930), p. 72.

souls, while the two bodies are themselves, as it were, infused with and animated by one composite soul, could be the source of a similar conceit that concludes Secundus' *Basium XIII*:

> Pars animae, mea vita, tuae hoc in corpore vivit
> Et dilapsuros sustinet articulos;
> Quae tamen impatiens in pristina iura reverti
> Saepe per arcanas nititur aegra vias
> Ac nisi dilecta per te foveatur ab aura,
> Iam conlabentes deserit articulos.
> Ergo age, labra meis innecte tenacia labris,
> Assidueque duos spiritus unus alat,
> Donec, inexpleti post taedia sera furoris,
> Unica de gemino corpore vita fluet.[1]

But if the image was at all inspired by Castiglione's words, it has been bereft of any spiritual veneer, for Secundus quite unabashedly and deliberately utilizes the soul-in-the-kiss conceit in order to give expression to the purely voluptuary delights of osculation. This is evidenced in another of his poems (*Elegia*, I, 5) which contains the image of the soul being sucked up by a kiss and, again, the concept of an exchange whereby each of the lovers lives by virtue of the other's soul or breath. Again, however, the sensual note is so intense that one hesitates to speak of it as an example of the psychic exchange or transformation of lovers.[5]

But another of Secundus' poems which needs to be mentioned because of the many imitators it was to have is *Basium II*. Besides its conceit of the lovers clinging together in one long eternal kiss, the poem is important for its development of the theme of the lovers dying together glued to that kiss and then passing into an Elysium for lovers who remain forever together in a love that is stronger than death. The poet and his lady will be especially honored by the dwellers of that blissful afterlife.[6] The theme of an Elysium for lovers derives ultimately from the classic poets (cf. Tibullus, I, 3), but one wonders

---

[1] "A part of your soul, my life, lives in this body and sustains my limbs [that are] on the point of dissolution. But it, unable to bear more, often strives, poor thing, to return to its former kingdom by hidden ways, and were it not warmed by you with your dear breath, it would leave my collapsing limbs. Come, therefore, and join your clinging lips to mine and let one breath-spirit continually nourish both of us, until after the late weariness of unassuaged passion, a single life flows from a twin body." *Ibid.*, p. 84.

whether Secundus was not deliberately contrasting his kiss unto Elysium with the kiss unto Hell of Paolo and Francesca. Secundus, however, was not one to restrict the possibilities of the soul-kiss conceit, and in still another poem (*Elegia*, I, 3) he prays that even in old age he may know the titillating sensation of kisses. Then, when it is time for his soul to depart from his body, may his soul come forth in kissing his lady; haply it will be sustained by her lips where it will prefer to linger wantonly rather than make its way to Elysium.[7]

The popularity of Secundus' *Basia* was such as to create a vogue for poems on kisses to which both vernacular and Neo-Latin writers contributed. But there is little variety among the Neo-Latin poets who subsequently used the soul-kiss conceit. They derive the image primarily from Secundus, although Pontano and Marullo are certainly to be counted among their sources. In addition to this, a familiarity with the Platonic epigram and its elaboration in Aulus Gellius was now also at work. Invariably the image is given a strictly erotic and even salacious value. This is so even when the poet is also drawing quite clearly on Ficinian or other Neoplatonic ideas as well. Such, for example, is the case of Sir Robert Aytoun (1570–1638), a Scottish writer of amatory complaints who deserves to be remembered here. In singing the praise of the passionate tongue kiss, Aytoun claims that it is the vehicle whereby souls are exchanged, and he adds the thought that in this way the lover lives in the body of the beloved and vice versa.[8] But it is quite likely that Aytoun was also influenced by vernacular poets of the Renaissance, for he was writing at a time when these amatory images had become almost indispensable and inevitable commonplaces in the love poetry of Italy, France, and England.

Italian Authors: The Kiss and Death as a Sexual Metaphor

The earliest instances of the soul-in-the-kiss conceit among the Renaissance vernacular poets of Italy are by Serafino Aquilano (1466–1500). Since Serafino was a court poet, it is not surprising to find him giving an air of witty if erotic gallantry to the image in one of his *strambotti*. Having stolen a kiss from his offended lady, the poet assures her that she may take her revenge without protest from him. In kissing, the poet's soul was so attracted by the sweetness of her lips that his soul was ready to take flight. If she would but grant him a second kiss, his soul would surely come wholly forth. This, of course, is to die, and his lady might well account herself satisfied with his death. The poet, we know, would like nothing better than so to die in ecstasy on a kiss:

> Incolpa, donna, amor, se troppo io volsi
> Aggiungendo alla tua la bocca mia.
> Se pur punir voì di quel ch'io tolsi,
> Fa che concesso replicar mi sia:
> Che tal dolceza in quelli labri accolsi,
> Che 'l spirto mio fu per fugirsi via.
> So che al secondo tocco uscirà fora;
> Basta ti de', che per tal fallo io mora.[m]

The fame of Serafino in his own time and in the sixteenth century was so widespread that we are apt to be amazed by it today. But our contemporary skepticism must not prevent us from recognizing his extraordinary influence as a transmitter of conceits and rhetorical devices. Hence the second example of his use of the soul-kiss theme deserves to be made known here, especially in view of the accompanying erotic motifs that are brought into play.

> Quando per dar al mio languir conforto
> Tua bocca con la mia dignò toccarse,
> Poco mancò che io non restasse morto,
> Chè in su le labre mie l'anima apparse;
> Et se più stava, e ben non era accorto,
> Intrava in voi per mai più separarse.
> Novo caso era esser di vita privo
> Et pur dentro da voi rimaner vivo.[n]

First to be remarked here is the traditional medieval motif of the poet seeking health or balm for his lovesickness in his lady's kiss. But this

---

[m] "Lay the blame on love, lady, if I dared too much in joining my mouth to yours. But if you wish to punish me for what I took, let me be allowed to do it again. For I plucked such sweetness from those lips that my spirit was ready to take flight, so that at a second touch it would come forth; it should suffice you that through such a fault, I die." *Die Strambotti des Serafino Dall'Aquila*, ed. Barbara Bauer-Formiconi (Munich, 1967), p. 318.

[n] "When, to comfort my languishing, your mouth deigned to touch mine, I was close to being left for dead, for my soul appeared on my lips, and if it stayed there longer and I had not been careful, it would have entered into you never to be separated from you again. A wonderful thing it would have been to be deprived of life and yet still remain alive within you." *Die Strambotti*, pp. 317–318.

is followed by the idea that rather than being restored the poet came close to death—a welcome one, it seems—for again his soul was drawn from within him to his lips. Finally, we meet with the idea that had the kiss lasted a bit longer, the poet's soul would have passed over and lodged itself within the lady's bosom, with the marvelous result [*novo caso*] that the poet dying unto himself would continue to live in the beloved. The latter thought, we know, is a characteristic Ficinian motif, but the fact that Serafino has worked it into the kiss conceit may mean that he was also adapting it directly from the poem in Aulus Gellius. Given their great contemporary popularity, Serfino's two *strambotti* on the kiss may well have had an influence on the *Basia* of Johannes Secundus as on vernacular poets.

In Ariosto's *Orlando Furioso* there is a well-known stanza (VII, 29) describing the sexual embrace between the lovers Ruggiero and Alcina. It contains an apparent allusion to the soul-kiss conceit, followed by a pun upon the lingual kiss. The poet would leave the telling of their joy to the lovers, who could be expected to have the required eloquence since, in kissing, each was in possession of two tongues:

> Non così strettamente edera preme
> Pianta ove intorno abbarbicata s'abbia,
> Come si stringon li due amanti insieme,
> Cogliendo de lo spirto in su le labbia
> Suave fior, qual non produce seme
> Indo o sabeo ne l'odorata sabbia.
> Del gran piacer ch'avean, lor dicer tocca;
> Che spesso avean più d'una lingua in bocca.°

The reference to the plucking of the sweet flower of the spirit from the lips may be an echo from the verses in Aulus Gellius. For the rest, the verses are a superior rendition of a stanza from Boiardo's *Orlando Innamorato*.[9]

Also to be remembered in connection with Ariosto's poem is the beautiful scene where Isabella kisses into herself the vital spirit (or soul-breath) of her dying lover Zerbino:

° "Ivy does not press the plant on which it is entwined as tightly as the two lovers clasped themselves together, plucking on their lips the spirit's sweet flower, such as is not produced by Indian or Arab seed in perfumed sands. It is for them [the lovers] to tell of the great pleasure that they felt for they often had more than one tongue in their mouths." Cf. Ariosto, *Capitoli*, VIII, vss. 13–15; 22–24.

> Cosí dicendo, le reliquie estreme
> De lo spirto vital che morte fura,
> Va ricogliendo con le labra meste,
> Fin ch'una minima aura ve ne reste.[p]

Like Tristan, Zerbino is content to die in his lady's arms. So too, like Iseult, Isabella wishes to die with her lover; unlike what happens in the Tristan story, Zerbino dissuades her from doing so by appealing to faith in God's succour. But besides this general similarity with the medieval romance, one can find a distant source for the particular adaptation of the soul-kiss conceit in the old Roman belief that the soul-breath which was expired from the mouth at the moment of dying could be captured by a survivor. As Franz Cumont wrote: "When Virgil shows us Dido's sister, at the time of the queen's suicide, receiving the last breath which floats on her dying lips, he is lending a Roman custom to the Carthaginians, the custom of the last kiss, which, according to a widely held belief, could catch on its way the soul which was escaping into the atmosphere."[10] In addition to the famous Virgilian passage (*Aeneid*, IV, 684–685), the thought is to be found in Ovid (*Met.*, VIII, 860–861) and in Seneca's tragedy *Hercules Oetaeus* (1340–1342) where Alcmena desires to receive through her mouth the spirit of her dying son Hercules. In the case of Ariosto, however, this image has become eroticized by being placed in the context of a lover's death in the lap of his mistress. In this respect it is more in keeping with the scene from Bion's *Lament for Adonis* (I, 45) where Venus in fact desires a last kiss from the dying Adonis in order that she might suck in and preserve within herself her lover's spirit (see Introduction).

We have already pointed out that it is after the promulgation of the kiss as a Neoplatonic sacrament in the *Book of the Courtier* that the soul kiss overruns amatory verse. The examples to follow are from writers who knew or could have known Castiglione's key passage, although not all apply the image to a description of pure or Platonic love. One who does so is Benedetto Varchi (1503–1565), in his time a much respected theorist of love and poetry. When he himself wished to describe oscular sensation, he was mindful of the courtly and

[p] "With these words she proceeds to gather with grieving lips the last remnants of the vital spirit that death is stealing as long as the slightest breath remains." XXIV, 82.

Neoplatonic dictum that a chaste lover desires nothing beyond the kiss. This is because the kiss brings the true lover the greatest gift he can hope for—an exchange of souls with the beloved:

> Quel ch'io sentii non so ridir: so bene
> Ch'io lasciai l'alma e ricevetti invece
> Cosa che avanza in terra ogni altro bene.
> O santissimo Amor, l'ultima spene
> È il baciar casto in te, ch'altro non lece
> A cortese amator, nè più conviene.^q

The poet Orsatto Giustinian seems to have written the sestet of a sonnet, in which he begs a kiss, fresh from a reading of Castiglione. In it we find Neoplatonic amatory conventions like the kiss regarded as a reward granted to chaste lovers and the idea that the desire to kiss derives from the yearning of souls to unite:

> Le dolci labbra (don ch'Amor destina
> A' più casti desir) l'anima brama
> Per unirsi a la vostra omai vicina:
> Nè voi punger devria men calda brama
> D'unir, provando gioia alta e divina,
> L'alma vostra a la mia, che tanto l'ama.^r

Such "Neoplatonizing," needless to say, is not always to be taken seriously when found in the poets. Giustinian, for example, is simply being amorous and gallant in the style and language of his day. The same poet could and did just as easily write uninhibited sensual love poetry, as his fine sonnet "Godianci amando, o mia diletta Flora" reveals.

For the most part, in fact, the Italian poets using the soul-kiss image and other "mystic" conceits reduce them to sensual terms. At the same time, these amatory *topoi* are often colored with the Petrarchan preciosity characteristic of the Cinquecento, an inevitable enough circumstance given the fusion and even confusion of Platonism

---

^q "I do not know how to describe what I felt; I do know that I left my soul and in return received something that is greater than all other good on earth. O most blessed Love, whose ultimate hope is the chaste kiss, beyond which nothing is lawful or fitting for a courtly lover." In *Lirici del Cinquecento*, ed. D. Ponchiroli (Turin, 1958), p. 241.

^r "The soul yearns for the sweet lips (gift that Love reserves for the most chaste desires), in order to be united to your [soul] ever near; nor should you feel a less intense desire for union—tasting deep and divine joy—between your soul and mine that loves it so." *Lirici del Cinquecento*, p. 165.

and Petrarchism in Renaissance poetry. This will be noted in the following verses by Girolamo Parabosco (1524–1557), in which the poet describes the state of ecstasy that would be his in kissing his lady.

> Quei bei coralli, anzi que' bei rubini,
> Che chiudon quelle perle Orientali;
> Falli a la bocca mia, falli vicini,
> Mentre punto e'l mio cor da mille strali
> Et mentre l'alma già sopra i confini,
> Per uscir fuor si stà, battendo l'ali,
> L'alma che tocca da quei labri bei
> Lieta sen volarà fra mezzo a Dei.[s]

Here are the precious trappings such as coral and rubies and Oriental pearls to indicate the lips and teeth of the lady. Here too is the ancient but perennial image of the amorous heart wounded by Love's arrows. But the soul-in-the-kiss image is presented in a way that is interesting enough to merit a brief elucidation. Even before the kiss, the poet feels his soul, attracted by the jewel-like mouth of the beloved, beating its wings at his lips from within as it seeks an egress. This introduces a metaphor of death, for the conceit of the soul's wings is clearly dependent upon the old image of the soul as a bird, which was especially common in representations of the soul departing by way of the mouth at the moment of death, usually to make its flight to the abode of the blessed. Hence the poet is saying that he is dying from desire or is close to a deathlike lover's swoon. If his lips (where his soul lies) were to be touched by his lady's lips, his soul would then be released and fly happily to the gods. All of which is the author's way of saying that his lady's kisses enrapture him to a Paradise of sensual delights.

More in keeping with the Fescennine vein of Neo-Latin poetry is Giovanni Mazzarelli who adapted the themes of the soul kiss and the transformation of lovers to a context of a wholly lascivious nature, although the verses are not without a redeeming touch of wit:

> I dolci basci e replicati spesso,
> Mille tronchi, amorosi e brevi detti,
> Tenersi i volti e corpi insieme stretti,

---

[s] "These fair corals, or rather, these fair rubies that enclose those Oriental pearls—bring them to my mouth, bring them near, while my heart is pierced by a thousand darts, and while my soul, already at its bounds, is ready to issue forth, beating its wings, my soul that if touched by your fair lips, will joyfully fly into the midst of the gods." *Quattro libri delle lettere amorose di M. Girolamo Parabosco* (Venice, 1607), Libro secondo, pp. 172–173.

Suggersi de le labbra il core espresso:
Un languir dolce e un mormorar sommesso,
Un star dubioso in qual de' nostri petti
Sian l'alme proprie, e 'n gli ultimi diletti
Non saper de nui dui qual sia se stesso.[t]

This seems to have been written in the teeth of Ficino's protest that the union and mutual indwelling of lovers can in no way be effected by a contact between bodies. But if at first the verses appear to be a travesty of the Neoplatonic theme of psychic exchange, in point of fact they effectively describe the character of the sexual ecstasy of lovers: the sharing of pleasure and the sensation of the fusion of the pair into one with an ensuing loss of identity of the self as each feels he has become the other.

With this we may turn to a particularly ribald example of the soul-in-the-kiss by the notorious and brilliant Pietro Aretino. In erotic literature, as we have seen, the expression "to die" had assumed the value of a sexual metaphor signifying the culmination of the love act. In a similar way the expiration of the soul in a kiss was a metaphor of the death of the self at the height of ecstasy. In the following prose passage from the *Ragionamenti*, the description of the sexual embrace is brought to a close with the kiss conceit used to signify precisely the moment of this sexual dying:

> Già i lor petti si congiungono sì fermamente insieme che i cuori di tutti e due si sbasciarono con uguale affetto. In quello essi si beccano dolcemente gli spiriti corsi ne le labbra per diletto, e beendosigli, gustavano le dolcezze del cielo, e i supradetti spiriti fecero segno di alle-grezza, mentre gli ahi, ahi, gli oimè, oimè; e, vita, e anima, il cuor mio, il muoio, lo aspetta che io fo, finirono. Onde cadde questo e quella lentamente, spirandosi l'un l'altro in bocca l'anima, con un sospiro.[u]

---

[t] "Sweet and oft-repeated kisses, a thousand broken loving and brief phrases; holding faces and bodies tightly together; sucking from each other's lips the heart's essence: a sweet languor and a subdued murmuring; a being in doubt as to which of our own souls are in; and in the ultimate delights not knowing which of us two is oneself." *Lirica d'amore italiana*, ed. S. Quasimodo (Milano, 1957), p. 379.

[u] "Their breasts were now joined so firmly together that the hearts of both of them kissed one another with equal affection. Whereupon they fed themselves gently on each other's spirit that had rushed to their lips because of the pleasure, and drinking them [the spirits] in, they tasted the sweet pleasures of heaven, and the aforesaid spirits gave signs of happiness during the 'ohs' and 'ahs'; and 'life,' 'soul of mine,' 'my heart,' 'I'm dying,' 'wait for me' were over. Whereupon both he and she sank slowly down, expiring their souls into one another with a sigh." *Piacevoli e capricciosi ragionamenti*, ed. A. P. Stella (Milan, 1944), p. 186.

Without doubt, Aretino took a satanic delight in so desecrating the soul-in-the-kiss conceit, for he was very much aware of its role as a Neoplatonic love sacrament, which he also parodied in a comedy entitled *Il filosofo*. The philosopher (whose name is nothing less than Plataristotile), for all his metaphysical acuity, is deceived by his wife, who has the following exchange with her lover after being greeted by him with a kiss:

POLIDORO: Ho basciato la vostra anima corsavi tra i labbri.

TESSA: Et io il vostro spirito apparso in mezzo de la bocca vostra.[v]

Among Italian writers, the supreme virtuosi of the poetry of kissing are Torquato Tasso, Battista Guarini, and Giovanni Battista Marino; in their verses, where kisses (of all varieties) know no end, the soul kiss occupies a particularly important place. The conceit was especially suited to the imagination of Tasso and his inimitable vein of elegiac sensuality. We may note it first in the following madrigal, where the poet, finding himself left with but a part of his soul after a kiss, entreats the beloved either to return the part she has enraptured from him or else draw from him the rest. It goes without saying that to do either requires another kiss:

> Baciami dolcemente.
> Ahi! che la debil vita
> Recidi e n' hai gran parte a me rapita.
> Crudel, perchè mi struggi?
> Rendi a la parte ancisa
> L'alma scevra e divisa,
> O l'avanzo di lei m'invola e suggi.[w]

It is typical of the declining age of the Italian Renaissance and especially of Tasso that even poetry in the manner of a courtier-like gallantry is often permeated with a languorous sensuality of a melancholy hue. Such a sensibility permeates the madrigal just quoted as it does these verses from a bucolic sonnet where we find Aminta, clasped in the arms of his beloved, offering her his soul expiring from him in sweet kisses:

[v] "Polidoro: I have kissed your soul as it rushed between your lips. Tessa: And I your spirit as it appeared in the middle of your mouth." *Teatro italiano antico*, IX (Milan, 1809), 342.

[w] "Kiss me gently. Alas! for you cut short my feeble life and have snatched the greater part of it from me. Cruel one, why do you destroy me? Return to the tormented part the separated and divided soul, or suck and steal from me the rest of it." *Lirici del Cinquecento*, ed. Carlo Bo (Milan, 1945), p. 391.

Cogliete, anima mia, quest'alma ch'io
Vi spiro in braccio. Ahi, che mi giunge al core,
Al core, ahi lasso, un venen dolce e rio!
Io 'l sento, ohimè: da queste labbra amore
Per troncar la radice al viver mio
In dolcissimi baci il manda fòre.[x]

This, of course, is yet another example of the voluptuous death of the lover. So, too, in the *Gerusalemme liberata*, Armida's kisses are such as to cause Rinaldo's death-ecstasy by drawing his soul from him into the enchantress's own body:

> . . . . Or l'alma fugge
> E 'n lei trapassa peregrina.[y]

Tasso is the great poet of the death of heroic and pastoral lovers. Invariably an aura of sensuality pervades his representations of death; or perhaps it would be better to say that in his romantic and elegiac vision, love always walks in the shadow of death. For him love's fulfillment is inseparable from death whether the latter is metaphorical or literal. The most famous case of this, as every reader will agree, is the description (*Ger. lib., XII*) of the fatal combat between Tancredi and Clorinda. No one can miss the parallel between the literal wounding and death of Clorinda and the metaphorical death of the act of love. There is no kiss in that episode, but elsewhere in the great epic we find the poet applying the soul-in-the-kiss image to another scene of a lover's death when Erminia discovers the wounded Tancredi and, believing him to be dead, kisses him in the hope that she will be able to exhale her own soul upon his lips. Her wish, however, is not that she may in this way revive her beloved, as so often is the case in the poetry of kissing, but rather that her own soul may be sent from Tancredi's lips to follow the path taken by his soul:

> Lecito sia ch'ora ti stringa, e poi
> Versi lo spirto mio fra i labri tuoi.
>
> Raccogli tu l'anima seguace;
> Drizzala tu dove la tua sen gio.[z]

---

[x] "Pluck, my soul, this spirit (soul) that I breathe to you in your arms. Alas, how my heart, my heart, alas, is filled with sweet and evil poison! I feel it, ah me! from these lips love sends it forth in sweetest kisses to cut the root of my life." *Opere di Torquato Tasso*, II, ed. B. Sozzi (Turin, 1956), 90.

[y] "Now the soul takes flight and like a pilgrim passes into her." XVI, 19.

[z] "Let me be allowed to clasp you now, and then to pour my spirit between your lips. Gather up my following soul, guide it whither yours has gone." XIX, 108:7–8; XIX, 109:1–2.

Erminia's wish, we see, is like that of heroines before her from Thisbe and Iseult to Isabella: to die with a kiss and so be joined with the beloved ever after.

Of the many Tassian examples of the soul-kiss image connected with the theme of the love-death, the most significant and beautiful one occurs at the beginning of canto II of the *Liberata*, in an episode charged with a mixture of religious and sexual imagery. In Jerusalem, where Christ suffered his mortal anguish ("la 've Cristo soffrì mortale affanno," I, 80:8), a chaste and stately virgin, Sofronia, is about to die the death of a martyr for the faith. By order of the Saracen ruler, she is to be burned at the stake. When the youth Olindo seeks to win her freedom by generously claiming responsibility for the act for which she has been condemned, the order is given for him to be tied to the same stake. It is at the moment of their imminent death (it matters little that they are eventually released) that Olindo makes known to Sofronia the extent of his love and desire. Though he could not share her bed, he will be her consort at the funeral pyre. His pity is not for himself but for her, since he will after all have the satisfaction of dying beside her. Yet his bliss would be complete and his martyrdom sweeter if, instead of being bound thus back to back, they could face one another; then in a kiss he could expire his soul into her, and she dying with him at the same time could breathe into him her last sigh:

> Ed oh mia sorte avventurosa a pieno!
> Oh fortunati miei dolci martìri!
> S'impetrerò che giunto seno a seno
> L'anima mia ne la tua bocca spiri:
> E venendo tu meco a un tempo meno
> In me fuor mandi gli ultimi sospiri.[a]

Olindo, it is true, is a martyr for a love that is not Christ's cause. His words are a confession of sensual love and a vision of sexual fulfillment; however, unlike many examples by writers punning on the sexual connotation of dying, they convey no prurient suggestion. On the other hand, the sincerity and the intensity of his desire and of his willingness to be love's holocaust is such that his passion can be said to merge into that mystical yearning to die and pass into the

---

[a] "And oh, completely blessed [would be] my lot! How fortunate my sweet martyrdom! If I could be granted that, joined breast to breast, I might breathe my soul into your mouth; and you, dying at the same moment with me, might send into me your final sighs." II, 35:1–6.

beloved which is characteristic of the deepest experience of sexual as of spiritual and divine love.[11]

Without being facetious or sacrilegious, one may compare Olindo's vision with a madrigal in which Tasso plays upon the theme of the dying of lovers to make of it throughout a sexual metaphor within which the expiration of the soul-breath in the kiss is used to signify the culmination of the sexual act. The motif is thus much like what we found in Aretino in idea and imagery, although the tone is withal more lyrical:

> Nel dolce seno de la bella Clori
> Tirsi, che del suo fine
> Già languendo sentìa l'ore vicine,
> Tirsi, levando gli occhi
> Ne' languidetti rai del suo desìo,
> —Anima, disse, omai beata mori.—
> Quand'ella—Ohimè! ben mio,
> Aspetta,—sospirò dolce anelando.—
> Ahi! crudo, ir dunque a morte
> Senza me pensi? io teco, e non me 'n pento,
> Morir promisi, e già moro, e già sento
> Le mortali mie scorte
> Perché l'una e l'altr'alma insieme scocchi.—
> Si stringe egli soave e sol risponde
> Con meste voci a le voci gioconde.
> Oh fortunati! l'un entro spirando
> Ne la bocca de l'altra, una dolce ombra
> Di morte gli occhi lor tremanti ingombra:
> E sì sentian, mancando i rotti accenti,
> Agghiacciar tra le labbra i baci ardenti.[b]

[b] "In fair Clori's sweet breast, Thyrsis, already failing, felt the hour of his end to be near; Thyrsis, raising his eyes to the languid beams of his desire, said: 'My soul, die blest at last.' Whereat she: 'Woe is me! Dear friend, wait for me,' she sighed, gasping softly. 'Alas! cruel one, will you then go to death without me? I promised to die with you and have no regrets. I am already dying, already feel my mortal escorts, so that both souls may depart together.' So he clasps her gently and replies only with mournful words to her words of joy. Oh happy [pair]! One expiring into the other's mouth, a sweet shadow of death darkens their trembling eyes; and as their broken voices fail, they feel their burning kisses congeal upon their lips." *Opere di T. Tasso*, II, ed. B. Sozzi (Turin, 1956), 92. As for the erotic death motif in Tasso's poem, there is a version in a madrigal by Battista Guarini, which, however, does without the soul kiss. Guarini's madrigal ("Tirsi morir volea"), which was often attributed to Tasso, is perhaps more nicely if frivolously turned than Tasso's own and was to enjoy the greater popularity in the seventeenth century when it was translated or imitated by several French and English authors, most notably by John Dryden in his song "Whil'st Alexis lay prest." See

There was a time—for more than a century—when Battista Guarini's *Pastor fido* was the most widely quoted book of Europe. It is so little read today, however, that we are likely to smile at rather than try to understand Cardinal Bellarmine's remark to Guarini that the play was more pernicious to Christianity than were the Lutherans, although this was something more than a boutade. Indeed, both Platonic love and Christian order are seductively subverted in this pastoral by a sensualistic immanentism where love appears in Lucretian style as a thoroughly natural and all-pervasive force driving things to seek sexual union. In this context (Act II, scene 1) Guarini offers us one of the most exquisite renderings of the soul-in-the-kiss conceit. The "shepherd" Mirtillo has been expatiating to his friend Ergasto on the delicious sensations of taste, smell, and touch that he experienced when he kissed the nymph Amarilli. His madrigalesque peroration terminates with a description of the climactic ecstatic swoon in which the lover's entire life was reduced to the enervating sensation of the kiss itself:

> Su queste labbra, Ergasto,
> Tutta sen venne allor l'anima mia;
> E la mia vita, chiusa
> In così breve spazio,
> Non era che un bacio,
> Onde restar le membra,
> Quasi senza vigor, tremanti e fioche.[c]

Chandler B. Beall, "A Quaint Conceit from Guarini to Dryden," in *Modern Language Notes*, LXIV (November, 1949), 461–468.

In Dryden's own *Don Sebastian* we read the thought "How can we better dye than close embrac'd / Sucking each other's souls while we expire," which seems to be inspired by Olindo's words in the *Gerusalemme liberata*.

[c] "On these lips, Ergasto, all my soul came forth then; and my life, contained in so small a space, was no more than a kiss. Wherefore my limbs remained almost without strength, trembling and weak."

Guarini's conceit is not entirely original, for something of it is found earlier in a madrigal by Gian Francesco Fabri, who speaks of his life being enclosed within the lips of his lady:

> Dolci basci soavi,
> Che quella parte, ond'io
> Vivo, et respiro, hor mi togliete, hor date,
> Candide perle amate,
> Ch'accogliete tra voi lo spirto mio,
> Et voi labra rosate
> Dolci amorose chiavi
> Ch'in poco spatio mia vita chiudete.

Rime di diversi nobili huomini et eccellenti poeti nella lingua Thoscana (Venice, 1547), Libro secondo, fol. 60[vo].

In view of the fact that Guarini appears in Romei's dialogue as the expounder of the spiritual Neoplatonic kiss (see chapter 5), the thoroughly sensualistic interpretation accorded the motif in his own work is all the more suggestive; and it is a matter of considerable interest that in his commentary to the play Guarini explicated his kiss passage in terms of the psychology of his time in order to justify the image of the soul being on the lips and in the kiss. His discourse amounts to a scientific definition of the physical ecstasy or *ravissement* he was describing: "Although the soul cannot be separated from any part of the body, nevertheless, it seems experientially that it may be in that part whither desire carries it, and therefore he says that it was wholly in that kiss and wholly in that mouth; and as in evidence of this, the other parts of the body remained faint, as if they had been abandoned by it [the soul], and, as he says, trembling."[12] There can be no real separation of the soul from the body while one is of this life, but experientially it seems that the soul betakes itself to where it is led by desire or love. In this case desire has carried the soul to the lover's lips, or rather to the kiss itself; hence the rest of the body appears trembling and lifeless. This, we note, is old psychology indeed, and still valid. It is exactly what we found in the medieval Christian formula of ecstatic love: "Puto, anima mea, quod verius es ubi amas quam ubi animas." But here, too, Dante—an invaluable and inevitable touchstone for the expression of the amoristic psychology of any period—impinges upon our mind. How can we not think that in Guarini's description of a lover trembling in an ecstatic kiss, Francesca's terse, dramatic, and compelling hendecasyllable—"La bocca mi baciò tutto tremante"—has been transposed into another key and another (totally hedonistic) ethos.[13]

Giambattista Marino, the Italian baroque virtuoso, aspired to outdo all other poets in all themes. Such an ambition was bound to include in its sphere the theme of the kiss, which Marino perhaps more than any other poet, including Johannes Secundus, was to elaborate *ad nauseam*. It is no wonder then that the particular conceit of the soul kiss recurs with high frequency in his verse; and, as may be expected, with Marino the image is used in the most venereal contexts. It is symptomatic that one of his best-known poems—it is the poem that catapulted him to an early and massive popularity—is precisely the

Canzone dei baci (beginning "O baci avventurosi") in which he refers wittily but salaciously to the kissing lovers as having two "souls" in one mouth, "E più d'un'alma in una bocca asconde," a pun easily enough understood on its own, but which is the more appreciated by recalling Ariosto's tonguing couple (see above).

The *Canzone* describes an interminable oscular orgy in which, among other things, the lover's heart and life is bandied to and fro by the kisses of his mistress:

> Alfin col bacio il cor mi porge e prende
> E la vita col cor mi fura e rende.[d]

But the poet is led finally by those kisses to that pleasure which fuses souls and grafts bodies together:

> Di bacio in bacio a quel piacer mi desta,
> Che l'alme insieme allaccia e i corpi innesta.[e]

It is then that the poet's soul, drawn and overcome by so irresistible a delight, comes in a sigh to its passageway—the poet's mouth—ready to escape. Fortunately, it is met and stopped by his lady's soul. But a happy "death" ensues nonetheless, as his soul drowns in the sweet "shower" of joy that is infused into him from the lovely one's ruby lips:

> Vinta allor dal diletto
> Con un sospir se 'n viene
> L'anima al varco, e 'l proprio albergo oblia;
> Ma con pietoso affetto
> La 'ncontra ivi e ritiene
> L'anima amica, che s'oppon tra via;
> E 'n lei, ch'arde e desia
> Già languida e smarrita,
> D'un vasel di rubin tal pioggia versa
> Di gioia, che sommersa
> In quel piacer gentile,
> Cui presso ogni altro è vile,

---

[d] "Finally with the kiss she gives and takes my heart, and with the heart steals and restores my life."

[e] "From kiss to kiss she awakens me to that delight which binds souls and grafts bodies together."

> Baciando l'altra, ch'a baciar la 'nvita,
> Alfin ne more, e quel morire è vita.[f]

Kissing the soul that has invited it to kiss, the lover's soul dies but finds its life in that voluptuous death.

In another canzone which is a lesson in philematology (*Baci dolci, et amorosi*), Marino borrowed from Guarini the remarkable conceit of the lover being transformed not into the beloved but into the kiss itself, as an expression of the hedonistic principle of reducing life to pure sensation. The speaker is Thyrsis whose heart has been tossed between death and life in the kisses of Phyllis:

> Tanto diletto io sento
> Mentre bacio, e ribacio,
> Che per farmi contento
> A pien quand'io ti bacio
> Trasformarmi vorrei tutto in un bacio.[g]

Phyllis's desire for sensual delights is equal to that of Thyrsis, and in a literal rage of voluptuousness she replies that in the kiss, souls no less than mouths can kiss and bite one another. The image may strike us as grotesque, but it is not without efficacy and not without foundation in the anthropophagic character of the kiss:

> Qualhor con dolce rabbia
> Bocca si bacia, o morde,
> Su le baciate labbra

---

[f] "Vanquished then by pleasure, my soul comes with a sigh to the passageway, and forgets its own dwelling place; but with compassion, my lady's soul, putting itself in the way, meets it and keeps it there. And into it [my soul], that now languid and bewildered burns and desires, she pours such a shower of joy from a ruby cup that, drowned in that gentle pleasure compared to which all else is base, and kissing the other soul that invites it to kiss, finally dies, and that death is life." *Marino e i Marinisti*, ed. G. Ferrero (Milan, 1954), pp. 354–355.

[g] "I feel such great delight while I kiss and kiss again, that to become completely happy when I kiss you I would wish to be transformed entirely into a kiss." *La lira, rime del Cavaliere Marino* (Venice, 1678), p. 262. Along with Guarini's passage, Marino's conceit that the lover be fully transformed into the kiss may be contrasted with a Neoplatonizing conceit in Michelangelo's sonnet "Ben posson gli occhi mie presso e lontano" where because it is the eyes that enjoy the beauty of the beloved the poet concludes with a prayer to be transformed wholly into an eye so that every part of him will be able to enjoy her:

> Deh, se tu puo' nel ciel quante tra noi,
> Fa' del mie corpo tutto un occhio solo;
> Né fie poi parte in me che non ti goda.

Van con voglia concorde
A mordersi, a baciar l'anime ingorde.[h]

But where this and like amatory conceits are most cloyingly exploited by Marino is in the extraordinary love scene between Adonis and Venus in the *Adone* (VIII, stanzas 116–149), which is the last spectacular effort of the Renaissance-Baroque world to represent nature in pagan sensualistic terms. In making her invitation to Adonis, Venus employs such familiar commonplaces as love's power to unite two souls or two hearts in one, the psychic exchange of lovers' hearts, and the dying unto the self so as to live in the beloved:

Fansi in virtù d'un'amorosa fede
Due alme un'alma e son due cori un core.
Cangia il cor, cangia l'alma albergo e sede,
In altrui vive, in se medesma more.[i]

But the invitation soon passes from a spiritual to a carnal level. If there is an exchange and union of hearts, why not then of bodies too?

Se ti prendi il mio core e 'l tuo mi dai,
Perchè de' corpi un corpo anco non fai?[j]

Love is the maker or inspirer of the kiss, the heart distils it, the lips effect it, but it is the soul more than the mouth that enjoys it. The kiss couples souls, but the context is anything but Neoplatonic or mystical. Indeed, the soul kiss is at the same time the lingual kiss for Marino. Hearts and tongues are exchanged simultaneously, and the sexual orgasm of the lover is what is intended when it is said that the kiss incites the soul to die. But clever lovers hold back their death until both can expire together:

[h] "Whenever with sweet frenzy mouths kiss or bite each other, upon the kissed lips greedy souls come with mutual desire to bite and kiss."
[i] "Through the power of an amorous faith two souls are made one soul. Two hearts are one heart. The heart changes, the soul changes dwelling place and seat, lives in another and dies in itself." 116:1–6.
[j] "If you take my heart and give me yours, why do you not then make one body of our bodies?" 119:7–8. Compare the following verses from Robert Browning's *The Ring and the Book*, where the same casuistry appears:

Because of our souls' yearning that we meet
And mix in soul through flesh, which yours and mine
Wear and impress, and make their visible selves,
All which means, for the love of you and me,
Let us become one flesh, being one soul!
(VII, 774–778)

211

> Treman gli spirti infra i più vivi ardori
> Quando il bacio a morir l'anima spinge.
> Mutan bocca le lingue e petto i cori,
> Spirto con spirto e cor con cor si stringe.
> Palpitan gli occhi e de le guance i fiori
> Amoroso pallor scolora e tinge;
> E morendo talor gli amanti accorti
> Ritardano il morir per far due morti.[k]

Venus then explains to Adonis that as they lie dying and their souls are escaping by their mouths (the typical image of real death), they can convert their mutual death into new life by way of yet another kiss in which the departing soul of each will pass into the other:

> Da te l'anima tua morendo fugge,
> Io moribonda in su 'l baciar la prendo,
> E 'n quel vital morir, che ne distrugge,
> Mentre la tua mi dai la mia ti rendo.[l]

Adonis is an apt pupil, and since he is being initiated into these mysteries of love in deed as well as word, he himself is able to exult in this life-giving death (*vital morir*) wherein the dying lover is re-suscitated in the beloved:

> Morendo io vivrò in te, tu in me vivrai,
> Così ti renderò quanto mi dai.[m]

After many kisses, deaths, renewed kisses, and resuscitations, the lovers are finally rapt into the heaven of love (Venus's own) in a last sexual spasm:

> Stillansi l'alme in tepidetto umore,
> Opprime i sensi un dilettoso oblio.
> Tornan fredde le lingue e smorti i volti,
> E vacillano i lumi al ciel travolti.

---

[k] "The spirits tremble under most intense ardors when the kiss spurs the soul to die. Tongues change mouths, hearts [change] breasts, spirit embraces spirit, heart [embraces] heart. Eyes flutter, and an amorous pallor drains the color and paints again the flowers of the cheeks; and the able lovers as at times they die withhold their dying to make two deaths." 131:1–8.

[l] "Your soul as you die flees from you; I, dying, catch it in kissing, and in that vital death that destroys it, while you give me yours I give mine back to you." 132:1–4.

[m] "Dying, I shall live in you, you in me will live. Thus I shall return as much as you give me." 135:7–8.

> Tramortiscon di gioia ebre e languenti
> L'anime stanche al ciel d'amor rapite.[n]

Again one naturally calls to mind the artistic representations of the ecstatic deaths and love-wounds of saints as well as that spiritual eroticism of religious writers which received some of its most intense accents in the Counter Reformation or the Baroque age. The analogy and the interplay, perhaps even the confusion, between religious and sexual love were as characteristic of this period as of the late Middle Ages. But in this central episode of Marino's *Adone*, as in his *Canzone dei baci*, the secularization of mystic (Christian and Neoplatonic) amatory conceits has reached extravagant proportions, utterly unredeemed by anything like the psychophysical love symbiosis found in certain of the medieval love legends (e.g., Tristan and Iseult) as it is lacking in the rich ambiguity of the Tassian elegiac-voluptuous surrender to the love-death.[14]

We must end this excursion into Italian poetry with Marino's osculatory bravura, for although kissing continued to be a common subject with Italian authors, nothing new was added to the particular images that interest us.[15] Hence it will be more profitable to turn to the fortune of the conceits in French literature.

French Authors: Badinage and Ravissement

The earliest Renaissance poet of France in whom the soul-in-the-kiss motif occurs is Clément Marot, who applied it neatly to his blending of sensuality and badinage, witness these verses from the charming rondeau "Du baiser de s'amie" (1524):

> Bref mon esprit sans cognoissance d'ame
> Vivoit alors sur la bouche à ma Dame,
> Dont se mouroit le corps enamouré:
> Et si la levre eust gueres demouré
> Contre la mienne, elle m'eust succé l'ame
> En la baisant.[o]

[n] "The souls are distilled in a warm moisture, a delightful oblivion weighs upon the senses. Tongues turn cold and faces pale, eyes waver, faced toward the heavens. The weary souls, languishing and drunk with joy, now swoon, ecstasied into love's heaven." 147:5–8; 148:1–2.

[o] "My spirit, in a total trance, lived then on my lady's mouth, whereby my body full of love was dying; and if her lip had stayed a little longer against mine, she would have drawn out my soul in kissing it." *Poètes du XVIe siècle*, ed. Albert-Marie Schmidt (Paris, 1953), p. 35.

Here already is something of the theme we saw perfected in Guarini and Marino. In kissing, the lover's spirit (vital spirit) has left the body lifeless because it makes its life on the lady's lips. If the kiss were to last any longer, the lover's soul would be drawn into his lady's body.

Less "innocent" is a quatrain (*Epigrammes*, cclxix) in which Marot, punning on the theme of love as a desire for union, defines the kiss as an incitement to lovers to fuse into one in the sexual embrace:

> Baiser souvent, n'est ce pas grand plaisir?
> Dites ouy, vous aultres amoureux:
> Car du baiser vous provient le desir
> De mettre en un ce qui estoit en deux.[p]

After Marot, the kiss conceit appears briefly and in simple form in verses from Maurice Scève's *Délie*. The kiss has drawn the poet's soul to his lips:

> L'esprit vouloit, mais la bouche ne peut
> Prendre congé, et te dire: à Dieu, Dame!
> Lors d'un baiser si tres doulx se repeut,
> Que jusqu'au bout des levres tyra l'Ame.[q]

There are several places in Scève's *Délie* where Neoplatonic love conventions are evident, but inasmuch as the kiss conceit does not figure in them, we may forgo treatment of them here. However, their presence and the overall context of the work would seem to indicate that the poet has used the kiss conceit primarily as a Neoplatonic convention rather than as a sensual image, although it also partakes of the latter.

A writer who, like Scève, was active at Lyons and who does demand our closer attention is the poetess Louise Labé. In her passionate love poetry the kiss conceit is used to remarkable and vital effect in conjunction with the themes of the union and psychic exchange of lovers and the lover's ecstatic death. There are two sonnets to consider, of which the first deserves to be quoted in its entirety if we would appreciate the personal and original way in which the amatory conceits are employed:

---

[p] "Kissing often—is not this a great pleasure? Say yes—all you lovers; for from the kiss arises the desire in you to make into one that which was two." *Oeuvres complètes*, III, ed. P. Jannet (Paris, 1873), 112.

[q] "The spirit is willing, but the mouth cannot take leave and say to you, 'Farewell, my lady.' When one may have again so sweet a kiss that it draws the soul to the tip of the lips." *Delie*, CCCLXIV, in *Poètes du XVIe siècle*, p. 196.

Oh si j'estois en ce beau sein ravie
    De celui là pour lequel vois mourant:
Si avec lui vivre le demeurant
    De mes cours jours ne m'empeschoit envie:
Si m'acollant me disoit, chere Amie,
    Contentons nous l'un l'autre! s'asseurant
    Que ja tempeste, Euripe, ne Courant
Ne nous pourra desjoindre en notre vie:
Si de mes bras le tenant acollé,
    Comme du lierre est l'arbre encercelé,
    La mort venoit, de mon aise envieuse,
Lorsque, souef, plus il me baiseroit,
    Et mon esprit sur ses levres fuiroit,
    Bien je mourrois, plus que vivante, heureuse.[r]

The sonnet is built upon a series of conditions that takes up the first thirteen lines of the poem (*si j'estois . . . , si avec lui . . . , si m'accollant . . . , si de mes bras . . . , lorsque . . .*) and prepares the last line's apparently paradoxical conclusion that the lover would be happier in death than in life. The paradox, however, resolves itself by a play on the meanings of the word *die*. At the outset the lover is "dying" in the unrealized desire to be joined to or, better, rapt into the beloved. Dying here (vs. 2) signifies the anguish resulting from unfulfillment and separation. The various images that are presented in the following verses to line ten develop the idea of reciprocity and the union of the lovers (in a sensual Ovidian fashion) against possible sources of division. In line eleven death is again introduced, not now, however, as signifying the languishing and suffering of the unrequited lover of line two, but as a threat to the union envisaged in the lover's daydream ("la mort . . . de mon aise envieuse"). But death as a threat may be more apparent than real, or it may by a pun be turned into victory. The fact is that the union fancied by the lover is the sexual union (the image of entwining the beloved as ivy entwines a tree is, of course, quite clearly a sexual symbol); and death is to intervene just

---

[r] "Oh, if I were rapt into that fine breast of him for whom I am dying; if envy did not prevent me from living with him for the rest of my short days; if, embracing me, he would say: 'Dear beloved, let us make each other happy, being confident that neither storm, nor [straits of] Euripus, nor [ocean] current can disunite us while we live.' If, while I held him in my arms as a tree is encircled by ivy, death, envious of my happiness, should come, while he sweetly continued to kiss me and my spirit took flight upon his lips—why then, I would be happier in so dying than I am in life." *Poètes du XVIᵉ siècle*, p. 285.

here. The literal sense of death is merged into its metaphorical meaning of the climax of the sexual embrace. The clinch or punning image by which this is effected is nothing less than the soul-in-the-kiss conceit, which is employed to signify the ecstatic death, that is, orgasm, of the lover. What the poem says in the sestet is this: If, while I am clasped in a close embrace with my beloved and he is kissing me sweetly, my soul should flee from me to his lips (i.e., if I should *die*), I would in so *dying* be happier than I am in life. The poetess has set up the conditions in which she would be content to die, or, we may say, she has specified and set up the kind of death she desires against the kind of death she undergoes in reality (languishing in unrequited love). What she wishes is the death desired by all lovers, that which comes at the moment of fulfillment and which, mystically or sexually, is both a possessing of the beloved and a surrendering of the self. To expire her spirit on the lips of the beloved would be to die the perfect death of the lover. Like the mystics of the *mors osculi*, but in a quite different context, the poetess dreams of dying by the kiss of her *lord* and being rapt into his bosom.

The sonnet "Baise m'encor, rebaise moy et baise" is an unusually fine example of the Renaissance revival of the Catullan invitation to osculatory delights, availing itself of a Neoplatonic mystico-amatory convention. The last eight verses are especially relevant to our interest:

> Ainsi meslans nos baisers tant heureus
> Jouissons nous l'un de l'autre à notre aise.
> Lors double vie à chacun en suivra.
> Chacun en soy et son ami vivra.
> Permets m'Amour penser quelque folie:
> Tousjours suis mal, vivant discrettement,
> Et ne me puis donner contentement,
> Si hors de moy ne fay quelque saillie.[8]

In the previous sonnet the vision was one of being rapt into the beloved by a kiss; here the poetess imagines a mutual indwelling of the

---

[8] "And so mingling our kisses so happily, let us enjoy each other at our pleasure. Then a double life will come to each. Each will live in himself and in the beloved. Permit me, my Love, to entertain some mad thoughts; I am always unhappy, living discreetly, and cannot give myself ease unless I make some leap outside of myself." *Ibid.*, p. 287. Louise Labé's sonnets have received much attention of late. For a full account and for an eloquent interpretation see Enzo Giudici, *Louise Labé e l'école lyonnaise* (Naples, 1964), especially the chapter "Il messaggio amoroso e poetico della Belle Cordelière." The sonnet "Baise m'encore . . ." is given particular attention.

lovers. Although there is no explicit mention of souls, it is clear that the idea depends on the soul-in-the-kiss conceit: the double life of these lovers—each living in himself and in the other—results from a mingling of kisses. At this point the erotic fantasy is called a "folie" for which Louise asks the indulgence of her beloved. As in the previous sonnet, we are told here that in the world of reality she knows nothing but the anguish of unrequited love which she can alleviate only occasionally by "going outside herself." That, one would think, is her "folie"; and so it is, except that it too refers to the fantasy's wish-fulfillment of living in the beloved. To go, indeed, "to leap" outside oneself (in a kiss) is to experience an ecstasy (which is also a "folie"). Thus the sonnet concludes with a witticism that colors the whole. The "saillie" of the poetess is indeed a *saillie d'esprit*.

Even before Guarini and Marino in Italy, the French poets of the Pléiade, taking their cue chiefly from Johannes Secundus and the Italian Neo-Latin poets, wrote ad infinitum on the delights of kissing.[16] It is not surprising therefore that the soul-kiss motif and the accompanying conceits of the union, transformation, and ecstasy or sexual dying of lovers should be well represented in their verse.[17] Among French poets, in fact, the soul kiss is generally laden with the heaviest sensual significance, and it may even be said that they outdo the Italians in their scabrous punning on the theme. In connection with this, it is to be remembered that in France, Platonism or Neoplatonism (in matters of love) never became as deeply entrenched or as widespread as in Italy and England. As a fad among the French poets, its heyday lasted but a few years around the middle of the sixteenth century, and its love conventions were for the most part rejected with irreverent delight by those poets of the Pléiade who had themselves first indulged in many of the Neoplatonic themes imported from Italy.[18] Joachim Du Bellay's famous attack in the poem "Contre les Pétrarquistes" is directed against "Platonic love" as much as against the Petrarchizing mannerism of style:

> J'ay oublié l'art de Pétrarquizer
> Je veulx d'Amour franchement deviser.[t]

Petrarchism and Neoplatonism, as we have already noted, were in fact interwoven into one general poetic mannerism. In the revulsion

[t] "I have forgotten the art of Petrarchizing. I wish to talk realistically of love."

against Petrarchizing Neoplatonic concepts of love, Du Bellay's muse could go to the other extreme of Ovidian sensuality, as in the following verses from a *Baiser* ("Quand ton col de couleur de rose") where the poet revels in the nectarine tongue kiss, and, perhaps partly with Ariosto's verse in mind (see above), speaks of gathering the flower of the beloved's breath from her lips:

> Puis quand j'approche de la tienne
> Ma levre, et que si pres je suis,
> Que la fleur recueiller je puis
> De ton haleine Ambrosienne:
> Quand le soupir de ces odeurs,
> Ou noz deux langues qui se jouënt
> Moitement folastrent et mouënt,
> Evente mes doulces ardeurs,
> Il me semble estre assis à table
> Avec les Dieux, tant suis heureux,
> Et boire à longs traicts savoureux
> Leur doulx breuvage delectable.[u]

This is the closest Du Bellay comes to the soul-in-the-kiss image as such, although one notes that the poet develops with considerable efficacy the theme of being made an equal of the gods by virtue of the ecstasy-inducing ambrosia of his lady's kisses.

The poetry of Pierre Ronsard offers so many examples of the soul-kiss conceit—invariably as a mark of a frankly sensual love—that we are faced with an embarrassment of riches in selecting a few significant examples. Generally, Ronsard's use of the image can be traced to a specific source—Marullo and, more often, Secundus—but even when he seems to be translating, Ronsard is so genuinely a poet that the result never seems slavishly derivative. This may be seen, for example, in the chanson "Harsoir, Marie, en prenant maugré toy / Un doux baiser," a poem closely modeled on Marullo's popular poem "Suaviolum invitae rapio dum, casta Naera" quoted above.[19] So too the ode "Ma dame ne donne pas," although patterned on Secundus's

---

[u] "Then when I bring my lip to yours and am so close that I can pluck the flower of your ambrosian breath. When the sigh of these scents, where our two tongues playing with each other moistly sport and pout, fans my sweet ardors, I am so happy that I seem to be sitting at table with the gods, and drinking with long delicious draughts their sweet delectable beverage." *Divers jeux rustiques*, ed. H. Chamard (Paris, 1947), pp. 92–93.

Basia IV–V, has a uniquely Ronsardian freshness, especially in the lighthearted play on the idea of the soul being sucked up in a kiss.[20] The latter image, which is frequent in Ronsard, is sometimes invoked in order to express a paroxysmal passion:

> Marie, baisez-moy: non, ne me baisez pas,
> Mais tirez moy le coeur de vostre douce haleine;
> Non, ne le tirez pas, mais hors de chaque veine
> Succez-moy toute l'ame esparse entre vos bras.[v]

The kiss coupled with the image of dying as a sexual metaphor is likewise found more than once in Ronsard's poetry. In the ode "O pucelle plus tendre" the poet's life clings to his beloved's lips, and in a mutual embrace and kiss the lovers will die together:

> Un baiser mutuel
> Nous soit perpetuel.
> Ny le temps, ny l'envie
> D'autre amour desirer,
> Ne pourra point ma vie
> De voz lévres tirer;
> Ains serrez demourrons,
> Et baisant nous mourrons.
> Tous deux morts en mesme heure.
> Voirrons le lac fangeux,
> Et l'obscure demeure
> De Pluton l'outrageux,
> Et les champs ordonnez
> Aux amans fortunez.[w]

The poem, inspired by Secundus' *Basium II*, develops the motif of the lovers being transported after their mutual death to the Elysian fields of fortunate lovers, a realm where, unlike that of Dante's Francesca and Paolo, "les amans ont de bien." This motif was especially

[v] "Kiss me, Marie; no, do not kiss me, but draw out my heart with your sweet breath; no, do not draw it out, but from each vein suck all my soul, languid between your arms." *Oeuvres complètes*, I, 150. Similarly in the ode "Ma petite Nymphe Macée," the poet says of his lady's kiss: "Tu suces l'ame et le sang" (*ibid.*, I, 433). Cf. Aulus Gellius: "sugis animam," and Secundus: "animam sugere suaviolis" (*Eleg.*, I, 5).

[w] "May a mutual kiss be forever ours. Neither time nor the desire to long for other love will ever draw my life away from your lips; and so shall we stay embraced and we shall die while kissing, both of us dead in the same hour. We shall see the muddy lake of Pluto's dark abode, and the fields decreed for fortunate lovers." *Ibid.*, II, 702.

popular with Ronsard and the other French poets. For example, in the chanson "Plus estroit que la vigne à l'ormeau," the same erotic dream occurs: the lovers die on a kiss and are borne in the same bark to Elysium where they are honored by the holy band of ancient lovers—"la troupe sainte autrefois amoureuse."[21]

That to die on a kiss was a constant desire in the poet's erotic dream-world is attested by the opening quatrain of a sonnet where Ronsard asserts that he would gladly die in the embrace of his beloved if he could, while kissing her, expire his soul into her body:

> Se je trespasse entre tes bras, Madame,
> Je suis content: aussi ne veux-je avoir
> Plus grand honneur au monde, que me voir,
> En te baisant, dans ton sein rendre l'ame.[x]

It is not easy to say whether there is here a punning on dying, kissing, and *sein* which would make for a *double entente* ambiguity. The verses contain a thought that is similar to what we have found in Louise Labé, although in their somewhat formal gallantry they are quite different from the intellectual yet highly emotionally charged conceits of the poetess.

Among other poets of the Pléiade, Jean-Antoine Baïf and Rémy Belleau pillaged the *Basia* of Secundus for their own kiss poetry. The *Second livre des amours* of Baïf consists chiefly of *baisers* with occasional references to the soul-in-the-kiss motif, which the author manages to treat with a scurrilous inventiveness second to none.

It was an ancient belief of the Stoics that the male seed contained the soul-stuff, and it was evidently something of the sort that was in Baïf's mind when, describing the sexual embrace within the metaphors of the mingling of souls and dying, he spoke of his soul passing over into his mistress by way of seminal emission. This left him dead. Fortunately, however, his mistress knew the art of reviving him by returning his soul to him in kisses:

> O doux plaisir plein de doux pensement,
> Quand la douceur de la douce meslée,
> Etreint et joint, l'ame en l'ame mellée,
> Le corps au corps accouplé doucement.

---

[x] "If I die in your arms my lady, I am happy; therefore I wish to have no greater honor in the world than to see myself, while kissing you, give up my soul in your breast." *Ibid.,* I, 34.

O douce mort! ô doux trepassement!
Mon ame alors de grand' joye tremblée,
De moy dans toy s'ecoulant a l'emblée,
Puis haut, puis bas, quiert son ravissement.
Quand nous ardentz, Meline, d'amour forte,
Moy d'estre en toy, toy d'en toy tout me prendre,
Par celle part, qui dans toy entre plus,
Tu la reçoys, moy restant masse morte:
Puis vient ta bouche en ma bouche la rendre,
Me ranimant tous mes membres perclus.^y

In another of Baïf's poems ("Vivons, Mignarde, vivons . . ."),
lover and beloved "die" not simultaneously, but alternately. The advantage of this is that there is always one surviving partner ready to
revive the other by means of the soul kiss. Even more than the preceding poem, the "douce rage d'amour continuel" expressed by this
dithyramb is a riotous desecration of the Neoplatonic kiss and the
Ficinian theory of the transfusion of lovers' souls into each other with
accompanying deaths and resuscitations.[22] Yet Baïf has merely done
what we have seen other poets do in their rejection of Platonic love:
he has seized upon the equivocal Neoplatonic sacrament, the soul kiss
(although it also came to him from libertine sources) and put it to work
in the cause of an unambiguous sensual love. But he has done it with
even less reserve than most. This is a good place to remark that when
Italian and French poets of a parodistic or sensually oriented vision
adopted the image of death as a metaphor to signify sexual orgasm,
they were shooting barbs not only at the current Neoplatonic love
psychology but also at the "Petrarchan" convention of the lover's
daily and multiple deaths because of unrequited love.

The same procedure can be observed in certain poems by Rémy
Belleau, although in the following verses, inspired by Secundus, the
motifs of the kiss and the exchange of souls are handled in a more
subdued and elegant fashion. As the lovers kiss, their souls will live

---

^y "O sweet pleasure, full of sweet thought, when sweetness from the sweet
mingling, embraces and unites soul mixed with soul, body sweetly joined with
body. O sweet death! O sweet passing! My soul then shaken by great joy,
flowing at once from me into you, now high, now low, seeks its ecstasy. When we
are on fire with powerful love, Meline, I to be in you, you to take me wholly into
you, by that part which goes farthest into you and you receive it [i.e., my soul],
while I remain a lifeless mass; then your mouth comes to return it within my
mouth, bringing life back to all my paralyzed limbs." *Les amours de Jean-Antoine
de Baïf*, ed. M. Augé-Chiquet (Paris, 1909), p. 147.

in one another, and one same breath will animate their bodies or hearts:

> Quant je presse en baisant ta levre à petis mors
> Une part de mon ame est vivante en la tienne,
> Une part de la tienne est vivante en la mienne,
> Et un mesme soupir fait vivre nos deux cors.[z]

These lines echo *Basium XIII* of Secundus. But perhaps Belleau is better remembered here for the way in which he elaborated the kiss of the Song of Songs in his paraphrase of that book of the Bible. He has the bride speak at the outset in the following manner:

> Doncques mon cher Espous, mon mignon, ma chere ame
> En fin est de retour: que sa bouche de basme
> Me donne promptement pour ma flamme appaiser,
> Le nectar ensucré d'un amoureux baiser.[a]

In the dedicatory preface to his paraphrase, which he called *Eclogues sacrées prises du Cantique des Cantiques*, the author says that the bride is the Church and the Bridegroom is Christ. Readers, he adds, ought not to appropriate these verses "to their own personal advantage and according to their particular [earthly] affection," for the theme is that of "a love that is totally divine and spiritual." Be that as it may, Belleau's rendering is such that its manner is hardly to be distinguished from that of his secular love poems, and one can best evaluate the above verses by applying to them the terse comment Belleau made on a sonnet by Ronsard ("Marie, levez-vous . . ."): "Ce ne sont que mignardises."

Over and over the Pléiade poets meet with the erotic life-in-death kiss that enraptures them out of themselves and into the beloved— "ainsi ravi / Hors de moy dans elle je vy."[23] But it were best to give some brief attention to writers not in their orbit, since, after all, such conceits were universal.

---

[z] "When I press your lip kissing it with little bites, one part of my soul is living in yours, one part of yours is living in mine, and one same sigh [of love] makes both our hearts [or bodies] live." *La Bergerie*, ed. Doris Delacourcelle (Geneva, 1954), p. 121. Belleau's verses echo *Basium XIII* of Secundus. Other examples of the conceit in *La Bergerie* are common. See *ibid.*, pp. 118–119. Belleau also has the theme of lovers dying on a kiss and passing together over Styx. See the first poem of the *Premiere journee de la Bergerie*.

[a] "Then my dear Spouse, my love, my dear soul has returned at last; let his mouth full of balm quickly give me to quench my flame the sweetened nectar of a loving kiss." *Oeuvres poétiques de Rémy Belleau*, II, ed. Ch. Marty-Laveaux (Paris, 1878), 297, 299.

A poet who dallied with the soul-kiss conceit on several occasions was Jean Vauquelin. At least once he manages to add an original note of piquancy to the well-worn theme. In a poem in which a lady is invited to embraces and kisses, we have the idea of love reducing duality to mutuality and unicity by joining souls in a kiss; since there is no longer any thine and mine in such a fusion, in kissing one another each of the lovers will be kissing himself:

> Faisons encor s'entrebaiser
> Nos ames pour les appaiser:
> Amour puissant qui les assemble
> Les sçaura bien lier ensemble:
> Ouvrier il les detrempera,
> Et de deux une il en fera,
> Qui n'aura plus, ô belle Iolle,
> Qu'en [sic] mesme esprit mesme parolle.
> Me baisant vous vous baiserez,
> Et me Salmacis vous serez.[b]

The oscular-sexual fantasy indulged in by the poet is in truth a vision of a perfect psychophysical symbiosis. The Salmacis the poet would have his lady be to him was the nymph who, finding herself spurned by Hermaphroditus, threw herself upon him while he was bathing and clung so tenaciously and strongly as to become fused with him, resulting in the creature partaking of both sexes.

One of the better-known French examples of the soul-kiss commonplace is found in a poem by Vincent Voiture. Although there is nothing original or unusual about the treatment of the conceit itself, it is freer than most French examples from an oppressive sensuality, being toned down by Voiture to the key of elegant drawing-room eroticism.

> Mon ame sur ma lèvre estoit lors toute entiere,
> Pour savourer le miel qui sur la vostre estoit;

[b] "Let us also make our souls kiss one another to bring them peace; mighty Love who brings them together will be able to bind them to each other; like a craftsman he will temper them and from the two of them he will make one, which, o fair Iolle, will no longer have but one same spirit, one same word. In kissing me you will kiss yourself, and you will be my Salmacis." *Les diverses poésies de Jean Vauquelin Sieur de la Fresnaie*, II, ed. J. Travers (Caen, 1870), 547. See also p. 566 where the lover says to the beloved while kissing her: "de moy ravi / Tout entier dans toy ie vi."

> Mais en me retirant, elle resta derriere,
> Tant de ce doux plaisir l'amorce l'arrestoit.[c]

With Tristan l'Hermite we are again in the Ovidian-Catullan spirit of the Pléiade poets. In a poem appropriately entitled "L'extase d'un baiser," he adds to the cases of erotic "death" resulting from the enrapture of the soul overcome by the intense pleasure of the kiss. A baroque witticism introduced by the poet is not without efficacy. The kiss, which is supposed to be a bearer of life and health (the play is on the word *salut*), hastens this lover to his tomb:

> Ah! mon âme s'envole en ce transport de joie!
> Ce gage de salut, dans la tombe m'envoie;
> C'est fait! je n'en puis plus, Elise je me meurs.[d]

Jean de Lingendes, a poet who deserves to be better known, adopted the soul-kiss conceit several times, most enchantingly in verses that seem to have been written under the inspiration of the kiss passage in Guarini's *Pastor fido*. Here, too, the lover recalls that, in kissing his beloved, his soul came to her lips to surrender his life. In that moment the lover's entire being was concentrated into the ecstatic sensation itself so that he felt that his very life was transformed into a kiss:

> Mon esprit se vint rendre alors,
> Enchanté sur ces rouges bors,
> Ma vie en ceste douce envie
> Pour ma passion appaiser,
> N'estant plus pour tout qu'un baiser,
> Mais un baiser qui fut ma vie.[e]

---

[c] "My soul was then wholly upon my lip to taste the honey that was on yours; but as I withdrew, it stayed behind, so strongly did the lure of this sweet pleasure hold it back." *Les oeuvres de Monsieur de Voiture*, ed. A. Roux (Paris, 1856), p. 471.

[d] "Ah, my soul takes flight in this transport of joy! This promise of salvation [health] sends me to the tomb; it is done! I can no more resist, Elise, I die!" *Les amours, la lyre, les vers héroiques* . . . (Paris, 1909), p. 147. The Catullan spirit of Secundus and the Pléiade poets is present in the poem "Les baisers de Dorinde." See *ibid.*, p. 76.

[e] "My spirit came to give itself up then, enchanted on these red borders, [and] in this sweet desire to allay my passion my life was worth no more than a kiss, but a kiss that was my life." *Oeuvres poétiques*, ed. E. T. Griffiths (Paris, 1916), p. 34. The verses are from the poem "Des changemens de la bergere Iris" where the soul-kiss image is repeated; and in the poem "Tirsis," we read of lovers embracing long and nourishing themselves on each other's soul by kissing (p. 140).

As a last example from the libertine poets, we note that in the last four stanzas of his famous lyric "Le promenoir des deux amants," Théophile De Viau develops the death-from-the-kiss motif. Playing on the concept of dying, the poet wittily concludes that if he does not die (i.e., if he is not ecstasied) by his lady's kisses, then he really deserves to die:

> Climeine, ce baiser m'enyvre,
> Cet autre me rend tout transi.
> Si je ne meurs de celuy-cy,
> Je ne suis pas digne de vivre.[f]

Although almost no credence is given to the Neoplatonic interpretation of the kiss by the French poets, there are at least two cases in novels of the early seventeenth century in which it is invoked. In *Le Quatrième livre des Bergeries de Juliette* by Nicolas de Montreux, the kiss is real enough but "spiritualized" by a Neoplatonic veneer:

> . . . les [amants] avoyent passé iusqu'au baiser, qui sans doubte est la perfection du plaisir que l'amour peut apporter à ceux qui le suyvent. . . . Et durant la douceur du baiser, qui colle les bouches fermement ensemblent, dont les douces haleines, portent ce bien dans tous nos esprits vitaux, qui s'entresent, cela faict que les ames mesmes, en mesme temps s'entrelient, et se baisent, ravies en ioye, d'une si douce chose.[g]

[f] "Climeine, this kiss intoxicates me, and this one completely chills me [i.e., to death]. If I do not die from the latter, I am not worthy to live." *Oeuvres poétiques* (Paris, 1926), p. 53.

Before leaving the French poets, we may take note of some verses from a jocularly libertine poem ("L'occasion perdue et retrouvée") by the dramatist Pierre Corneille. Like other poets, Corneille employs the soul-in-the-kiss motif in connection with the metaphorical dying and resuscitation—five or six in number—of a closely embraced couple:

> Ce fut alors qu'ils se pasmèrent
> De l'excez des contentemens:
> Que cinq ou six fois ces amans
> Moururent et rescusitèrent;
> Que bouche à bouche et corps à corps,
> Tantost vivans et tantost morts,
> Leurs belles ames se baisèrent.

In *De l'amour au voyage, anthologie thématique de la poésie française* (Paris, 1958), p. 281.

[g] ". . . the [lovers] had reached the kiss, that is undoubtedly the most perfect pleasure that love can give to those who follow it. . . . And during the sweetness of the kiss that cements mouths firmly together, and whose sweet breaths convey this good to our vital spirits that feel in harmony, it happens that the souls themselves are simultaneously intertwined and kiss each other, enraptured with the joy of so sweet a thing." *Le Quatrième livre des Bergeries de Juliette* . . . (Paris, 1595), p. 361.

It is interesting to note that here the kiss is said to be love's perfect pleasure much in the way the courtly and Neoplatonic tradition consider it to be the utmost intimacy allowed to pure lovers. It is obvious, however, that the kiss is analyzed for the voluptuous sensations it offers, and the thought that souls are led by the sweetness of the kiss to mingle actually figures here as an image that conveys the idea of the intensity of the pleasure experienced.

In a second novel, Hélie Decoignée's *Silene insensé ou, l'estrange Metamorphoses des Amans fidelles*, Elydor, a shepherd wasting away for love, asks a kiss of his nymph, assuring her that kissing is but the union of spirits and the soul's way of communing:

> . . . il n'ira rien du vostre en me baisant, puisque le baiser n'est rien qu'union des esprits, qu'un langage de l'ame, et un discours muet de la passion d'amour, que debrez vous donc craindre, en parlant à moy de ce langage de coeur et de pensée?[h]

But here too, more than that of a simple shepherd, it is the voice of the voluptuary that speaks, borrowing the language of spiritual love to promote a hedonistic end.[24]

English Authors: Platonicks and Antiplatonicks

That the soul-kiss image was bound to capture the imagination of Elizabethan and seventeenth century Englishmen is understandable when we consider that in England osculatory salutations between the sexes seem to have been rather common, even promiscuous, if we are to believe the reports of some observers. Readers will perhaps remember the remarks of the young Erasmus in a letter (1499) describing his indulgent amazement at the great liberty in kissing among the English:

> Nevertheless, did you but know the blessings of Britain, you would clap wings to your feet, and run hither . . . To take one attraction out of many; there are nymphs here with divine features, so gentle and kind, that you may well prefer them to your Camenae. Besides, there is a fashion which cannot be commended enough. Wherever you go, you are received on all hands with kisses; when you take leave, you

---

[h] ". . . you will lose nothing of your own in kissing me, since the kiss is nothing but a union of spirits [minds], a language of the soul, and a silent discourse on the passion of love; what then should you fear in speaking to me with this language of hearts and mind?" *Silene insensé ou, l'estrange Metamorphoses des Amans fidelles* (Paris, 1613), foll. 50ᵛ–51ʳ.

are dismissed with kisses. If you go back, your salutes are returned to you. When a visit is paid, the first act of hospitality is a kiss, and when guests depart, the same entertainment is repeated; wherever a meeting takes place, there is kissing in abundance; in fact, whatever way you turn, you are never without it. Oh Faustus, if you had once tasted how sweet and fragrant those kisses are, you would indeed wish to be a traveller, not for ten years, like Solon, but for your whole life in England.[25]

This philematological propensity of the English is abundantly reflected in their own literature where the number of kisses seems almost to equal the combined output of French and Italian writers. As to the soul-in-the-kiss image, it is at least as easy to come by in English poetry as in French and Italian. It is to be noted, however, that this particular motif did not become popular in England until the time of the Elizabethans, so that numerous continental sources for it were available as models. Chief among these must have been Castiglione's famous passage, which was known not only in Italian but also in Sir Thomas Hoby's influential translation (1560) of the *Book of the Courtier*. Owing to its importance, Hoby's English version deserves to be given here:

> Therefore the woman to please her good lover, beside the graunting him mery countenance, familiar and secret talke, jesting, dalying, hand in hand, may also lawfully and without blame come to kissing: which in sensuall love according to the Lord Julian's rules, is not lawfull. For since a kisse is a knitting together both of bodie and soule, it is to bee feared, lest the sensuall lover will be more inclined to the part of the bodie, than of the soule: but the reasonable lover woteth well, that although the mouth be a parcell of the bodie, yet is it an issue for the wordes, that be the interpreters of the soule, and for the inwarde breath, which is also called the soule: and therefore hath a delite to joyne his mouth with the womans beloved with a kisse: not to stirre him to any dishonest desire, but because hee feeleth that that bonde is the opening of an entrie to the soules, which drawne with a coveting the one of the other, poure themselves by turne the one into the others bodie, and bee so mingled together, that each of them hath two soules.
>
> And one alone so framed of them both ruleth (in a manner) two bodies. Whereupon, a kisse may be saide to be rather a coupling together of the soule, than of the bodie, because it hath such force in her, that it draweth her unto it, and (as it were) separateth her from the bodie. For this doe all chaste lovers covet a kisse, as a coupling of

soules together. And therefore Plato the devine lover saith, that in kissing, his soule came as farre as his lippes to depart out of the bodie. And because the separating of the soule from the matters of the sense, and the through coupling her with matters of understanding may be betokened by a kisse, Salomon saith in his heavenly booke of Balates, O that he would kisse me with a kisse of his mouth, to expresse the desire he had that his soule might be ravished through heavenly love to the beholding of heavenly beautie, in such manner, that coupling her selfe inwardly with it, she might forsake the bodie.

As for English poetry, the earliest example of the conceit may be that found in a free translation of Serafino Aquilano's *strambotto* "Incolpa, donna, amor" (see above, among Italian examples). This is Sir Thomas Wyatt's short lyric, "Alas! Madame, for steyling of a kysse." As in the Italian poem, here too the poet advises the indignant lady that the best way to punish him for his theft is to give him yet another kiss, for then he would surely die:

> Then revenge you, and the next way is this:
> An othr kysse, shall have my life endid.
> For to my mowth the first my hert did suck,
> The next shall clene out of my brest it pluck.[26]

There is a reference to the motif in the *Hecatompathia* (1582) of Thomas Watson, an interesting fact inasmuch as this volume of poems was admittedly a pastiche of the love conventions of the Petrarchan-Neoplatonic poetic tradition of the continent, and the author proudly points to all his Greek, Latin, Italian, and French sources in a prose commentary to the poems. In poem 20, Watson exults in the memory of a kiss bestowed upon him by his beloved, and to express the bliss then experienced, he writes:

> Forthwith my heart gave signe of joye by skippes,
> As though our soules had joynd by joyning lippes.[27]

Though he gives no direct source for the conceit, Watson does have a marginal note in Latin: "Siquidem opinati sunt aliqui, in osculo fieri animarum combinationem," a commentary suggesting that at this time the conceit was still new and daring in England.

The motif, however, was being picked up by others, such as Sir Philip Sidney, who introduced it in his famous sonnet on the kiss (*Astrophel and Stella*, 81) in rather orthodox Neoplatonic fashion:

> O kiss which souls, even souls, together ties
> By links of love and only Nature's art.

Considerably more sensuality envelops Sidney's use of the image in a song ("O dear life, when shall it be") from the same *canzoniere*. Suffering because of a separation from Stella, Astrophel consoles himself with thoughts of the delights that will be his when he is reunited with his beloved:

> Think of that most grateful time
> When my leaping heart will climb
> In thy lips to have his biding,
> There those roses for to kiss
> Which do breathe a sugared bliss,
> Opening rubies, pearls dividing.

This is anything but the dream of a Platonic lover. Rather it is a vision of a bliss not unlike that which we have found expressed in Guarini's *Pastor fido*. The lover's heart would dwell on his lips to enjoy the lips of his lady. Conventional preciosity is present in the rubies and pearls; and also to be noted is the rhyme of *kiss* and *bliss*, which in amatory verse (in English) is perhaps only slightly less inevitable and common than the association between *love* and *dove*, which latter term has its own close connection with the kiss. For the English, in fact, the kiss conceit nearest at hand and most easily exploited consisted of the idea that the touch of the beloved's lips equaled a paradisal state of blessedness. The conceit as such, of course, was no invention of the English, but in developing it they seemingly had an advantage over the Italians and the French in this purely linguistic accident which provided them with the binominous rhyme made up of the two key terms, *kiss* and *bliss*. By the same token they would be less favored in exploiting the erotic connection between the flower and love—less favored, say, than the Italians, who had *fiore* and *amore* in rhyme, which binominal received its apotheosis in Dante's *Divine Comedy* (*Paradiso*, XXX, 7–9). But that the *kiss-bliss* rhyme was also an easy occasion for abuse is known to any reader of English love poetry. Even within the limits of our concern, we will meet with it several times.[28]

The Neoplatonic idea of the chaste kiss in reciprocal love is played out fully in an ode by Robert Greene. Meditating on the treasured

values of life—wealth, honor, friendship, perfect health, power—
Philomela concludes that pure love surpasses all others because of the
wonderful quality of the kiss enjoyed by its practitioners. It will be
seen that Greene, like many other authors, points to the connection
between breath and soul which is at the origin of the conceit:

> Love 'twixt lovers passeth these,
> When mouth kisseth and heart grees,
> With folded arms and lippës meeting,
> Each soul another sweetly greeting;
> For by breath the soul fleeteth
> And soul with soul in kissing meeteth.[29]

The handling of the image by Ben Jonson is less didactic, more
sensually and wittily orientated, but quite engaging despite its de-
pendence on previous models. In the *Sad Shepherd* (I, 6) the following
dialogue takes place:

MARION: You are a wanton.

ROBIN HOOD: One, I do confess,
I wanted till you came; but now I have you
I'll grow to your embraces till two souls,
Distilled into kisses through our lips
Do make one spirit of Love.

And in the author's *Volpone* (III, 6) the image is put into service by
Volpone himself in anything but a Platonic sense when, in an effort
to seduce Celia with "sensual baits," he promises her all the voluptuous
joys of love, culminating in those pleasures of kissing,

> Where we may so transfuse our wandering souls
> Out at our lips . . . ,

which seems to be a veiled allusion to dying in the sexual sense.
Robert Tofte was openly willing to "die" kissing his lady:

> Content am I to lose this life of mine,
> Whilst I do kiss that lovely lip of thine.[30]

Perhaps the most famous of all instances of the conceit in English
literature is the ecstatic exclamation of Christopher Marlowe's Faustus:

> Was this the face that launch'd a thousand ships,
> And burnt the topless towers of Ilium?
> Sweet Helen, make me immortal with a kiss. (*Kisses her*)

> Her lips suck forth my soul; see where it flees!
> Come, Helen, come, give me my soul again.
> Here will I dwell, for heaven is in these lips,
> And all is dross that is not Helena.

It is remarkable how in the space of a few lines Faustus has managed to refer to several aspects of the kiss conceit: immortality bestowed by the beloved's kiss; the soul ravished by the kiss and passing over to the beloved; the request for the soul's return (through another kiss); the paradisiacal life enjoyed by the lover on the beloved's lips. The debt of this passage to an indefinite number of possible sources takes nothing away from the perennial magic and freshness with which Marlowe has imbued it.

The many allusions to kissing in Shakespeare would themselves fill a little volume, but here we need only pause on those—they are the most interesting—that are of immediate relevance to our study. On at least two occasions the soul-kiss image intensifies the sense of pathos and/or passion in a scene depicting the forced separation of lovers. In *King Henry VI, Part II*, the banished Suffolk takes leave of his mistress, Queen Margaret, with anguish in his heart and words of despair on his lips. His ardent wish at this moment is reminiscent of similar requests made by French and Italian poets: to die by expiring his soul into his lady's body by way of a kiss. That would be a glorious death, for then his soul could do without the need of an afterlife journey to Elysian fields. There in his lady's bosom, in fact, it would be dwelling in its true Elysium:

> If I depart from thee I cannot live;
> . . . .
> Where, from thy sight, I should be raging mad,
> And cry out for thee to close up mine eyes,
> To have thee with thy lips to stop my mouth:
> So shouldst thou either turn my flying soul,
> Or I should breathe it so into thy body,
> And then it liv'd in sweet Elysium
>
> (III, 2)

If the conceit here seems somehow less trivially gallant and more vital than in so many other examples, that is because it has found its way into a context that is so much more charged with the true stuff of life and human passion.

231

In the play *Richard II*, during the farewell scene between the king and his wife, the important theme of the mystic exchange of hearts through the kiss is likewise revitalized by a context depicting the real suffering of lovers. After receiving the king's heart and giving hers in a kiss, the Queen requests her own again, for in her anguish she fears she would cause the death of her husband's heart in her breast. In a second kiss the hearts are returned to their respective bodies. It is her own heart that will break in the Queen's bosom:

RICHARD: Come, come, in wooing sorrow let's be brief,
Since, wedding it, there is such length in grief.
One kiss shall stop our mouths, and dumbly part;
Thus give I mine, and thus take I thy heart.

(They kiss)

QUEEN: Give me my own again, 'twere no good part
To take on me to keep and kill thy heart.

(They kiss again)

So, now I have mine own again, be gone,
That I may strive to kill it with a groan.

(V, 1)

In Shakespeare's *Romeo and Juliet*, the story of the young lovers may be said to begin and end with a kissing scene. At the outset the couple's first kisses are, in a literal sense, wittily exchanged. The following dialogue occurs as Romeo takes a kiss from Juliet's lips:

ROMEO: Then move not, while my prayer's effect I take.
Thus from my lips, by thine, my sin is purged.
JULIET: Then have my lips the sin that they have took.
ROMEO: Sin from my lips? O trespass sweetly urged!
Give me my sin again.
JULIET: You kiss by the book.

(I, 5)

Act V of the play opens with Romeo's account of a dream which presages the unhappy fate of the lovers, although, ironically, Romeo interprets it as an augury of happiness:

I dreamt my lady came and found me dead
And breathed such life with kisses in my lips,
That I revived, and was an emperor.

(V, 1)

Every reader knows the play's ending: the double suicide, with Romeo slaying himself over what he takes to be the dead Juliet, and the latter awakening beside her dead lover only to join him in death. The deaths, real as they are, like the deaths of Pyramus and Thisbe and of Tristan and Iseult (and of other lovers), have erotic significance. Here is death on a kiss. Romeo's words as he takes his poison and dies are:

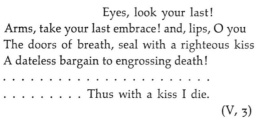

> Eyes, look your last!
> Arms, take your last embrace! and, lips, O you
> The doors of breath, seal with a righteous kiss
> A dateless bargain to engrossing death!
> . . . .
> . . . . Thus with a kiss I die.
>
> (V, 3)

And when Juliet seeks to die by kissing Romeo in the fond hope that some poison may yet be on his lips, she would effect the opposite of what her lover's dream had been. She even manages another pathetic witticism by which the kiss (inasmuch as Romeo's lips may yet have poison on them), normally thought of as a restorative, and dreamed of as such by Romeo, becomes in fact a way of death, which, of course, it also is on occasion:

> I will kiss thy lips;
> Haply some poison yet doth hang on them,
> To make me die with a restorative.[31]

Though Juliet is denied this manner of dying, her end is no less erotic, for like Dido and Thisbe, she brings herself death with her lover's sword (or dagger). When she dies falling on Romeo's body, we may be sure that she does so pressing her lips to his.

It is this same love-death that Shakespeare attributes to one of the most remarkable figures in the world of the theatre when he has Othello stab himself and fall on the wife he has slain:

> I kiss'd thee ere I kill'd thee: no way but this;
> Killing myself, to die upon a kiss.

Finally, we would not forget Cleopatra's stunning line, "Eternity was in our lips and eyes" (*Antony and Cleopatra*, I, iii), which recalls something of Marlowe's Faustus on Helen's kiss. And Antony, it will be remembered, was yet another lover who desired to die upon a kiss.[32]

Moving on from Shakespeare, we note first that the soul-in-the-kiss conceit is used by Bishop Henry King in "The Surrender," a poem dealing with the separation of lovers. Its unusual feature is that the parting is not caused by any external force but is the result of an end of reciprocal love. The lovers, who have been holding one another (i.e. each other's heart) in keeping, are returned to themselves in the farewell kiss:

> In this last kiss I here surrender thee
> Back to thyself, so thou again art free.
> Thus in another, sad as that, resend
> The truest heart that lover ere did lend.[33]

That frequent imitator of Italian poetry, William of Hawthornden, employed the image at least three times. In "The Quality of a Kiss," after inquiring of his lady whether a kiss he received from her was a sign of death or life, he decides that it must be understood as death because by it his soul left him and went out to her: "of life it could not be, / For I by it did sigh my soul to thee." In the lyric "To Thaumantia," he invites his lady to join lips with him so that while they are embracing, "to augment our bliss, / Let souls e'en other kiss." And in "Desired Death" he tells his lady that in kissing her, "all panting in my lips / My heart my life doth leave"; but it is so sweet a death that he would willingly surrender all sense of life if he could only so die forever![34]

The extraordinary popularity of the soul-kiss theme is also demonstrated by its presence in several airs of the early seventeenth century. By far the most charming of such songs is an anonymous madrigal printed in 1613:

> Hero, kiss me or I die.
> On thy lips my soul doth lie.
> There I left it, for in kissing
> Thee, I found my soul was missing.
>
> Quickly send it then to me
> By a kiss, or you undo me.
> If to send it you deny,
> I needs must die,
> And all the world shall know thy cruelty.[35]

This theme of losing one's heart or soul to the beloved in a kiss followed by the lover's request for its return or an exchange by the same means enjoyed particular favor with the English poets. James Shirley developed it in "A Kiss" with just the right amount of gallantry and wit to give the commonplace a delightful turn:

I could endure your eye, although it shot
Lightening at first into me;
Your voice, although it charm'd my ear, had not
The power to undo me:
But while I on your lip would dwell,
My ravished heart leap'd from his cell,
For, looking back into my breast,
I found that room without a guest.
Return the heart you stole thus with a kiss,
When last our lips did join,
Or I'll forgive the theft, to change a bliss,
And have your heart for mine.
I ne'er till now believ'd it truth,
That lovers' hearts were at their mouth,
Now by experience I may say,
That men may kiss their hearts away.[36]

The English, we have seen, found the kiss conceit especially well suited to poems about the temporary or permanent separation of lovers. The poet John Donne employs it in vigorous if brief fashion in such a context ("The Expiation"):

So, so, break off this last lamenting kiss
Which sucks two souls, and vapours both away.

Another fleeting allusion to the image occurs at the opening of Donne's poetic epistle "To Sir Henry Wotten, Knight":

Sir, more than kisses, letters mingle souls,
For thus, friends absent speak . . .

Used here as the term of a comparison, the motif presupposes familiarity with it on the part of readers. At the same time, it was still vital enough to offer Donne a witty and attractive figure by which to suggest the intimate nature of his epistle.

In the history of the soul-in-the-kiss motif a conspicuous place is occupied by Thomas Stanley, the indefatigable translator. Stanley translated a portion of Pico's commentary to Benivieni's *Canzona* under the title *A Platonick Discourse upon Love* (published in 1651) and so knew directly Pico's germinal kiss passage though it does not figure in his version. Moreover, he also translated fourteen of the nineteen *Basia* of Secundus and, in so doing, gave exquisite rendering to the soul-kiss image.[37] But Stanley claims our attention even more because also in his own poems (filled with echoes from other writers, to be sure) he frequently employs the conceit in a manner which suggests acquaintance with it from Plato and Aulus Gellius down to its presence in English poets of his own day. In "The Exchange: Dialogue," the kiss is the means by which the Ficinian love mysteries of psychic exchange and union are carried out. Each of the lovers' souls dwells simultaneously within its respective body and in that of the beloved; because the love is reciprocal, the two are one and each is two. Such is the miracle of love and the kiss:

> PHILOCHARIS: That kiss which last thou gav'st me, stole
> My fainting life away:
> Yet, though to thy breast fled, my soul
> Still in mine own doth stay.
> Weak Nature no such power doth know:
> Love only can these wonders show.
> CHARIESSA: And with the same warm breath did mine
> Into thy bosom slide,
> There dwell, contracted unto thine,
> Yet still with me reside.[38]

Another instructive employment of the image is found in a poem which in the 1647 edition of Stanley's *Poems* bore the significant title "The Killing Kiss." The first stanza of this poem develops the theme of the mystic death of lovers, that is, the dying to corporeal desires and sensations. As the lovers kiss, their souls come forth, escaping from the prison of the body (the "death" image) to commune with one another in a spiritual dialogue:

> When on thy lip my soul I breathe,
> Which there meets thine,
> Freed from their fetters by this death,
> Our subtle forms combine:
> Thus without bonds of sense they move,
> And like two cherubim converse by love.[39]

Stanley, however, does not sustain this idea of a spiritual communion which is soon contaminated by kisses desired for the languorous sensations they bring. What the lover goes on to plead for is hardly in keeping with the angelic life referred to in the first stanza. It is, as he says, the very moment of "pleasing death" that alone "gives ease unto [his] pain." Thus he desires to die again and again, as is indicated in the Serafino-like rather than seraphic conceit at the end of stanza four:

> Kill me once more, or I shall find
> Thy pity than thy cruelty less kind.

The poem then is another illustration of how the soul kiss could easily fall away from its Neoplatonic meaning to express a love which is its very opposite. But it would be wrong to conclude from this that Stanley was a militant antiplatonist. His use of the conceit in association with the metaphor of dying never reaches the extremes of sexuality, let alone the licentiousness, of such poets as Baïf and Marino. He seems rather to be representative of the degeneration of Platonic love into a not too dangerous erotic gallantry.

The Neoplatonic bias is clear enough in the following lines from a poem by Charles Cotton (the famous seventeenth century translator of Montaigne):

> Each kiss of thine creates desire,
> Thy odorous breath inflames love's fire,
>   And wakes the sleeping coal:
>   Such a kiss to be I find
> The conversation of the mind,
>   And whisper of the soul.[40]

But again, if this is the "Platonic" kiss, then it must be admitted that a certain ambiguity is present. Here, in fact, it would be proper to speak of a glaring contrast between the sense of ardent passion associated with the kiss in the first three lines and the spiritual interpretation given to it in the next three. In medieval Christian symbolism of the kiss this symbiosis was possible and even encouraged for, the lovers in question being God and the human soul, there was no real danger of misunderstanding the nature of the love and the kind of kiss involved. But Cotton and others like him are speaking of love and kisses between two human beings. The verses are still another testimony to the dangers that lurked within the "blameless" Neoplatonic kiss.

A more sober Platonic coloring is given the kiss by Lord Herbert of Cherbury in the poem entitled "The First Meeting." As the poet reminds his beloved of their first meeting, he explains how his soul was ravished and made to dwell in her, where it found new joys. Then in a kiss the poet received in exchange his lady's soul, much more refined than his own. It is a case of the Neoplatonic wedding of minds (or souls) effected by the kiss of pure lovers:

> Nor here yet did your favours end,
> For whil'st I down did bend,
> As one who now did miss
> A soul, which grown much happier than before,
>   Would turn to more,
> You did bestow on me a Kiss,
>   And in that Kiss a soul infuse,
> Which was so fashion'd by your mind,
> And which was so much more refin'd,
>   Than that I formerly did use,
> That if one soul found joys in thee,
> The other fram'd them new in me.[41]

Despite the spiritualization of the kiss in such cases as this by Lord Herbert of Cherbury and other English writers, the talk is nonetheless about a real kiss. The ultimate refinement or aberration (depending on the poet's amorous and metaphysical disposition) comes when it is felt that souls may kiss without the actual meeting of lips as the vehicle. As in Italy and France, so too in England it was this extreme of nonsensual passion that was becoming known rather loosely as Platonic love. From the poets Spenser and Sidney on, the Neoplatonic psychology and philosophy of love were favorite topics more and more among English poets and courtiers.[42] And in 1634 James Howell noted that "The Court affords little News at present, but that there is a Love call'd Platonick Love, which much sways there of late; it is a Love abstracted from all corporeal gross Impressions, and sensual Appetite, but consists in Contemplations and Ideas of the Mind, not in any carnal Fruition."[43] This is the love exalted by Theander in Sir William Davenant's delightful satire *The Platonick Lovers*: "How! marry her! Your souls are wedded, Sir, I'm sure you would not marry bodies too; that were a needless charge" (II, i).

It is in the expression of this angelistic conception of love that the soul kiss becomes that lifeless kiss of souls or minds which completely does away with *oscula corporalia*. This was well enough for the mystics, who could kiss only in this way since God was one of the partners, and the Divinity, of course, is approachable only in the spirit. If there is any advantage to this disembodied osculation among humans, it is in the belief that it may be enjoyed even in absence. Carew's lyric "To My Mistress in Absence" is a case in point:

> Yet let our boundless spirits meet,
> And in Love's sphere each other greet . . .
> There, whilst our souls do sit and kiss,
> Tasting a sweet and subtle bliss . . .
> Let us look down, and mark what pain
> Our absent bodies here sustain.[44]

Here there is at least the suggestion that the bodies of the separated lovers may be uncomfortable; but then that is of no consequence because this love wishes to be contemplative and ethereal to the point of creating disdain for the weak flesh. Thus, Donne, who knew both kinds of love, in his "Valediction, Forbidding Mourning," writes:

> But we by a love so far refined
> That ourselves know not what it is,
> Inter-assuréd of the mind,
> Care less eyes, lips and hands to miss.[45]

For the Platonistic amorist sufficiently refined by love, the wedding or kiss of souls is not thwarted by spatial obstacles. There is a charming rendition of the theme in a Song ("Soul's joy, now I am gone") formerly attributed to Donne but now generally considered to belong to the Earl of Pembroke. Forced to leave his lady, the poet, instead of asking for an exchange of hearts in a farewell kiss, addresses these reassuring words to her:

> Let not thy wit beweep
>   Words, but sense deep:
>   For when we miss
> By distance our life's joining bliss,
>   Even then our souls shall kiss.[46]

Concerning the vogue of Platonic love among English poets, John Smith Harrison long ago pointed out that "this idea of restricting love to the experience of soul as opposed to the enjoyment of sense is the one notion which runs beneath many of the love lyrics written in the seventeenth century; and it is the point attacked by opponents."[47] The attacks, in fact, were many, as in John Suckling's *Aglaura* (c. 1638), where one of the characters, Orsames, asked to give his opinion concerning "the Platonics" or "those of the new religion of love," replies curtly that their love philosophy is "a mere trick to enhance the price of kisses."

A focal poem in this debate is John Donne's famous and much discussed poem "The Ecstasie." In "A Valediction, Forbidding Mourning," we saw that the lovers "care less" about doing without gazing, kissing and holding hands. To "care less," however, could suggest that even for Donne's lovers there is not an absolute eschewal of the pleasure of all bodily contact; it is just that these lovers are able to forego corporeal intimacies to a greater degree than those who are not so refined as to be "inter-assured of the mind." "The Ecstasie," the experience of which unperplexed the lovers of that poem but has ever since perplexed its readers, does not really seem too far removed from this concept. Indeed, whatever specific interpretation one wishes to give to Donne's aim (was he playing the role of a cynical voluptuary or was he a sincere, perfectly ethical Aristotelean realist?) in this poem, it can hardly be denied that the following verses argue that even "pure" lovers who have attained a spiritual union cannot or should not long forego the expression of their love in physical terms. While earthly existence endures, the usefulness—perhaps the rightness and the need—of physical intimacies as vehicles for the communication of souls is seen as a stubborn though not a repugnant fact of reality:

> So must pure lovers souls descend
> T'affections and to faculties
> Which sense may reach and comprehend,
> Else a great Prince in prison lies.

Although this is not a total repudiation of Platonic love, it does argue against the "Platonic" idea that the body is by necessity the soul's tomb.[48]

Among those directly attacking the Neoplatonic love conventions, William Cartwright, in his poem "No Platonique Love," made a frontal assault precisely on the themes of the bodiless embrace of minds, the exchange of hearts, and the disembodied kiss of souls:

> Tell me no more of Mind's embracing Minds,
> And heart exchang'd for hearts;
> That spirits spirits meet, as Winds do Winds,
> And mix their subt'lest parts;

> That two unbodi'd Essences may kiss,
> And then like Angels, twist and feel one Bliss.[49]

And the poet Abraham Cowley, in "The Injoyment" (1647), as though in a rebuttal to those who, like Donne, could "care less lips and hands to miss," turns the soul-kiss conceit into a metaphor expressing rabid sensual passion and desire:

> Nought shall my hands or lips controule,
> I'll kisse thee through, I'll kiss thy very Soule.[50]

Within the framework of the epithalamium, a genre allowing for the enumeration of physical pleasures legitimized by marriage, the poets could freely recommend the soul kiss in its quality of voluptuous sensation. Thus Phineas Fletcher gives newlyweds the following counsel:

> Give the first onsett with delightful kisses
>   Not such as sliding light
>   Onlie salute the brimme
> And those faire lippes doe lightlie overswimme
>   But such as sucke the sprite
>   From his retyred seate.[51]

So too in Robert Herrick's "An Epithalamium," the groom is told to proceed quickly to kisses because

> Soules, and breaths, and lipps excite
> Sweetes, to rouse up appetite.[52]

Jasper Mayne was also among those who turned the conceit into a metaphor expressing the acme of sensual pleasure. Cosmic participation is what he wants from the ecstatic soul kiss:

> Let's number out the hours of blisses,
> And count the minutes by our kisses;
> Let the heavens new motions feel
> And by our embraces wheel.
>   And whilst we try the way
>   By which lover doth convey
>   Soul into soul,
>   And mingling so
> Makes them such raptures know
> As makes them entrancéd lie

> In mutual ecstasy,
> Let the harmonious spheres in music roll.[53]

Finally, John Cleveland, author of a lyric entitled "Antiplatonick," could have given the same name to another of his poems ("To the State of Love, or The Senses' Festival"), where the image is used in rollicking fashion to express the sensual pleasures of lovemaking:

> Our mouths incountering at the sport
> My slippery soul had quit the fort
> But that she stopped the sally-port.[54]

Then later in the same poem, he intimates what must have sent a shudder through all Neoplatonic amorists when he refers to this "soul kissing" as but a light, preliminary skirmishing in the war of love, whose major battle is elsewhere:

> Yet that's but a preludious bliss,
> Two souls pickeering in a kiss.

One could continue to enlist examples of the kiss in support of either the Platonics or anti-Platonics. But theirs is perhaps an endless quarrel which it is now time to transcend. To this purpose I would quote again from John Donne who, besides using the kiss conceit sparingly as a poet, gave it much attention as a preacher. One of his sermons ("Preached upon Trinity-Sunday"), is in fact a long disquisition on the meaning of the kiss. The following passage is particularly relevant here, because in it Donne touches on several points we have discussed in the course of the present work:

> In the Old Testament, at first God kissed man, and so breathed the breath of life, and made him a man; In the new Testament Christ kissed man, he breathed the breath of everlasting life, the Holy Ghost, into his Apostles, and so made the man a blessed man. *Love is as strong as death:* As in death there is a transmigration of the soule, so in this spirituall love, and this expressing of it, by this kiss, there is a transfusion of the soule too: And as we find in *Gellius* a Poëm of Platoes, where he says, he knew one so extremely passionate, *Ut parùm affuit quin moreretur in osculo,* much more it is true in this heavenly union, expressed in this kisse, as *S. Ambrose* delivers it, *Per osculum adhaeret anima Deo, et transfunditur spiritus osculantis.* In this kiss, where *Righteousnesse and Peace have kissed each other,* In this person, where the Divine and the human nature have kissed each other, In this Christian Church, where Grace and Sacraments, visible and invisible

means of salvation, have kissed each other, *Love is as strong as death*; my soule is united to my Saviour, now in my life, as in death, and I am already made *one spirit with him*: and whatsoever death can doe, this kisse, this union can doe, that is, give me a present, an immediate possession of the kingdome of heaven.[55]

It is fascinating to see Donne quoting side by side the Platonic kiss conceit (as given by Aulus Gellius) and St. Ambrose on the divine kiss, and just as fascinating to find him making the connection between the kiss and death as ways or metaphors for the soul's spiritual migration and union with God. But perhaps the most compelling idea we find here associated by Donne with the kiss—as indeed it was in the Song of Songs and in medieval writers—is that *love is as strong as death*. For it is the "kiss" that does now what otherwise only death can do: unite the soul with God.

Epilogue

brief survey of the aftermath is in order so that we may be brought up to date. The kiss *topos* and the conceits attached to it continued to be used in secular and religious amatory writing alike, albeit with less frequency and less creativeness or depth of feeling, save perhaps in the area of devotional literature. This was the state of affairs until the Romantic age, when the kiss motif was strikingly revitalized.

The prelude to this later stage is perhaps to be found in the retelling of the story of Abélard and Héloïse by the neoclassical Alexander Pope. In the verse epistle *Eloisa to Abelard* (1717), Pope has Héloïse (now a nun) imagine her own last moments taking place in the presence of Abélard. Her first impulse is to invite her former lover to kiss her as she expires and so suck up her fleeing soul; but this thought gives way to a more pious one as she urges him rather to be present in clerical garb and to hold before her uplifted eye the crucifix:

> Thou, Abelard! the last sad office pay,
> And smooth my passage to the realms of day;
> See my lips tremble, and my eyeballs roll,
> Suck my last breath, and catch my flying soul!
> Ah no—in sacred vestments mayst thou stand,
> The hallowed taper trembling in thy hand,
> Present the Cross before my lifted eye,
> Teach me at once, and learn of me to die.
>
> (321–328)

The passage brings to mind both Tasso and Crashawe, in its vision and theme if not in sensuous appeal. It is followed by verses in which Pope, perhaps influenced by Italian seventeenth century paintings depicting the ecstatic death of saints, has Héloïse imagine the manner of Abélard's death (vss. 337–342). After the vision of her lover's death, Héloïse, in keeping with the medieval legend, prays that she and Abélard may be entombed in one same sepulchre, there to be forever together:

244

> May one kind grave unite each hapless name,
> And graft my love immortal on thy fame.
>
> (343–344)

The image of *grafting* her *immortal love* on his *fame* is pregnant with erotic suggestiveness. In addition to its first meaning—her name forever linked with his in a "tender story" (vs. 364) that she hopes will survive and (vss. 359–366) find a poet worthy of its telling (i.e., Pope) —the line evokes a sexual fantasy of a physical union, and one can easily slip in the reading and hear *frame* as the rhyme word. The situation (or fantasy) is much like that in which Francesca and Paolo find themselves. Francesca's "immortal love" (bad though it be) is grafted onto Paolo's fame (which is also infamy, to be sure) in a "tender story" that found a sympathetic listener (Dante the wayfarer) and a worthy if uncompromisingly righteous poet (Dante the author of the *Divine Comedy*). At the same time, her immortal love is grafted, as it were, to Paolo's beautiful but damned frame in an eternal carnal embrace which is figured by a kiss. In the context of Pope's poem, if Héloïse and Abélard are in one *kind* grave, then we may assume (and here the knowledge of the medieval legend assists us) that they are locked in a "face to face" embrace, and Héloïse, in all her love, "grafted" to Abélard's frame.

Leaving Pope, we must stop somewhat longer on the astonishing figure of Jean-Jacques Rousseau, and first on his modern day (eighteenth century) Héloïse. One of the most clamorous episodes of *La nouvelle Héloïse* proved to be the scene in which the "philosophical" hero, Saint-Preux, kisses Julie (the heroine) for the first time (Part I, letter 14). In describing the overpowering and disordering effect of that kiss, Saint-Preux referred to it by the startling expression "baiser âcre," an acrid kiss. The phrase did more than scandalize linguistic purists, but even Voltaire's raillery was unable to check the sensational effect of that kiss. It has even been said that the "baisers âcres" that Saint-Preux found on the lips of Julie revolutionized hearts and imaginations which until then (i.e., during the eighteenth century) had been accustomed to think of love either in the manner of a badinage or, at best, as a harmless pastime.[1] Despite its exaggeration, there is an element of truth in this statement. What needs to be added, however, is that the hearts and imaginations—especially the feminine ones— were won over not only by the idea of the acrid yet longed-for kiss Saint-Preux knew, but also and perhaps more so by the quality of that

245

same kiss as experienced by Julie. In his directions for an engraving to be made in illustration of that first kiss of the lovers, Rousseau described its nature and effect on the heroine, and here the kiss is said— in Italian—to have been *così saporito* (so savory) as to cause her to swoon. This scene was in fact represented over and over by artists through the latter half of the eighteenth century and the early years of the nineteenth, and it is the union of the two elements, the *âcre* and the *saporito*, making for the rediscovery of the kiss (i.e., love) as a *bittersweet* and profound experience that had the greatest impact on the sensibility of the time.

In connection with this *baiser âcre-così saporito*, mention should be made of an equally significant episode from the life of Rousseau. In the *Confessions* (Part II, Book 9), the author narrates the circumstances attending the first tremulous kiss he exchanged with Mme. d'Houdetot after a long, frustrating courtship. After that Rousseau goes on to tell of his daily visits to the countess and how he would be welcomed by her with a kiss that had the character of a sacred rite. But it was the very thought of the kiss awaiting him that was enough to ecstasy him much in the manner of the medieval troubadours: "As I went along, I dreamed of her whom I was going to see, of the affectionate welcome she would give me, of the kiss awaiting my arrival. That single kiss, that fatal kiss [*baiser funeste*], even before I received it, so enflamed my blood that my head was swimming; a dazzlement blinded me, my trembling knees were unable to support me." Here then is a *baiser funeste* to match the *baiser âcre* experienced by Saint-Preux. We may add here that after their necessary separation Rousseau wrote a long, emotionally charged letter (which he did not send) to Mme. d'Houdetot in which he despairs at the thought that he can no longer expire his soul upon her heart in ardent kisses.[2]

Returning briefly to *La nouvelle Héloïse*, it is of great interest to find that the hero at one point has a Tasso-like (let us call it so) vision or desire of plunging a dagger into the breast of his beloved Julie, of mixing his blood with hers and then expiring his breath-soul on her lips while receiving hers (Part III, letter 16).[3] For this fantasy, coupled with the *baiser âcre-così saporito*, was a motif taken up and adapted by Goethe in *The Sorrows of Young Werther*, an epistolary novel that owes not a little to Rousseau. In Goethe's book events move toward a climax which is nothing less than the kiss that Werther gives to Charlotte. With that kiss we are near the end of the young hero's life and of the novel. Following quickly upon it, as Werther prepares for suicide, his thoughts are that by that kiss he and Charlotte are forever joined; his vision or hope is that of an eternal embrace and kiss in the afterlife. One feels that Goethe had in mind not only Rousseau's work but medieval literature as well—the Tristan-Iseult and Abélard-Héloïse legends, and the couple from Rimini.

The Romantic apotheosis of the soul kiss is perhaps to be found in Ugo Foscolo's *Ultime lettere di Jacopo Ortis*, an epistolary novel which in turn owes something to both *La nouvelle Héloïse* and *Werther*. Here, upon kissing the beloved Teresa for the first and only time, the hero is blasted with ecstasy in a manner that recapitulates the entire amoristic tradition from the troubadours, the *dolce stil novo* poets, and Dante to Rousseau and Goethe. Paradisal nympholepsy has seldom received such glowing eloquence as here where the kiss of the beloved transfers all of nature into Eden regained and transforms the hero from a Saturnian into a Uranian type. And like Tristan at the moment of his first kiss with Iseult, Jacopo invokes voluptuous death:

> Everything I saw seemed to me joyous laughter of the universe: I gazed with grateful eyes at the sky and it appeared to have been opened wide to welcome us: Ah! why did death not come? and I invoked it. Yes, I kissed Teresa; the flowers and plants at that very moment exhaled a sweet fragrance; the breezes were all in harmony; the streams echoed from afar; and all things were made fair by the brightness of the moon that was filled with the infinite light of divinity. . . . Teresa embraced me, trembling all over, and transfused her sighs into my mouth, and her heart beat on this breast; gazing at me with her large languishing eyes, she kissed me, and her moistened lips, half-closed, murmured on mine.
>
> After that kiss I became divine. My ideas are more sublime and joyous, my face more gay, my heart more compassionate. I feel that everything becomes beautiful before my eyes; the complaints of the birds, the whispering of the breezes in the leaves are sweeter than ever; plants flourish, flowers take on color at my feet; I no longer flee from men and all nature seems to be mine. My mind is all beauty and harmony. If I had to carve or paint that beauty I would disdain all earthly model and find it in my imagination.[4]

In *Jacopo Ortis* the paradisal kiss occurs near the middle of the novel, but its effect is long and the episode can be said to mark the book's psychological and emotional center. As the hero notes, it is a celestial kiss that is forever on his lips and dominates all his thoughts. One more kiss and he would in fact die (letter of May 27). But although Jacopo is denied the luxury of dying on Teresa's lips, his real, self-inflicted death is eroticized in view of his last thoughts, which revolve around the memory of that one kiss by which his soul was poured into the beloved's bosom: "And our lips and our breaths were intermingled, and my soul was transfused into your breast."[5]

In addition to the obvious Dantean echoes in Foscolo's passages, the kiss episodes of *Werther* and *Jacopo Ortis* bear a significant similarity to the story of Dante's Francesca in a detail worthy of note. Paolo and Francesca, we remember, were brought to their damning kiss by the reading of a romance. Werther and Charlotte are led to their fatal kiss under the spell of a passage from Ossian. And Jacopo and Teresa come to their ecstatic and fatal kiss after a discussion of Petrarch as a poet of love and a recital, by Jacopo, of the odes of Sappho!

It would be strange indeed if, at this point, we were able to pass on without mentioning Percy Bysshe Shelley. One of this English Romantic's most passionate transports was recorded by him in the poem *Epipsychidion*, where, in the context of what is meant to be an expression of the highest degree of Platonic love felt by the poet for Emily Viviani, we read of his desire for the soul-mingling kiss. As the vision has it, by that kiss and the love it expresses, the two will merge into a psychophysical oneness which is to carry them to one same life and one same death:

> Our breath shall intermix, our bosoms bound,
> And our veins beat together; and our lips
> With other eloquence than words, eclipse
> The soul that burns between them, and the wells
> Which boil under our being's inmost cells,
> The fountains of our deepest life, shall be
> Confused in Passion's golden purity,
> As mountain-springs under the morning sun.
> We shall become the same, we shall be one
> Spirit within two frames, oh! wherefore two?
> .   .   .   .
> One hope within two wills, one will beneath
> Two overshadowing minds, one life, one death,
> One Heaven, one Hell, one immortality,
> And one annihilation.
>
> (565–574; 584–587)

The poem comes to a close here, for, just as in the culminating moment of Dante's experience of mystic communion (with God), words, or the poet's high fantasy itself, are unable to sustain and express the ineffable vision of "Love's rare Universe." Like the preceding passage by Foscolo, Shelley's verses will bring to mind medieval and Renaissance writings. But among them in this case will be the legend of Tristan and Iseult. And yet, once again it is chiefly Dante who claims our attention, not only as the author of the *Vita Nuova*, which work is referred to in the poem's Advertisement, but also as the poet-chronicler of the kiss (i.e., love) of Paolo and Francesca. Shelley might well have thought of Dante's couple as sharing as one both life and death and, beyond that, a state that was both Heaven and Hell, both immortality and annihilation.

Again, there is little that is especially striking about the use of our amatory conceits by the writers since the Romantics, except the fact itself that they have continued to be part of the language of love. Undoubtedly, each reader will have in mind a passage or two meriting attention. We must be content here to cite but one case from a relatively recent author. I choose it from among the many because it is one of the most fascinatingly decadent, I am tempted to say sacrilegious, examples of the kiss-and-death image known to me. It occurs when Marcel [Proust] likens the "soul kiss" of Albertine to the gift of the Holy Spirit, the receiving of the communion and the viaticum. Even her kisses on Marcel's neck are first spoken of in religious terms as kisses of peace:

> It was Albertine's turn to bid me goodnight by kissing me on both sides of my neck; her hair caressed me like a wing with sharp sweet feathers. As incomparable one to the other as these two kisses of peace were, Albertine yet slipped into my mouth, bestowing on me the gift of her tongue, like a gift of the Holy Spirit, giving me thus the viaticum, and leaving me with a store of tranquillity almost as sweet as did my mother when she used to place her lips on my brow in the evening at Combrey.

Perhaps we ought not to be surprised to learn that these words occur only among the variants of Proust's monumental work; the passage corresponding to them in the established text makes no reference to the kiss of peace, the Holy Spirit, and the viaticum.[6]

By way of bringing this study to a close, it may be profitable to refer to a curious and significant connection between the kiss conceit and the history of modern sculpture. One of the best-known works of sculpture in the Western world is Rodin's *Kiss*, of which there are several versions (Fig. 17). It is to be noted that this sculpture was inspired by Dante, Rodin's first study of the motif being the group Paolo and Francesca, meant for the artist's Dantean *Gates of Hell*. But other considerations are to be made here. It has been said that "*Le Baiser* is the only great work by a Western artist that approximates in spirit to the *mithuna* couples of Indian art."[7] The group, in fact, represents the psychophysical merging of lovers into one during a kiss. The further point of unique interest is that with this famous piece, Rodin may be said to have closed an era of art that was chiefly inspired in its forms and manner by classical standards. One may see this immediately by a comparison with a late Hellenistic (first century B.C.) bas-relief now in the Museo Archeologico at Venice (see Fig. 18).[8]

But if the old or classical basis of sculpture reached its modern apogee with Rodin's *Kiss*, the new age of sculpture, at least in one of its most significant and pervasive directions, was ushered in by an even more remarkable handling of the theme. In 1908 or 1910 the Romanian sculptor Constantin Brancusi, working in Paris, carved his own extraordinary *Kiss*, a work that is suggestive of preclassical, or better, of primitive or primeval forms (Figs. 19, 20). The fact that Rodin's *Kiss* supplied Brancusi with the idea of this motif that was to occupy him for some thirty years makes the contrast between the two treatments of the theme all the more dramatic.[9] Brancusi's piece is a powerful representation of the motif of the merging of two into one in a kiss and embrace. Here the figures are carved in such a way that they remain part of the *one* block. But not the least significant feature of this sculpture is the fact that it either was made or was allowed by Brancusi to serve as a memorial for the grave of a Russian girl in the Montparnasse cemetery.[10] The meaning the *Kiss* acquires in this setting is one with which we are now familiar enough: it is an affirmation of a love unto and beyond the grave, an assertion that love is as strong as—nay, stronger than—death.

In this connection we may observe that the motif is to be found in tomb sculpture of a much earlier period. Touching on the development of sepulchral effigies representing husband and wife, Henriette s'Jacob notes that in the later Middle Ages, "whereas previously they stared straight in front, apparently unaware of each other's presence, they now sometimes turn towards each other. This emotional element was not unknown either to the Etruscans, as is seen in a sarcophagus, found at Vulci with husband and wife lovingly embracing. The strong bonds of life are maintained beyond the grave."[11] I would substitute the word *love* for *life* unless, as is very likely the case here, the two are an inseparable binomial. For if, as I think, the piece referred to by the author—who does not identify it beyond what is said above—is the splendid sarcophagal sculpture now in the Boston Museum of Fine Arts, then we have to do with an everlasting love-union beyond the grave (Fig. 21). In this piece the two-in-one motif is heightened by the fact that the two are wrapped in the same winding sheet in such a way that the separate contours of the pair from the waist down are discernible, but not in sharp outline, and give the impression of merging or being about to intertwine. In addition, the wife has one arm clasped around the neck of her bearded husband in such fashion that her hand placed on the back of his neck seems to be drawing him toward her into an even closer embrace and, perhaps, a kiss. Referring to this and a second Etruscan sarcophagus from Vulci, Erwin Panofsky makes the following suggestive comment: "Two famous sarcophagi from Vulci in South Etruria go so far as to show couples linked in an everlasting embrace so that the roof-shaped lid, characteristic of the Punic type, appears transformed into a *lectus genialis*."[12]

The reader who has accompanied me thus far will be indulgent enough to let me close with a poem after all. It is one of the most poignant expressions to be found in all of literature on our concluding theme, and such that it must have been placed as a proem to this book were it not to have its place here. The poem is Emily Dickinson's "If I may have it, when it's dead," where the impersonal pronoun conceals a very personal object: the beloved [lover] and his love:

> Think of it Lover! I and Thee
> Permitted—face to face to be—
> After a Life—a Death—We'll say—
> For Death was That—
> And This—is Thee.

"Face to face to be" in the afterlife—or in the same grave—suggests, as we have seen the expression used in mystic eroticism, a kiss and an embrace throughout eternity.

The Dove, the Kiss, and the Trinity

"He breathed on them," it is said (*John* 20, 22), that is, Jesus on the Apostles, the primitive Church; and he said, "Receive the Holy Spirit." That was indeed a kiss he gave. What? Was it the corporeal breath [*flatus*]? No, rather the invisible Breath [*Spiritus*] which was given by way of the Lord's breathing, so that we would understand that he proceeds from him [the Son] equally as from the Father, like a true kiss that is common to the one who kisses and to the one who is kissed.

St. Bernard, *Serm. s. Cant.* VIII, i, 2.

The idea that the Holy Spirit is the Kiss that unites the Father and the Son indicates specifically the Latin Church doctrine of the double procession of the Holy Spirit, the teaching that in the mutual indwelling or coinherence of the three divine Persons of the Godhead the Spirit proceeds both from the Father and the Son as a single principle of spiration. Spiration (the theological term) here, like a kiss, is itself the principle of an active and mutual love. It is one of the purposes of this appendix to show that the motif of the Holy Spirit as the Kiss of the Father and Son may have figured in Christian iconographical representations of the Trinity in a way that is not at first immediately apparent.

When, in the fourth century, St. Ambrose considered the relation of the Holy Spirit to the Father and Son, he accommodated his discussion of the absolute unity of the three Persons to an anthropomorphic imagery and spoke of the Spirit (Breath) of the mouth: "When the Holy Spirit proceeds from the Father and the Son, He is not separated from the Father nor is he separated from the Son. For how can He be separated from the Father who is the Spirit of His mouth. This surely both is proof of His eternity, and expresses the unity of the God-head."[1] It is to St. Augustine, however, that Latin Christianity chiefly owes the idea that makes of the Holy Spirit the bond of love uniting the Father and Son, a view depending on the concept of the Spirit proceeding *ab utroque*. It has been rightly noted that "no part of Augustine's Trinitarian doctrine has had a more profound or more lasting influence upon Christian thought than his 'appropriation' of the divine love to the Person of the Holy Spirit."[2] The Holy Spirit is the Breath common to the first two Persons, the Love that knits them together: "quia Spiritus est Patris et Filii, tanquam caritas substantialis et consubstantialis amborum" (In Joan., CV, 3). "Et si charitas qua Pater diligit Filium, et Patrem diligit Filius, ineffabiliter communionem demonstrat amborum; quid convenientius quam ut ille dicatur charitas proprie, qui Spiritus est communis ambobus?"[3] In Augustine's words, the Holy Spirit is the subsistent and consubstantial unitive Love of the Father and the Son. Thus the Breath or Love of Father and Son is one and the same Breath or Love.

The particular iconographical depiction to be discussed in connection with these ideas is the anthropo-zoomorphic representation of the Holy Trinity. Although this has many variations, its essential features are the portrayal of the Father and the Son in human form whereas the Holy Spirit is figured as a dove. From the twelfth to the seventeenth century, this motif had one of its most popular treatments in a special vertical arrangement which modern iconography refers to as the *Throne of Grace*. The Father appears seated on a throne, arms outstretched and holding by the ends of the transverse beam the Cross upon which Christ is nailed. The size of the Father is often such that his head is above the top of the Cross while his feet are at or near its base. The dove hovers between the heads of the Father and of the Son, sometimes "proceeding" downwards from the Father's mouth to the Son, sometimes "proceeding" upwards, its bill touching the Father's mouth. Frequently, that is, there is a depiction or suggestion of a mouth to mouth union of Father and Son by way of the dove, either by bill and tail or by the wing tips. The earliest known representation of this particular type of the vertical Trinity is found in a Missal at Cambrai dating from the first half of the twelfth century (Fig. 22). In this remarkable miniature the dove is horizontal in its bill to tail position, but its outstretched wings give to it the form of another cross. For us, however, the most important feature is the very decided way in which the dove unites the Father and Son by having the tips of its wings touching, indeed, actually issuing from or entering into the mouths of the first two divine Persons. In this way the Holy Spirit is seen to be the divine Breath of Love shared in common and reciprocally spirated and eternally present in the Father and the Son. There is no question, then, that such representations illustrate the theological concept of the double procession of the Spirit. Here we need not pause on the well-known use of the dove to symbolize the Holy Spirit. Suffice it to say that this usage has an important Scriptural basis (Luke 3:21–22) and that especially since the sixth century the dove has been the most common symbol of the Holy Spirit in Christian art, a feature quite in keeping with the ancient and widespread representation of the soul or spirit as a bird, particularly in funerary symbolism.[4] What I wish to suggest is that the motif of the dove-Holy Spirit as it appears in depictions of the Trinity such as the one discussed here may also be an illustration of the Holy Spirit as the kiss that unites the Father and Son. To support such an interpretation, in addition to the medieval references to the Holy Spirit as a kiss, we must also show that the dove itself was intimately associated with the kiss—a notion, I think, that can be amply demonstrated.

From ancient times the habits of certain birds were held to indicate an amatory nature ranging from tender affection to lasciviousness. Pigeons in general, and doves in particular, had the reputation of having both characteristics to an extreme. The dove was the bird of Ishtar and of Venus; indeed at times it was itself a symbol of a female goddess. Having reminded ourselves of this association, we may pass directly to the question of the connection between the dove and the kiss. One could plead the obviousness of such a connection by remarking that the English language still preserves the verb *to bill*—formed on the noun *bill* for the beak of a bird—as a term for kissing. Moreover, the dove is the bird that comes to mind with the use of this word. Thus the Oxford English Dictionary gives the following definition for the noun *billing*: "the caressing of doves; kissing; lovemaking." For the verb *to bill*, the complete Webster gives as the two current meanings: "to touch and rub bill to bill (a pair of doves gently billing)" and "to caress affectionately: show affection through fondling and kissing (lovers billing and cooing)." Hence a particular kind of passionate kiss is known as "the billing kiss" or even, from the Latin word for dove, *columba*, "the columbine kiss." But it was in the Latin writers that this association was first clearly established, and it will be well to note some pertinent examples.

In an Elysium where a variety of birds dwell, it is the dove that Ovid portrays in the characteristic act of kissing its mate: "oculo dat cupido blanda columba mari" (*Amores*, II, 6, 56). But Ovid offers us an even more interesting passage when, as a preceptor of love, he explains that kissing is the way a lover may placate the fury and tears of a jealous mistress. The kisses of love will bring peace, and although there is nothing "spiritual" about this kiss and the peace it brings, the connection between the two cannot but be striking to us. The principle involved is not really so different from that found in the Christian kiss of peace which is understood to bring about a reconciliation: "Osculo da flenti; Veneris da gaudia flenti; Pax erit; hoc uno solvitur ira modo" (*Ars Am.*, II, 459–460). In an analogy to this principle of peace effected by kisses after a struggle, Ovid reports the same behavior in doves who are cited as an example to be followed:

> Quae modo pugnarunt iungunt sua rostra columbae,
> Quarum blanditias verbaque murmur habet.
> (*Ars Am.*, II, 465–466)

The inimitable epigrammatist Martial also presents us with pertinent texts. In one place he speaks of Issa, a pet dog, being more playful than Catullus' sparrow and more pure than the kiss of a dove: "Issa est purior osculo columbae" (I, 109, 2). In another poem, where he decries the frigidity of a wife in contrast to his own amorous disposition, he says that he needs kisses like those of the lascivious dove: "Basia me capiunt blandas imitata columbas" (XI, 65, 7). And elsewhere he tells of being embraced and kissed long like the caressing kiss of doves:

> Amplexa collum basioque tam longo
> Blandita, quam sunt nuptiae columbarum.
> (XII, 65, 7–8)

As a complement to the references to the dove-kiss in Latin erotic poetry, we may consider those found in a "scientific" treatise—the *Naturalis Historia*—of the elder Pliny. From this book, which was one of the most influential of all Latin texts, we learn that doves have the habit of kissing each other as a prelude to copulation: "Columbae proprio ritu osculantur ante coitum" (X, ch. 58). More interesting yet is the fact that Pliny has a description of dove behavior that confirms Ovid's observations on the restoral of peace by love kisses. Doves, says Pliny, practice chastity, neither the male nor the female being given to "adultery." This faithfulness to mate and nest lasts until death. At the same time, however, the males are imperious and given to jealousy; thus the females suffer injustices because they are suspected of that which is against their very nature—infidelity. When the male is querulous, he strikes cruelly with the bill, but then, to make amends he gives the female kisses, pressing around her in order to obtain amorous favors (X, ch. 34).

The motif of lovers' kisses bringing peace is of importance, for we find that in the Christian perspective too, love, kisses, and the dove have a similar relationship. Of course, with the Latin poets the motif is related to the concept of the attainment of peace in a context of sexual love. It is in this sense that the erotic poets saw love as a god of peace and Venus as the conqueror of Mars.

> Pacis Amor deus est, pacem veneramur amantes;
> Sat mihi cum domina praelia dura mea.[5]

In returning to the Christian tradition let us first recall that the *spiratio* (represented by the dove) of the Trinity is a principle of love. Thence it is not a great step from Augustine's concept that the Holy Spirit is the subsistent and consubstantial link of love in the Trinity to St. Bernard's thought that the Holy Spirit is "the very sweet kiss between Father and Son," inasmuch as He is "the reciprocal knowledge and love of Father and Son" (*Serm. s. Cant.* VIII, i, 1). In the same context in which he speaks thus, Bernard says that the Holy Spirit is "the imperturbable peace of Father and Son, their unique love and indivisible bond of union." Now all these thoughts have a special relevance to the dove in Christian thinking. The dove, which in paganism was the bird associated with Venus and sexual love (but also, at times, with tenderness and faithfulness), continued in Christianity to be associated with the amatory life primarily, but by no means exclusively, in a spiritualized sense. In this respect, once again we find that the Song of Songs with its several references to the Shulamite as a dove has significant bearing (see Song: II: 10–14; V: 2; VI, 8). The dove of the Song is the soul-bird (or the Church, frequently referred to as a dove by Christian writers). It figures then as another name for the "bride." To be sure, it is a term of endearment, but one used by lovers. It need not seem captious if we add that this is a dove that desires to be kissed by its Mate: "Osculetur me osculo oris sui."

Thus among Christians the image of the dove was likely to bring to mind not only the idea of the Holy Spirit, but also thoughts of love, kisses, tenderness, and harmony, or, indeed, peace. In short, a symbolic equivalence obtained among the concepts of breath, spirit, dove, kiss, love, and peace, which concepts were in turn all readily and early associated with the Holy Spirit. When, in the third century, St. Cyprian sought to explain the propriety of the Holy Spirit's coming in or as a dove, and the nature of the love the brethren should have for one another, he had recourse to the belief that doves practice the unifying kiss of peace: "So the Holy Spirit came in a dove. It is a simple and happy animal, not bitter with gall, not cruel with its bites, not violent with lacerating claws. . . . [Doves] spend their lives in mutual intercourse, *they recognize the concord of peace by the kiss of the beak;* they fulfill the law of unanimity in all things. This is the simplicity which ought to be known in the Church; this the charity to be attained, that the love of the brethren imitate the doves."[6] In a similar vein St. Augustine said that kissing doves are an image of the concord and peace that the brethren should have in their relations with one another: "simplicem se essere debere sicut columbam, habere cum fratribus veram pacem quam significant oscula columbarum."[7]

One cannot fail to be struck by the way in which the Christian writers, no less than Ovid, point to the example of doves to inculcate a lesson of love which deals with the attainment of peace by way of kisses. It is needless to spell out the different value that Christian and pagan give to the same terms and images, but once again we may point out that the "principle" involved is the same for both: the kiss is reconciliation, love, and peace.

With this background before us, we may now consider a second type of the anthropo-zoomorphic Trinity, that which follows a horizontal arrangement. In this type, which began in the late twelfth or early thirteenth century, the Father and the Son are identical or only slightly different and are shown seated side by side. The Son is on the right of the Father in keeping with the verse of Psalm 109: "*Dixit Dominus Domino meo: sede a dextris meis.*" Again the dove is portrayed as hovering or "proceeding" between them, and, as in the vertical Trinity, sometimes uniting them mouth to mouth with the tips of its wings. An example that is of particular interest to this discussion comes from a fourteenth-century miniature in the *Petites Heures* of Jean, Duke of Berry (see fig. 23). Here we see that the Father and the Son are also joined by a handclasp made with the right hand. The dove is in a vertical position in its tail to bill direction, the bill making contact with the clasped hands of Father and Son. A strong horizontal line is also created by the dove's extended wings, the tips of which go to (or proceed from) the mouths of the Father and Son.[8] This representation then is highly suggestive of a conjugal union. The *dextrarum junctio*, for example, was part of the early Christian nuptial ceremony. Inherited by the Church from Greeks, Romans, and Jews, it was used to signify the union of the marrying couple; its place in the wedding ceremony, though not easily documented throughout the centuries, was not lost.[9] Indeed, the joining of the right hands of the couple is still common during religious wedding ceremonies. As to the kiss, we have already amply noted its importance in the betrothal or nuptial ceremony (see chapter 1). Here we will only recall Tertullian's reference to both the *immixtio manuum* and the kiss as part of the pagan betrothal rite: "Si autem ad desponsationem velantur [virgenes], quia et corpore et spiritu masculo mixtae sunt per osculum et dexteras. . . ."

My point is, then, that the dove in these depictions of the Trinity is first of all a breath symbol (*spiratio*), but one with a unique amatory or affective value attached to it. This being so, in those cases where it is made to join Father and Son mouth to mouth, we can hazard the conclusion that a kiss of some kind is to be understood. In the course of this book we have noted several examples in which the spiritual kiss of union depends upon the concept of the real kiss as a means by which two lovers become as one by mingling and joining their spirits (breaths). But here I would also recall the Mexican pre-Columbian depiction of the copulation of two gods or the original human couple (see the Introduction and fig. 3). This picture has a striking resemblance to our horizontal Trinity, specifically in the joining of hands (more precisely the hand of one clasping the wrist of the other) and in the "kiss." Here too the kiss is not shown as a direct labial conjunction, but is indicated by means of what is apparently a breath symbol going from mouth to mouth. It seems clear that in order to pictorialize the idea of an exchange or union of breath-spirits via a kiss, some such breath symbol is of the greatest advantage if not absolutely necessary. In the Christian iconographical representations we have been considering, the dove is precisely that. Its truly exceptional advantage as a breath symbol in the depiction of a kiss is its traditional association with love and with the kiss itself.[10]

Christian Elements and the Kiss Motif in the Troubadour Lyric

Christian Elements in the Love Poetry of the Troubadours

The stressing of the Christian elements in the love poetry of the troubadours has been undertaken by several critics in the present century. Among the most significant studies in this direction are the following: Ed. Wechssler, *Das Kulturproblem des Minnesangs: Studien zur Vorgeschichte der Renaissance*, Bd. I, Halle a. S., 1909 (a pioneer work which, for all its debatable points and exaggerations, remains highly suggestive); D. Scheludko, "Religiöse Elemente im weltlichen Liebenslied der Trobadors," in *Zeitschrift für französiche Sprache und Literatur*, LIX (1935), 411 ff., and "Uber die Theorien der Liebe bei den Trobadors," in *Zeitschrift für romanische Philologie* LX (1940), 191–234 (in which the "religious" elements of the language of Guillaume IX are studied. Augustinian and other Christian elements are accentuated); Myrrhe Lot-Borodine, "Sur les origines et les fins du Service d'Amour," in *Mélanges de linguistique et de littérature offerts à M. Alfred Jeanroy*, Paris, 1928, pp. 223–242 (an excellent study despite the tendency to seek for *the* common source of mystics and troubadours in the writings of the Pseudo-Dionysius); Guido Errante, *Marcabru e le fonti sacre dell'antica lirica romanza*, Florence, 1948 (For Errante, too, troubadour love poetry is a transposition of the *expression* of Christian motives but not of the motives themselves. The singularity of his view is that he sees the poet Marcabru—who except for Guillaume IX is the earliest of the troubadours we are able to read—as the transmitter of this manner. Marcabru himself, says Errante, sang not of courtly love but of *amor Dei* or *caritas* in conscious opposition to *amor mundi* or *cupiditas*. The troubadours who followed continued to use this religiously informed amatory language of Marcabru—and also of Guillaume—but applied it only to their profane love, *amor mundi*, forgetful of the contrast *caritas-cupiditas* in which it originated); D. Zorzi, *Valori religiosi della letteratura pro-*

venzale: la spiritualità trinitaria, Milan, 1954 (not an inquiry into the origins, but a study of special religious elements, chiefly in Provençal poetry following the first and second generations of troubadours. Nonetheless, the author goes far in demonstrating that the *forma mentis* of the troubadours was distinctly Christian). A vigorous rebuttal to the theory of filiation between Bernardine mysticism and courtly love (especially as advanced by Wechssler) was made by Etienne Gilson in *The Mystical Theology of Saint Bernard* (London, 1940), pp. 170–197. In general Gilson's arguments are, as usual, cogent, but while granting that they are strong in repudiating the idea of a specific, i.e., Bernardine, parentage, I do not find them definitive in the overall question of Christian influence which they seek to underplay and even deny.

In his criticism of any suggestion of an important likeness between divine love and troubadour love, E. Gilson insisted that "the courtly poet, putting the problem of love between two beings of flesh and blood, can conceive of purity only in the exclusion of all real union between these beings, so that the purity of courtly love keeps the lovers apart, while that of mystical love unites them." *The Mystical Theology*, p. 193. Mme. Lot-Borodine also thought that was so and felt that in addition to being one of the clearest marks of the distinction between divine and courtly love, it proved that there could have been no significant influence by the one on the other; "Une première différence les sépare, assez imprévue et combien importante: tandis que l'un connaît le secret d'atteindre, procure l'apaisement, dans l'autre l'équilibre se trouve rompu et le bonheur n'est plus qu'un mirage, fuyant devant le coeur inassouvi. . . . C'est dans l'amour profane que les deux termes—le sujet et l'objet de l'amour—tendait à s'éloigner de plus en plus, tandis que dans l'amour divin, un rapprochement se fait insensiblement, l'épouse devenant de plus en plus semblable à l'époux" ("Sur les origines . . .," in *Mélanges . . . Jeanroy*, p. 234).

It seems to me that these eminent scholars have greatly exaggerated the differences between the two loves in this particular question which they find so crucial. For my part I find a profound similarity between the divine and the courtly lover on this matter. The difference is really once again in the beloved with whom one desires to be united, but for both kinds of lover, love, whether it be *caritas* or *cupiditas*, like the Eros of the Greeks drives one to seek union, even fusion. Furthermore, mystic and courtly lover alike know both frustration and fulfillment. In fact, we have seen (chapter 3) such authoritative Christians as Augustine, Gregory of Nyssa, and Bernard of Clairvaux insist that there is no complete attainment and that there is no real end to desire. The perfection of joy is in the desire to seek the face of the beloved evermore. Except for some rare moments of foretaste here and now, quiescence is, in the ultimate analysis, an eschatological reality. So too for courtly love, there is perhaps no better way to refer to it than to say it is a dream of a paradisiacal bliss.

In his study *Medieval Latin and the Rise of European Love Lyric,* I (Oxford, 1965), Peter Dronke criticizes those who would look for the origins of courtly love, it being his contention that "the new feelnig" that critics have generally held to exist in the twelfth century troubadours "is at least as old as Egypt of the second millenium B.C., and might occur at any time or place" (p. ix). This itself is not a new idea, but Dronke has argued for it at length. His arguments, however, and his concept of courtly love do not seem convincing to me. Few scholars, I think, would be unwilling to acknowledge that, like sophistry, the sentiments of "romantic" and even "courtly love" have existed in earlier times and in different climes. But leaving aside the confusion that arises from the word *origins,* the problem of the forces influencing or shaping the sentiments and specific coloring of courtly love in the twelfth century, as thorny as it may be, cannot be an idle matter.

I cannot go deeply into another of Dronke's principal assertions, namely, that the feelings of adoration that the poets of courtly love experience in connection with woman "imply that human and divine love are not in conflict with each other, but on the contrary can become identified" (p. 5). That some of the poets thought this to be so and strove to make the identification may be true, but they could never do so without the full awareness of the tension or conflict between *caritas* and *cupiditas* involved in the very attempt. Even Guinizelli's famous canzone, *Al cor gentil,* of which Dronke makes so much, leaves the reader with a statement of the conflict rather than with its resolution. It should not be difficult to see that a lady, however angelicized, cannot be a legitimate rival of God and the Virgin Queen of Heaven, though a rival she may be. Precisely this question, incidentally, is dealt with in the third chapter of Charles S. Singleton's *Essay on the Vita Nuova* (Cambridge, 1949), a work which seems to have escaped Dronke's attention. But all this is not meant to belittle Dronke's study. In point of fact, I think he has made his own valuable contribution to the kind of scholarship which he claims is fruitless—that which points to the Christian patterns of thinking that influenced the poetry of courtly love—although he could rightly protest that he has done so not in order to indicate specific origins but rather to point to some of the factors determining "the sophisticated and learned development of courtois themes" (p. ix).

Some Pertinent Theories of the Origins of Courtly Love

In connection with the important place occupied by the kiss in medieval amatory literature it is necessary to touch here on some theories of the origins of courtly love that are pertinent to the present study. The first is the proposal, advanced by Father Denomy, that courtly love has its source in a specific work of Arab mysticism—a *Treatise on Love* by Avicenna. Avicenna's treatise, which reflects a certain current of Arab love metaphysics, puts forth a theory of a pure and ennobling rational love between human lovers that has several points of agreement with the troubadours' conception of *fin' amors*, among them the idea that intercourse, being a desire arising from the animal nature of man, is forbidden as impure and abominable, and that love is right only when such animal desires are subdued; this is because pure love consists in the union of the souls and hearts of the lovers.[1] Now it is precisely the significance given to the kiss and embrace within this conception of pure love that is crucial in assessing the similarity between the two concepts of love. Avicenna writes:

> As for embracing and kissing, the purpose in them is to come near to one another and to become united. The soul of the lover desires to reach the object of his love with his senses of touch and sight, and thus he delights in embracing it. And he longs to have the very essence of his soul-faculty, his heart mingle with that of the object of his love, and thus he desires to kiss it. However, feelings and actions of excessive lust happen to follow them frequently, and this makes it necessary that one should be on guard against them, except if the complete absence of physical appetite and immunity even from suspicion is beyond doubt.[2]

Although it is not my aim here to offer a detailed critique of Denomy's claim that the troubadours acquired their doctrine of pure love from Avicenna's treatise, I must say that it seems to me highly improbable that this could be so. For one thing, the notion of the kiss as a vehicle for the union of souls or hearts is a thought which is present in the earliest Christian exegetes of the Song of Songs. Moreover, in connection with this question, I believe it is somewhat misleading to say, as Denomy does, that *fin' amors*, in allowing the delights of kissing and embracing (and of seeing and touching the beloved in the nude), was encouraging "all that provokes and fans desire," that *fin' amors*, in short, is "that doctrine of pure love which allows to the lover any carnal solace short of consummation of his love."[3] It is Andreas who speaks of stopping short of a final solace, not the poets, at least not those who precede him. My point is, as I have stated in chapter 3, p. 116, that in a number of cases the troubadours, far from considering the kiss and embrace as a fanning of desire, think of these intimacies as the terminus of their love, as the solace they desire, as the attainment of that mysto-magical union of two in one that is the ultimate aim of lovers. The particular character of the kiss motif in the Provençal examples I have cited in chapter 3 (I believe they are the most significant ones to be found in the earliest troubadours) is such as to show us the poets of *fin' amors* considering the kiss in much the same spirit as does the bride in the Christian reading of the Song. That the troubadours could have known of the kiss conceit and other mystico-erotic images from Avicenna and other Arabic (or Hispano-Arabic) sources is certainly possible. Such a contact, however, could have been contributory at best, not decisive, in the formulation of the conceits and attitudes associated with courtly love. The more pervasive influence was the troubadours' own Christian heritage.

A second theory concerning the nature of courtly love that is worth touching on here because of its bearing on the question of the kiss is that which has been presented by René Nelli in his book *L'érotique des troubadours* (Toulouse, 1963). Nelli's study, which emphasizes an ethno-sociological approach, is rich with valuable and suggestive observations to which I cannot do justice here. The author sees the conception of courtly love as the development of a relationship between the sexes that is modeled on the nature and the rites of male friendship found in primitive and advanced societies. "Chez tous les peuples primitifs l'amitié et l'amour sont dans les mêmes rapports: doctrinal et chronologique. C'est de l'amitié et non de la sexualité qu'est issue l'amour épuré, l'on peut affirmer, sans crainte de généraliser indûment qu'il ne s'est jamais éprouvé comme tel, c'est à dire, comme transcendant—ou même refusant—le fait charnel, qu'après avoir emprunté à l'amitié masculine, préalablement idealisée, ses mythes et ses rites, et s'être, pour ainsi dire, greffée sur elle" (p. 277). Such bonds of friendship are made or solemnized among primitive peoples by means of various rites, one of which is an incision allowing two men to exchange blood. This is the establishment of blood brotherhood. At times, in place of the exchange of blood, the rite of brotherhood consists of an exchange of saliva or perhaps of breath. Nelli suggests that in the medieval tradition of courtly love the interchange of blood by an incision (the prototype of the eventual idea or myth of the exchange of hearts) was replaced, under the influence of women, by a kiss, perhaps in imitation of the kiss exchanged by medieval knights in those ceremonies where a bond of comradeship was established.[4] "Il était inévitable que dans l'affrèrement érotique les incisions fussent remplacées—peut-être sous l'influence des femmes—par le baiser qui est naturellement plus galant et qui, d'ailleurs, avait été déjà adopté comme rite d'union par les *compagnons* eux-mêmes; inévitable aussi que les troubadours—du fait que l'amour était resté tributaire, dans le monde arabe et en Occident, de son expression poétique—missent surtout l'accent, dans le temps qu'il passait du libertinage chevaleresque à l'idéalisme courtois, sur les métaphores du coeur. De toute façon ce qui s'imposait à l'imagination des femmes, quand elles pensaient l'amour pur (en tant qu'il conditionnait pour elles les relations sexuelles), c'était le 'phantasme' de la fusion des coeurs plutôt que celui du mélange des sangs: il était doué, à leurs yeux, d'une véritable efficacité opératoire" (p. 314).

That the progressive "purification" of the troubadour love was the result of a changing attitude in the relationship between the sexes, namely the raising of the lady to a rank in which she qualified for "friendship" with a male on equal terms is, I think, only part of the story. In this respect we may call to mind an analogous but much earlier development in the erotic attitudes of Catullus and the Roman elegists of "personal" poetry. In a short but rich article written in 1945, Luigi Alfonsi pointed to the borrowings made by Catullus, Propertius, and Tibullus of a number of concepts and images from the language of male friendship (in particular as found in Cicero) which the elegists transposed to the description of their amatory relationship with a woman. In this process, for all the sensuality that remained in their love, the Roman elegists were contributing to an idealization of woman.[5] In considering Catullus to be the originator of the new amatory attitude, Kenneth Quinn writes: "In his poetry, and in some way also in actual experience, Catullus became involved in a kind of love that, in his view of it, transcended the usual pattern, that lifted him out of the circle of *amici* into a more deeply passionate relationship with a woman who, because he wanted her as his intellectual companion as well, gave shape to a new conception of a kind of *amor* that could also be *amicitia*."[6]

That something along these lines took place in the development of medieval love poetry is, I think, certainly true. But the situation is more complex than that. The fact is that medieval amatory poetry reveals that what the poets really needed and what they created was a creature approximating or possessing the character of a divinity. It is no accident that the cult of the Virgin and the idealization of the lady in profane love were contemporaneous developments and that they should have had a reciprocal influence. (The question of precedence is a moot one.) Both reflect the need and offer something of an answer to the need that for so long had been felt in the Christian world for a female element in the Divinity. As an offshoot of the religion of the Hebrews, Christianity inherited the strong patriarchal and masculine-centered concepts of Judaism regarding God. The Virgin and, to a lesser degree, Sophia notwithstanding, the fundamental lack of a female deity that Christians could adore perhaps facilitated the idealization of woman. At any rate, both the cult of the Virgin and that of woman were to continue side by side down through the centuries, and in doing so, the two principals were to be rivals.

In returning to Nelli's views, one can also object to the excessive importance the author gives to woman as an active agent in determining the nature of courtly love. The latter, in the final analysis, was so dominantly a masculine "invention" that even the "divinization" of the lady can almost be considered a by-product of the true center of its love psychology, which was an awareness, cultivation, and exaltation of the male's own capacity for loving. As to what Nelli says about the use of the kiss as part of the rite by which a medieval lady and her lover sealed a spiritual union, I would agree that there is a connection between it and the "primitive" idea of the kiss as a joining of breaths which establishes a union. But it is puzzling to me that the author should so completely neglect any reference to the Christian symbolism of the mystic kiss and the kiss of the Song of Songs in the sacred and secular poetry of the age. It is clear that he is interested more in a "ceremony" which allegedly took place than in the troubadours' own allusions to the kiss. He does not, in fact, discuss the lyrics in which they refer to kisses.[7]

The playing down or even the neglect of Christian elements and, we may add, of the classico-Christian theme of *amicitia* as influences in the development of courtly love constitutes, for me, a defect in Nelli's otherwise very valuable book. On the other hand, the author is in at least partial agreement with the proponents of the Arabic origins of courtly love. According to him the most significant themes that make up the common substance of Arabic and Provençal love are "la théorie du coeur séparable et de l'échange des coeurs, la surestimation de la femme, la soumission absolue de l'amant à sa dame, l'exaltation du long désir et l'idée de mort-par-amour" (p. 52). In a note Nelli rightly observes that these characteristics were not exclusively Arabic and that they can be found (at times only in a germinal state) in all sufficiently advanced societies. However, he says, "Nous les appelons arabes parce que c'est sous l'influence de ces conquérants et dans l'Espagne musulmane qu'ils ont été formulés avec le plus de précision et le mieux 'valorisés,' en un temps [X–XIe siècles] ou, en Occident, ils n'avaient encore aucune existence 'sociale' " (p. 52, n. 80). Now all the characteristics Nelli speaks of are an integral part of Christianity. All, that is, with the exception of the presence of the lady as the beloved. (I leave aside the question of the cult of the Virgin.) But that is just what the profanation in Provençal love is about: the lady has usurped the place that belongs to God. The motif of the separability, movement, or exchange of the hearts of lovers which is considered central by Nelli was, we have seen, a commonplace in Christian thinking. "Inquietum est cor nostrum donec requiescat in te," said Augustine. And St. Anselm of Canterbury wrote: "Ecce, domine, coram te est cor meum. Conatur, sed per se non potest. Admitte me intra cubiculum amoris tui. Peto, quaero, pulso" (*Meditatio* 3, ending, in *Opera omnia*, III, Edinburgh, 1946). The Johannine Gospel has such mystic expressions referring to mutual indwelling as "qui manet in me et ego in eo" (15:5) and "qui manducat meam carnem et bibit meum sanguinem, in me manet et ego in illo" (6: 57).

If it is true that many of the amatory conceits and attitudes of courtly love occur before troubadour poetry in the Arabs (both in the mystic writings of the Muslims and in the eleventh century Hispano-

Moorish court poets), it is also true, by Nelli's own admission, that they do not appear significantly in Provençal poetry until 1130 and after. And that is at a time when such conceits and attitudes were receiving full and renewed expression in the words of Christian mystics and exegetes. As a matter of historical fact, such conceits were part of a Christian tradition that preceded and even influenced early Islam mysticism. In itself this would not exclude a later counterinfluence upon the West from the Arabic sources. But are we to assume also that twelfth century Christian mystics were influenced by Islam's erotic mysticism? Regarding the troubadours, Nelli is really at a loss to explain the presence of the *sentiments* of courtly love in the poets. "Ainsi donc, si l'érotique d'oc a suivi à peu près le même destin que l'erotique arabe, elle n'en est pas, pour autant, la copie pure et simple. Elle a du évoluer pour la rejoindre. Elle résulte d'un long effort pour faire cadrer les concepts fournis par l'Espagne musulmane avec le renouvellement progressif de la sensibilité, car on peut importer directement des modèles poétiques mais non point des sentiments" (pp. 62–63). Just so. But where should these sentiments have come from if not from the very heart of Christian spirituality itself, a tradition which made available to the poets both the sentiments and the erotico-religious conceits by which they were expressed?

Another theory concerning the nature of troubadour love which would seek to capitalize on the role of the kiss as part of its argument is that which considers troubadour love poetry to be a veiled allegory of the beliefs of the Cathar heresy. "The ring of gold or the single kiss the lady grants the poet is his *consolement*—a reflection of the kiss of peace exchanged at the ceremony of final entrance of a heretic into the Catharist church—the *consolamentum*."[8] This is a far-fetched theory. As for the kiss of peace, its place in the religious ceremonies of the medieval Church of Rome was still widespread and of a solemn nature. The medieval penitentials, for example, indicate that one of the ceremonies marking the re-entry of a penitent into the Church was the kiss of peace. We may also recall here that among the ceremonies associated with the contract of vassalage was the *osculum* which sealed the obligations made by lord and vassal. In this ceremony it was the lord who conferred the kiss. In the love-service ritual, when the lady finally consented to accept the suppliant lover as her faithful man, the act of amatory homage was modeled on the ceremony of the feudal contract of vassalage. The oath of service and homage made by the *drut* (faithful love-servant) was solemnized by a kiss from the lady.

Another study to be mentioned here is Moshé Lazar's *Amour courtois et fin' amors* (Paris, 1964). The characterization of *fin' amors* offered by Lazar appears untenable to me. Speaking of the troubadours and specifically of their conception of *fin' amors*, he writes: "Quels que soient les sentiments et les idées que le poète exprime, ils viennent tourner en fin de compte autour d'une seule et même exigeance: la récompense finale, c'est à dire le rendez-vous, le baiser, 'et le reste': *del sorplus*, comme dit le troubadour" (p. 66). And again, after his analysis of a few poems, I find he is quite unjustified in stating that the troubadours, *without exception*, seek to go beyond the kiss and embrace and to obtain "the rest": "Passer la nuit auprès de la dame dévêtue, dans l'intimité de son alcôve; caresser sa peau blanche: baiser et étreindre son noble corps: demander à la dame de ne pas être parcimonieuse 'del plus,'—telles sont les expressions caractéristiques du désir amoureux que tous les troubadours, sans exception, nous présentent chacun dans le style qui lui est propre" (p. 133). Lazar denies any spiritual value to troubadour love in any case, and he seems to have been led to this position as a result of a not very cogent argument against the idea of the existence of any connection at all between the troubadour love-lyric and Christianity.

Notes

[The abbreviations *PL* and *PG* indicate J. P. Migne's *Patrologiae cursus completus*, Series Latina and *Patrologiae cursus completus*, Series Graeca; Numbers refer to volume and column.]

Introduction

1. A complete history of the kiss in general, that is, a history of its various manifestations in life and in literature, would constitute a project of no small length. The studies known to me that ostensibly have such an end are, for the most part, rather amorphous and fall far short of fulfilling the promise of their titles. This is particularly true of one of the latest books on the subject, E. Scerbo's *Il bacio nel costume e nei secoli* (Rome, 1963), pp. 255, its division into twenty-three short chapters notwithstanding. The same is to be said of Christopher Nyrop's *The Kiss and its History*, trans. Wm. F. Harvey (London, 1901), and of an anonymous nineteenth century French study of which only three hundred copies were printed: *Le basier: étude littéraire et historique* (Nancy, 188?). Such studies inevitably end up being a collection of random references with incidental digressions on topics ranging from the life of the Greek hetaerae to homosexual love. The longest expatiation on the kiss is without doubt a seventeenth century work, Martin von Kempen's *Opus Polyhistoricum, dissertationibus XXV de osculis, subnexisque de Judae ingenio, vita et fine, sacris epiphyllidibus, absolutum*, etc. (Frankfurt, 1680). This is an incredible volume of 1040 pages. The seventeenth and early eighteenth centuries saw several studies on the kiss, with a special emphasis on the use of the kiss in Christian rites. In general the most rewarding studies on the kiss are those that have limited themselves to a specific usage or idea connected with the kiss. Such a work is Karl-Martin Hofmann's *Philema Hagion*, Beiträge zur Förderung christlicher Theologie, 2 Reihe, 38 Band, Gütersloh, 1938. My first chapter is indebted to Hofmann's study for some leads if not for its method and ultimate scope. At the end of the present volume the reader will find a selective bibliography of works bearing on the nature and history of the kiss.

2. P. d'Enjoy, "Le baiser en Europe et en Chine," *Bulletin de la Société d'Anthropologie*, IVe Série, VIII (1897), 181 ff.

3. Sigmund Freud "The Sexual Aberrations," in *Three Essays on the Theory of Sexuality*, trans. and ed. James Strachey (New York, Avon Library Book, 1965), p. 38. My italics.

4. Havelock Ellis, *Studies in the Psychology of Sex: Sexual Selection in Man* (Philadelphia, 1914), Appendix A, p. 215.

5. *Ancient Near Eastern Texts Relating to the Old Testament*, ed. James B. Pritchard, 2d ed. (Princeton, 1955), p. 383. On the sense of taste in the erotic kiss, one may confidently read Th. H. Van de Velde's classic treatment of *Ideal Marriage*, trans. Stella Browne (New York, 1941, 1962), pp. 154–155. Van de Velde observes that "This is a factor [i.e., taste] which most people fail definitely to perceive, and there are only very few connoisseurs who can discriminate and describe the individual flavour of their beloved's kisses" (p. 154). The true poets, we know, are precisely those who are gifted far beyond the average man in matters of intuition and sensory perception. Pages 152–161 of Van de Velde's work constitute the sanest and most salutarily uninhibited treatment known to me on the physiology and technique of the erotic kiss.

6. Robert Briffault, *The Mothers: A Study of the Origins of Sentiments and Institutions* (New York, 1927), I, 120. In a note (no. 6) to this quote, Briffault writes: "Liking, or judging a thing to be 'good' is throughout the greater part of the biological scale equivalent to regarding it as 'good to eat.' All other forms of attraction, of desire, are derivatives of that primary value. That fundamental value is never entirely obliterated."

7. *The Sexual Life of Savages in North-Western Melanesia* (New York, 1929), p. 333.

8. *Méditations sur l'Evangile: Sermons de Notre-Seigneur*, XXIVe journée, in *Oeuvres complètes de Bossuet*, VI (Paris, 1862), 369.

9.
> Denique cum membris conlatis flore fruuntur
> Aetatis, iam cum praesagit gaudia corpus
> Atque in eos Venus ut muliebria conserat arva,
> Adfigunt avide corpus iunguntque salivas
> Oris et inspirant pressantes dentibus ora,
> Ne quiquam, quoniam nihil inde abradere possunt
> Nec penetrare et abire in corpus corpore toto;
> Nam facere inter dum velle et certare videntur.
> *De rerum natura* (IV, 1105–1112)

This Lucretian description is to be compared to what Malinowski says about the erotic mouth play of his Melanesian savages. But an even more exact parallel to the latter may be read in four lines from the poem "Dolores" by the decadently primeval Swinburne:

> By the ravenous teeth that have smitten,
> Through the kisses that blossom and bud,
> By the lips intertwisted and bitten,
> Till the foam has a savour of blood.

10. R. Mukerjee, *The Flowering of Indian Art* (New York, 1964), p. 189.

11. Mircea Eliade, *Le Yoga immortalité et liberté* (Paris, 1954), p. 267.

12. Hebrew scholars interpret the biblical text to say either into man's

nostrils or into man's face. The Septuagint speaks of God's breathing into man's face, as does the Latin Vulgate version. This allows more easily for the idea of the kiss. Indeed, even within the Jewish rabbinical tradition the episode is referred to as a kiss. It is said to be one of the two kisses that God gives man. This one is "the kiss in this world"; the kiss in the hereafter is promised in these words from Ezechiel 37:12–14: "I mean to open your graves and revive you, my people . . . Will you doubt, then, the Lord's power, when I open your graves and revive you? *When I breathe my spirit into you, to give you life again.*" See: *Shir Hashirim Zuta*, ch. 1, T. S. 21, 144.

In connection with such breath-power or miracle-working of "spirit," we may also note the account of one of the greatest miracles performed by Elisius: the restoring of life to the dead son of the woman of Sunam, recorded in IV Kings 4:32–35. This miracle is effected by a *mouth-to-mouth* resuscitation, a method of reviving persons at death's door which is, in fact, popularly known as the "kiss of life." I have already referred (see p. 2) to the early Babylonian hymn that speaks of the source of life as being in the mouth of the great goddess Ishtar. I may mention here a remarkable episode from the ancient Babylonian *Epic of Gilgamesh*. The hunter exhorts the "harlot-lass" to welcome the savage-like Enkidu:

> There he is, O lass! Free thy breasts,
> Bare thy bosom that he may possess thy ripeness!
> Be not bashful! Welcome his ardor!

The key phrase here, "Welcome his ardor," literally says "Welcome his *breath*," the word being *na·pis·su*, which is repeated soon after in the same expression: "She was not bashful as she welcomed his ardor." What is actually involved here is a hierogamotic rite in which one may picture a kiss preceding or accompanying the ritual coition. Significantly, when it is over Enkidu has been transfigured. The harlot says to him: "Thou art wise, Enkidu, art become like a god." *Ancient Near Eastern Texts Relating to the Old Testament*, ed. James B. Pritchard, 2d ed. (Princeton, 1955), p. 75. The episode is recorded in Tablet I, iv, of the epic. An ancient Egyptian *Hymn to Amon-Re* alludes to the myth that the gods came into being from the spittle of the supreme god, Amon-Re, creator and sustainer of life. See in *Ancient Near Eastern Texts . . .* , p. 366. On the matter of the connection made in the Old Testament between the respiration of man and God's "breath," a number of parallels in Babylon and Egypt have been noted by Paul van Imschoot in "L'esprit de Yahweh, source de vie dans l'Ancien Testament," *Revue Biblique*, IV (October, 1935), 481–501, but see esp. pp. 492–496.

13. Wilhelm Wundt, *Völkerpsychologie*, IV, Part I (Leipzig, 1920), 135. This work is to be consulted on the whole question of the breath-soul and primitive ideas on spittle, blood, and the wanderings of the soul.

14. The scene of this copulating couple is found in the pictographic manuscript known as the Codex Borgia. It is reproduced in color in the recent Spanish translation of Eduard Seler's *Comentarios al Códice Borgia*, III (Mexico 12, D.F., 1963), Pl. 61.

The nature of the couple and the scene is not without question. Eduard Seler, whose interpretation of the Codex Borgianus is still generally accepted as the most authoritative, considered the nude pair to be the first human couple and the "blood" symbol passing from the mouth of the male to that of the woman to be a sign of the mixture of blood and the vital energies. Eduard Seler, *Codex Borgia: Eine altmexicanische Bilderschrift der Bibliotek der Congregatio de Propaganda Fide*, II (Berlin, 1906), 212. More recently C. A. Burland speaks of the scene as a couple, male and female, "with tongues joined together symbolizing sexual intercourse. The man has a ball of incense to show the holiness of the act." *The Gods of Mexico* (New York, Capricorn Books), p. 204 and fig. 6d.

Now in point of fact there are no features that clearly distinguish the couple as male and female, whereas in the Codex Borgia representations of the female figure are invariably made clear by anatomical features. The scene could conceivably be a depiction of the god of life (or sustainer of life)—distinguished as a god by the headdress—infusing the blood-spirit of life into man.

15. A picture of this may be seen in Charles Waldemar, *Magie der Geschlechter* (Munich, 1958), Pl. LXVI. In connection with such scenes, we may note in passing that one of the earliest representations of the kiss between man and woman is to be found among the Iberian stone reliefs discovered at Osuna, Spain. The piece, dating from the fourth to the second century B.C. and now in the Madrid National Archaeological Museum, is unrelated to anything else from Osuna, and one cannot be sure of the exact nature or intent of this kiss. The busts of a man and woman are seen in profile. Contact between them is made at the breast, and their faces meet in a light mouth-to-mouth kiss (Fig. 4).

16. James Frazer, *The Belief in Immortality* . . . , II (London, 1922), 11.

17. Christopher Nyrop, *The Kiss and its History*, p. 182.

18. *The Greek Anthology with an English Translation*, ed. W. R. Paton (Cambridge, Mass., and London, 1950), p. 168.

19. "The Soul in the Kiss," in *The Criterion*, II (April, 1924), 349–359.

20. See Franz Cumont, *After Life in Roman Paganism* (New York, Dover Publications, 1959), p. 59. Also, Richard Broxton Onians, *The Origins of European Thought* (Cambridge, Eng., 1951), pp. 172–173.

21. There seems little doubt that Gaselee took the passage from Burton's book, which also gives examples from Petronius and Aulus Gellius. In the body of his text Burton gives the Castiglione passage in English: "They breathe out their souls and spirits together with their kisses, saith Balthasar Castilio; change hearts and spirits, and mingle affections as they do kisses; and it is rather a connexion of the minde than of the body" (Partition Three, Section Two, Member III, Subsection IV, where Burton is speaking of the

artificial allurements involved in love, and, at this point, particularly of the role of kissing). Burton's Castiglione reference is not exact. Since the important page on the kiss in the *Book of the Courtier* must be analyzed in its context, an effort to do so is made in chapter 4 of the present study.

22. *European Literature and the Latin Middle Ages*, trans. W. R. Trask (New York, 1953), p. 292.

23. James Hutton, *The Greek Anthology in Italy to the Year 1800* (Ithaca, 1935), and *The Greek Anthology in France and in the Latin Writers of the Netherlands to the Year 1800* (Ithaca, 1946).

24. Wilhelm Bölsche, *Love-Life in Nature: The Story of the Evolution of Love*, trans. from the German by Cyril Brown, ed. Norman Haire (London, 1931), p. 520.

1. The Early Christian Centuries

1. Old Testament references to the kiss are found in the following passages: Genesis 27:27; 29:11; 29:13; 31:28; 31:55; 33:4 (the reconciliation and kiss of Jacob and Esau); Exodus 4:27 (Aaron and Moses greeting each other with a kiss); 18:7 (the kiss accompanied by words of peaceful welcome); Ruth 1:9; 1:14; I Kings 20:41 (the kiss of affection between David and Jonathan); II Kings 19:39–40; 20:9; Proverbs 27:6; Song of Songs 1:1; 8:1; Tobias 7:7; 10:12; 11:11.

2. The use of the kiss to conceal a treacherous act is found in the Old Testament at II Kings 20:9; and at Proverbs 27:6 it is written: "Better the love that scourges, than hate's false kiss." The New Testament references to the kiss of Judas are in Matthew 26:48–50, in Mark 14:44–46, and in Luke 22:48 where the words of Jesus to Judas are "Judas, wouldst thou betray the Son of Man with a kiss?"

3. The references occur in the following Epistles: Romans 16:16; I Corinthians 16:20; II Corinthians 13:12; I Thessalonians 5:26; I Peter 5:14.

4. Paul's Epistles refer to the "holy kiss," whereas the Petran Epistle speaks (in the original Greek) of a "kiss of love." But it is the same kiss and the same custom that is intended. The holy kiss is a kiss of love (charity).

5. See also Romans 8:9; II Timothy 1:14; Ephesians 2:22.

6. Philo, *Questions and Answers on Exodus*, translated from the Ancient Armenian Version of the Original Greek by Ralph Marcus (London; Cambridge, Mass., 1953), pp. 128, 169.

7. F. C. Conybeare, "New Testament Notes," in *The Expositor*, 4th series, IX (London, 1894), 460–462.

8. See Erwin R. Goodenough, *Jewish Symbols in the Greco-Roman Period*, VIII (New York, Bollingen Series, XXXVII, 1958), 12–15.

9. Hugo Rahner writes on the relationship between the mystery religions and Christianity in respect to cultic practices: "Many elements that were formerly declared to be direct borrowings from the mystery cults entered into Christian life through the cultural heritage held in common with the Greeks. It was the same with the cultic words and usages with which the Greeks fashioned their mysteries; here, too, symbols were formed of elements taken from everyday life. . . . The use of identical and similar words, gestures, rites in the Christian and the Hellenistic cults does not imply derivation of one from the other but a common source in domestic and civil life." In *Pagan and Christian Mysteries: Papers from the Eranos Yearbooks*, ed. Joseph Cambell (New York, Harper Torchbooks, 1963), p. 173. As for the kiss, it is clear that both the Palestinian and Greek worlds knew it in its several functions.

10. *Plutarch's Moralia*, VI, with an English translation by W. C. Helmbold (London; Cambridge, Mass., Loeb Classical Library, 1939), 303.

11. *Apology*, I, 65; in *PG* 6, 427. A little later Origen also noted that it was a practice to exchange the kiss after prayers in the Church (*PG* 14, 1282). Tertullian refers to the kiss as a "signaculum orationis," a signal for the prayer (*De oratione* XVIII), *PL* 1, 1176.

12. "Martyrdom without mysticism is impossible. That martyrdom is not just asceticism, but also mysticism, is implied in the fact that in the martyr ecstasy is realized to the full extent. He steps completely out of this life to unite himself with God." Anselm Stolz, O.S.B., *The Doctrine of Spiritual Perfection*, trans. Aidan Williams, O.S.B., S.T.D. (St. Louis and London, 1948), p. 213. St. Thomas Aquinas speaks of martyrdom as "maximae charitatis signum," a sign of the greatest love, and says that its perfection necessitates the suffering of death (*Summa Theol.* II–II, q. 124, a. 3–4).

13. *The Passion of S. Perpetua*, newly edited from the MSS. with an Introduction and Notes by J. Armitage Robinson (Cambridge, 1891), p. 93.

14. *Apostolic Tradition*, 4; 18; 21. The most trustworthy edition of this precious work which offers many difficult textual problems is *La Tradition Apostolique de Saint Hippolyte, Essai de Reconstitution par Dom Bernard Botte, O.S.B.*, in the series Liturgiewissenschaftliche Quellen und Forschungen, Heft 39, Münster Westfalen, 1963. For the places we have referred to, see pp. 10–11; 40–41; 54–55. There is also the important English version with critical appraisal by the Rev. Gregory Dix, *The Treatise on the Apostolic Tradition of St. Hippolytus of Rome* (London, 1937), pp. 6, 29, 39.

15. Sermo XLII (De Elisaeo, II). *Sermones supositos*, in *PL* 39, 1830. We shall see that S. Bernard of Clairvaux was also to adapt the kiss image to the Johannine passage.

16. St. Augustine was fond of confronting the two insufflations. In one place he does so in order to show that the resurrected Christ who breathed

the Holy Spirit into the disciples is the same God the Creator who breathed the spirit of life into the first man. As God vivified and gave a soul to Adam whom he had first fashioned out of slime, so Christ gave the Spirit to the disciples that they could come forth from the slime of the world: "Et insufflavit in faciem eorum, qui flatu primum hominem vivificavit, et de limo erexit, quo flatu animam membris dedit; significans eum se esse, qui insufflavit in faciem eorum, ut a luto exsurgerent, et luteis operibus renuntiarent." In *Joannis Evangelium*, Tractatus XXXII, 6; in *Oeuvres complètes de Saint Augustin*, IX (Paris, 1869), p. 602. The two biblical insufflations are also the subject of Book XIII, chapter 24 of *The City of God*. There Augustine explains that Genesis 2:7 speaks not of the transmission of the Holy Spirit to man but refers rather to the infusion of the rational soul by God in man.

In connection with this (and the kiss image) there comes to mind Dante's description of the direct infusion of the rational or spiritual soul by God into each human embryo (which has been fashioned by God's child, Nature):

> Apri alla verità che viene il petto;
> E sappi che, sì tosto come al feto
> L'articular del cerebro è perfetto,
> *Lo motor primo a lui si volge lieto*
> Sovra tant'arte di natura, *e spira*
> *Spirito novo di vertù repleto.*
>
> (*Purgatorio*, XXV, 67–72)

Here then is the picture of God the Creator bending affectionately over the human creature (be it yet an embryo) and insufflating into it the soul. Dante's image and the very words *spira* and *spirito* reveal that he had the Vulgate of Genesis 2:7 in mind: "*Inspiravit* in faciem eius *spiraculum* vitae."

17. Eusebius, *The Ecclesiastical History*, I, with an English translation by Kirsopp Lake (London and New York, Loeb Classical Library), 126–127.

18. The Odes of Solomon were discovered in 1909 by J. Rendel Harris. Written in Syriac, an Aramaic dialect, they are a product of the second century. The definitive study with an accompanying literal translation (English) of the Odes remains that of J. Rendel Harris and Alphonse Mingana in two volumes which appeared in 1916 and 1920: *The Odes and Psalms of Solomon* (Manchester, England). The translation is reprinted in *The Oldest Christian Hymn-Book*, Introduction by Michael Maryosip (Temple, Texas, 1948).

19. Hans-Martin Schenke, "Das Evangelium nach Philippus," *Theologische Literaturzeitung*, 84 (1959), n. 1, 1–5. This preface is followed by Schenke's German translation of the Gospel of Philip from the Coptic. Schenke's was the first modern translation of Philip. Though the Coptic manuscript dates from around A.D. 400, the lost Greek original is thought to be of the second or third century. For a discussion of the discovery of the Coptic manuscript and for the present views on the document, see the work referred to in the next note.

20. *The Gospel of Philip*, translated from the Coptic text by R. McL. Wilson (London, 1962), pp. 34–35. The numerical division into "sayings" was first made by Schenke in his German translation.

21. *Ibid.*, pp. 39–40.

22. "Das Evangelium nach Philippus," p. 5.

23. *Five Books of S. Irenaeus Against Heresies*, trans. Rev. John Keble (Oxford and London, 1877), p. 41.

24. "Alexander the False Prophet," 41. In *Lucian, with an English Translation by A. M. Harmon*, IV (London and New York, Loeb Classical Library, 1925), 229.

25. The *Pistis Sophia*, which is a miscellany of several documents, purports to reveal an esoteric learning given by Jesus after the Resurrection to Apostles and women disciples. It has been preserved in a Coptic manuscript. Authorship and dates of the various parts are questions that are still debated. However, there seems to be general agreement that the first document—in which our kiss image occurs—is of the second or third centuries. See the introduction by F. Legge in *Pistis Sophia*, literally translated from the Coptic by George Horner (London, 1924), pp. vii–xlviii. For the episode of the kiss between Jesus and the Holy Spirit in this edition, see pp. 59–60. There exists a highly regarded German translation in Carl Schmidt, *Koptisch-gnostische Schriften*, I Bd (Leipzig, 1905). For the kiss passage, see the recent reprint of this work edited by W. Till (Berlin, 1954), p. 78.

26. From *The Discourse of Theodosius*, in *The Apocryphal New Testament, being the Apocryphal Gospels, Acts, and Apocalypses, with other Narratives and Fragments Newly Translated by Montague Rhodes James* (Oxford, 1924; corrected edition 1955), p. 199.

27. The question of the place and manner of the kiss in the liturgy is complex, and to speak of it would be to fill these pages with minutiae that are important in their own right but really outside my main concern. It is not easy to determine when the kiss was given on the mouth. Some rites prescribed the kiss as an *osculum oris* into the Middle Ages. On the other hand, the kiss or *pax* eventually was reduced to a mild embrace occasionally accompanied by a touching of the cheeks. At the same time, outside the liturgy the kiss tended to become restricted to meetings between the highest ecclesiastical dignitaries or noble personages. An interesting development in the ceremony of the liturgical kiss was the introduction in the thirteenth century—first in England and soon after on the Continent—of the *osculatorium* or *pax board*, a plaque bearing a painted or graven image of Christ or of some other holy and symbolical figures. Because this could be kissed by all, the laity was once again made to participate in the kiss of peace. Gradually, however, the imparting of the kiss in this way also ceased. For particulars on these and other matters concerning the liturgical use of the

kiss, the following may be consulted: F. Cabrol, "Baiser," in *Dictionnaire d'archéologie chrétienne et de liturgie* (fasc. XII), Vol. II, Part I (Paris, 1907), Cols. 117–130; Dom Gregory Dix, *The Shape of the Liturgy* (Glasgow, 1945), pp. 105–110; Joseph A. Jungmann, S.J., *The Mass of the Roman Rite: Its Origins and Development*, translated by Francis A. Brunner, C.S.S.R., II (New York, 1955), 321–332.

28. Catechetical Lecture, XXIII, 3. From *The Catechetical Lectures of Saint Cyril* (Oxford, 1839), pp. 273–274. See *PG* 33, 1112.

29. Sermo CCXXVII (*In die Paschae, IV*); in *Oeuvres complètes de Saint Augustin*, XVIII (Paris, 1872), 190.

30. Sermo CCIV (*In Epiphania Domini, VI*); in *Oeuvres complètes*, XVIII, 100.

31. *Miscellanea Agostiniana: testi e studi pubblicati a cura dell'ordine eremitano di S. Agostino* . . . , I, *Sermones post Maurinos Reperti* (Rome, 1930), 31.

32. Sermo CCLXVII, 4 (*In die Pentecostes, I*); *Oeuvres complètes*, XVIII, 377.

33. *The Ecclesiastical Hierarchy*, III, 3, 8; in *PG* 3, 437. In keeping with Christ's command that the faithful love one another, Christians insisted on the necessity of love and unity in order to approach Christ. To love others is to love Christ. To be with Christ who is the Head, one must be united by love to all who are the body. For this reason Augustine somewhere compares the desire to come to Christ without this all-embracing love to the desire of one who would kiss the head of a beloved while treading on his feet.

34. *On Compunction*, I, 3; in *PG* 47, 398.

35. *Baptismal Instructions*, trans. Paul W. Harkins (Westminster, Md. and London, 1963), pp. 171–172. The passage is from the Eleventh Instruction, the original of which was published by A. Papadopoulos-Kerameus in a rare Russian series of the former University of St. Petersburg: *Varia graeca sacra. Sbornik grečeskikh neisdannikh bogoslovskikh tekstov I–IV věkov* (St. Petersburg, 1909), pp. 154–183.

36. "Homily 44 on the First Epistle to Corinthians," in *PG* 61, 376.

37. "Homily 30 on the Second Epistle to Corinthians," in *PG* 61, 606.

38. *Loc. cit.*

39. *Baptismal Instructions*, p. 172.

40. *Constitutions of the Holy Apostles*, II, vii (lvii). In *The Ante-Nicene Fathers*, ed. A. Roberts and J. Donaldson, VII (Buffalo, 1886), 422.

41. "Magnum sacramentum osculum pacis: sic osculare, ut diligas. Ne sis

Iudas; Iudas traditor Christum ore osculabatur, corde insidiabatur." *Miscellanea Agostiniana*, I, *Sermones post Maurinos Reperti* (Rome, 1930), 31–32.

42. Epistola 41 (*Frater sorori*); in *PL* 16, 1164–1165.

43. *Hexaemeron*, VI, ix, 68. In *Bibliotheca Patrum Ecclesiasticorum Latinorum Selecta*, IX, pars II (Leipzig, 1840), 180. In the text I have used the translation by John J. Savage in *Hexameron, Paradise, and Cain and Abel* (New York, 1961), p. 278.

44. *PG* 6, 964. The passage occurs in a context in which Athenagoras is replying to the charge of incest brought against the Christians.

45. *PG* 8, 660–661. The English translation used is from *The Ante-Nicene Fathers*, ed. A. Roberts and J. Donaldson, II (Buffalo, 1885), 291. The dangers in kissing (between the sexes) were evidently always present. In the ninth century, Amalarius of Metz also admonished his flock that when the *Pax* is to be given at the Mass, the men are not to kiss the women and vice versa for fear that unholy carnal desires be aroused. *De Ecclesiasticus officiis*, in *PL* 105, 1153 A–B.

The comparison that Clement made between the sting of certain spiders and licentious kisses calls to mind a similar judgment made by Socrates when the latter pointed to the dangers that lurk in the kiss. The episode is recorded by Xenophon in the *Memorabilia* (I, iii, 11–13): "Unhappy man!" exclaimed Socrates, "and what do you think that you incur by kissing a handsome person [youth]? Do you not expect to become at once a slave . . . ? And to be compelled to pursue what not even a madman would pursue?" "By Hercules," said Xenophon, "what extraordinary power you represent to be in a kiss!" "Do you wonder at this?" rejoined Socrates; "are you not aware that the Tarantula by just touching a part of the body with his mouth, wears men down with pain, and deprives them of their senses?" "Yes, indeed," said Xenophon, "but the Tarantula infuses something at the bitten part." "And do you not think, foolish man," rejoined Socrates, "that beautiful persons infuse something when they kiss, something which you do not see?" *The Memorabilia of Socrates*, trans. Rev. J. S. Watson (Philadelphia, 1899), pp. 36–37. See also Xenophon's *Banquet*, IV, 25–26.

46. Hermas, *Le Pasteur*, Introduction, texte critique, traduction et notes par Robert Joly (Paris, 1958); Sources Chrétiennes, No. 53, pp. 312–314. A modern English translation of *The Shepherd of Hermas* by Joseph M.–F. Marique, S.J., is printed in the series The Fathers of the Church: *The Apostolic Fathers*, trans. Francis X. Glimm, Joseph M.–F. Marique, S.J., Gerald G. Walsh, S.J. (New York, 1947–48), pp. 225–352.

47. See Hermas, *Le Pasteur*, ed. Joly, pp. 48 and 312, n. 1. The Rev. F. Crombie, author of an earlier translation into English of the *Shepherd*, writes in connection with the episode: "We have in it [the early experiment of living as brothers and sisters] an example of the struggles of individuals out of heathenism,—by no means an institution of Christianity itself." *The Ante-Nicene Fathers*, II (New York, 1913), 58.

48. Hermas, *Le Pasteur*, pp. 300–303. Both the identity of the tall Master and the meaning of the tower are made manifest to Hermas *after* his experience with the virgins. It is then too that Hermas is told who the twelve virgins themselves are. They are nothing less than holy spirits, the twelve powers of the Son of God without which one cannot enter into the Kingdom of God. Their names are: Faith, Continence, Fortitude, Patience, Simplicity, Innocence, Purity, Cheerfulness, Truth, Understanding, Concord, and Love. The question arises as to whether this allegorization has a bearing on the erotic episode between Hermas and the virgins. Joly and some other scholars deny this to be so. Joly rejects the interpretation that would see the episode as an allegorical representation of the joys of heaven. See Hermas, *Le Pasteur*, pp. 48 and 315, n. 1. The arguments against any allegorical intention at all, however, are not conclusive. It seems to me that we may well have an awkward attempt at an adaptation of an erotic pagan theme to a Christian allegory. In a similar way, but much later, Boccaccio, in his *Ameto*, was to make a clumsy attempt at allegorizing the figures of seductive nymphs whose sensual charms are perceived by a young and as yet uncouth shepherd.

49. Epistula VI, 4. In Saint Cyprian, *Correspondance*, I, ed. Le Chanoine Bayard, 2nd ed. (Paris, 1962), 17.

50. *The Passion of S. Perpetua* (see n. 13 above), p. 80.

51. Maxime Collignon, *Essai sur les monuments grecs et romains relatifs au mythe de Psyché*, in *Bibliothèque des écoles françaises d'Athènes et de Rome*, fascicule second (Paris, 1877), pp. 285–446. For the list of Christian sarcophagi bearing the Psyche and Eros embrace, see pp. 436–438.

52. See Collignon, p. 364.

53. Filippo Buonarotti, *Osservazioni sopra alcuni frammenti di vasi antichi di vetro ornati di figure trovati ne' cimiteri di Roma* (Firenze, 1716), p. 201. More recently, Franz Cumont, touching on the presence of the Eros and Psyche myth in funerary art, wrote that the group "symbolise cet amour divin dont l'âme doit être saisie pour s'élever vers le séjour des dieux;" and in a note to this he interpreted the overall myth as symbolizing the soul's winning of Paradise "Le conte moral suivant lequel Psyché après de dures épreuves et une sévère pénitence obtenait, grâce à l'intercession d'Eros, d'être transportée dans l'Olympe, où un mariage l'unissait pour toujours à son amant, devint à l'époque paienne et resta pour les chrétiens un symbole de l'âme pénétrée de l'amour divin, qui, après avoir expié ses fautes, est admise au ciel." *Recherches sur le symbolisme funéraire des romains* (Paris, 1942), pp. 319–320, n. 8.

54. Epistula XXXVII, 3, in *Correspondance*, I, 94. The accommodation of certain pagan myths to Christian ideas, especially in funerary art, included such figures as Hermes and Orpheus as young shepherds, in which guise they were types of Christ. More in line with the Psyche-Eros myth was the legend of Ganymede abducted by Jupiter, which was allegorized into the Christian

idea of the soul's ascension to Heaven. Such myths were to be revived in the same key by the Italian Neoplatonists and artists of the Renaissance.

55. *Symposium*, 192. It is worthwhile remembering that in Genesis, Judaism and Christianity had an androgyne myth also. Both versions of the Genesis account (1:27–28; 2:21–24) of the creation of man consider the original man to be androgynous or hermaphroditic.

56. "Quid est ergo amor, nisi quaedam vita duo aliqua copulans, vel copulare appetens, amantem scilicet, et quod amatur? Et hoc etiam in externis carnalibusque amoribus ita est." *De Trinitate*, VIII, x, 14; in *Oeuvres de Saint Augustin*, XVI, ed. P. Agaësse, S.J. (Paris, 1955), 70.

57. *De ordine*, II, xviii, 48; in *Oeuvres de Saint Augustin*, IV, ed. R. Jolivet (Paris, 1948), 446.

58. I would refer, for example, to one of the most widely read psychological enquiries concerning love in our day. It is easy to see that Erich Fromm's *The Art of Loving* (New York, Harper Colophon Books, 1962) is centered on the concept that true love—in whatever form it takes—is the result of the human creature's sense of alienation and an urge to find at-one-ment. "The desire for interpersonal fusion," Fromm writes, "is the most powerful striving in man. It is the most fundamental passion, it is the force which keeps the human race together, the clan, the family, society. The failure to achieve it means insanity or destruction" (p. 18). Within this existential need for fusion or oneness is included the specific biological need for union between the masculine and feminine poles. And Fromm observes further that "The basis for our need to love lies in the experience of separateness and the resulting need to overcome the anxiety of separateness by the experience of union. The religious form of love, that which is called the love of God, is psychologically speaking, not different. It springs from the need to overcome separateness and to achieve union" (p. 63).

59. "De Substantia Dilectionis" (*Institutiones in Decalogum*, ch. IV); in *PL* 176, 15.

60. *Loc. cit.*

61. It may be pointed out that Paul's words indicate that it is the earthly conjugal union which is a *copy* of the mystic marriage between Christ and the Church. This is a "Platonic" feature, if one likes, in Paul's passage. Some time after Paul, the Neoplatonic philosopher Plotinus has the same manner of considering a supernal union to be the *model* of the union of earthly lovers. Speaking of the soul's attainment of union with the divine, he says that then there is "no longer a duality but a two in one; for so long as the presence holds, all distinction fades: it is as lover and beloved here, in a copy of that union, long to blend" (*Enneads* VI, vii, 34). Plotinus, *The Enneads*, trans. Stephen MacKenna, 3d ed. revised by B. S. Page (London, 1956), p. 588. We will find the same thing later in medieval Jewish mysticism.

62. *Mysticism* (New York, 1960), p. 426. This work was first published in 1911.

63. As for the nuptial idea, it is already conspicuous in the Old Testament; it becomes a major metaphor in the Gospels of the New Testament (where we even find the portrayal of Christ's awareness of himself as a Bridegroom), and is fully confirmed by St. Paul, most dramatically in the passage from Ephesians. For a close examination of this motif in the prophetic books of the Old Testament, see André Feuillet's *Le Cantique des Cantiques: Étude de théologie biblique et réflexions sur une méthode d'exégèse* (Paris, 1953), pp. 140–192. The concept as it developed from the Old to the New Testament and then in the early Church Fathers has been studied by Claude Chavasse in *The Bride of Christ: An Enquiry into the Nuptial Element in Early Christianity* (London, 1940), a work that stresses the idea of the Bridegroom and bride as referring to Christ and the Church (which is the Mystical Bride and the Mystical Body of Christ). Chavasse is unsympathetic to the interpretation that considers the individual soul to be the bride, this being a development that reached its apogee in the twelfth century. Thus he does not do justice, or so it seems to me, to the richness of St. Bernard's sermons on the Song. On the other hand, the chapter on St. Augustine's use of the bride motif is excellent. Augustine, who does not adopt the soul-bride theme, save perhaps with one exception (*Serm.* LXXXVII, 9), frequently in his writings applies the idea of the bride as the Church.

64. The interpretation of the Song of Songs in the Jewish tradition has been studied by Paul Vulliaud in *Le Cantique des Cantiques, d'après la tradition juive* (Paris, 1925), a book which is, however, often disconcerting. Besides giving over half of his time to ridiculing almost everything that had hitherto been written about the Song, the author seems not to care about matters of chronology, and frequently ascribes medieval Jewish mystical trends to earlier periods, in some cases to the time of St. Paul. The reader will find a succinct and reliable account of the Jewish tradition vis-à-vis the Song in *The Jewish Encyclopedia* under the entries "Bride" and "Song of Songs." For a view of the major Christian interpretations of the Song through the centuries, see the invaluable *Dictionnaire de Spiritualité Ascétique et Mystique*, II (Paris, 1953), 86–109. However, the most definitive single study of patristic and medieval Christian exegeses of the Song in the West is that by Friedrich Ohly, *Hohelied-Studien: Grundzüge einer Geschichte der Hoheliedauslegung des Abendlandes bis um 1200*. Schriften der Wissenschaftlichen Gesellschaft an der Johann Wolfgang Goethe-Universität Frankfurt am Main, Geisteswissenschaftliche Reihe Nr. 1 (Wiesbaden, 1958). Another important though more specialized study is Helmut Riedlinger's *Die Makellosigkeit der Kirche in den lateinischen Hoheliedkommentaren des Mittelalters*, (Muenster, 1958). A survey which is especially valuable for some of the more modern interpretations is H. H. Rowley's "The Interpretation of the *Song of Songs*," in that author's volume *The Servant of the Lord and other Essays on the Old Testament* (London, 1952), pp. 189–234. The bulk of Rowley's essay is devoted to

a cogent criticism of the view that the Song is closely connected with the liturgy of the Babylonian Adonis-Tammuz fertility cult. The latter is a view that has been favored by many in one form or another, especially since it was put forth by T. J. Meek in 1922. The latest somewhat modified presentation of this view by Meek is found in *The Interpreter's Bible*, V (New York, 1956), 91–98. There (p. 94) the author still maintains that "The *Song of Songs* is the survival in conventionalized form of ancient Hebrew New Year liturgies that celebrated the reunion and marriage of the sun god with the mother goddess, which in the ancient world typified the revival of life in nature that came with the return of the growing season." For a consideration of the possible relationship between the Song and love poetry of the East as well as for a refutation of the cultic and literalist interpretations (both ancient and modern, for the controversy over the Song is as vital today as ever), see the edition of the Song in the series of *Études Bibliques: Le Cantique des Cantiques*, traduction et commentaire par A. Robert, P.S.S., et R. Tournay, O.P. avec le concours de A. Feuillet, P.S.S. (Paris, 1963). This volume includes an essential bibliography.

65. The attitude of Christianity toward marriage in the early centuries and in the Middle Ages is notorious. For the theologians, virginity and absolute chastity were the highest ideals as conditions which would preserve one from a defection from God; marriage was at best held to be a necessary evil. It was a lawful concession to weakness, and it was necessary to the propagation of the species, but otherwise it was deplorable. Rather than Christ's approval of marriage, early Christianity remembered Paul's begrudging tolerance: "I wish you were all in the same state as myself . . . To the unmarried and to the widows, I would say that they will do well to remain in the same state as myself, but if they have not the gift of continence, let them marry; better to marry than to feel the heat of passion" (melius est enim nubere quam uri. I Cor. 7:7–9). The voices echoing this sentiment were many, but among the most forceful was St. Jerome's in his *Adversus Iovinianum*, a work that enjoyed great fame in the Middle Ages because of its antifeminist pronouncements. Jerome reminds his readers that it is a great blessing not to be bound to a wife because then one is free to serve Christ. As for those who are married, he warns them that ardent love of one's wife is equivalent to adultery or fornication. A man should love his wife with judgment, not with feeling (Sapiens vir judicio debet amare conjugem, non affectu). Married men should behave toward their wives not as lovers, but as husbands. PL 22, 281.

Paul's attitude toward marriage was declared the official position of the Catholic Church at the Council of Trent in a decree that anathematized those who held celibacy and virginity to be an inferior state to marriage. Nonetheless, it would be wrong to deny that the overall effect of Catholic teaching has been to spiritualize and sanctify marriage, and it was precisely Paul's use of the conjugal union of man and wife to figure the union of Christ and the Church which was a key text in this development. Besides this general development, there were voices in the Middle Ages that spoke of the positive side of marriage and sex in a naturalistic key.

66. *PG* 44, 776 C.

67. *Ibid.*, 780 C-D.

68. As an illustration of this point we may refer to a passage from the great seventeenth century Spanish mystic St. John of the Cross, who exalts the sense of touch as the highest in the order of the spiritual senses, and the kiss as the greatest touch that God gives to the soul. "For these are the touches that the Bride entreated of Him in the Songs, saying *Osculetur me osculo oris sui.* Since this is a thing which takes place in such close intimacy with God, whereto the soul desires with such yearnings to attain, it esteems and longs for a touch of this Divinity more than all the other favours that God grants it. Wherefore, after many such favours have been granted to the Bride in the said Songs, of which she has sung therein, she is not satisfied, but entreats Him for these Divine touches, saying: 'Who shall give Thee to me, my brother, that I might find Thee alone without, sucking the breasts of my mother, so that I might kiss Thee with the mouth of my soul.' " *Dark Night of the Soul*, trans. and ed. E. Allison Peers, 3d rev. ed. (New York, Image Books), p. 188.

69. *De IV Gradibus Violentae Caritatis*, 18. I have used the critical edition of Gervais Dumeige (Paris, 1955), p. 145.

70. The significance of the need for such a language was admirably stated by Evelyn Underhill in a work on mysticism which, although written half a century ago, remains a classic in its field. The author writes: "At this point we begin to see that the language of deification, taken alone, will not suffice to describe the soul's final experience of Reality. The personal and emotional aspect of man's relation with his Source is also needed if that which he means by 'union with God' is to be even partially expressed. Hence, even the most 'transcendental' mystic is constantly compelled to fall back on the language of love in the endeavour to express the content of his metaphysical raptures: and forced in the end to acknowledge that the perfect union of lover and Beloved cannot be suggested in the precise and arid terms of religious philosophy. Such arid language eludes the most dangerous aspects of 'divine union,' the pantheistic on the one hand, the 'amoristic' on the other; but it also fails to express the most splendid side of that amazing experience. It needs some other, more personal and intimate vision to complete it; and this we shall find in the reports of those mystics of the 'intimate' type to whom the Unitive life has meant not self-loss in an Essence, but self-fulfilment in the union of heart and will." *Mysticism* (New York, 1960), pp. 425–426.

What is said here of Christian mystical language is true of other religions as well. Muslim mysticism in particular is to be compared with Christianity in this matter. A. J. Arberry writes: "Many anecdotes of the early Sufis relate how fond they were of quoting love poetry, often in the first place of a purely human character, which they interpreted allegorically to accord with their own passionate spiritualism . . . . Fully to understand the later poetry of Sufism . . . . it is necessary to keep in mind how fundamental in Sufi thought is this allegory of love, and how readily in their minds human and Divine imagery is interchanged." *Sufism, An Account of the Mystics of Islam* (London, 1950), p. 61.

71. *De virginibus velandis*, XI, 7. In *Stromata patristica et mediaevalia, Fasciculus quartus: Q. Septimi Florentis Tertulliani De oratione et De virginibus velandis libelli*, ed. G. F. Dierks (Utrecht/Antwerpt, 1956), p. 53. Cf. *De oratione*, XXII, 10, *ibid.*, p. 32.

72. *PL* 16, 1165.

73. The important document relative to this topic is a decree by Constantine concerning the question of donations *ante nuptias* (*Codex Theodos.* ed. G. Haenel, 1842 Bonn, III, 5, 6). For its significance and impact see G. Tamassia, "Osculum interveniens: Contributo alla storia dei riti nuziali," in *Rivista storica italiana*, II (1885), 241–264. For matrimonial rites under the Empire see also Mario Righetti, *Manuale di Storia Liturgica*, IV (Milan, 1953), 335. It is not known when the use of the kiss as the seal or perfecting of betrothal among the Romans was begun. Tamassia notes that by the time of Constantine's decree Roman customs had perhaps lost even the memory of the austerity of the early years of the Republic, which evidently would not have approved of such usage. However, it is not so much as an erotic symbol that the betrothal kiss seems to have been used, but rather as a magical rite establishing a psycho-physical union. In this sense it could have been quite ancient. It is also to be noted that Tertullian's reference to the usage precedes the decree by a century.

74. Until the ninth century, writes W. M. Foley, "the *sponsalia* and actual nuptials were still regarded as distinct ceremonies, between which an interval of time might elapse. . . . It is, however, most probable that from much earlier times the two ceremonies had been generally combined in practice. Formal *sponsalia* were not required by Roman law, and were frequently omitted. In such cases . . . espousal ceremonies would take place at the actual marriage." "Marriage," in *The Encyclopedia of Religion and Ethics*, ed. J. Hastings, VIII (New York, 1928), 436. It is curious that the author does not mention the kiss specifically as being among the chief features of the ancient betrothal ceremony: "The solemn troth-plight, the joining of hands and the giving and receiving of a ring or rings with certain gifts of money—the arrhae, pledge of the dowry—were the principal features of the betrothal ceremony" (p. 435).

75. The Evreux Pontifical of the eleventh and twelfth centuries, in its description of the marriage ceremony, indicates that after the *Agnus Dei*, "the bridegroom goes up to the altar to receive the Pax from the priest, and then carries it to his bride, whom he kisses." A. Villien, *The History and Liturgy of the Sacraments*, trans. H. W. Edwards (New York, 1932), pp. 323–324. Villien also notes that the Ambrosian Ritual likewise declares that at the marriage Mass the Pax is given first to the bridegroom, then to the bride (*In missa datur pax sponso primum, deinde sponsae*). *Ibid.*, p. 324. There was also an effort to exclude the nuptial kiss entirely, especially in the post-

Tridentine period. For example, a Synod of Turin in 1647 declared: "Nulli sponso liceat in ecclesia sponsam osculari" (Synod. I Taur, 1647, p. 104). Quoted in M. Righetti, *Manuale*, IV, 345. The nuptial kiss is once again in current usage as part of the wedding ceremony in the Church.

76. Before or contemporaneously with Origen, in the early part of the third century, Hippolytus of Rome had written a commentary in which the bride was the Church, and the bridegroom was the Incarnate Word. Of this work, which was very likely the first full Christian spiritual allegorization of the Song, only fragments remain. In it, there is at least the suggestion of the soul as bride. See *Dictionnaire de Spiritualité* (above, n. 64), II, 94.

77. In *Canticum Canticorum* I, 1; *PG* 13, 85. Except for a few Greek fragments, Origen's Commentary on the Song comes down to us in the Latin translation of Rufinus. Similarly his Homilies on the Song were saved for posterity by way of the Latin version of St. Jerome.

78. *PG* 13, 86.

79. "Il saute aux yeux qu'on est ici [la littérature hermétique] aux antipodes de la conception philonienne et gnostique, d'après laquelle le pneuma est consideré comme une lumière divine accordée à l'homme en vue de lui révéler des vérités qu'il ne pourrait pas connaître par les seules forces de son intelligence humaine." G. Verbeke, *L'évolution de la doctrine du pneuma du stoicisme à S. Augustin* (Paris and Louvain, 1945), p. 321.

80. In *Liber de Isaac et anima*; *PL* 14, 531.

81. *Epistola* 41, 15. In *PL* 16, 1165. The same verse from the Psalm had been referred to as a kiss by Origen in speaking of the kisses of the Word as the illuminating of obscure meanings for the perfected soul. See *PG* 13, 85–86.

82. *De Sacramentis*, V, ii, 5–7; *PL* 16, 466–467.

83. *PG* 81, 53.

84. The Eucharistic-bridal union is in fact a frequent thought in Christian writers. Without seeking to multiply examples, we may note that one of the most ecstatic waxings on the Eucharist as a marital union between the communicant and Jesus Christ occurs in the works of Bossuet. The eating of the God-man is a marriage in body and spirit between bride and Bridegroom. Building on the fundamental Johannine text (John 6:57), Bossuet reminds us that the union and the indwelling is reciprocal, and, he says, "l'Eucharistie nous explique toutes les paroles d'amour, de correspondance, d'union, qui sont entre Jésus-Christ et son Eglise, entre l'Epoux et l'Epouse, entre lui et nous." *Oeuvres complètes de Bossuet*, VI (Paris, 1862), 369. These words are immediately followed by the remarkable passage in which Bossuet explains the bridal-alimentary image of eating and assimilating the Host by an analogy with the rage of human lovers who seek desperately to unite in an embrace and kiss that have an anthropophagic quality and intent.

The Eucharist is the divine Banquet, and it is worthwhile noting that in the Church's liturgical chants, Psalm 33, which urges us to "taste and see how sweet the Lord is," has commonly been linked with the Eucharist. The invitation to taste and so experience the sweetness of the Lord is easily connected with the kiss image, as is done, for example, in the eleventh century by John of Fécamp, who brings the verse from the Psalm into conjunction with the kiss of the Song: "Osculetur me osculo oris sui. Quae osculum divinae veritatis felicissimo amore expetis, vaca et vide quoniam Deus est suavis." Quoted in *Un maître de la vie spirituelle au XIe siècle: Jean de Fécamp, par Jean Leclercq et Jean-Paul Borines* (Paris, 1946), p. 205.

85. A. M. La Bonnardière, who has recorded Augustine's citations from the Song, gives no entry for the verse that speaks of the Shulamite's request for kisses. See "Le Cantique des Cantiques dans l'oeuvre de saint Augustin," in *Revue des Études Augustiniennes*, I, no. 3 (1955), 225–237.

86. *De libero arbitrio*, II, xiv, 37; in *Oeuvres de Saint Augustin*, VI, ed. F. Thonnard (Paris, 1941), 286.

87. "Nunc illud quaerimus, qualis sis amator sapientiae, quam castissimo conspectu atque amplexu, nullo interposito velamento quasi nudam videre ac tenere desideras, qualem se illa non sinit, nisi paucissimus et electissimis amatoribus suis." *Soliloquia*, I, xiii, 22; in *Oeuvres de Saint Augustin*, V, ed. P. de Labriolle (Paris, 1948), 70. This idea of the lover desiring to behold and embrace chastely the beloved *Sapientia* in the nude is strikingly like the medieval troubadour concept of *fin' amors* which speaks of touching and embracing the beloved in the nude. See chapter 3 for remarks on the connection between troubadour love and the Christian tradition.

88. In the fourteenth century, Henry Suso, the German "troubadour" of divine love, has Eternal Wisdom use such expressions as: "My faithfulness is so made to be loved, so lovely am I to be embraced, and so tender for pure languishing souls to kiss, that all hearts ought to break for My possession"; "My love is of that sort which is not diminished in unity, nor confounded in multiplicity"; "I go forth to meet those who seek Me, and I receive with affectionate joy such as desire My love." Quoted from *The Soul Afire*, ed. H. A. Reinhold (New York, 1944), pp. 234–235.

89. The translation is that of J. C. Pilkington in *Basic Writings of Saint Augustine*, ed. Whitney J. Oates, I (New York, 1948), 166.

90. "But what is it that I love in loving Thee? Not corporeal beauty, nor the splendor of time, nor the radiance of the light, so pleasant to our eyes, nor the sweet melodies of songs of all kinds, nor the fragrant smell of flowers, and ointments, and spices, not manna and honey, not limbs pleasant to the embracements of flesh (*non membra acceptabilia carnis amplexibus*). I love not these things when I love my God; and yet I love a certain kind of light, and sound, and fragrance, and food, and embracement in loving my God, who is the light, sound, fragrance, food, and embracement of my inner man" (X, 6). *Basic Writings of Saint Augustine*, I, 151.

2. *Medieval Mystics*

1. *PL* 177, 563.

2. See R. Javelet, "Psychologie des auteurs spirituels du XIIe siècle," in *Revue des Sciences Religieuses*, 33, 3 (1959), esp. 266–267. See also in our chapter 1 the remarks concerning love as a desire for at-one-ment.

3. *Sermones super Cantica Canticorum*, I, iv, 6. For Bernard's Sermons on the Song I have translated from the critical edition of the *Opera*, Vols. I and II prepared by J. Leclercq, C. H. Talbot, H. M. Rochais (Rome, Editiones Cistercienses, 1957, 1958). The first quote is from Vol. I (1957), p. 5. Other references to this work will be given as *Opera*, followed by the volume number and page.

4. Origin's use of this etymology of Solomon as the Peaceful One occurs in the prologue of his own Commentary on the Song. See *PG* 13, 80.

5. *Sermones super Cantica*, II, ii, 3. In *Opera*, I, 9–10.

6. *Sermones super Cantica*, II, iii, 4–7. In *Opera*, I, 10–12. The application of the kiss image to the Incarnation itself was made by St. Jerome in the exposition of Psalm 84:11, a verse which uses the term *kiss* to refer to the fusion of justice and peace into one, which in turn is interpreted as referring to the Incarnate God (*Dei et hominis filius*). "*Misericordia et veritas obviaverunt sibi: justitia et pax osculatae sunt*. Misericordia et veritas obviaverunt. Duas res video, quae conveniendo et obviando unum fiunt. Iustitia et pax osculatae sunt. Hoc totum in mysterium Domini Salvatoris coaptatur: hoc est Dei et hominis filius, qui est nobis veritas misericordia pax atque iustitia, in quo iustitia prioris populi et misericordia sequentis in unam pacem coniunguntur. 'Ipse enim est, ait apostolus, pax nostra, qui fecit utraque unum.' Hoc est mysterium, quod ecclesia desiderat, et clamat in Canticis canticorum dicens 'Osculetur me osculo oris sui.' Hoc est osculum, quod Paulus apostolus dicit 'Salutate invicem in osculo pacis.' " *S. Hieronymi Presbyteri Opera, Pars II Opera Homiletica.* Corpus Christianorum: Series Latina, LXXVIII (Turnholti, 1958), p. 398. Here then, it is an ecclesiastical interpretation that Jerome gives to the Song of Songs. The connection made with the Pauline holy kiss of salutation among the brethren is clear. The *osculum pacis* is Christ. The faithful greet, love, and kiss one another in Christ.

St. Bonaventura perhaps remembered Jerome's words when he also referred Psalm 84:11 and the *osculum amoris* of the Song to the Incarnate Word: "Osculum . . . signum est amoris et pacis . . . Hoc osculum amoris et pacis petit sponsa in Canticis . . . Benedictionis plenitudo ex hoc osculo procedit. Unde in Psalmo 'Benedixisti, Domine, terram tuam;' et subditur: 'Misericordia et veritas obviaverunt sibi, justitia et pax osculatae sunt.' Istius deosculationis origo est in Verbo incarnato, in quo est unio summi amoris, et connexio duplicis naturae, per quam Deus nos osculatur, et nos Dominum deosculamur." "Expositio in Evangelium S. Lucae," in *Sancti Bonaventurae Opera omnia*, XI, ed. A. C. Peltier (Paris, 1864), 16.

Bernard's contemporary and fellow Cistercian, William of Saint-Thierry, although he prefers to see the soul as the bride of the Song, nonetheless recognized that the Incarnation was itself a celestial kiss given by Christ to his bride the Church. In that kiss—that is, in joining himself with the human nature—he united himself so intimately with the bride that he became one with her, God having become man, and man having become God. *Exposé sur le Cantique des Cantiques*, ed. J.-M. Déchanet, O.S.B. (Paris, 1962), p. 112. Also in *PL* 180, 483 C.

7. In point of fact, in Bernard's Sermons the bride is alternately the Church and the individual soul; sometimes he passes unexpectedly and imperceptibly from the one to the other. In the same way, although the Bridegroom of the soul-bride is usually the Word, at times it is the Word made flesh, Jesus Christ. Ordinarily, though not constantly, for the mystics of spiritual marriage, when Christ is the Bridegroom the Church is the bride.

8. *Sermones super Cantica*, III, iii. In *Opera*, I, 17.

9. *Sermones super Cantica*, VIII, i, 2. In *Opera*, I, 37.

10. Bernard notes that the Kiss of the Mouth is the indwelling of the Father in the Son and of the Son in the Father, the texts referring to this being the mystic utterances from the Johannine Gospel: "I and the Father are one" and "I am in the Father and the Father is in me" (John 10:30; 14:10). This, says Bernard, is the Kiss from Mouth to Mouth. No creature can lay claim to such a kiss: "Audi siquidem osculum de ore: *Ego et Pater unum* sumus (John 10:30); item: *Ego in Patre, et Pater in me est* (John 14:10). Osculum est ore ad os sumptum." *Sermones super Cantica*, VIII, vii, 7. In *Opera*, I, 40.

11. *Loc. cit.* For further discussion of the Holy Spirit as Kiss motif in connection with the Trinity and dove symbolism, see Appendix I.

12. *Sermones super Cantica*, VIII, ii, 5. In *Opera*, I, 38.

13. *Sermones super Cantica*, VIII, vii, 8. In *Opera*, I, 41.

14. Such, for example, is what we find in a page from St. Gregory the Great: "Hoc autem, quod generaliter de cuncta ecclesia diximus, nunc specialiter de unaquaeque anima sentiamus. Ponamus ante oculos esse animam quandam donorum studiis inherentem, intellectum ex aliena praedicatione percipientem: quae per diuinam gratiam etiam ipsa inlustrari desiderat, ut aliquando etiam per se intellegat: quae nihil se intellegere nisi per uerba praedicatorum considerat; et dicat: OSCULETUR ME OSCULO ORIS SUI. 'Ipse me tangat intus, ut cognoscam intellegentia, et non iam praedicatorum uocibus sed internae eius gratiae tactu perfruar.' Quasi osculo oris sui osculabatur Moysen dominus, cum ei per fiduciam familiaris gratiae intellectum porrigeret. Unde scriptum est: *Si fuerit propheta, in somnium*

loquar ad eum, et non sicut famulo meo Moysi: os enim ad os loquor ei [Num. 12:6–8]. Os quippe ad os loqui quasi osculari est et interna intellegentia mentem tangere." *Expositiones in Canticum Canticorum, In Librum Primum Regum,* ed. Patricius Verbraken, O.S.B. Corpus Christianorum: Series Latina, CXLIV (Turnholti, 1963), pp. 17–18. Here too, the kiss indicates an infusion of special grace whereby the soul is illuminated and *touches*—knows in an intimate way—the deeper mysteries of the Deity. The same thought and the same transposition from intellectual to affective imagery is what we find in a passage from William of Saint-Thierry. Yearning for insight into the secrets of the Kingdom of God, he desires to have a clear revelation of the Father made to him, he says, *face to face, eye to eye, kiss to kiss.* "Mysterium regni Dei desidero, palam nihi annuntiari de Patre deposco; faciem ad faciem, oculum ad oculum, osculum ad osculum. *Osculetur me osculo oris sui.*" *Exposé sur le Cantique des Cantiques* (Paris, 1962), pp. 118–120.

15. *Sermones super Cantica,* VIII, iv, 6. In *Opera,* I, 39.

16. *Sermones super Cantica,* VII, ii, 2. In *Opera,* I, 31–32.

17. *Sermones super Cantica,* IX, ii, 2. In *Opera,* I, 43.

18. *Sermones super Cantica,* VIII, iv, 6. In *Opera,* I, 39.

19. The great mystics such as Bernard and Gregory of Nyssa think of the grace they may receive not as a private gift, but as a privilege carrying the joyous responsibility of assisting others by it. Grace, that is, has an apostolic and charismatic character attached to it. See the observations made by J. Danielou on this matter in connection with the mystic theology of Gregory of Nyssa, in *Platonisme et Théologie Mystique: Doctrine spirituelle de Saint Grègoire de Nysse,* Nouvelle édition (Paris, 1954), p. 310.

20. *Sermones super Cantica,* IX, v, 7. In *Opera,* I, 46.

21. One of the best-known Latin religious songs of the Middle Ages is often attributed to Bernard. It is the beautiful *"Jesu, dulcis memoria"* in which we hear of the soul's yearning for the sweetness of union with Christ. The union is pictured as the embracement and honeyed kisses of lovers:

> Tunc amplexus, tunc oscula
> Quae vincunt mellis pocula:
> Quam felix, Christi copula!

22. It is true, however, that William first acknowledges the celestial kiss Christ gave the Church when the Word assumed flesh and thereby joined himself so intimately with her that the two became one. What William is saying is that the Incarnation is a kiss: "Sponsus vero Christus, sponsae suae Ecclesiae, quasi osculum de caelo porrexit, cum Verbum caro factum, in tantum ei appropinquavit, ut se ei conjungeret; in tantum conjunxit, ut uniret, ut Deus homo, homo Deus fieret." *Super Cantica Canticorum,* in *Exposé sur le Cantique des Cantiques,* texte latin, introduction et notes de J.-M. Déchanet, O.S.B. (Paris, 1962), Sources Chrétiennes No. 82, p. 112. Also in *PL* 180, 483.

23. *Exposé*, p. 144. Also in *PL* 180, 483.

24. The passage occurs in connection with William's exegesis of the words "Lectulus noster floridus" from the Song (1:16). It is in this bed, says William, that the embrace and the unitive kiss are consummated. *Exposé*, pp. 220–222. Also in *PL* 180, 506. There is a similar passage in William's *Epistola ad Fratres de Monte-Dei* (108) where again the bond joining the soul and God is said to be the Holy Spirit itself, the Charity that is God, the unity, kiss, embrace, that binds the Son to the Father and vice versa. This same bond or kiss binds the soul and God. The blessed soul finds itself rapt into that Trinitarian kiss and embrace: "cum in amplexu et osculo Patris et Filii mediam quodammodo se invenit beata conscientia." But no more than Bernard can William be accused of confusing the creature with the Creator. Great as the gift of the Spirit is, the fact remains that in this ineffable manner man is like God because of that gift of grace, whereas God *is* what he is by virtue of his nature: "cum modo ineffabili incogitabili fieri meretur homo Dei non Deus, sed tamen quod est Deus, homo ex gratia, quod Deus [est] ex natura." *Un traité de la vie solitaire: Epistola ad Fratres de Monte-Dei de Guillaume de Saint-Thierry*, Edition critique du texte latin, par M.-M. Davy (Paris, 1940), p. 146. Also *PL* 184, 349 A-B. On the other hand, the German mystic Meister Eckhart, in using the kiss image to indicate the mystic union, apparently suggests that the creature spiritually joins with God in essence, thus losing its creaturely condition: "They say no property (or union) is closer than that of the three Persons being one God. And next they put the union of the soul with God. When the soul, being kissed by God, is in absolute perfection and in bliss, then at last she knows the embrace of unity, then at the touch of God she is made uncreaturely, then with God's motion, the soul is as noble as God is himself." Sermon 83: St. Germanus' Day, in Franz Pfeiffer, *Meister Eckhart*, trans. C. De B. Evans, I (London ,1924), 209.

25. "Et sicut solet in amantium osculis, suavi quodam contractu mutuo sibi spiritus suos transfundentium, creatus spiritus in hoc ipsum creanti eum Spiritui totum se effundit; ipsi vero Creator Spiritus se infundit, prout vult, et unus spiritus homo cum Deo efficitur." *Exposé*, p. 222. Also *PL* 180, 506.

26. "Ideo quaecumque Sponsa est, hoc solum desiderat, hoc affectat, ut facies ejus faciei tuae jungatur jugiter in osculo caritatis; hoc est, unus tecum spiritus fiat per unitatem ejusdem voluntatis." *Exposé*, p. 280. Also *PL* 180, 520. "Et Sponsus quidem in Sponsa etiam nesciente, eo pascitur, quo illa cruciatur; cum illa citra amplexum et osculum, citra mutuae conjunctionis suavitatem, non recipiat consolationem." *Exposé*, p. 356. Also *PL* 180, 535. The kiss (and, at times, the embrace with it) remains the image describing the attainment of the lover's desire: union and peace. St. Gregory the Great had said: "Anima ergo, quae iam per amorem conpungi desiderat, quae iam contemplari visionem sponsi sui appetit, dicat: *Osculetur me osculo oris sui.* Vel certe osculum oris eius est ipsa perfectio pacis internae: ad quam cum pervenerimus, nihil remanebit amplius, quod quaeramus." *In Cant.* 18–19. Corpus Christianorum: Series Latina, CXLIV, p. 21.

27. "Simul etiam nota, in petitione osculi, supremum in oratione humanae possibilitatis affectum, in lumen illud vultus Dei suum direxisse aspectum." *Exposé,* p. 124.

28. *PL* 195, 672. Again we find here the echo of the great theme from Acts 4:32, where it is said that in the believers in Christ "there was one heart and one soul." We may point out that in speaking of friendship as uniting in equality those who love one another, Aelred says that such friendship reaches its highest joy when it embraces many friends. See *PL* 195, 687–692.

29. *PL* 195, 672–673.

30. *PL* 195, 673.

31. "Quomodo avulsus es ab amplexibus meis, subtractus oculis [osculis?] meis, subductus oculis meis. Amplexabar te, dilecte frater; non carne sed corde. Osculabar te, non oris attactu, sed mentis affectu." *PL* 195, 543.

32. *PL* 195, 673.

33. *PL* 16, 192.

34. *Basic Writings of Saint Augustine,* I, ed. Whitney J. Oates (New York, 1948), 47.

35. *Sermones super Cantica,* XXVI, vi, 9. In *Opera,* I, 177.

36. *PL* 195, 619.

37. Meanwhile we may note that one of the most beautiful testimonies to the two-in-one sentiment and the ecstatic or quasi-mystical character of friendship comes from that least mystical-minded of Frenchmen, Montaigne. Recalling his relationship with his dead friend, La Boëtie, Montaigne writes: "En l'amitié dequoy je parle, elles [les âmes] se meslent et confondent l'une en l'autre d'un mélange si universel, qu'elles effacent et ne retrouvent plus la couture qui les a jointes. Si on me presse de dire pourquoy je l'aymois, je sens que cela ne se peut exprimer qu'en respondant: 'Par ce que c'estoit luy; par ce que c'estoit moy.' " From the essay "De l'amitié," in *Essais,* ed. M. Rat (Paris, 1952), I, 203–204.

With this we may compare what we read in Dryden's *All for Love,* where Antony speaks of his friendship with Dollabella in the following way:

> He lov'd me too,
> I was his Soul; he liv'd not but in me,
> We were so clos'd within each others breasts,
> The rivets were not found that join'd us first
> That does not reach us yet: we were so mixt,
> As meeting streams, both to our selves were lost;
> We were one mass; we could not give or take,
> But from the same; for he was I, I he.

For the concept of friendship in antiquity the fundamental study remains L. Dugas, *L'amitié antique d'après les moeurs populaires et les théories des philosophes* (Paris, 1894). One may also consult, for later developments, Laurens J. Mills, *One Soul in Bodies Twain: Friendship in Tudor Literature and Stuart Drama* (Bloomington, 1937). Mills's book is good for the period it is primarily concerned with, and there is a useful review of the theme of conventional male friendship in the Middle Ages. Too much is left unsaid, however, of the special friendship motif in Christian medieval literature. Strangely, there is no mention at all of Ficino or of Montaigne.

38. See Paul Zumthor, *Miroirs de l'amour: Tragédie et Préciosité* (Paris, 1952), p. 51.

39. "Vultis ergo a me audire, quare et quomodo diligendus sit Deus? Et ego: Causa diligendi Deum, Deus est; modus, sine modo diligere." St. Bernard, *De Diligendo Deo* (PL 182, 974). Discussing Augustine's concept of love of God, Etienne Gilson writes: "To love such a good [God] as it deserves to be loved, we must love it unreservedly, without equality; indeed we must, on the contrary, love it with utter inequality. That same justice which, in love between men, demands equality between ourselves and the object of our love, demands that God be the object of an unqualified love even though our own good cannot be compared with Him. In this case, the measure is to love without measure: *ipse ibi modus est sine modo amare* . . . This formula, which will recur frequently during the Middle Ages, is not from Augustine but from his friend Severus, summarizing Augustine's own thought with great felicity of expression (*Epist.* 109, 2; *PL* 33, 419)." *The Christian Philosophy of Saint Augustine* (New York, 1960), pp. 138–139.

40. *PL* 176, 972, 975.

41. *PL* 184, 267. In the *Symposium,* Plato has Phaedrus indicate love's power by stating that love makes men—and even women—dare to die for their beloved.

42. The idea is so fundamental to Christianity that the very first and most basic of the sacraments, baptism, has always been explained as a dying with Christ and an assurance of a new life with him: "You know well enough that we who were taken up into Christ by baptism have been taken up, all of us, into his death. In our baptism, we have been buried with him, died like him, that so, just as Christ was raised up by his Father's power from the dead, we too might live and move in a new kind of existence. We have to be closely fitted into the pattern of his resurrection, as we have been into the pattern of his death" (Rom. 6:3–5). I have used the Knox translation here. On the importance of the role of a ritual dying and resurrection in religions, I can only quote here one of the most authoritative scholars on such questions: "L'histoire des religions et l'ethnologie connaissent un nombre considérable d'initiations, mais il n'en existe pas une seule qui ne comporte, comme élément constitutif, la mort et la résurrection rituelle. *Mort et initiation* sont deux notions si proches qu'en plusieurs langues les termes qui les expriment sont les mêmes ou sont dérivés de la même racine." Mircea Éliade,

"Chasteté, Sexualité et Vie Mystique chez les Primitifs," in *Mystique et Continence* (*Études Carmélitaines*, 1952), p. 32.

43. *De Genesi ad litteram*, XII, 5, 14, and XII, 27, 55. In *PL* 34, 453 and 477–488.

44. For this passage I have quoted from *The Confessions*, trans. Sir Tobie Matthew, revised and edited by Dom Roger Hudleston (London, 1931), p. 6. The Latin of the last line reads: "Noli abscondere a me faciem tuam: moriar, ne moriar, ut eam videam."

45. *On the Divine Names*, IV, xii–xiii. In *PG* 3, 773–776.

46. *Sermones super Cantica*, LII, ii, 4. In *Opera*, II, 92.

47. *Loc. cit.* In a fascinating development of this idea, Bernard distinguishes between two "deaths" as he describes the two highest peaks of mystic contemplation. Like Augustine, but in a more truly mystic context, Bernard prays that he might undergo the bride's death so as to be saved from a more terrible death. The death desired is that in which the soul is transported out of itself [*a seipsa abripitur*] so that it may rise above the ordinary modes of thought and beyond all material impressions and temptations. Though this is a good death by which our life is translated into something better, Bernard says that it is a death peculiar to "men," that is, something less than that death by which not only is desire transcended, but the soul is rid of all conceptual thinking and the memory of corporeal imagery that keep it from pure spiritual vision and communion with angelic intelligence. This death, in fact, is called by Bernard the "death of angels."

48. *Exposé sur le Cantique des Cantiques*, p. 114. Also in *PL* 180, 483.

49. In St. Bonaventura we read the following: "He who with full face looks to this propitiatory [Christ] by looking upon Him suspended on the cross in faith, hope, and charity, in devotion, wonder, exultation, appreciation, praise, and jubilation, makes a passover—that is, the phase or passage with Him—that he may pass over the Red Sea by the staff of the cross from Egypt into the Desert, where he may taste the hidden manna and with Christ may rest in the tomb as if outwardly dead, yet knowing, as far as possible in our earthly condition, what was said on the cross to the thief cleaving to Christ: *Today thou shalt be with me in Paradise.*" *The Mind's Road to God*, trans. George Boas (New York, 1953), pp. 43–44. For some remarks on Franciscan Christianity in relationship to poetry, see F. J. E. Raby, *A History of Christian-Latin Poetry* (Oxford, 1927), pp. 415–451. For the influence of Franciscan piety on late medieval art, see Emile Mâle, *L'art religieux de la fin du moyen âge en France* (Paris, 1909), and Etienne Gilson, "Saint Bonaventure et l'iconographie de la Passion," in *Revue d'histoire franciscaine*, I (1924), 405 ff.

50. *De perfectione vitae*, in *Opera*, III (Florence, Quaracchi, 1898), 123–124. The ascription to Bernard is, I believe, unauthenticated. This erotic interpretation of the crucified Christ was common in the Middle Ages. It occurs

in a writing that was even attributed to St. Augustine. We are told that there is no more efficient remedy against the ardor of our passions than to meditate on the death of the Redeemer. His arms and hands are stretched out on the cross as a sign that he is prepared to embrace sinners. It is in the arms of the Savior that one should wish to live and die. At his death the Savior inclined his head so as to give a kiss to his beloved. And so we kiss him whenever for love of him we are repentant. "Nullum tam potens est, tam efficax contra ardorem libidinis medicamentum, quam mors Redemptoris mei. Extendit brachia sua in cruce, et expandit manus suas paratus in amplexus peccatum. Inter brachia Salvatoris mei et vivere volo, et mori cupio . . . Salvator noster caput inclinavit in morte, ut oscula daret suis dilectis. Toties Deum osculamur, quoties in ejus amore compungimur." *Manuale*, ch. 23. In St. Augustine, *Opera omnia*, VI, Pars altera (Paris, 1837), 1399. This quote, along with the first twenty-four chapters of the Manual, is also found in the fourth book of Hugh of Saint-Victor's *De Anima*.

The particular image in question was carried to an extreme by the Italian mystic Domenico Cavalca (1270–1342) when he made a detailed comparison between the figure of the crucified Christ and the dress and manner of a secular swain going to a love tryst. When lovers go to visit their beloved, they put on colored raiment and, as a token of love, wear garlands on their heads. So Christ willed to be dressed in purple and have a garland of thorns as a mark of his love. Lovers bear oranges and roses in their hands, and Christ bore vermillion wounds in his own hands. As lovers are wont to sing sweet words, so too from the cross Christ spoke words of love and of such sweetness as to draw all hearts. Lovers are wont to stretch out their arms and lean their heads down so as to greet and embrace the beloved, and they give other such signs of their love. All such signs were manifested by Christ, the soul's Bridegroom, whose head is bent downwards to greet us, his mouth now closed to kiss us, his arms and hands outstretched to embrace us, his whole body extended to love us. The Italian text, which occurs in Cavalca's *Specchio di croce* (ch. 33), may be read in Arrigo Levasti, *I Mistici*, I (Florence, 1925), 190–191.

51. *Sermo suppositus* 120:8 (*In Natali Domini*, iv). In *PL* 39, 1987.

52. Taking this passage (and others like it) which speaks of embracing and dying with Christ on the cross, and thinking of the early Gnostic text (Gospel of Philip) which spoke of Mary Magdalene as the consort of Christ, who kissed her often, and thinking also of early depictions of the Magdalene embracing the foot of the cross, one is brought to the daring conception of Auguste Rodin's sculpture in the late nineteenth century. Rodin depicts a sensuously nude Magdalene literally embracing Christ on the cross and swooning away. It is quite more blatantly sexual than anything in the Baroque age, or at least it fails to show that spiritualization of the sensual that the best Baroque art achieves in its sensuous interpretation of religious ecstasy, witness Bernini's famous sculpture of the transverberation of St. Theresa.

53. A discussion of the various manifestations of the religio-erotic ecstasy of the mystical marriage in visions of the nuns would take us far beyond the scope of this study. How far that language could go may be sampled here by one case which, it is true, is even chronologically beyond the period I am interested in in this section. Nonetheless it is an extreme example of the matter at hand, and yet, it will be seen, it is directly connected with earlier expressions we have noted. The passage is from St. Maria Maddalena de' Pazzi (1566–1607): "I saw how Jesus united with His bride in closest embrace. He laid His head over the head of His bride, His eyes upon her eyes, His mouth upon her mouth, His feet upon her feet, all His members upon hers so that His bride became one with Him and wanted all her Bridegroom wanted, saw all that her Bridegroom saw, and savoured all that her Bridegroom savoured. And God wants nothing but that the soul unite with Him in such wise, and that He may be utterly united with her." Quoted in *The Spear of Gold: Revelations of the Mystics*, ed. H. A. Reinhold (London, 1947), p. 274. The union of the soul with God is here imaged in as realistic a picture of the *hieros gamos* as one can get. And yet we note that the expressions "His head over the head of His bride, His eyes upon her eyes, His mouth upon her mouth" are what we found in William of Saint-Thierry, who desired to have the revelation of God made to him "face to face, eye to eye, kiss to kiss" (see last part of n. 14 to this chapter).

54. *The Exercises of Saint Gertrude*, Introduction, Commentary, and Translation by a Benedictine Nun of Regina Laudis (Westminster, Md., 1956), pp. 77–78.

55. *Ibid.*, p. 90. My italics.

56. The Latin document was printed in the *Acta Sanctorum, Octobris*, XII (Brussels, 1884), pp. 403–404, where it appears in the Life of Blessed Joanna Soderini, one of the persons present at the miracle of the Host at Juliana's death.

The practice of offering the Crucifix to be kissed by the moribund naturally leads to the idea of one dying *in, on,* or *by* the kiss of the Lord. An example in point is the ecstatic death of St. Francis Xavier. In secular literature just such a scene is recorded in a nineteenth century Italian novel which is permeated with sensuality and religious yearnings: Niccolò Tommaseo's *Fede e Bellezza* (1840) concludes with the death of one of the two chief protagonists. As Maria is about to breathe her last, her husband (Giovanni) places the Crucifix to her lips: "La pace eterna, disse ella, e mosse le labbra a baciare il crocifisso offertole da Giovanni; *e nel bacio dell'Amico suo immortale spirò*" (my italics). Another example of the motif in Romantic literature occurs in Alphonse Lamartine's poem entitled "Le crucifix" (from *Nouvelles Méditations*), an elegiac meditation on the death of a woman he loved. Readers will recall the better known episode of Flaubert's *Madame Bovary* when, as the crucifix is offered to the dying Emma, she urges her lips to it like one seeking to slake a thirst and, with all her expiring force, imprints upon it "le plus grand baiser d'amour qu'elle eût jamais donné."

297

Still current in parts of Italy are the expressions "morire nel bacio del Signore" and "addormentarsi nel bacio del Signore" (i.e., to die and/or to sleep in the kiss of the Lord) which signify "to die in the grace of God" and "to die peacefully." See for example, *Garzanti Comprehensive Italian-English, English-Italian Dictionary*, ed. Mario Hazon (New York-Toronto-London: McGraw Hill, 1961), at *morire* and *bacio*; also *Dizionario Enciclopedico Sansoni*, I (Florence, 1952), 307.

57. During the late Middle Ages stories of the death of saints by divine rapture were common. In the seventeenth century, St. Francis of Sales carried a notice of a number of them in his treatise *On the Love of God* (Bk. VII, chap. 9–13). Among those he passes in review as having died for and by love in this way are: St. Ambrose, said to have died in ecstasy just after having received the blessed sacrament; St. Thomas Aquinas, who died during a great act of devotion singing the words of the Song: "Come my beloved, let us go into the fields" (7:11); and Jean Gerson, the great theologian and chancellor of the University of Paris, who is said to have died while reciting as an ejaculatory prayer a variant of the remarkable line from the Song: "Oh Lord, *your* love is strong as death." But it is the Virgin Mother who is, after Christ, the greatest example of one dying of and for love; and she died in a rapture, her soul being ravished and transported into the embrace of her Son's love. Francis' discussion is made to illustrate precisely the idea that not only is there a mystic love and rapture which causes a temporary death, but also a mystic or divine love that is sometimes so "violent" that it causes a bodily death by rapture, which definitively separates the soul from the body.

58. See Hilda Graef, *Mary: A History of Doctrine and Devotion*, I (New York, 1963), 85.

59. *Expositio Psalmi CXVIII*, 1, 16. In *Corpus Scriptorum Ecclesiasticorum Latinorum, LXII. Sancti Ambrosii Opera*, ed. M. Petschenig (Leipzig, 1913), Pars quinta, p. 16.

60. Henri De Lubac, S.J., *The Splendour of the Church*, trans. M. Mason (New York, 1956), p. 279. This book includes a discussion of the Marian exegesis of the Song and the scriptural bride motif. See the chapter "The Church and Our Lady," esp. pp. 257–285.

61. An explanation of Bernard's avoidance of a Marian interpretation of the Song is offered by Y. Congar, O.P., in "L'Ecclésiologie de S. Bernard," *Analecta sacri ordinis cisterciensis* IX, nos. 3–4 (Roma, 1953), 152–154. Father Congar suggests that whereas others tended to equate Mary and the Church (the ecclesial interpretation of the bride was, of course, traditional), Bernard lifts the Virgin above the Church as mediatrix between the Church (all the souls of the faithful making up the Church) and the Lord. We may note, however, that in his other Sermons, Bernard does apply various verses of the Song to the Virgin.

62. *Expositio in Cantica Canticorum;* in *PL* 202, 1255. The long disquisition on the kiss occupies some twenty-three columns: 1149–1172.

63. *Homiliae Festivales,* LXVII; in *PL* 174, 1025.

64. *PL* 167, 1577. Elsewhere Rupert exclaims: "Tibi autem, o Maria, semetipsum revelavit, et osculans, et osculum et osculantis." *PL* 168, 839–840.

65. Amédée de Lausanne, *Huit Homélies Mariales* (Paris, 1960), Sources Chrétiennes No. 72, p. 174.

66. "Festina, noli tardare, quia ille non tardabit . . . Festina et tu, obliviscere populum tuum, et domum patris tui, occurrens obviam ei, ut osculeris osculo oris Dei, eiusque beatissimis immiscearis amplexibus. Egredere, quia iam thalamus collocatus est, et sponsus venit tibi, venit tibi Spiritus sanctus . . . *Spiritus sanctus superveniet in te,* ut attactu eius venter tuus contremiscat, uterus intumescat, gaudeat animus, floreat alvus. Macta, id est magis aucta, quae tanta suavitate perfrueris, tam caelesti osculo dignaberis, tali sponso coniungeris, a tali marito fecundaberis." *Ibid.,* p. 104.

67. On the hesitancy of medieval writers to refer to Mary as *Sponsa Christi* and their preference for insisting on her role as *Mater Christi,* thereby keeping the Church as the bride, see H. Barré, C.S.Sp., "Marie et l'Église du Vénérable Bède à Saint Albert le Grand," in *Bulletin de la Société Française d'Etudes Mariales,* 9 (1951), esp. 66–71.

68. "Sermo VIII in Anuntiatione Beatae Mariae"; in *PL* 195, 254.

69. *Commentarius in Cantica,* II, xi; in *PL* 203, 271.

70. *PL* 203, 194–195. Like other writers who use the mystic kiss symbolism, Philip explicates the principle of infusion of the Spirit into the soul (here the Virgin) by a comparison to a real kiss which is, he says, something more than a meeting of lips. There is also the sweetness of the inner breath which is infused by the kisser into the one kissed: "In osculo quidem oris non fit sola exteriora junctura labiorum, sed etiam percipitur et sentitur quaedam exhalatio internorum, quae si munda et referta fuerit sapore dulcorato, suavem quasi spiritum infundit osculans osculato." *Ibid.,* 194.

71. The theme of the Virgin as mother, daughter, and bride at one and the same time was not restricted to the writings of the theologians. In those moments of recantation of earthly ladies, when poets turned to this greater Lady, they too recognized her threefold character. Thus in the early thirteenth century, the troubadour Aimeric de Belenoi, in a poem addressed to Mary, *Domna, flor d'amor,* speaks of her having received a precious reward when at the birth of Jesus she was mother, daughter, and bride: "Ric jovnal / Aguetz, tal / Benedeita, gloriosa, / Q'a Nadal / Fos engal / Marie, filha, espoza." *Poésies du Troubadour Aimeric de Belenoi,* ed. Maria Dumitrescu (Paris, 1935), p. 119. The Virgin as mother and daughter of God is sung in the majestic opening of Dante's great hymn commencing the last canto of the

Paradiso: "Vergine madre, figlia del tuo figlio." Likewise Petrarch, in his *canzone* to the Virgin (*Vergine bella, che di sol vestita*), which closes his long history of tormented love, writes: "Vergine pura, d'ogni parte intera, / del tuo parto gentil figliuola e madre"; but also a little farther on he speaks of the "three sweet names" that are Mary's in her relation to God: "tre dolci e cari nomi ài in te raccolti, / madre, figliuola e sposa." Thus she is also called "Donna del Re," Spouse of the celestial King.

We may add a word here about the depiction of the Virgin and Child in the manner known in iconography as "Our Lady of Tenderness." This rendering, which became popular in the twelfth century, shows Mary and the Infant kissing tenderly. One of the most beautiful and justly famous versions is the Russian icon generally called "The Virgin of Vladimir," now in the Tretyakov Gallery at Moscow. A fine plate may be seen in Tamara Talbot Rice's *Russian Icons* (London, 1963), p. 41. Although this particular treatment is frequent, the tender love—maternal and filial—is more commonly manifested by caressing and tender gazing than by the kiss. See Maurice Vloberg, *La Vierge et l'Enfant dans l'art français* (Paris, 1954), esp. Ch. IV, "Les tendresses de la Vierge-Mère," pp. 143–177.

72. *Iconographie de l'art profane au moyen-âge et à la Renaissance*, I (La Haye, 1931), 474.

73. I am not here concerned with Jewish usage of the kiss between persons and the conventions and regulations governing the kiss that are to be found in rabbinical sources. Such questions have been dealt with by Auguste Wuensche, *Der Kuss in Bibel, Talmud und Midrasch* (Breslau, 1911), pp. 59.

74. *Pentateuch with Targum Onkelos, Haphtaroth and Prayers for Sabbath and Rashi's Commentary*, II, trans. Rev. M. Rosenbaum and Dr. A. M. Silberman (London, 1946), 95 b.

75. Moses Maimonides, *The Guide of the Perplexed* [III, 51], translated with an Introduction and Notes by Shlomo Pines (University of Chicago Press, 1963), p. 625.

76. In a study of one such interpretation, A. S. Halkin suggests that even at a very early period there possibly was "a more philosophic or mystic approach to the Song than the allegoric method" [i.e., the God-Israel relationship]. "Ibn 'Aknin's Commentary on the Song of Songs," in *Alexander Mary Jubilee Volume: English Section* (New York, 1950), p. 396. However, there is no documentation in support of this view, nor does the author say what such an approach could have been like. His study, in any case, is concerned with the philosophic approach, which was a medieval development, and here he has some observations that are of value to us. This approach, he says, "came from the impact of Hellenized Islam on Jewish culture," which fostered a new emphasis on the individual in Jewish theological speculation. Moreover, "the spiritual father of the group of commentators who substituted the individual for the nation as the theme of the allegory is Maimonides" (p. 396) in an occasional reference to the Song in his works.

Halkin excludes an influence of Maimonides on ibn 'Aknin's commentary which was claimed by its author to be the first philosophic commentary on the Song of Songs. In this commentary, says Halkin, "the hero of the Song is the Active Intellect and man's rational soul is the heroine" (p. 409). Ibn 'Aknin interprets the Song in this light from the first mention of kisses, a fact which Halkin feels "leaves much to be desired from the point of view of development and the other principles of literary composition" (p. 411). For some observations on other interpreters of the Song in this philosophic key, see Georges Vajda, *L'Amour de Dieu dans la théologie juive du moyen âge* (Paris, 1957), esp. pp. 242–246 on Immanuel ben Salomon of Rome (1265–1330). This book may be profitably consulted for the question of individual and collective love of God in medieval Judaism.

77. This concern for propriety is found in Rashi. When he glossed the biblical words "and Miriam died there" to signify that like Moses and Aaron she too died by a Kiss, he went on to ask and answer: "But why is it not said with reference to her: [she died] 'by the command [lit. mouth] of God?' Because this would be no respectful way of speaking about the Most High God [as it would have reference to a woman]. But of Aaron it says in the *Sedrah* [*Numbers* XXXIII, 38] 'by the mouth of the Lord.'" *Pentateuch . . . and Rashi's Commentary*, II, 95 b.

78. The exhaustive studies made by Gershom G. Scholem led him to conclude that the *Zohar*, written in Aramaic, was chiefly the work of Moses de Leon, a Spanish Jew of the late thirteenth century. The work, however, draws vastly from earlier sources, i.e., the *Babylonian Talmud*, the *Midrasch Rabbah*, and esoteric texts and traditions not easily identifiable. See Scholem's views in *Major Trends in Jewish Mysticism* (New York, Schocken Paperback Edition, 1961), pp. 156–243.

79. *The Zohar*, translated by Harry Sperling, Maurice Simon, and Dr. Paul P. Levertoff (London, 1949), III, 293. Quotes from the *Zohar* are from this version which, although not a translation of the entire work, is, according to Scholem, a "solid and workmanlike translation" as opposed to the "deliberate falsifications of the French translator, Jean de Pauly." Scholem, *Major Trends*, pp. 387–389, n. 34.

80. *The Zohar*, III, 348–349.

81. Scholem, *Major Trends*, p. 235. My discussion of the background of the "mystery of sex" at this point necessarily leans upon Scholem, the most authoritative modern scholar on Jewish mysticism. Besides Scholem and the English version of the *Zohar* itself, I have also found useful Henri Sérouya's *La Kabbale* (Paris, 1947) and A. E. Waite's *The Holy Kabbalah* (New York, n. d.).

82. Of the many passages from the *Zohar* in which this idea and the interrelated idea that a man is not one unless he has a wife (i.e., is joined with the feminine principle) occur, the following may serve as an example:

"So in the exposition of the verse, 'Hear, O Israel, the Lord our God, the Lord is one,' we have learnt that 'one' signifies the Community of Israel who clings to the Holy One, blessed be He, since, as Rabbi Simeon said, the union of male and female is called 'one,' the Holy One, blessed be He, being called 'one' only in the place where the Female also is, since the male without the female is called half the body, and half is not one. When, however, the two halves are united, they become one body and are called one. At the present day the Holy One, blessed be He, is not called 'one.' The inner reason is that the Community of Israel is in exile, and the Holy One, blessed be He, has ascended aloft and the union has been broken so that the Holy Name is not complete and is therefore not called 'one.' " *The Zohar*, IV, 340.

83. In the *Zohar* the only case of sexual symbolism applied to the relation of a human being to God is that of Moses' "marriage" and "intercourse" with the Shekhinah, the female principle of the Divinity. G. Scholem writes: "But while in all other instances the Kabbalists refrain from employing sexual imagery in describing the relation between man and God, they show no such hesitation when it comes to describing the relation of God to Himself, in the world of the Sephiroth. The mystery of sex, as it appears to the Kabbalist, has a terribly deep significance. This mystery of human existence is for him nothing but a symbol of the love between the divine 'I' and the divine 'You,' the Holy one, blessed be He and His Shekhinah. The *hieros gamos*, the 'sacred union' of the King and the Queen, the Celestial Bridegroom and the Celestial Bride, to name a few of the symbols, is the central fact in the whole chain of divine manifestations in the hidden world. In God there is a union of the active and the passive, procreation and conception, from which all mundane life and bliss are derived." *Major Trends in Jewish Mysticism*, p. 227. It is in the context of this mystery of sex symbolism that the kiss image acquires its special kabbalistic significance.

84. See above, n. 82. In another place the *Zohar* says: "The male is not even called man till he is united with the female" (I, 177). The *Zohar* lays down regulations on a man's duty to have sexual union with his wife, and it refers to this as "the glad performance of a religious precept" (I, 159).

85. See *The Zohar*, IV, 400–401.

86. See Henri Sérouya, *La Kabbale* (Paris, 1947), pp. 266–267; also S. Karppe, *Etude sur les origines et la nature du Zohar* (Paris, 1901), pp. 67 and 429.

87. *The Zohar*, IV, 14.

88. *Loc. cit.*

89. One is reminded of Ezechiel's great vision of God on the chariot. There too the number four figures prominently. The intricate celestial chariot which is knit together and guided by the Spirit of God is supported by four cherubin and four wheels which have one likeness. See Ezechiel 1:1–21 and 10:9–17.

90. *The Zohar*, IV, 14–15.

91. *Ibid.*, IV, 16.

3. The Medieval Love Lyric

1. This is not the place to attempt a summary of the controversy over the question of origins. As to the theory of Arabic origins or dominant influence, it is again being championed by some scholars; my opinion of it within the limits that concern this study is given in the body of my text. In aligning myself with those who have stressed Christian sources, I have no intention of denying the existence, even the importance of non-Christian elements. One need not agree in the detail with those critics who seek to limit and pinpoint *the* specific Christian sources upon which the troubadours are sometimes said to depend. But one must, I think, acknowledge the overwhelming importance of what Leo Spitzer referred to as the "Christian *a priori*" for the full understanding of the troubadour love lyric. Even Etienne Gilson, in the midst of a virgorous attack against the idea of a Christian influence, asserts that "courtly love is inconceivable save in a Christian atmosphere" (*The Mystical Theology of Saint Bernard* [London, 1940], p. 186). My own choice of passages from Christian authors is meant to be generally indicative of what the troubadours had readily available to them, as part of their Christian heritage, by way of a psychology of love and amatory conceits. Here, too, I have naturally focused on what has most relevance to the present study. In this connection, much of what has been said in the first two chapters has bearing. As to the kiss image in particular, I find it surprising that so little attention has been given to its use in troubadour poetry. Its importance, I think, will become clear in the pages of this chapter, which aims at studying it in a meaningful context.

2. "*Fin' Amors*: the Pure Love of the Troubadours, its Amorality, and Possible Sources," in *Medieval Studies*, VII (1945), 153 (my italics). Gilson writes: "It is chimerical to seek out an influence of mystical on courtly love, beyond a few verbal borrowings. Of all that which defines the one nothing passed into the definition of the other because no passage from the one to the other was possible at all" (*The Mystical Theology*, p. 193). This is as excessive in its own way as the interpretation (Wechssler's) that it attacks.

3. "An Inquiry into the Origins of Courtly Love," in *Medieval Studies*, VI (1944), 176. J. Huizinga writes: "When in the twelfth century unsatisfied desire was placed by the Troubadours of Provence in the centre of the poetic conception of love, an important turn in the history of civilization was effected. . . .Courtly poetry makes desire itself the essential motif, and so creates a conception of love with a negative ground-note" *The Waning of the Middle Ages* (New York, 1954), p. 107.

4. *In Epistolam Joannis ad Parthos*, Tract. IV, 6; in *Oeuvres complètes de Saint Augustin*, X (Paris, 1869), 496–497.

5. *In Joannis Evangelium*, Tract. XXVI, 4; in *Oeuvres complètes de Saint Augustin*, IX (Paris, 1869), p. 549. No less than the body, says Augustine, the soul has its intense pleasures: "An vero habent corporis sensus voluptates suas, et animus deseritur a voluptatibus suis?"

6. *PG* 44, 404. Also in *La vie de Moise*, ed. and trans. Jean Daniélou (Paris, 1955), p. 107.

7. *PG* 44, 404. Also in *La vie de Moise*, pp. 107–109.

8. *From Glory to Glory: Texts from Gregory of Nyssa's Mystical Writings*, ed. Jean Daniélou, S.J., and Herbert Musurillo, S.J. (New York, 1961), pp. 200–201.

9. *Ibid.*, p. 270.

10. *Sermones super Cantica*, LXXXIV, i, 1. In *Opera*, II (Rome, 1958), 303.

11. The author of the *Epistola ad Severinum de Caritate* insists on the theme. Because God is of an infinite nature his lovers must know neither measure nor end in their love. Blessed is the hungry soul that hungers only for what he holds and holds only what causes his hunger. Let your Charity be persuaded that no one can in the future be satiated by the sweetness of love just as no one can be filled with it in the present. By this impossibility your solace will be to have no solace: "De qua impossibilitate solatium tibi sit nullum habere solatium." And Richard of Saint-Victor notes that in the fourth and last degree of the "violence" of Charity there is nothing that can henceforth satisfy the soul's desire. The soul thirsts and drinks, yet in drinking, its thirst is not quenched; the more it drinks the more it thirsts. Ives, *Epître à Séverin sur la Charité*; Richard de Saint-Victor, *Les quatre degrés de la violente Charité* (Paris, 1955), pp. 61–63, 139–141. As the Song of Songs has it: "Aquae multae non potuerunt extinguere caritatem" (8:7). William of Saint-Thierry also says that in divine love satiety does not diminish desire in the soul, but rather increases it, although anxiety is removed. And in a mood that is much like that found in Gregory of Nyssa, William asserts that the way is eternal and to journey forever is to arrive: "Sic semper ire: hoc est pervenire." *De contemplando Deo*, ed. Dom Jacques Hourlier (Paris, 1959), p. 80. In like manner Juliana of Norwich exclaimed: "I saw him and searched for him, and I had him and I wanted him. And this, it seems to me, ought to be our common experience. . . . For he will be seen, and he will be sought" (Revelations, ch. 10). In Ecclesiasticus (24:29), Wisdom says, "Eat of this fruit, and you will yet hunger for more; drink of this wine, and your thirst for it is still unquenched." One of the most famous hymns of the Middle Ages, *Jesu, dulcis memoria* (or in its third part, *Jesu decus angelicum*) which deals precisely with the praise and the search by the soul for its Beloved, echoes this thought and imagery with the words: "Those who taste you hunger still, those who drink of you yet thirst" (Qui te gustant, esuriunt,/Qui bibunt, adhuc sitiunt).

The same concept of the endless search for the Beloved runs through

Muslim mysticism. Abu Yazîd was quoted by Al-Ghazâlî as saying: "If it were granted unto you to talk with God face to face as Moses did, and to be filled with the Spirit, and to enjoy the Divine friendship, like Abraham, yet should you seek what is beyond that, for there is infinitely more to be given by Him, and if you rest content with that, you are veiled thereby, and this is the test for such as these, and one who is like them, for they are in the highest rank." Quoted in Margaret Smith, *Al-Ghazâlî, the Mystic* (London, 1944), p. 126. One would think this passage to have been inspired by the writings of Gregory of Nyssa himself. It is clear, in any case, that early Sufi mysticism was influenced by Christianity, even in its Platonism.

12. In connection with this idea it is customary to cite the example of Virgil's Dido and Aeneas. Aeneas forsakes love for something more important; Dido cannot do without Aeneas. One of the most telling and widely known denunciations of the sentiment which would make one a slave of passion is that found in Book IV of Lucretius' *De natura rerum*. There "romantic" love is painted as a degrading affair which leads to madness and disorder. Lucretius' recommendation (which we may take as the "typical" attitude of antiquity) is that a man should satisfy his craving for sensual pleasure without becoming sentimentally involved, as we would say. But of course the question is much more complex than this and even to offer but a brief summary would lead to an impossibly long digression. Yet some mention, however inadequate, must be made of Catullus and the Roman elegists Propertius and Tibullus, who deliberately go counter to the traditional view that held that love (insofar as the male was concerned) should never involve the whole personality of man. Those that went too far in love were *miseri*; but these poets present the case of those who find a new and secret pleasure in being so. This attitude brought with it a certain amount of idealization of the lady who was being raised to a plane of equality with the male insofar as she was thought to be not only an instrument for the satisfaction of sensual needs but worthy also of being one's companion. At this point there showed itself an inevitable psychological development in which the male lover felt that he "needed" his lady. See L. Alfonsi, "Otium e vita d'amore negli elegiaci augustei," in *Studi in onore di Aristide Calderini e Roberto Paribeni*, I (Milan, 1956), 187–209; A. W. Allen, "Elegy and the Classical Attitude toward Love," in *Yale Class. Stud.*, 11 (1950), 257 ff.; George Luck, *The Latin Love Elegy* (London, 1959). Luck observes that with the Roman elegists "the mistress becomes the *domina*, the lover her 'slave' (a metaphor which is as rare in Greek erotic poetry as it is frequent in Latin elegiac verse). The earliest evidence for this inversion is found in Catullus" (p. 122). It is worth recalling also that in the first century A.D. Plutarch was advancing such extraordinary ideas as that a woman was worthy of man in all respects and that in the conjugal relationship love between man and woman could lead to the highest spiritual values. On Plutarch see L. Dugas, *L'amitié antique d'après les moeurs populaires et les théories des philosophes* (Paris, 1894), esp. pp. 142–150; and Robert Flacelière, *Love in Ancient Greece*, trans. James Cleugh (New York, 1962), pp. 182–186.

13. *The Emergence of Christian Culture in the West* (New York, Harper Torchbook, 1958), p. 191. The original title of this work is *The Classical Heritage of the Middle Ages.*

14. *Conf.* VI, 15. *Basic Writings of Saint Augustine,* I, ed. Whitney J. Oates (New York, 1948), 89.

15. *Oeuvres spirituelles,* ed. Edouard des Places, S.J., in the series *Sources chrétiennes* (Paris, 1955), p. 84.

16. *PG* 45, 940–941.

17. Bernard's words are from *De praecepto et dispensatione* (60); in *PL* 182, 892, but also now in Volume III of *Opera,* ed. J. Leclercq and H. M. Rochais (Rome, 1963), 292. The adaptation by Bonaventura that follows above in the text is from the *Soliloquium,* in *Opera omnia,* VIII (Quaracchi, 1898), 49. For both quotations I am indebted to the study by Jean Orcibal, "Une formule de l'amour extatique de Platon à Saint Jean de la Croix et au Cardinal de Bérulle," in *Mélanges offerts à Etienne Gilson* (Toronto-Paris, 1959), p. 451.

18. Bruno Snell, *The Discovery of the Mind: The Greek Origins of European Thought,* trans. T. G. Rosenmeyer (New York, Harper Torchbook, 1960), p. 66.

19. *Des Minnesangs Frühling,* ed. Carl von Kraus (Zurich, 1950), p. 1.

20. Chrétien de Troyes, *Cligès,* ed. Alexandre Micha (Paris, 1957), pp. 85–86. The relevant verses are 2777–2814.

21. *L'érotique des troubadours* (Toulouse, 1963). I discuss Nelli's work in Appendix II to this book.

22. Et purus quidem amor est, qui omnimoda dilectionis affectione duorum amantium corda coniungit. Hic autem in mentis contemplatione cordisque consistit affectu; procedit autem usque ad oris osculum lacertique amplexum et verecundum amantis nudae contactum, extremo praetermisso solatio; nam illud pure amare volentibus exercere non licet. Hic quidem amor est, quem quilibet, cuius est in amore propositum, omni debet amplecti virtute. Amor enim iste sua semper sine fine cognoscit augmenta, et eius exercuisse actus neminem poenituisse cognovimus: et quanto quis ex eo magis assumit, tanto plus affectat habere. Amor iste tantae dignoscitur esse virtutis, quod ex eo totius probitatis origo descendit." *De amore,* ed. S. Battaglia (Rome, 1947), p. 212.

23. *De amore,* p. 38. The fact that Andreas does suggest that a man and a woman who have dwelt long and patiently in *pure love* may, without loss of their affection, pass on to *mixed love* does not erase the theoretical distinction between the two kinds or forms of love. Nor, for that matter, does any interpretation that would see Andreas's explication of pure love as a satirical polemic or boutade.

24. See Ernst Robert Curtius, *European Literature and the Latin Middle Ages* (New York, 1953), pp. 512–514.

25. James J. Wilhelm, *The Cruelest Month: Spring, Nature, and Love in Classical and Medieval Lyrics* (New Haven and London, 1965), p. 132.

26. On the *gloriosa mors*, see Christine Mohrmann, "Le latin commun et le latin des chrétiens," in *Vigiliae Christianae*, I, 1 (January, 1947), 11. The word *gloria*, of course, has a long history, and like many other fundamental words and ideals of the Christian vocabulary it underwent a rich and complex semantic development in passing from the pagan sphere of ideas into the area of Christian spirituality. This transposition has been fruitfully studied by A. J. Vermeulen, *The Semantic Development of Gloria in Early-Christian Latin* (Nijmegen, 1956). As is to be expected, the author gives much attention to the phrase and the idea of the *gloria martyrum*. Pertinent to the present discussion, and indeed to the whole question of the influence of Christianity on the development of medieval secular love literature, is Erich Auerbach's "*Passio* als Leidenschaft," *PMLA*, 56 (1941), 1179–1196.

27. *The Cruelest Month*, p. 132.

28. Peter Dronke, *Medieval Latin and the Rise of European Love Lyric*, I (Oxford, 1965), 285.

29. *PG* 13, 54.

30. "Multi jam in suis praecordiis sagittas tuas infixas portant, et altius adhuc eas infigi desiderant. Delectabiter enim et suaviter vulnerati sunt, et plagas tuas se percepisse, nec dolent, nec erubescunt. O charitas! quanta est victoria tua! unum prius vulnerasti, et per illum omnes postmodum superasti." *De laude Caritatis*, in *PL* 176, 975.

31. "Christus amore Ecclesiae vulneratus est in cruce. Prius vulnerasti cor meum, quando causa amoris tui flagellatus sum, ut te facerem mihi sororem . . . iterum vulnerasti cor meum, quando amore tui in cruce pendens vulneratus sum, ut te sponsam mihi facerem gloriae participem." *PL* 172, 419.

32. See the edition by G. Dumeige (Paris, 1955), p. 127.

33. "It [*fin' amors*] was a love that yearned for and, at times, was rewarded by the solace of every delight of the beloved except for the physical possession of her by intercourse. Far from being pure in the accepted sense, or disinterested, it is sensual and carnal in that it allows, approves and encourages the delights of kissing and embracing, the sight of the beloved's nudity and the touching and lying beside her nude body—in short, in all that provokes and fans desire." "*Fin' Amors*: The Pure Love of the Troubadours," *Medieval Studies*, VII (1945), 142–143.

34. The phrases in quotes are from A. Denomy, "*Fin' Amors*: the Pure Love of the Troubadours," *Medieval Studies*, VII (1945), 164, and Leo Spitzer, "L'amour lointain de Jaufré Rudel et le sens de la poésie des troubadours," in

Romanische Literaturstudien 1936–1956 (Tubingen, 1959), p. 364. (Spitzer's study first appeared separately in 1944.)

35. The same is true of the poetry of the Sufi mystics, of whom R. A. Nicholson writes that "unless we have some clue to the writer's intention, it may not be possible to know whether his beloved is human or divine—indeed the question whether he himself always knows is one which students of Oriental mysticism cannot regard as impertinent." *Studies in Islamic Mysticism* (Cambridge, Eng., 1921), pp. 163–164.

36. Peter Dronke, *Medieval Latin,* I, 271.

37. Hanns Swarzenski, *Monuments of Romanesque Art*: *The Art of Church Treasures in North Western Europe,* 2d ed. (University of Chicago, 1967), p. 18.

38. Heinrich Kohlhaussen, "Das Paar vom Bussen"; in *Festschrift Friedrich Winkler* (Berlin, 1959), pp. 29–48, but esp. p. 39.

39. George Fenwick Jones, "The Kiss in Middle High German Literature," in *Studia Neophilologica,* XXXVIII, 2 (1966), p. 207. I owe the references to the kisses in the Minnesänger that follow in the text to Jones's article, which mentions them. Jones, however, seems not to have suspected the real significance of these kiss allusions, for he says of them that they are an "idle speculation rather than a *fait accompli*" (*loc. cit.*). Moreover, he does not refer to one of the most important (form our point of view) cases of the kiss in the medieval German lyric, one dealing with the exchange of hearts by way of the kiss in a poem by Ulrich von Winterstetten which we are soon to consider. Likewise he makes no mention of the kiss in the Provençal poets, and he somewhat misses the point when he writes: "The scarcity of erotic kisses in courtly literature reflects the prevailing attitude of this genre toward eroticism in general; for the courtly poets show considerable moral restraint (or is it social decorum?) in their treatment of amorous themes" (*ibid.,* p. 205). Jones refers to a number of cases of the kiss, particularly between men, in medieval German literature, and although here too I think he has not seen the ultimate significance of the kiss, his article is valuable for its treatment of the theme of the kiss as a sign of reconciliation. An interesting observation he makes on this score is that "the mental association between kisses and reconciliation was so close that the Middle Dutch word for reconciliation (*soene*) acquired the meaning of 'kiss'" (p. 204). We have noted a similar development in the Gaelic word which comes from *pax*.

40. *Des Minnesangs Frühling,* ed. Lachmann, M. Haupt, F. Vogt, newly edited by Carl von Kraus (Zürich, 1950), pp. 46, 187.

41. *The Greek Anthology with an English Translation by W. R. Paton,* I (Loeb Classical Library, 1960), p. 173. Compare the poem by Straton of Sardis (second century A.D.) in *The Greek Anthology* (XII, 177).

42. Maurice Valency, *In Praise of Love* (New York, 1961), p. 26.

43. There is a poem in Latin, the charming *"Lydia, bella puella candida,"* which contains an allusion to the image of the soul being drawn by a kiss. This image is connected with the highly sensual columbine kiss:

> Porrige labia, labra corallina;
> Da columbarum mitia basia:
> Sugis amantis partem animi;
> Cor mi penetrant haec tua basia.

An Anthology of Medieval Latin, ed. Stephen Gaselee (London, 1925), pp. 68–69. The date of this poem is uncertain, and as Gaselee pointed out in his brief introduction to it, "scholars are not yet agreed whether the little poem is of late imperial days or a medieval Italian production."

Also to be noted here are the final verses from a poem ("Ecce redit species et amoris grata voluptas") dating from the late eleventh century according to its editor, Peter Dronke, in *Medieval Latin and the Rise of European Love Lyric,* II (Oxford, 1966), 449. The poem is found in two manuscripts: Roma, Vat. Reg. lat. 585, fol. 5^v, and Escorial, O. III. 2, fol. 101^r:

> Murmure grata suo tura favumque ferunt,
> Guttura melle fovent, penetrant precordia, replent
> Pectora, rimantur viscera, corda traunt.
> Alternant animas, laqueataque corpus in unum
> Corpora spiritibus pervia corda parant.
> Corpora spirituum transfusio languida reddit,
> Dumque sibi moritur vivit uterque pari.

Unlike what we find in Lucretius (see the Introduction), here are lovers whose entwined bodies do seem to merge into one. Moreover, there is an exchange of *souls,* and their hearts become penetrable by way of their *spirits;* they transfuse or exchange *spirits* by which their bodies are revived. And thus each dying to itself lives in the other. These motifs make it necessary, I think, to see the lovers as kissing; it is by the kiss that the exchange of souls and spirits takes place.

4. Medieval Love Legends

1. The situational irony of this episode of the *Flamenca* was first touched on briefly but pointedly by Phillip Damon whose observations have served to stimulate my own comments on the scene. Besides reminding us that puns on the liturgical phrase "to offer the *Pax"* were a commonplace of the medieval French *sermo amatorius,* Damon notes of the *Flamenca* that "The various stages and crises of the courtship are all ingeniously drawn into analogies with the forms of the liturgy or the facts of church history. The narrative explores the full range of ironic incongruity between the sacred format and the profane intention of Guillaume's enterprise." "Courtesy and Comedy in *Le Roman de Flamenca,"* *Romance Philology,* XVII (February, 1964), 609–610.

2. The ritualistic nature of this kiss and the role of Galehaut as a witness in a ceremonial sense were perceived by Vincenzo Crescini, who noted the resemblance to the use of the kiss in the betrothal ceremony and in the ceremony attached to the act of feudal homage. "Il bacio di Ginevra e il bacio di Paolo," in *Studi Danteschi*, III (1921), 5–57. Crescini's article is more than a confrontation of the kiss in the *Lancelot* romance and the kiss of Paolo and Francesca in Dante's *Divine Comedy* (*Inferno*, V). The second part (pp. 26–49) has some references to the attitude to the kiss in the Middle Ages, with mention of a few examples of the kiss having the character of a rite in the literature of profane love. It cannot be said, however, that the author realized the full scope of the significance of the kiss in medieval culture. There is, for example, no mention of the religio-erotic kiss of the mystics nor of the Song of Songs.

3. See F. L. Ganshof, *Feudalism*, trans. Philip Grierson (New York, Harper Torchbooks, 1961), p. 78.

4. See A. Restori, *Letteratura provenzale* (Milan, 1891), p. 52. The *Vida* of Raimon-Jordan speaks of the lady receiving the poet-lover as her *cavalier* in a ceremony of homage. The acceptance of the homage is solemnized by a kiss and a ring bestowed by the lady upon the poet.

5. *Le Roman de Tristan et Iseut renouvelé par Joseph Bédier* (Paris, 1946), p. 39.

6. *Ibid.*, p. 41. This part of Bédier's reconstruction comes from Eilhart von Oberg's German version. In the romance *Gui de Warewic*, written around the middle of the thirteenth century, there occur two kisses that have an interest for us. As Terry lies suffering from a wound, he is lamented over by a damsel who says that should he die she will join him. She then falls in a swoon upon him, kissing his mouth and face:

> Sur le cors chai, si se pasma,
> Deus! quel doel ele demena!
> La boche li baisa e la face.
> (5007–5009)

Witnessing this scene is Guy, who consoles the maid and then takes it upon himself to heal Terry. When this is done, the two men become fast friends. Guy makes it known that he would like for them to become sworn brothers (*compaignuns*) and so forever faithful to one another. Terry is overjoyed and the two seal this pact with the solemn rite of the kiss:

> Atant se sunt entrebaisez,
> De lur compaignie ben assurez.
> (5061–5062)

Quoted from *Gui de Warewic: Roman du XIIIᵉ siècle*, ed. A. Ewert, I (Paris, 1932), 152, 154.

7. Bédier, pp. 49–50. But see especially the early thirteenth century German poem *Tristan und Isolt* by Gottfried von Strassburg, vss. 12042 ff. I see no

point in taking up Denis De Rougemont's fanciful notion that Tristan and Iseult are really in love with annihilation; it is on a par with his theory that the love poetry of the troubadours was an allegorization of the Manichean-Catharist heresy.

8. Thomas, *Les Fragments du Roman de Tristan*, ed. Bartina H. Wind (Geneva and Paris, 1960), p. 33.

9. It is worth noting that almost in direct contrast with this is a passage in the *Vita Nuova* in which Dante, protesting the absolutely pure nature of his love for Beatrice, takes the trouble to explain his affirmations that no one can look steadily at his lady's mouth and that the eyes are the beginning while the mouth is the end or aim of love. Lest anyone think evil of this, Dante says, be it known that his lady's salutation, which was an operation of her mouth, was the only end of his love: "Questa seconda parte [Dante is analyzing a poem of his own] si divide in due: che ne l'una dico de li occhi li quali sono principio d'amore; ne la seconda dico de la bocca, la quale è fine d'amore. E acciò che quinci si lievi ogni vizioso pensiero, ricordisi chi ci legge, che di sopra è scritto che lo saluto di questa donna, lo quale era de le operazioni de la bocca sua, fue fine de li miei desiderii mentre ch'io lo potei ricevere" (XIX, 20). For Dante there was to be no ambiguity in the word *saluto* that would cause it to be equated with the idea of a kiss, for, in this context at least, his purpose is precisely that of making it plain that it was not kisses from his lady that sustained him or to which he aspired, but verbal greetings. Dante's beatitude was indeed for a while in his lady's salutations.

10. *Les Fragments*, pp. 161–162. We may mention here the frequent medieval motif of the saint curing a leper by kissing him. In the Abbey of Saint-Martin de Metz, among the miniature drawings illustrating a *Recueil de textes sur saint Martin* is one dating from the early twelfth century which portrays the saint in the act of exorcising two possessed persons and, at the same time, healing a leper by kissing him on the mouth. (Epinal, MS 73, fol. 5v) The illustration is reproduced in Jean Porcher, *L'enluminure française* (Paris, 1959), p. 21, fig. 19.

11. See Francesco A. Ugolini, *I cantori d'argomento classico* (Geneva and Florence, 1933), pp. 97 ff.

12. Thomas, *Les Fragments*, pp. 153, 155. There is a remarkable similarity to this ending in the twelfth century lai *Narcisus*. It is such that Thomas may have had the latter poem in mind when he wrote the death scene of his own poem. The French lai changes the Ovidian story of Narcissus in a significant way by introducing a real nymph, Dané, who is desperately in love with the youth. As Narcissus lies near death from his languishing over his unattainable image, the nymph comes upon him. She kisses and embraces him, raises her lament, and vows that she will die with him. At the moment of Narcissus' death, she lies beside him, embraces him tightly and thus expires her own soul: "Ele le baise, ele le tient; / Ele se pasme, puis

revient; / Ele l'acole, ele l'embrace; / Baise les eus, baise la face. / 'Ahi! fait ele, dous amis, / Com estes de la mort soupris! / . . . . / Lasse, ma proiiere est la mort! / Or n'i a mais autre confort; / Morir m'estuet de compagnie, / Car assés mius aim mort que vie.' / Li vallés muert, l'ame s'en vait. / La pucele plus pres se trait. / Vers lui se trait par tel aïr, / Du cors se fait l'ame partir. / Ç'a fait Amor qui l'a souprise, / Andui sont mort en itel guise. / Or si gardent tuit autre amant / Qu'il ne muirent en tel samblant!" *Narcisus* (*poeme du XIIᵉ siècle*), ed M. M. Pelan and N. C. W. Spence (Paris, 1964), pp. 72–73. The verses, which close the lai, are 987–992 and 999–1010.

In a way, the love-death in the French *Narcisus* is closer than that in the *Pyramus* to what we have in Thomas. The maid does not employ a weapon to kill herself, but dies by tightly embracing her beloved. The chronology of the *Narcisus* and the *Pyramus* is not ascertained. One theory holds that they appeared simultaneously. See *Narcisus*, ed. Pelan and Spence, p. 34. Without becoming involved in the question of which came first, I would here only point out that the endings of the two poems suggest a borrowing from the *Pyramus* on the part of the Narcisus author. The French *Pyramus*, after all, has its ending grounded in the tale as it was told by Ovid, whereas the *Narcisus* ending has no foundation in the story as given by Ovid.

13. I borrow the language of this sentence from two different passages in the poetry of John Keats: "We might embrace and die: voluptuous thought" (*Endymion*, IV, 759), and "That I may die a death of luxury" (*Sleep and Poetry*, 58–59).

14. In this connection, an Italian rifacimento of the French prose romance adds a detail that speaks almost too plainly. As in the French version, we read that the lovers remained in their embrace even after death; but now we also learn that those present in the room (including Iseult's husband, King Mark!) thought the motionless figures to be not dead but in a love swoon or languor: "A braccia a braccia e a bocca a bocca morirono li due pazienti amanti. E dimorano in tale maniera abracciati; tanto che tutti quelli di là entro credeano che fussero tramortiti ambendue per amore. Altro riconforto non v'hae." From the *Tristano Riccardiano*, in *La prosa del Duecento*, ed. C. Segre and M. Marti (Milan and Naples, 1959), p. 661.

15. The law which says that love constrains a loved one to love in return is not only mentioned in Francesca's line from the *Inferno* ("Amor, ch'a nullo amato amar perdona"); it is also seen exemplified in the encounter between Dante and Casella on the shores of the isle of Purgatory. When Casella, emerging from the company of newly arrived shades, moves to embrace Dante, the poet, even before he recognizes his friend, is moved to reciprocate:

> Io vidi una di lor trarresi avante
> Per abbracciarmi, con sì grande affetto,
> Che mosse me a fare il simigliante.
>
> (*Purgatorio*, II, 76–78)

The idea is stated again in a later canto from the *Purgatorio*:

> . . . Amore,
> Acceso di virtù, sempre altro accese,
> Pur che la fiamma sua paresse fore.
> (XXII, 10–12)

The principle enunciated by Francesca is perhaps more Christian than courtly, the great texts on the matter being I John 4: 10–13 and 19. In the *De catechizandis rudibus*, which through the centuries was to be one of the chief texts for the inculcation of Christian instruction, St. Augustine tells us that because God loved us first we are under an obligation, as it were, to love him in return. Such is the law of love, in fact, that one can offer no greater invitation to love than to take the first step in loving. Nobody should be so cold that though he may refuse to initiate a love he would refuse to reciprocate a love shown to him. Moreover, this principle is so true, says Augustine, that we can observe it even in bad love. Thus, those who would be loved reveal their love. There is no better way to be aroused to love than to be loved. *De catechizandis rudibus*, IV, 7. In *Oeuvres de Saint Augustin*, XI (Paris, 1949), p. 32. In his *De diligendo Deo* (III, 7), St. Bernard writes that those who know they are loved much find it easier to love more in return: "Facile proinde plus diligunt, qui se amplius intelligunt: cui autem minus donatum est, minus diligit." *Opera*, III (Rome, 1963), 124.

16. As for the Pyramus and Thisbe legend, the theme of the burial in one tomb is already found in Ovid's treatment. There, as Thisbe is about to follow Pyramus in suicide, she expresses the wish that though she and Pyramus have been kept apart in life, they may be entombed together. The wish, in fact, is carried out (*Metamorphoses*, IV, 155–166), almost as a confirmation, as it were, of Thisbe's assertion that Pyramus, who it seems could be separated from her only by death, cannot after all be separated from her: ". . . quique a me morte revelli / heu! sola poteras, poteris nec morte revelli" (IV, 152–153). In Thomas's *Tristan*, when Iseult was fearful she might die in a shipwreck, separated from her lover, she lamented that she had hoped to die in his arms and be buried with him in one coffin: "Car en vos bras quidai murrir, / En un sarcu enseveiliz" (1650–1651), and in the verses that follow we learn that her desperate fancy led her to imagine that they could still have one sepulchre. The tomb motif became more and more elaborated in the Tristan legend. The prose versions give much attention to the burial accorded the pair by King Mark. One version has it that the lovers were buried in adjoining tombs but that during the night a plant grew out of the tomb of Tristan and burrowed its way into the tomb of Iseult. See *Le Roman de Tristan et Iseut, renouvelé par Joseph Bédier* (Paris, 1946), p. 220. This particular motif has been studied by Giuseppe Cocchiara, "Sulla tomba di Tristano ed Isotta," in his *Genesi di leggende*, terza edizione riveduta (Palermo, 1949), pp. 153–183.

It is not without significance that the same legend of the burial of lovers in one tomb developed around Dante's couple from Rimini. We find it, in fact, in Boccaccio's commentary on the *Divine Comedy*. After describing how Francesca's husband Gianciotto murdered the adulterous pair and then fled, Boccaccio concludes: "Furono poi li due amanti, con molte lacrime, la mattina seguente seppelliti e in una medesima sepoltura." *Trattatello in laude di Dante e pagine scelte dal "Commento,"* ed. G. Gervasoni (Milan, 1960), p. 88. The phrase "con molte lacrime" inserted by Boccaccio bespeaks the sympathy that readers were prone to give to ill-fated lovers even when their love was "illicit."

It would be unpardonable to fail to mention another unforgettable medieval pair of lovers—Héloïse and Abélard. The most tender and even the most significant legend to develop around this extraordinary couple is that of a burial in the same tomb. But that is not all. A thirteenth century manuscript of the *Chronicle of St. Martin of Tours* records the following miracle: "She [Héloïse], indeed, it is said, as she was lying in her last illness, directed that when she was dead she should be laid in the tomb of her husband. And when her dead body was carried to the open tomb, her husband, who had died long before her, raised his arms to receive her, and so, embracing her, closed them fast about her." Quoted from Enid McLeod, *Héloïse, A Biography* (London, 1938), p. 226. Concerning this legend, E. Gilson wrote: "The story, thus related is beautiful. But matching legend for legend, we would much prefer to believe that when Héloïse joined her lover in their tomb, she was the one who opened her arms for the embrace." *Héloïse and Abelard*, trans. L. K. Shook (Chicago, 1951), p. 123. But then, we may note, the story would not correspond to the death scene of Tristan and Iseult. However, we need not quibble here. Surely this last embrace was a mutual one.

It is also instructive to compare the character of love in Héloïse and Abelard with that of the great love legends of the Middle Ages. What strikes us greatly is the fact that in this real-life story of medieval passion it is the woman alone who loves totally, unreservedly; it is Héloïse who makes the true sacrifice in giving all for love. On the other hand, Abelard, as a lover, is much closer to Aeneas than he is to a Tristan or to a number of troubadours. Héloïse's superiority (if I may so call it) in love has been recognized by modern critics. Suzanne Lilar, for example, writes that "there was no common measure—there never had been—between Abélard's love and that of Héloïse. Abélard always subordinated love to his career and his own glory." *Aspects of Love in Western Society*, trans. J. Griffin (London, 1965), p. 79. The same point is made by Aldo Scaglione: "There was in this woman that perfect harmony of spirituality and naturalism that is the hallmark of medieval love literature at its best, and the condition for all truly great love between man and woman: body and soul in unity without quarrel. But Abelard was no match for her." *Nature and Love in the Late Middle Ages* (Berkeley-Los Angeles, 1963), p. 29. Professor Scaglione makes the further point that "public opinion was against this woman in love, and the time had not yet come for public sympathy toward great sinners. The sympathy of some of her contemporaries (for example, Peter the Venerable) for Héloïse was purely a movement of exquisite hearts and humane understanding, and did not imply recognition of her revolt, rather strove to cover it up officially" (p. 29). This is a significant matter. Public sympathy, as is spoken of here, was not accorded to real persons. In the world of fiction and the imagination, however, a private sympathy was fast growing, witness the development of the great love legends in medieval literature. In fact, even the story of Héloïse and Abelard, as we have seen, was taken over by legend and an accompanying sympathy. And it was the legend that lent to their love that element that Suzanne Lilar feels it lacked. "Their great love lacked only one dimension, the mystical. Héloïse and Abélard remain realists—great and powerful characters, but earthly" (*Aspects of Love*, p. 79). The legend was to correct that.

17. That Dante was influenced by the Tristan legend in its character of a story of love unto death and beyond is also indirectly evidenced by the repercussion Dante's episode in turn had on the Italian development of the Tristan legend. The author of the important fourteenth century *Tavola ritonda* says of the love potion drunk by Tristan and the queen that "il detto beveraggio fue ordinato a sforzare la natura, e a sottomettere la ragione e la volontà, e dare volontà di piacere." In these words we hear an echo of Dante's reference to the carnal sinners of the second circle of Inferno as those who "la ragion sommettono al talento." But even more interesting is what the *Tavola ritonda* says about the effects of the love potion: "E gli due amanti ebbono una vita e fecione una morte, e credesi che le anime abbiano uno luogo stabilito insieme." The phrase *una morte* and the idea that the souls of Tristan and Iseult are together (or at least in one same place) throughout eternity were surely suggested by Dante's episode. The author of the Italian prose romance, however, was careful not to frighten or disillusion his readers by revealing just where the lovers' souls were in eternity. The text is quoted from *La Tavola Ritonda e l'istoria di Tristano*, ed. F.-L. Polidori, I (Bologna, 1864), 122.

18. *Exposé sur le Cantique*, p. 102. Also *PL* 180, 481.

19. The interpretation of the union of the lovers in Hell as a sign of the mitigation of punishment goes back (at least in its modern form) to Ugo Foscolo. For a pointed refutation of the Foscolian type interpretation see Michele Barbi, "Con Dante e coi suoi interpreti," in *Studi Danteschi*, XVI (1932), p. 6. As for Dante's pity, it is certainly real, but he has pity for some other souls in Hell also whose punishment is none the less unmitigated. Even in the present canto it is not restricted to the lovers from Rimini. The poet expressed his sorrow before discovering Paolo and Francesca among the carnal sinners when Virgil first numbered to him a countless horde of the dames and knights of old:

> Poscia ch'io ebbi il mio dottore udito
> Nomar le donne antiche e i cavalieri,
> Pietà mi giunse, e fui quasi smarrito.
>
> (70–72)

20. For example, one medieval codex turns the ending of the Pyramus and Thisbe tale into an appeal for pity for the young couple and a warning that efforts to thwart the course of true lovers can only prove futile and tragic, for those who love loyally and *strongly* will love unto *death*:

> At ainsi fina l'amistié
> Des duex amant dont fu pitié.
> Cest excemple doit bien noter
> Tous ceux qui cuident destourner
> Aux vrais amans qu'il ne s'entraiment;
> Mais fous sont touz ceux qui s'en pament
> Car riens ni vault clef ne fermeure
> Ne grief menace ne bateure
> Car qui loialment aime et fort
> Il amera jusqu'a la mort.

In *Piramus et Thisbé*, ed. F. Branciforti (Florence, 1959), pp. 307–308.

21. *De ordine*, VIII, 24. In *Oeuvres de Saint Augustin*, IV, ed. R. Jolivet (Paris, 1948), 340.

22. Of course, despite Dante's significance as a summing-up of medieval attitudes—the value of such statements is always relative—the rehabilitation and renewed sympathy for such lovers, in particular for the heroine, was not long in coming, if, indeed, there was any need for it. Precisely in connection with Thisbe, for example, Boccaccio's retelling of the tale in his work *Concerning Famous Women* (*De claris mulieribus*) is in the vein of the medieval French poem. At the end of the tale he comments: "Whoever feels no pity for them and does not shed at least a tear must be made of stone. They had loved each other from the time they were children, and for this they did not deserve a bloody death." *Concerning Famous Women*, translated, with an Introduction and Notes, by Guido A. Guarino (New Brunswick, N. J., 1963), p. 27. We may also recall that in *The Legend of Good Women*, Chaucer "atoned" for his earlier misogyny by exalting heroines like Thisbe, Dido, and even Cleopatra as saints and martyrs of the religion of love (i.e., of Cupid).

23. The relationship or parallel between the Paolo-Francesca episode and the medieval love romances, especially the Lancelot-Guinevere legend, has received much attention. Among the more rewarding studies of this question is Renato Poggioli's "Tragedy or Romance? A Reading of the Paolo and Francesca Episode in Dante's *Inferno*," in *PMLA*, LXXII, 3 (June, 1957), of which see especially pp. 336–355. At the conclusion of his study, Poggioli writes: "There is no doubt that the poet derived the idea that the reading of the Lancelot romance had been 'the first root' of the passion and ruin of the two lovers, not on the authority of any external tradition, but solely on the inner urgings of his own imagination. If the 'how' and 'why' of Francesca's fall is an invention of Dante's, then its supposed occasion becomes highly suggestive and significant. The real kiss of Paolo and Francesca follows the imaginary kiss of Lancelot and Guinevere, as an

316

image reflecting its object in a perspective similar and different at the same time. . . . The 'romance' of Paolo and Francesca becomes in Dante's hands an 'antiromance,' or rather, both things at once. As such, it is able to express and to judge romantic love at the same time" (pp. 357–358).

However, in the matter of love and kisses being inspired by certain readings, Dante was, in fact, working within a medieval tradition. There is a passage from the thirteenth century French romance *Floris et Lyriopé* by Robert de Blois that has some interesting points of similarity with Dante's infinitely superior episode. Floris, in the guise of his twin sister Florie, has intimate access to the company of the beautiful princess Lyriopé. At an appropriate occasion he kisses her: "Souef vers la bele s'encline / Doucement l'estraint à deux bras. / Emmi la bouche, par soulas, / La baise sept fois par loisir; / Li grans doucors les fait fremir . . . / Un roman aportei avoient / Qu'eles moult volentiers lisoient, / Pour ce que tout d'amors estoit. / Et au comencement avoit / Coment Piramus et Tisbé / Furent de Babilonie né, / Coment lor pere destornerent / Le mariage des enfans; / Coment en avint dues si grans, / Qu'en une nuit furent ocis, / Amdui en une tombe mis." *Histoire littéraire de la France* (Paris, 1895), XXIII, 746. (But see also now the recent edition prepared by Paul Barrette, University of California Press, 1968, p. 105.) Here then is the motif of a kiss (seven, in fact) inspired by the reading of a tender love story. Not the least interesting thing here is that the reading which moved this couple to foresake reserve was the story of Pyramus and Thisbe. The motif of couples being led to love under the spell of a book was well known in the Middle Ages. The "author" is generally Ovid, although the particular story is not usually specified.

24. *Dante e la cultura medievale* (Bari, 1942), pp. 83–84. Nardi writes that "la storia di Francesca è una storia di passione e di peccato, troncata nell'attimo stesso del primo ed ultimo bacio." And so too in our romantic moments we are tempted to see the couple eternally united by that kiss even in the terrible blast of Hell. John Keats, whose own poetry has a remarkably high number of references to the kiss image in literal and figurative employment, illustrates this point for us. In the midst of despondency he found relief by luxuriating in the dream of being in Paolo's place, as we learn from a passage in one of his letters: "The fifth canto of Dante pleases me more and more—it is that one in which he meets with Paolo and Francesca. I had passed many days in rather a low state of mind, and in the midst of them I dreamt of being in that region of Hell. The dream was one of the most delightful enjoyments I ever had in my life. I floated about the whirling atmosphere, as it is described, with a beautiful figure to whose lips mine were joined as it seemed for an age" (*Letters*, 1952, p. 325). The reading also led him to write his sonnet *A Dream, after reading Dante's episode of Paolo and Francesca*.

25. In *Purgatorio*, XXVII, 37–42, Dante compares the effect the name "Beatrice" has on him to that produced on the dying Pyramus at hearing the name of Thisbe:

> Come al nome di Tisbe aperse il ciglio
> Piramo in su la morte, e riguardolla,
> Allor che 'l gelso diventò vermiglio;
> Così, la mia durezza fatta solla,
> Mi volsi al savio duca udendo il nome
> Che nella mente sempre mi rampolla.

The second allusion to the death of Pyramus occurs in *Purgatorio*, XXXIII, 69, where the phrase "Piramo alla gelsa" is used to refer to the spotting or offuscation of Dante's mind. The metaphor depends on the allusion to the myth that the mulberry fruit which was white became red by being stained or offuscated with the blood that spurted from Pyramus when he slew himself. More blood was spilled when Thisbe also killed herself by the mulberry tree beside Pyramus. Is there perhaps a connection between this allusion to Pyramus' letting of blood for love ("allor che 'l gelso diventò vermiglio")—which carries with it the idea of the same death of Thisbe— and Francesca's reference to the death of herself and Paolo by murder (for love) with the words "noi che tignemmo il mondo di sanguigno" (90)? It is interesting to note that in his circumstantial account of famous lovers, Petrarch sees Pyramus and Thisbe as a pair: "Vedi Piramo e Tisbe inseme a l'ombra" (*Triumphus Cupidinis*, III, 20). That they are thought of in connection with their death is evidenced by the reference to the shadow they stand in, the shadow of the mulberry tree beneath which they slew themselves. Francesca and Paolo are also specifically referred to as a *pair* in Petrarch's listing, and, incidentally, in a way which shows how closely they were associated with the two illustrious couples, Lancelot and Guinevere, and Tristan and Iseult, who are present though not clearly paired:

> Ecco quei che le carte empion di sogni,
> Lancilotto, Tristano e gli altri erranti,
> Ove conven che 'l vulgo errante agogni.
> Vedi Ginevra, Isolda e l'altre amanti,
> E la coppia d'Arimino che 'nseme
> Vanno facendo dolorosi pianti.
>
> (*Tr. Cup.*, III, 79–84)

26. Pio Rajna, "Dante e i romanzi della Tavola Rotonda," in *Nuova Antologia*, CCVI (May–June, 1920). The pertinent pages are 239–241.

27. Gottfried von Strassburg, *Tristan und Isold*, ed. Friedrich Ranke (Berlin, 1958), p. 149. Vss. 11897–11920.

28. A medieval manuscript at Paris, B.N., fr. 9561, fol. 8v, has a miniature with a dual scene on two levels. Above are Adam and Eve, naked and in the act of eating the forbidden fruit from a tree around which a bicephalous serpent has entwined itself. The scene below represents a robed couple embracing and kissing. The man caresses the face of the woman. Behind the woman a kneeling demon is tieing the two ends of a cloth with which he has encircled the couple a little below their waists signifying their

carnal two-in-one union. It is, like the Amiens relief, a dramatized scene of Concupiscence or *Luxuria*. An illustration of the miniature may be seen in Millard Meiss, *French Painting in the Time of Jean de Berry*, Plate Volume (London and New York, 1967), fig. 408.

29. I am not moved to modify my interpretation by a recent argument that presents Francesca as a wily, unscrupulous wanton who first took the initiative in the matter of the kiss, "made advances to her brother-in-law," and then in Hell deliberately lies to Dante in her relation of the event in order "to cover up the part [the leading one] she played in bringing disaster upon her and her lover." According to this view, Francesca seeks to put the blame on Paolo in the matter of the kiss, and "in order to offer [to Dante] a convincing parallel that might have served to influence Paolo, she must reverse the roles played by Lancelot and Guinevere." The view is that of Anna Hatcher and Mark Musa, in "The Kiss: *Inferno V* and the Old French Prose Lancelot," *Comparative Literature*, XX (Spring, 1968), pp. 97–109. Its aim is to explain why Dante has Francesca say, contrary to what is said in the known versions of the *Lancelot* story, that it was Lancelot who gave the kiss to Guinevere when she knew (according to the authors) that it was the other way around.

30. It will be noticed that in the matter of yearning—for the *mouth* of the beloved—it is the man Dante who is shown to be the greater yearner, here in the earthly paradise as in the Florence of the *Vita Nuova*. Thus we have a perfect correspondence with the psychology of love as found in the Lancelot-Guinevere and Paolo-Francesca relationships centered around the kiss motif.

5. The Renaissance Neoplatonic Phase

1. "Une formule de l'amour extatique de Platon à Saint Jean de la Croix et au cardinal de Berulle," in *Mélanges offerts à Etienne Gilson* (Toronto and Paris, 1959), p. 462.

2. I quote from W. C. Helmbold's translation of the passage in the Loeb Classical Library edition of Plutarch's *Moralia*, IX (Cambridge, Mass., and London, 1961), 367–369.

3. In Book III, 32, of *Lives of Eminent Philosophers*.

4. *Convivium*, ed. R. Marcel, p. 156. The idea has a curious precedent in the early fourteenth century Italian *Tavola ritonda*. Ghedino, having fallen in love with Iseult, continued to live—between life and death—as long as he had hope of having his love returned. But when no hope was left to him, he died (literally). This, says the author, is proof that he who loves and is loved in turn lives, but he whose love is without hope of being reciprocated dies without fail: "E in ciò dimostra che chi ama ed èe rimunerato, campa e vive; e quegli che di suo amore non èe rimunerato,

muore sanza niuno rimedio." *La prosa del duecento*, ed. G. Segre and M. Marti (Milan and Naples, 1959), p. 690.

5. *Convivium*, ed. R. Marcel, pp. 156–158.

6. Dionysius the Areopagite, *On the Divine Names*, trans. C. E. Rolt (New York, 1951), pp. 105–106. (Bk. IV, 12–13.)
That love in the tradition of Christian spirituality is ecstatic by definition, we have seen. However, we may record a reminder of the fact by St. Albert the Great, who used the Pseudo-Dionysius as his authority: "It is of the nature of both spiritual and carnal love ever to proceed and flow and never to be stationary. Hence Dionysius maintains that divine love brings about ecstasy in the sense of transport: for it transports the lover into the beloved and does not permit him to remain in himself." Prima pars Summae theologiae: Tractatus VII, questio 31, membrum 4, in *Opera*, XVII (London, 1651), 185.

7. "Quamobrem amor dicitur, in amante extasim facere, id est, excessum quendam, quo quasi se traducitur in amatum." *In Dionysium Areopagitam*; in *Opera omnia*, II (Basileae, 1576), 1068. (Riproduzione in fototipia a cura di M. Sancipriano con presentazione di P. O. Kristeller, Turin, Bottega d'Erasmo, 1959.)

8. The reference to Dionysius' thought is made by Ficino at the end of *Oratio* III, cap. 1.

9. Paul Oscar Kristeller, *The Philosophy of Marsilio Ficino*, trans. Virginia Conant (New York, 1943), p. 287. (This fundamental work was reprinted in 1964.) More specifically in reference to this question in Ficino's Commentary, Kristeller says: "The notion that each lover has lost himself in the other and given himself to the other is developed in the *De Amore*, probably after the model of the Old Tuscan poets" (*ibid.*, p. 281). Ficino's statement, at the end of the Commentary, to the effect that *all* he has to say about love is condensed in Guido Cavalcanti's famous canzone, *Donna me prega*, is a magnanimous acknowledgment of a small debt, and certainly an exaggerated claim for Cavalcanti's poem.
Touching on Ficino's passage John C. Nelson asks: "Did Ficino say that the lover's soul lives in his beloved because Plato had said so or because early Tuscan poets said so?" (*Renaissance Theory of Love* [New York, 1958], p. 83.) Though Nelson asks the question merely to suggest the difficulty (a real one) involved in trying to trace the sources of many of the motifs found in Renaissance love treatises, he seems to limit the possibilities to the two he mentions and is content to note that "Ficino appears to credit Plato as his source." He does not inquire into what the Platonic source might be, nor does the nature of his book call for it.

10. *Tractatus ascetici*, IV, *De confabulatione et meditatione circa res divinas*, 2; in *PL* 184, 267. Of the two biblical texts juxtaposed in this passage, the first, from the Song 8:6, has already received attention in an

earlier part of this study; the second is from Colossians 3:3. Credit for calling attention to this motif of love wounding unto death in the medieval mystics must go to the classic study by Pierre Rousselot, *Pour l'histoire du problème de l'amour au moyen âge (Beiträge zur Geschichte der Philosophie des Mittelalters*, Band VI, Heft 6), Münster, 1908. The passage from Gilbert is quoted on p. 69 of Rousselot's study, which breaks it off, however, after the first two words of the text from Colossians (*Mortui estis . . .*). The importance of the Song in Gilbert's text is at once apparent in the motifs of languor, wound, and death resulting from love.

11. *Spiritus Domini*, consid. 2; quoted in Andre Combes's important study, *La theologie mystique de Gerson*, II (Rome, 1964), 139.

12. The passage occurs in *Phaedrus*, 255 ff. Part of it may be quoted here: "And thus he loves, but he knows not what; he does not understand and cannot explain his own state; he appears to have caught the infection of blindness from another; the lover is his mirror in whom he is beholding himself, but he is not aware of this. When he is with the lover, both cease from their pain, but when he is away then he longs as he is longed for, and has love's image, love for love (Anteros) lodging in his breast, which he calls and believes to be not love but friendship only, and his desire is as the desire of the other, but weaker; he wants to see him, touch him, kiss, embrace him, and probably not long afterwards, his desire is accomplished." Jowett trans., in *The Dialogues of Plato*, I (New York, 1937), 259. Such a passage would naturally be connected by Renaissance readers (or readers of any other period) with the androgyne myth of the *Symposium*, where there occurs the observation that love is the desire and search for the whole.

13. *Convivium*, p. 251.

14. The Lucretian passage in question—part of which I have quoted in the Introduction to the present study—is from Book IV, but it is too long to quote here. The important descriptions are contained within verses 1037–1121. Ficino himself only cites vss. 1052–56 and 1108–14, but the whole passage has a bearing on his views, especially Lucretius' idea that the lovers are bewildered in not knowing how to find peace and that they yearn to know what it is they really desire. (Compare this with what Aristophanes has to say in Plato's *Symposium*.) Following Ficino, poets and theorists of love often recall the verses of Lucretius as a source for the idea that the desire of lovers is to be transformed into the beloved. Among those who do so are F. Nobili, L. Domenichi, Tullia d'Aragona, and T. Tasso.

15. Thus immediately after his passage on the death and revival of lovers, Ficino attenuates the erotic and mystic elements of his discourse by an insistence on the purely intellectual aspect of the love relationship between a man and a youth. The exchange that takes place between them is precisely defined as an exchange of beauty. The mature man absorbs the beauty of the youth through the eyes, that is, by gazing upon it, while the

youth absorbs the beauty of the older person by way of the mind's activity. In this way both profit; the mature man, who has only the beauty of soul, acquires the beauty of body, and the youth, having only corporeal beauty, acquires the beauty of soul. This wonderful exchange is both honest and pleasant. It is perhaps more pleasant for the older man because he enjoys with both his eyes and his mind; on the other hand, it is more useful to the youth because, inasmuch as the soul is superior to the body, the attainment of intellectual beauty is more commendable and more precious than that of corporeal beauty. Any desire to touch (desire for carnal intimacies) is thus condemned by Ficino as being no part of love but rather an aberration of the passion of a man who is enslaved by the senses (II, ix). *Convivium*, p. 159.

16. *Convivium*, pp. 152–153.

17. For an appraisal of Ficino's concept of friendship and "Platonic love," one must, of course, read P. O. Kristeller, who analyzes Ficino's letters to his friends in *The Philosophy of Marsilio Ficino* (above, n. 9). He writes that for Ficino, "true love between two persons is by nature a common love for God. In both of them it is based on the original love for God, which constitutes the essence of human consciousness" (p. 279). In illustration of this Kristeller quotes from a letter to Giovanni Cavalcanti in which Ficino says: "Those who worship God with a pious mind, however, are loved by God. *Therefore there are not two friends only, but always necessarily three, two human beings and one God* . . . He unites us into one. He is the insoluble bond and perpetual guardian of friendship." In another letter quoted by Kristeller (p. 286) Ficino writes: "So why do you doubt, oh Alamanno, whether Plato believed that there were several Souls in one body? There are not several in one, but the contrary seems frequently to be true when we see that one Soul exists in the bodies of several friends as the result of the Platonic love." In all this, which is, as Kristeller says, Ficino's doctrine of "Platonic love," one cannot avoid a comparison with Christian love and friendship—for example, the idea of Christian fellowship in the Holy Spirit. As for the presence of a third Person, that is God, in friendship between two men, it is still a fact that Ficino does not call him Christ. For the text of the two letters mentioned in this note, see M. Ficino, *Opera omnia*, I, 2, pp. 634, 716.

18. "Marsilius Ficinus Michaeli Mercato Miniatensi dilecto conphilosopho suo," in *Opera omnia*, I, 2 (Basel, 1576), 611. (Riproduzione in fototipia a cura di M. Sancipriano con presentazione di P. O. Kristeller, Torino, 1959, p. 611.)

19. In the *Theologia Platonica*, too, Ficino makes use of the concept of the soul dying and reviving in God. Nesca Robb has summarized this aspect of Ficino's thought: "Beatitude for him consists in a supreme act of love by which the human soul gives itself to God and so becomes assimilated to Him. Such an act is a voluntary death; it entails the rejection of the life

of passion and opinion in which the soul is immersed while it is subject to earthly conditions. Yet the lover lives again in God and there finds his true self, and knows himself as he is known. He becomes at once a complete personality and a sharer of the divine life, since the inmost truth of his being is the divine activity that dwells in him. The two lives, God's and man's, are made one while yet remaining two. Since man is made in the image of God he carries on like though not identical activities. He can give himself in love to God, because God out of love created him. There is a reciprocal affection like that of parent and child, but it has its origin in the parent." *Neoplatonism of the Italian Renaissance* (London, 1935), pp. 68–69.

20. "Perchè se il buono amore, come io dissi, è di bellezza disio, e se alla bellezza altro di noi e delle nostre sentimenta non ci scorge che l'occhio e l'orecchio e il pensiero, tutto quello che è dagli amanti con gli altri sentimenti cercato, fuori di ciò che per sostegno della vita si procaccia, non è buono amore, ma è malvagio; e tu in questa parte amatore di bellezza non sarai, o Gismondo, ma di sozze cose. Perciò che sozzo e laido è l'andare di que' diletti cercando, che in straniera balía dimorano e avere non si possono senza occupazione dell'altrui e sono in se stessi e disagevoli e nocenti e terrestri e limacciosi, potendo tu di quelli avere, il godere de' quali nella nostra potestà giace e godendone nulla s'occupa, che alcuno tenga proprio suo, e ciascuno è in sè agevole, innocente, spiritale, puro." *Prose e rime di Pietro Bembo*, ed. Carlo Dionisotti (Turin, 1960), pp. 468–469.

21. "L'amore onesto . . . non è generato nel desiderio, come l'altro [sensual love], ma dalla ragione; ed ha per suo fine principale il trasformarsi nella cosa amata con desiderio che ella si trasformi in lui, tal che di due diventino uno solo o quattro; della qual trasformazione hanno favellato tante volte e così leggiadramente sì Messer Francesco Petrarca, sì il reverendissimo cardinal Bembo. La quale, perchè non si può fare se non ispiritalmente, quindi è che in cotale amore non hanno luogo principalmente se non i sentimenti spirituali, cioè il vedere e l'udire, e più assai, come più spiritale, la fantasia." *Dialogo della Signora Tullia d'Aragona: Della infinità di Amore*; in *Trattati d'amore del Cinquecento*, ed. G. Zonta (Bari, 1912), pp. 222–223.

I do not mean to suggest that the theorists of Platonic love were absolute and uncompromising in their repudiation of the "lower senses." In fact, several of them make a hierarchy of the modes of love between man and woman and allow that there is a form of love which remains good although it consents to an enjoyment of the senses that goes far beyond the kiss. This is true even of Tullia d'Aragona herself and of one of the most authoritative writers of the time, Benedetto Varchi, who inspired if he did not actually write Tullia's treatise. Varchi distinguishes five types of relationship pertaining to human love, each having its own character and boundaries. They go from bestial (or swinish) love to love of soul alone. But I do not propose to deal here with Varchi's system in detail. I would only point out that there is a moment when Varchi forgets himself so far as to say that it is impossible that good love between man and woman can be perfect if, along with their souls, they do not couple their bodies. The reason for this is that the soul forms a unit with the body. But as he goes on, he recovers and we see that again the thrust or aspiration of his system is towards a non-corporeal love which may at the most involve the sense of sight. Bodies simply cannot effect that transformation of lovers which is the aim of true love. In short, as I already suggested, where the highest form of "Platonic love" was concerned, the theorists excluded all bodily intimacies. In Varchi this reasoning occurs in a discussion of the question "Se nell'amore onesto si sentono passioni." See in *Opere di Benedetto Varchi*, II (Trieste, 1859), 542–43. Also see p. 499 in the same volume for Varchi's careful breakdown of the various modes of love, made in his discourse on Petrarch's sonnet "S'amor non è . . ." See too p. 199 of the present study for an example of Varchi's position as poet vis à vis the "holiest" form of human love and the role of the kiss.

22. Può dunque per la prima morte, che è separazione solo dell'anima dal corpo, e non per l'opposito, vedere lo amante l'amata Venere celeste e a faccia a faccia con lei, ragionando della divina immagine sua, e' suoi purificati occhi felicemente pascere; ma chi più intrinsecamente ancora la vuole possedere e, non contento del vederla e udirla, essere degnato de' suoi intimi amplessi e anelanti baci, bisogna che per la seconda morte dal corpo per totale separazione si separi, e allora non solo vede e ode la celeste Venere, ma con nodo indissolubile a lei s'abbraccia, e con baci l'uno in l'altro la propria anima trasfundendo, non tanto cambiano quelle, quanto che sì perfettamente insieme si uniscono, che ciascheduna di loro dua anime e ambedue una sola anima chiamare si possono." *Commento sopra una canzona de amore composta da Girolamo Benivieni secondo la mente et opinione de' Platonici*; in the volume *De hominis dignitate, Heptaplus, De ente et uno, e scritti vari*, ed. Eugenio Garin (Florence, 1942), p. 557. Further references to Pico's Commentary will be from this same edition, which will be referred to as *Commento*.

23. *Serm. s. Cant.* LII, ii, 4; in *Opera*, II (Rome, 1958), 92.

24. "Moriatur anima mea morte iustorum. . . . Bona mors, quae vitam non aufert, sed transfert in melius. . . . Verum hoc hominum est. Sed moriatur anima mea morte etiam, si dici potest, angelorum, ut praesentium memoria excedens, rerum se inferiorum corporearumque non modo cupiditatibus, sed et similitudinibus exuat, sitque ei pura cum illis conversatio, in quibus est puritatis similitudo." *Serm. s. Cant.* LII, ii, 4–5; in *Opera*, II, 92.

25. In a well-known passage from *De ente et uno* Pico tells his addressee, Angelo Poliziano, that we are prisoners of a madness of the intellect. For, he says, we can love God, and by loving him do more good for ourselves and more honor to him than we can by trying to know him intellectually; yet

we persist in the latter course, thereby failing to find what we seek and what can only be possessed by love. "Sed vide, mi Angele, quae nos insania teneat. Amare Deum dum sumus in corpore plus possumus quam vel eloqui vel cognoscere. Amando plus nobis proficimus, minus laboramus, illi magis obsequimur. Malumus tamen semper quaerendo per cognitionem numquam invenire quod quaerimus, quam amando possidere id quod non amando frustra etiam inveniretur." In the volume including the *Commento* (see n. 22 above), p. 418.

26. *Commento*, p. 558.

27. The *mors osculi* is also mentioned by Pico in the eleventh of the seventy-two *Conclusiones* "according to his own opinion" (*secundum opinionem propriam*): "Modus quo rationales animae per archangelum Deo sacrificantur, qui a Cabalistis non exprimitur, non est nisi per separationem animae a corpore, non corporis ab anima nisi per accidens, ut contigit in morte osculi, de quo scribitur praeciosa in conspectu domini mors sanctorum eius." *Opera omnia*, I (Basel, 1572), 108–109.

28. *Commento*, p. 558.

29. See *Phaedo* (67) where Plato speaks of the soul reaching pure knowledge only after death, an experience that is possible in this life by means of a temporary deliverance from the body. Real or pure knowledge is conceived of as a process involving the soul's catharsis or purification, hence a passing from an inferior condition (its imprisonment in the body) to a superior condition. Final physical death is a perfect catharsis. In this context, the especial study of philosophers is said to be the separation and release of the soul from the body. It is pertinent here to recall also that in the *Phaedrus* Plato notes that there are two kinds of *mania*: the one bad, being caused by disease, the other good, being caused by a divine enrapture or inspiration. Among the four manifestations of the second kind, the best is that which is attributed to Venus and her son Eros and is called erotic mania. This is a divine amatory delirium which does not so much prevent man from philosophical contemplation as it allows him to soar to and find out the supreme good which is the lover's quest.

30. In the *Symposium* (179), Phaedrus points out that whereas the gods rewarded Alcestis by allowing her to return to life because of her unflinching readiness to die for her husband, they sent Orpheus away only with a phantasm or apparition of Eurydice because he did not really dare to die for love as did Alcestis, but rather sought to enter Hades alive. Moreover, they afterwards punished Orpheus for this offense by causing him to be slain by women.

31. *Commento*, p. 555.

32. *Theologia Platonica* (XVI, cap. viii). In *Opera omnia*, I (Basel, 1576), 383. Reprinted in facsimile, Torino, 1962.

33. "Plato cum frequenter contemplationis intentione longe secessisset a corpore, tandem in ea ipsa abstractione a corporis vinculis decessit omnino." *Theologia Platonica* (XIII, cap. ii). In *Opera*, I, 286. Ficino's statement occurs in a context where he is speaking of philosophers who experienced ecstatic trances during contemplation. For example, he refers to Porphyry's testimony that Plotinus had undergone such an ecstasy four times.

34. How easily Pico associated Plato with the patriarchs and their death is made apparent for us also in a passage from the most famous of his writings, the *Oration on the Dignity of Man*. Speaking of the great Christian themes of peace and concord and the ideal of all humanity as being as one and finally restored into the One that is God, Pico adopts nuptial symbolism in elaborating on the motif of the coming of the King of Glory (i.e., Christ) into the soul that has been cleansed by philosophy and theology: "If she [i.e., the soul] shows herself worthy of so great a guest, she shall, by the boundless mercy which is his, in golden raiment like a wedding gown, and surrounded by a varied throng of sciences, receive her beautiful guest not merely as a guest but as a spouse from whom she will never be parted. She will desire rather to be parted from her own people, and, forgetting her father's house and herself, will desire to die in herself in order to live in her Spouse, in whose sight surely the death of his saints is precious—death, I say, if we must call death that fulness of life, the consideration of which wise men have asserted to be the aim of philosophy." I have used the translation by Elizabeth Livermore Forbes, in *The Renaissance Philosophy of Man: Selections in Translation*, ed. E. Cassirer, P. O. Kristeller, J. H. Randall, Jr. (Chicago, Univ. of Chicago Press, 1948, fourth impression 1956), p. 232.

The reference to the death of God's saints, although ultimately from the Psalms (115:15), is more specifically an allusion to the death by rapture (i.e., the kiss) that Pico found in the kabbalists. As in the *Commento*, what Pico means here is a death to the world and the false self in order to live in the Beloved. The idea that philosophy is a consideration or meditation of death as the fullness of life implies the same reference to Plato that we saw in Ficino.

35. That Pico's kiss of union with the celestial Venus refers to a union between the soul and the Deity as such is attested to by a passage that occurs in his treatise just before the detailed commentary on Benivieni's verses. The passage anticipates the later one describing the kiss of Venus. In it Pico explains that whereas some lovers do not get beyond the contemplation of the beauty of a particular person, the more perfect lovers "recall" a more perfect Beauty beheld before the soul was immersed in a body. This recollection causes a great desire in the lovers to see that Beauty again and spurs them to "depart" from their bodies (i.e., they are no longer subjected to their physical desires). In this love the movement is from perfection to perfection until the soul has become angelic, and, burning with this angelic fire, elevated above all earthly contingencies, is transformed into a pure spiritual flame, whereupon it soars into the heaven of pure intelligence,

finally attaining to its blessed peace in the arms (i.e., embrace) of the first Father. See *Commento*, ed. Garin, p. 526. Pico's metaphors are mixed, but the meaning seems clear enough. The ascensive process to union is described in basically the same terms as in the later passage except that in place of the celestial Venus, we have the first Father in heaven.

36. "Puoi dunque considerare, lettore, quanti errori nel primo congresso commetta el nostro Marsilio confundendo in tutto, sol per questo capo, e pervertendo ciò che d'amore parla. Benchè, oltre a questo, in ogni parte di questo trattato abbia commesso in ogni materia errori, come io credo nel processo chiaramente manifestare." *Commento*, p. 488.

Pico's words about those who misinterpret Plato's kiss image suggest that the Platonic epigram was a current *topos* in his time and that it was generally given a "profane" interpretation. The "many" that he refers to, could, of course, include Aulus Gellius also. But that he had Ficino in mind is evidenced by the fact that the critical allusion occurs among a cluster of criticisms aimed at "Marsilio." All these criticisms, including the one in which Ficino is not specifically named, were suppressed in the edition of the *Commento* printed under the aegis of Benivieni. This was almost inevitable, for at the beginning of the treatise Benivieni himself says that his poem was written in an effort to reduce to a few verses what Ficino had written of copiously.

It is also interesting to note, however, that not only is there no reference to the "wrong" interpretations of Plato's (or Agathon's) "kisses" in the first printed editions of the Commentary, but that even the specific allusion to those kisses is suppressed, except for a casual and oblique reference at the end of the kiss passage. The reading is as follows: "Mostra nel primo verso Salomone la intentione totale del libro, e l'ultimo fine del suo amore, ne più oltre ch'al bacio vedremo mai andare ne Salomone, ne Platone, ne qualunque altro d'amore parlando, del celeste ha ragionato." *Opere di Girolamo Benivieni* (Venice, 1524), p. 59.

37. It is not possible to say whether Castiglione is reporting the actual words or ideas of Bembo in the detail, although authors of such dialogues in the sixteenth century very likely tried to recall and give as authentic the statements of the participating interlocutors. At any rate, what Castiglione has Bembo say about the kiss is all the more interesting since in the *Asolani* Bembo does not attribute such remarks to any of the interlocutors, and even certain others of love's miracles are treated with a degree of skepticism, being seen as the feigning of poets. On the other hand, it is known that at Castiglione's request Bembo revised *The Courtier*, which suggests that the content of the part attributed to him did not meet with his disfavor.

38. For the original of Castiglione's text, I have used *Il libro del Cortegiano*, ed. V. Cian (Florence, 1947).

39. *Pagan Mysteries in the Renaissance* (New Haven, 1958), pp. 130–134. Wind feels that the Renaissance interpretation of the third century Roman

funerary symbolism is essentially right and he offers it as a "corrective" to some of the modern studies of Roman sepulchral art (e.g., Cumont). I agree with his view. In a previous chapter we noted that the use of the Psyche and Eros motif on early Christian sarcophagi indicated the idea of the blessed union of the departed soul with God in the afterlife; and as we suggested then, there is every reason to believe that its appearance on pagan sarcophagi (whence Christians borrowed it) must have had an analogous meaning. It is unlikely, however, that the Christians using the motif in those early centuries identified their figure of Eros with Death itself as such.

40. One wonders what Pico might have thought of the copulation scenes of Leda and Zeus in the form of a swan. In his own description of the kiss of the celestial Venus, we remember, he specified the kiss as the extreme image to be used in the depiction of divine love.

41. *Pagan Mysteries*, pp. 130–131. The translation is by Wind. I have read the Italian text in Giovanni Piero Valeriano's *Ieroglifici overo commentari delle occulte significationi de gli Egittij, et d'altre Nationi . . . accresciuti di due Libri dal Sig. Celio Augusto* (Venice, 1602), p. 898.

42. "Endimione addormentato sopra un monte, e basciato da Diana. Si legge appresso i Cabalisti, che senza la morte del bascio non ci possiamo unir di vera unione co' celesti, nè con Dio. Questo dico, perciochè fra il numero de' più morti . . . è questa del bascio, della quale Salomone così fa mention nel principio della Cantica: *Osculetur me osculo oris sui*. Il qual senso per altre parole è più apertamente detto da Paolo, quando dice: *Cupio dissolvi, et esse cum Christo*. . . . Adunque il corpo essendo quello che ci tien separati dalla union vera e dal bascio, che vorrebbono fare le cose celesti alle anime nostre raccogliendole a loro, segue che per la dissolution di quello si verrebbe a questo bascio. Il che i Theologi simbolici volendo aprire hanno lasciato nelle lor favole, che Diana . . . questa innamorata di Endimione, cioè dell'anima nostra, la quale si aspetta là su, desiderosa di poterlo basciare mentre fugge, l'addormenta di sopra un monte, e havendolo addormentato può nel basciarlo satiar le sue voglie." *Tutte l'opere di M. Giulio Camillo Delminio* (Venice, 1566), pp. 136–137.

43. Leone Ebreo presents the image as a rabbinical metaphor referring to the rapturous death of God's great saints, but at the same time, he himself applies it metaphorically to describe the climax of the mind's highest reach of contemplation, which is equated with a love ecstasy. See *Dialoghi d'amore*, ed. S. Caramella (Bari, 1929), pp. 173–178. Reuchlin and Agrippa are quoted in connection with the *mors osculi* by François Secret in *Les Kabbalistes chrétiens de la Renaissance* (Paris, 1964), pp. 39–40. Other examples referred to by Wind or Secret are in Celio Calcagnini's *Orationes*, Francesco Giorgio's *Harmonia mundi*, Guy le Fèvre de la Boderie's French translation of the preceding, and Giordano Bruno. Bruno's two allusions to the theme occur in his *De gl'heroici furori*. "Appresso descrive la morte de l'anima che da cabalisti è chiamata morte di bacio, figurata nella *Cantica* di Salomone."

Later, mention is made of "quella morte de amanti che procede da somma gioia, chiamata da cabalisti *mors osculi*. La qual medesima è vita eterna, che l'huomo può haver in dispositione [i.e., virtually] in questo tempo et in effetto nell'eternità." *Des fureurs héroiques* (*De gl'Heroici Furori*), ed. Paul-Henri Michel (Paris, 1954), pp. 211 and 331.

44. In *Opere*, ed. A. Seroni (Florence, 1958), pp. 555–556.

45. In *Trattati del Cinquecento sulla donna*, ed. G. Zonta (Bari, 1913), p. 199.

46. *Ibid.*, p. 329.

47. *Discorsi del Conte Annibale Romeo Gentil'huomo ferrarese, di nuovo ristampato* . . . (Ferrara, 1586), p. 30. Romeo's work was published in English in 1598 at London under the title *The Courtier's Academie*.

48. *Il trattato dell'Amore Humano di Flaminio Nobili con le postille autografe di T. Tasso*, ed. Pier Desiderio Pasolini (Rome, 1895), pp. 24–25. Long before Nobili, the friar Girolamo Savonarola had condemned the aestheticism of Ficino's amatory doctrine that one could rise from the contemplation of beautiful earthly bodies (of youths) to the contemplation of spiritual beauty. In one of his sermons (XXVIII) he says that he would not advise us to do as it is said Socrates did nor to gaze on a beautiful woman in order to think on God, for this would be to tempt God: "E' si dice di Socrate che andava contemplando la bellezza delli giovani per contemplare la bellezza spirituale per la corporale. Io non consiglio già te che tu facci così nè che vadi a vedere una bella donna per contemplare la bellezza di Dio: saria questo uno tentare Iddio." *Prediche sopra Ezechiele*, I, ed. Roberto Ridolfi (Rome, 1955), 375.

49. *Il trattato dell'Amore Humano*, pp. 23–24.

50. *Dialoghi piacevoli del Sig. Stefano Guazzo* (Piacenza, 1587), pp. 387–388.

51. *Ibid.*, p. 388.

52. From the dialogue "Dell'honore universale," in *Dialoghi piacevoli*, pp. 252–253. It will be noted that Guazzo seems to consider the kabbalistic *mors osculi* as a purely eschatological phenomenon rather than also as a mystic experience possible in this life, as Pico understood it.

53. *Opere volgari e latine del conte Baldassare Castiglione* (Padua, 1733), p. ii. Ciccarelli's prefatory letter and notes are reprinted in this edition.

54. *Ibid.*, p. 236, n.

6. The Renaissance-Baroque Age

1. See Introduction and further on in the present chapter.

2. One of the better recent dictionaries of sexology gives a definition of just these expressions: "*Soul Kiss*: French kiss; deep kiss. A kiss with tongue contact and stimulation of the interior of the mouth. The tongue kiss is an intimacy designed to arouse sexual excitement." Hugo G. Beigel, *Sex from A to Z: A Modern Approach to all Aspects of Human Sex Life* (New York, 1961), p. 387. The famous Kinsey report, *Sexual Behavior in the Human Female* (Philadelphia and London, 1953) also gives these same terms along with an even more detailed description of the amatory or sexual activity they refer to. It also makes the following observation: "Because of the abundant nerve supply in the lips, the tongue, and the interior of the mouth, the stimulation of these areas may be very effective, and orgasm occasionally results from such deep kissing, even though no genital contact is involved" (p. 252). What today is most often referred to as the "French kiss" was known to the French in the sixteenth century as the *baiser à l'Italienne*.

3. Concerning this erotic meaning of *perire*, Hans Licht notes an example in Martial. "The Greek word for lizard means also especially the male member. Now we have an epigram of Martial, which runs: 'Spare the lizard creeping towards you; it desires to fade away in your fingers,' *Ad te reptanti, puer insidiose, lacertae / Parce: cupit digitis illa perire tuis* (XIV, 172)." In this context, says Licht, *perire* means "to pass away in love." *Sexual Life in Ancient Greece* (London, 1932), p. 194.

As for the metaphorical sense of dying in an erotic context, classical antiquity may offer several examples. One occurs in Propertius I, x, where the poet evokes with enervating pleasure a night in which he beheld a friend "die" clasped in a sexual embrace: "Cum te complexa morientem, Galle, puella / Vidimus et longa ducere verba mora!"

For another example of the erotic employment of the soul-kiss motif in Petronius, see the prose fragment 132 of the *Satyricon*.

4. *The Love Poems of Johannes Secundus*, ed. F. A. Wright (London, 1930).

5. Te iuvet in nostris positam languere lacertis;
    Me iuvet in gremio, vita, cubare tuo,
    Et cum suaviolis animam deponere nostris
    Eque tuis animam sugere suaviolis,
    Sive meam, lux, sive tuam; sed sit tua malim
    Ipse tuo ut spirem pectore, tuque meo.

Ibid., p. 124.

6. *Ibid.*, pp. 40–42.

7. *Ibid.*, p. 116.

8. Nonne hoc amplexu linguarum alterna meantum
    Ora per et fauces, nodo constricta tenaci
    Feodera pangit amor; legemque hanc dicit amori,
    Ut quoties geminas libuit committere linguas,
    Oscula transfundant animas per aperta sequaces,

Et pariter curent ut amati in corpore totus
Vivat amans, atque hic versa vice vivat in illo?

Delitiae poetarum scotorum, I (Amsterdam, 1637), 59.

Among the Neo-Latin poets inspired chiefly by Secundus and who use the soul-kiss conceit, we may here recall Jean Bonnefon (1554–1614) and Janus Dousa the Elder (1545–1609). Bonnefon's *Pancharis* is a cycle of thirty-two *basia* in which the conceit is used several times. In the very first *basium,* the poet invites his mistress to draw his soul out by a kiss but then complains that this means death for him. This death is imaged by the vision of the poet wandering along the banks of the river Styx in the company of Catullus and Tibullus. But the poet will be avenged by drawing away his mistress' soul with a kiss, so that she too will die and so make her way to the world of the shades of famous mistresses, precisely those mistresses of Catullus and Tibullus. See *Delitiae C poetarum belgicorum,* I, ed. J. Gruter (Frankfurt, 1609), 658–659.

In one of the series of twenty-one *Basia* by Dousa the Elder, we find the transmission of the soul associated with the deep kiss of nectarine sweetness:

Tu vero dulces mecum coniunge salivas
Oris, et inspirans dentibus ora preme:
Transmittensque animae florem me nectare grate
Proluc, et in partem gaudia nostra iuva.

Delitia C poetarum belgicorum, II, ed. J. Gruter (Frankfurt, 1614), 142.

9.   Stavan sì stretti quei duo amanti insieme,
               Che l'aria non potrebbe tra lor gire;
               E l'uno e l'altro sì forte se preme,
               Che non vi serìa forza a dipartire.
               Come ciascun sospira e ciascun geme
               De l'alta dolcezza, non saprebbi io dire;
               Lor lo dican per me, poi che a lor tocca,
               Che ciascaduno avea due lingue in bocca.

Orlando innamorato, I, xix, 61. Boiardo's verses have no reference to the soul conceit. Compare III, vii, 29, where the octave concludes with these lines:

E credo che un bel baso a bocca aperta
Per la dolcezza ogni anima converta.

10. *After-Life in Roman Paganism* (New York, 1959), p. 59.

11. One of the most felicitous imitations of Olindo's vision is to be found in Girolamo Graziani's *Il conquisto di Granata* (1650). The enamored Consalvo tells Rosalba of his desire to die exhaling his anguished soul into her beautiful body (*bel seno*). Though in life he was denied the bliss of being her consort, he would account it a fortunate death if he could expire his life into Rosalba's mouth:

Soggiunge il cavalier: lieta mia sorte
Io chiamerei, se permettesse almeno

Ch'io potessi esalar con dolce morte
L'afflitta anima mia nel tuo bel seno.
Se poichè non fui vivo a te consorte
Fussi morendo, o me felice appieno!
Fortunato morir oggi mi tocca
La mia vita finir ne la tua bocca.

(XIV, 84)

Also Tassian in its motif and tone is the moment in which Osmino is mortally wounded by Silvera, of whom he asks the grace of her lips. Silvera com-
plies and "stops" Osmino's pain with her words, and his soul (evidently
ready to make its egress) with her kisses (XVII, 62–63).

12. "Tutto che l'anima non si possa separare da niuna parte del corpo,
nientedimeno intensivamente par, ch'ella sia tutta in quella parte, dove
l'appetito la porta, e però dice, che tutta era in quel bacio, e tutta in quella
bocca: e che sia vero restarono l'altre membra come se da lei fossero ab-
bandonate languide, e com'egli dice, tremanti." *Il Pastor Fido, Tragicommedia
pastorale del molto illustre sig. Cav. Battista Guarini* (Venice, 1602), p. 88.

13. The soul-kiss conceit is repeated by Guarini at the end of Act II of the
Pastor Fido, where it is said that the only responsive place to be kissed is on
the mouth because there souls themselves kiss: "Ove l'un alma e l'altra /
Corre e si bacia anch'ella." Guarini also wrote a canzone celebrating the
osculatory ingenuity of lovers. The poem terminates with the kiss on the
mouth and the idea that by such a kiss love joins both the souls and bodies
of lovers. See *Rime inedite del Cinquecento*, ed. L. Frati (Bologna, 1918), p.
143.

14. The closest Marino comes to exemplifying these tendencies is in his
scene of the dirge of Venus over the dead Adonis, although here, too, as so
often in this poet, a promising thought is vitiated by a play on words or
conceits. In a departure from Bion's lamenting Venus, who expresses the
desire to have Adonis' last breath kissed into her, in Marino's poem the
grieving goddess wishes to have her immortal spirit die and be entombed in
his breast, which would mean a new life for Adonis. Obviously the vehicle
of transmission of her spirit is the kiss:

Arresta il volo, aspetta tanto almeno
Che 'l mio spirto immortal ti mora in seno.

(XVIII, 161:7–8)

15. It will be well to note at least one more example in prose. In a *novella*,
Giovanni Battista Fusconi seems to have remembered Aretino's use of the
soul-in-the-kiss and death image as a witty euphemism for sexual orgasm.
When Cleria—a married woman—upbraids a would-be suitor for his too-
ardent attentions, the despairing gallant pleads with her to kill him. But the
cruel Cleria replies that she wants to enjoy his death, whereupon she accordingly leads him to a bed chamber: "Vuoi dunque ch'io t'uccida, ripigliò
Cleria: così risolvo; levati, e vien meco, che hora voglio delitiare nella tua

332

morte. Ciò detto aprì la porta di un'altra camera angusta, dove era un letto, e quivi gli fece un laccio con le sue braccia al collo, nè lo disciolse sino che egli non spirò l'anima ne la sua bocca." *Cento novelle amorose dei Signori Accademici Incogniti* (Venice, 1651), Parte seconda, p. 206.

The number of examples of the soul-in-the-kiss image would almost seem to be endless in Italian authors of the sixteenth and seventeenth centuries. I refrain from giving more instances of it even without commentary, for to do otherwise would be to make an interminable note. The cases already recorded are certainly sufficiently representative.

16. Secundus was much admired by the French poets of the sixteenth century. An anthology of imitations of the *Basia* was prepared some years ago by Henri Chamard: *Les Baisers de Jean Second, imités par Pierre de Ronsard et ses disciples 1500–1600* (Monaco, Editions du Rocher, 1947). This anthology consists of twenty-five poems by Ronsard; three by Antoine De Baïf; three by Jacques Tahureau; four by Olivier de Magny; two by J. Du Bellay; one by Jacques Grévin; one by Claude de Buttet; thirteen by Rémy Belleau; one by Amadis Jamyn; one by Philippe Desportes; one by Jean Bertaut.

For some examples of the imitation of the kiss motif from Secundus among the poets of the Pléiade, see Henri Weber, *La création poétique au XVIe siècle en France*, I (Paris, 1956), 369 ff. Of this theme in the Pléiade poets, Weber writes: "Dans l'ensemble, ce thème imposait à la Pléiade des schémas trop fixes et trop rigides pour que la poésie puisse s'y épanouir librement. Elle apparaît çà et là dans le jeu des images dont le baiser n'est plus alors que le simple prétexte" (I, 391). Whatever one thinks of the reasoning here, it is certain that in the use of the theme of the kiss these poets, with the exception of Ronsard, fail to achieve the intense poetic accents given to it by Louise Labé.

17. An abundance of poetry of kissing even at that time did not necessarily mean that the soul-in-the-kiss image was inevitable. For example, in the numerous verses (including a series of *Basia*) on kissing and its delights by Jacques Tahureau, I find no use of the conceit.

18. This is not to say that Platonic love and its conceits ceased thereafter. An undercurrent of Platonic love went on, finally gushing forth again in the following century with Thomas D'Urfée's *Astrée*.

19. For Ronsard's version see *Oeuvres complètes*, I, ed. G. Cohen (Paris, 1950), 162–163.

20. *Ibid.*, I, 442.

21. *Oeuvres complètes*, I, 294–295. But also worthy of note is the echo of a "mystic" tradition where the poet asks the beloved to inbreathe or transmit her "grace" into him. This motif is quickly followed by the poet's request for the return of his soul by a kiss:

> Inspire, en me baisant, ton haleine et ta grace
> Et ton coeur dedans moy.
> Puis appuyant ton sein sur le mien qui se pâme,
> Pour mon mal appaiser,
> Serre plus fort mon col, et me redonne l'ame
> Par l'esprit d'un baiser.

22. *Ibid.*, pp. 106–107. Also found in Baïf is the theme of the beloved's ambrosial kiss raising the lover to the equal of the gods. See the poem "Ce ne sont baisers que donne / Ma mignonne," in the *Diverses Amours*, 1573. The expression "douce rage d'amour continuel" comes from a Ronsard chanson on the kiss beginning

> Douce maistresse, touche,
> Pour soulager mon mal
> Ma bouche de ta bouche,

which verses have an almost medieval flavor and recall the medieval poets' use of the kiss motif of the Song of Songs. Ronsard's poem, however, quickly goes on in typical Renaissance pagan fashion.

23. Thus Oliver de Magny in *Les Gayetez*, ed. E. Courbet (Paris, 1871), p. 14. In the poem "A s'amie," de Magny also envisions himself and his lady kissing and embracing even in the afterlife as well as living in one another here. See *Les Odes amoureuses de 1559*, ed. Mark S. Whitney (Geneva and Paris, 1964), p. 42.

24. In this context we should record the case (late sixteenth century) of Marguerite de Valois, who in a letter to M. de Chauvalon gives voice to the Neoplatonic love conventions, including the idea of the kiss as the true vehicle for the pleasure of the soul: "Vostre ame veut ce que je veux, et luy complaisant c'est vous complaire; car l'ame est seule l'homme, qui estant liée avec le corps, ces deux sens luy suffisent, la veue et l'ouye, pour contenter son desir qui, tout different des appetits du corps, se sent son plaisir d'autant retranché, que l'on s'adhère aux autres qui ne peuvent estre causes d'amour, puisqu'ils ne sont desirs de beauté (car l'amour n'est autre chose), et la beauté ne peut estre desirée et aymée que par ce qui la connoist. . . . Ainsy remplie de cette divine et non vulgaire passion, je rens en imagination mille baisers à vostre belle bouche, qui seule sera participante au plaisir reservé à l'ame, le meritant pour estre l'instrument de tant de belles et dignes louanges où bientost me puissé-je ravir." *Memoires et lettres de Marguerite de Valois*, ed. M. F. Guessard (Paris, 1842), pp. 466–467. For this and the preceding two references I am indebted to my colleague Professor Leonard Johnson.

25. Epistle 98 in *The Epistles of Erasmus from His Earliest Letters to His Fiftieth Year*, I, trans. Francis Morgan Nichols (New York, 1962), 203. The letter was written to Erasmus' friend and champion, Faustus Andrelinus, a native of Italy, who had become both Court poet and Professor of Rhetoric and Poetry at the University of Paris.

26. *Collected Poems of Sir Thomas Wyatt*, ed. Kenneth Muir (London, 1949), p. 35.

27. *THE EKATOMPATHIA or Passionate Centurie of Love* (London, 1869), p. 34.

28. The rhyme was used several times by Giles Fletcher in his *canzoniere*, *Licia* (1593), and even twice in a single Elegy ("Distance of place, my Love and me did part"):

> Happy those lips, that had so sweet a kiss!
> For heaven itself scarce yields so sweet a bliss.
>
> And thus kind love, the sun of all my bliss,
> Was both begun, and ended, in a kiss.

In *An English Garner*, VIII, ed. Edward Arber (Westminster, 1896), 462.

29. "Philomela's ode that she sung in her arbor," from *Philomela* (1592). In *Poetry of the English Renaissance, 1509–1660*, ed. J. W. Hebel and H. H. Hudson (New York, 1929), p. 155. Philomela adds the warning:

> But if a kiss prove unchaste,
> Then is true love quite disgraced.

30. *Laura: The Toyes of a Traveller, or The Feast of Fancy* (London, 1597), in *An English Garner*, VIII, 279. Compare Giles Fletcher in sonnet XVI of *Licia*:

> Then as the vine, the propping elm doth clasp,
> Loth to depart, till both together die;
> So fold me, Sweet; until my latest gasp!
> That in thy arms, to death I kissed, may lie.

31. In *King Lear* (IV, vii) the "restorative" kiss of balm occurs when Cordelia puts her lips to those of her abused and mad father with these words:

> O my dear father! Restoration hang
> Thy medicine on my lips; and let this kiss
> Repair those violent harms that my two sisters
> Have in thy reverence made!

32. "I am dying, Egypt, dying; only / I here importune death a while, until / Of many thousand kisses the poor last / I lay upon thy lips." *Antony and Cleopatra*, IV, 15.

In Shakespeare's *Venus and Adonis* an interesting twist is given to the kiss motif usually found at the end of the story where Venus kisses the dying Adonis. In Shakespeare's version, as Venus is lamenting over the dead youth, a speckled white-and-purple flower springs up from the ground where Adonis' blood had spilled. This flower is a substitute for or the child of Adonis. In smelling it, Venus in fact identifies its scent with Adonis' *breath* and determines that it shall be kept by her in her breast. There she shall kiss it forever: "There shall not be one minute in an hour / Wherein I will not kiss my sweet love's flower" (1187–1188).

33. *Poems of Bishop Henry King*, ed. James R. Baker (Denver, 1960), p. 28.

34. *The Poems of William Drummond of Hawthornden*, ed. Wm. C. Ward, I (London, 1894), 154, 167, and *ibid.*, II, 147.

35. *The First Set of English Madrigals . . . Newly Composed by John Ward* (London, 1613), p. 499.

36. *The Dramatic Works and Poems of James Shirley*, ed. Wm. Gifford, VI (London, 1833), 499. The theme is also found in Shirley's poem "Taking Leave when his Mistress was to Ride" (p. 421). And in Act II of *The Arcadia, a Pastoral* (London, 1754), p. 21, Pyrocles, in love with Philoclea, says to her: "First let me give my life / Up to these Lips, and take a new one from / This Kiss."
Another poet who was familiar enough with the thought was Thomas Carew. In "A Pastorall Dialogue," Celia offers Cleon her lips with the words "This kisse, my heart, and thy faith keepe," to which Cleon replies in kind: "This breathes my soule to thee." But it is somewhat more refreshing to find Carew, in another poem, giving a new twist to the image by having the lover bitterly complain: "My soule enflam'd with thy false breath, / Poyson'd with kisses, suckt in death." *The Poems of Thomas Carew*, ed. Rhodes Dunlap (Oxford, 1949), pp. 44, 50.

37. For example, see in *Kisses, Being the Basia of Johannes Secundus Rendered into English Verse by Thomas Stanley, 1647* (London, 1927), pp. 2, 9.

38. *Thomas Stanley: His Original Lyrics Complete*, ed. L. I. Guiney (Hull, 1907), p. 60.

39. *Ibid.*, p. 49.

40. In Chalmers' *The Works of the English Poets*, IV (London, 1810), 750.

41. *The Poems English and Latin of Edward Lord Herbert of Cherbury*, ed. G. C. Moore Smith (Oxford, 1923), p. 41.

42. Concerning Spenser ("the greatest representative of Platonism in English poetry"), however, something more may be said concerning the kiss image. In the *Faerie Queene*, when Scudamour and Amoret are finally reunited following the rescue of Amoret from Busirane, they are "reunited" as much as is possible by means of a kiss and an embrace which make (literally) one of the two, as Spenser brings in the Hermaphrodite image also in a vision which seems to belie Lucretius' opinion (see the Introduction). It is significant that these verses were replaced in the 1596 version by others:

> Lightly he clipped her twixt his arme's twain
> And straightly did embrace her body bright,
> Her body, late the prison of sad pain,
> Now the sweet lodge of love and dear delight;
> But she, fair lady, overcommen quite

> Of huge affection, did in pleasure melt
> And in sweet ravishment of soul poured out her sprite:
> No word they spake, nor earthly thing they felt,
> But like two senseless stocks in long embracement dwelt.
>
> Had ye then seen, ye would have surely thought
> That they had been the fair Hermaphrodite
> Which that rich Roman of white marble wrought
> And in his costly bath caused to be site;
> So seemed those two, as grown together quite.
>
> (III, xii; 45–46)

43. "To Mr. Philip Warwick, at Paris, June 3, 1634"; in *James Howell's Familiar Letters*, 10th ed. (London, 1737), p. 255.

44. Chalmers' *The Works of the English Poets*, V, 596.

45. The same turning away from the senses and such intimacies as the real kiss is to be noted in some lines from Henry Vaughan which are close in spirit and language to Donne's verses:

> Whilst I by pow'rfull Love so much refin'd,
> That my absent soul the same is,
> Carelesse to misse,
> A glance, or kisse,
> Can with those Elements of lust and sence,
> Freely dispence,
> And court the mind.

The Works of Henry Vaughan, I, ed. L. C. Martin (Oxford, 1914), 13. See also *The Poems of William Habington*, ed. K. Alcott (London, 1948), p. 48.

46. *Poems of John Donne*, I, ed. E. K. Chambers (London, 1896), 76.

47. John Smith Harrison, *Platonism in English Poetry of the Sixteenth and Seventeenth Centuries* (New York, 1903), p. 161.

48. For a fine review of the discussions on Donne's "The Ecstasie" and, at the same time, a sound interpretation, see Merrit Y. Hughes, "Some of Donne's 'Ecstasies,' " *PMLA*, LXXV (Dec. 1960), 509–518. For a well-argued interpretation based on the demonstration of the influence of Leone Ebreo's *Dialoghi d'amore*, see Helen Gardner's "The Argument of 'The Ecstasy,' " in *Elizabethan and Jacobean Studies Presented to Frank Percy Wilson* (Oxford, 1959), pp. 279–306. But see also A. J. Smith's cogent article, "Donne in His Time: A Reading of 'The Extasie,' " in *Rivista di letterature moderne e comparate*, X (July–Dec. 1957), 260–275.

49. *The Poems and Plays of William Cartwright*, ed. G. Blakemore Evans (Madison, Wisconsin, 1951), p. 494. In Cartwright's *The Royal Slave* there is a scene in which the lovers, who are listening to strains of beautiful music, feel their souls being drawn to their ears and in danger of evaporating into the magical harmony. The lover, in Neoplatonic fashion, suggests that he

and his lady kiss, for in this way their souls will return and then come to
their mouths. It also will give them the opportunity to exchange their souls
with one another:

> Let's kiss and call them backe againe.
> Now let's orderly conveigh
>   Our soules into each other's Brest
> Where interchanged let them stay
>   Slumbering in a melting rest.
>
> (II, iii)

The Poems and Plays of William Cartwright, p. 212.

50. *The Complete Works in Verse and Prose of Abraham Cowley,* I, ed.
A. B. Grosart (Edinburgh, 1881), 119.

51. *Venus and Anchises (Brittain's Ida) and other Poems,* ed. Ethel Seaton
(London, 1926), p. 27.

52. *The Poetical Works of Robert Herrick,* ed. L. C. Martin (Oxford, 1956),
p. 459. See also pp. 174, 240.

53. The song, from *The Amorous War,* is reprinted in *Seventeenth Century Lyrics,* ed. Norman Ault (New York, 1950), pp. 230–231.

54. *The Poems of John Cleveland,* ed. John M. Berdan (New Haven, 1911),
p. 68.

55. *The Sermons of John Donne,* III, ed. G. R. Potter and E. M. Simpson
(Berkeley, 1957), 320–321. That the kiss was sanctioned by a long Christian
tradition was known also to Joseph Beaumont, who finds the betrayal of
Christ the more reprehensible because it was carried out with a kiss which
should be a "mystick stamp" and a "conveyance of the Soul":

> Is not a Kiss that Mystick Stamp, which though
> It sinks not in, yet deep Impressions leaves:
> The smooth Conveyance of the Soul, which through
> The closed Mouth her thrilling self derives:
> Th' Epitome of genuine Salutation,
> And Modesty's most graceful Copulation?

The verses are from *Psyche: or Love's Mystery,* XI, 22 in *The Complete
Poems of Dr. Joseph Beaumont,* I, ed. A. B. Grosart (Edinburgh, 1880), 227.

The mystic kiss of the great contemplatives is remembered by John Davies
of Hereford: See *Mirum in modum: A Glimpse of God's Glorie, and the
Soules Shape,* in *The Complete Works of John Davies of Hereford,* I, ed. A.
B. Grosart (Edinburgh, 1878), 14.

We have already had occasion (chapter 2) to quote the verses by Richard
Crashawe in which he alludes to the ecstatic death by rapture of St. Theresa
of Avila: "By the full kingdome of that finall kisse / That seiz'd thy parting
Soul, and seal'd thee his."

Epilogue

1 Alexis François, *Le premier baiser de l'amour, ou Jean-Jacques Rousseau inspirateur d'estampes* (Geneva, 1920), p. 29. This book deals with the eighteenth and early nineteenth century engravings inspired by the descriptions Rousseau gave for a series of engravings to accompany his *Nouvelle Héloïse*. The first of the series is entitled *Le premier baiser de l'amour*, and François reproduces 25 examples of the theme.

2. "Quoi! tes yeux attendris ne se baisseroient plus avec cette douce pudeur qui m'enivre de volupté! Quoi! mes lèvres brulantes ne déposeroient plus sur ton coeur mon ame avec mes baisers? Quoi! je n'eprouverois plus ce frémissement céleste, ce feu rapide et dévorant qui, plus prompt que l'éclair . . . moment! moment inexprimable!" *Oeuvres complètes*, I (Paris, Bibliothèque de la Pléiade, 1959), 1502. For the passage quoted from the *Confessions* see *ibid.*, I, 444–445. Lord Byron understood Rousseau's passion to be a nympholeptic idealism which hallowed the ritual kiss of greeting he received daily from Mme. d'Houdetot:

> But his was not the love of living dame,
> Nor of the dead who rise upon our dreams,
> But of ideal beauty, which became
> In him existence, and o'erflowing teems
> Along his burning page, distemper'd though it seems.
>
> *This* breathed itself to life in Julie, *this*
> Invested her with all that's wild and sweet;
> *This* hallow'd, too, the memorable kiss
> Which every morn his fever'd lip would greet,
> From hers, who but with friendship his would meet.
> (*Childe Harold*, III:78, 5–9; 79, 1–5)

3. Rousseau had an undying passion for Tasso's *Aminta* and *Gerusalemme liberata*, works upon which his sensibility was nurtured. In *La nouvelle Héloïse* Tasso is one of only three or four Italian authors quoted (often, it must be said). The fact that chief among the others are Petrarch and Metastasio is telltale enough. Given Saint-Preux's desire for a Tassian type of love-death, it is significant and fascinating to discover that Rousseau made a French prose translation of the Olindo-Sofronia episode from the second canto of the Italian poet's great epic. We may sample it with part of the discourse Olindo addresses to Sofronia when the two are tied to the same stake and in imminent peril of the flames: "O que la mort me sera douce, que les tourments me seront délicieux, si j'obtiens qu'au dernier moment tombant l'un sur l'autre, nos bouches se joignent pour exhaler et recevoir au même instant nos derniers soupirs." *Oeuvres de J. J. Rousseau*, XIV (Paris, 1832), 265. The translation was first published in *Oeuvres posthumes de J. J. Rousseau*, II (Geneva, 1781), 283–319.

4. Letters of May 14–15; I translate from the 1802 edition, reprinted in *Ultime lettere di Jacopo Ortis*, ed. G. Gambarin (Florence, 1955), pp. 199–201. Jacopo's raptures were "experienced" by an even younger Foscolo in a juvenile literary exercise in terza rima. In *Le rimembranze* (46–58) the poet "recalls" his love for Laura [!] in verses that echo Dante's *Inferno* and *Paradiso*. Here the invocation to death comes as a conclusion to the ecstasy:

> Addio diceva a Laura, e Laura intanto
> Fise in me avea le luci, ed agli addio
> Ed ai singulti rispondea col pianto.
> E mi stringea la man: —tutto fuggío
> Della notte l'orrore, e radiante
> Io vidi in cielo a contemplarci Iddio,
> E petto unito a petto palpitante,
> E sospiro a sospiro, e riso a riso,
> La bocca le baciai tutto tremante,
> E quanto io vidi allor sembrommi un riso
> Dell'universo, e le candide porte
> Disserrarsi vid'io del Paradiso.
> Deh! a che non venne, e l'invocai, la morte?

Even in comparison with these immature verses, Lord Byron's own youthful lines on the "First Kiss of Love" sound flippant if not hollow:

> Oh! cease to affirm that man, since his birth,
> From Adam till now has with wretchedness strove;
> Some portion of paradise still is on earth,
> And Eden revives in the first kiss of love.

5. *Ultime lettere*, p. 287. There may be a Foscolian echo in the young Leopardi's account of the ecstasy of the kiss which, significantly enough in the case of this poet, was "experienced" in a dream: "E io baciarla [the lady's hand] senza ardire di toccarla . . . svegliatomi subito e riscosso pienamente vidi che il piacere era stato appunto qual sarebbe reale e vivo, e restai attonito e conobbi come sia vero che tutta l'anima si possa trasfondere in un bacio e perder di vista tutto il mondo, come allora proprio mi parve." *Ricordi d'infanzia e di adolescenza*, in *Tutte le opere*, I, ed. Francesco Flora, 5th ed. (Milan, 1956), 685.

6. The French text is printed in the Pléiade edition of *A la recherche du temps perdu*, III, ed. P. Clarac and A. Ferré (Paris, 1954), 1070. There is still a religious echo in the passage that appears in the established text near the beginning of *La prisonnière*: "Chaque soir, fort tard, avant de me quitter, elle [Albertine] glissait dans ma bouche sa langue, comme un pain quotidien, comme un aliment nourrissant et ayant le charactère presque sacré de toute chair à qui les souffrances que nous avons endurées à cause d'elle ont fini par conférer une sorte de douceur morale." *Ibid.*, III, 10.

7. Mervyn Levy, *The Moons of Paradise: Some Reflections on the Appearance of the Female Breast in Art* (London, 1962), p. 177.

8. Rodin himself commented thus on the marble version of his famous sculpture: "Undoubtedly the intertwining of *The Kiss* is pretty, but in this group I made no discovery. It is a theme treated according to the academic tradition, a sculpture complete in itself and artifically set apart from the surrounding world. My *Balzac*, on the contrary, by its pose and look makes one imagine the milieu in which he walked, lived and thought." Quoted thus in Albert E. Elsen's *Rodin* (New York, 1963), p. 102. With what I say in the text, I do not mean to contest Rodin's importance in the history of modern sculpture, the development of which owes much to the sculptor's *Balzac* pieces.

9. Malvina Hoffman reported the following conversation with Brancusi: " 'Here is my laboratory, and here are my pictures of the Temple du Baiser. You may have them for your book, they are recent ones. Tomorrow I shall go to see this gateway inaugurated in my country. Through this doorway one will enter a garden. . . . Do you recognize the patterns on the stone? Here are the plaster models of the supporting columns; what do you see in them? ' I thought for a few moments. 'I see the forms of two cells that meet and create life . . . like the revelation I once saw through a microscope when I studied embryology. The beginning of life . . . through love. Am I right?' 'Yes you are,' he answered, 'and these columns are the result of years of searching. First came this group of two interlaced, seated figures in stone . . . then the symbol of the egg, then the thought grew into this gateway to a beyond. . . .' " *Sculpture Inside and Out* (New York, 1939), p. 53. The *Gate of the Kiss* (1937) is the entrance to the public park of Tirgu-Jiu, in Romania. The columns of the *Gate* contain a decoration of two half-circles touching each other (the Kiss) and encompassed by a larger circle. The frieze of the *Gate* carries a series of the stylized kiss motif.

10. Athena Tacha Spear notes that "the dating of the Montparnasse *Kiss* presents a problem. . . . If Brancusi had carved that version of the *Kiss* in 1908, as is often said, then it was not commissioned especially for Tatiana's tomb. This assumption seems to be confirmed by the caption given to the Montparnasse *Kiss* in an early reproduction: 'Now in the Montparnasse Cemetery, although not originally intended as a memorial.' " In "A Contribution to Brancusi Chronology," *Art Bulletin* 48, no. 1 (March, 1966), 46.

11. Henriette s'Jacob, *Idealism and Realism: A Study of Sepulchral Symbolism* (Leiden, 1954), p. 38. The author adds: "Of this feeling the musée Adrien Dubouché at Limoges possesses a touching example in the rather mutilated group called 'bon mariage.' The wife, turning to the right, seems to invite her husband to the grave. On many tombstones one meets couples looking at each other with slightly inclined heads" (p. 38). For the idea of togetherness in death as suggested in a few epitaphs of Greek antiquity, see Richard Lattimore, *Themes in Greek and Latin Epitaphs* (Urbana, Illinois, 1962), pp. 58; 247–248.

12. Erwin Panofsky, *Tomb Sculpture*, ed. H. W. Janson (New York, n.d.),

341

p. 29. The text of this beautiful book is based on a series of public lectures delivered by Professor Panofsky at The Institute of Fine Arts of New York University in the fall of 1956.

Appendix I

1. *Theological and Dogmatic Works* (Washington, 1963), p. 78.

2. John Burnaby, *Amor Dei: A Study of the Religion of St. Augustine* (London, 1938, reprinted 1947), p. 166.

3. *De Trinitate*, XV, xix, 37. *Oeuvres de Saint Augustin*, XVI, 2me série (Paris, Desclée de Brouwer, 1955), 522. See also *De Trinitate*, VI, v, 7.

4. At times the dove also was an iconographical symbol of Christ, the Church, and Christians, as well as of the departed soul enjoying peace in Paradise. See Friedrich Sühling, *Die Taube als religiöses Symbol im christlichen Altertum*, Römische Quartalschrift für christliche Altertumskunde u. für Kirchengeschichte, 24 Supplementheft (Freiburg im Breisgan, 1930).

5. Propertius, *Elegies*, III, 1–2. Of course, love was also metaphorically associated with war, and the lover was seen as a soldier doing battle. This is especially true of Ovid who has a poem in which love is compared with the militia. It begins, "Militat omnis amans et habet sua castra Cupido."

6. St. Cyprian, *Treatises*, ed. and trans. Roy J. Deferrari (New York, 1958), p. 104. My italics.

7. *Tract. in Ioh.*, 6, 4. In *PL*, 35: 1427.

8. The presence of the angel holding the dove in this depiction of the Trinity and in some others like it has not, as far as I know, been explained. Even Millard Meiss, who speaks of the dove in such representations as "making more explicit the concept of the spiration of the Holy Ghost from the other two members of the Trinity," is at a loss to explain the angel: "A complication of meaning, however, appears with the introduction of a descending angel who seems almost to steer or steady the dove." He says of it only that it is a "puzzling notion." *French Painting in the Time of Jean de Berry*, text volume (London-New York, Phaidon, 1967), p. 152.

The figure of the angel with his function of supporting the dove is indeed curious. If I were to hazard a guess on the matter, I should say that he is a carry-over or superimposition of the angel of the Annunciation scene in which artists so often depicted the descent of the dove-Spirit upon Mary at the very moment the angelic minister is telling her that that event is soon to occur.

9. See *Dictionnaire d'Archéologie Chrétienne et de Liturgie*, ed. F. Cabrol and H. Leclercq, X, part 2 (Paris, 1925), 1881–1889.

10. In passing I would note that the dove may be connected with other

aspects of Christian kiss symbolism in iconographical representations. Such for example may be the case in some Annunciation scenes. Most medieval illustrations of this motif in which the dove is present as the Holy Spirit and divine impregnating force show the bird sent from the Father and moving or hovering near the lap or the ear of the Virgin. The impregnation of the Virgin by way of the ear, in fact, was the subject of a study by Ernest Jones, "The Madonna's Conception Through the Ear," in *Essays in Applied Psycho-Analysis* (London-Vienna, 1923), pp. 261–359. There are, however, examples of the Annunciation scene in which the dove is seen near the face or the very mouth of the Virgin. In this connection we need only recall that Ambrose had associated the kiss request of the Song with the impregnation of the Virgin and had spoken of the kiss as the Holy Spirit coming upon Mary: "Osculetur me ab osculis oris sui; significat spiritus sancti supervenientis gratiam sicut angelus ad Mariam dixit: spiritus sanctus superveniet in te . . ." (see p. 71). Another case in which the dove-Spirit may be a kiss is to be noted in those medieval miniatures which show the dove "inspiring" a Christian saintly writer. Here again, the dove is usually seen with its bill in or at the saint's ear, but occasionally at the saint's mouth.

Appendix II

1. A. J. Denomy, "*Fin' Amors*: The Pure Love of the Troubadours, its Amorality, and Possible Sources," in *Medieval Studies*, VII (1945), 189.

2. "A Treatise on Love by Ibn Sina, Translated by Emil L. Fackenheim," in *Medieval Studies*, VII (1945), 222. This translation was published in conjunction with Father Denomy's article (see previous note).

3. "*Fin' Amors*: The Pure Love of the Troubadours," in *Medieval Studies*, VII (1945), 142–143 and 157.

4. The French *chansons de gestes* and their Middle High German imitations offer many examples of men kissing one another. They have been enumerated and discussed by George Fenwick Jones in his article "The Kiss in Middle High German Literature" (*Studia Neophilologica* XXXVIII, 2, 1966, pp. 195–210). Jones notes that these kisses most often symbolize a reconciliation or otherwise are used with a legal or diplomatic aim, "usually that of sealing a truce or atonement" (p. 199). Jones, however, does not seem to be aware of the "primitive" myths or beliefs in the magico-physical nature of the kiss as a bond uniting breaths, blood-breaths, or souls, which lie behind such man-to-man kisses. Similarly he does not see the mystico-magical character of the kiss of parting between Tristan and Iseult. His only remark on this kiss is: "When Tristan and Isolde part in the love-grotto with a kiss, their kiss also serves to plight their pact to be true to each other" (p. 203). Thus Jones is led to what seems to me an oversimplification in his conclusion when he states that "sufficient to explain all the kisses in medieval literature, are the many kisses in Scripture . . . kisses of greeting, fare-

well, reconciliation, and contract" (p. 209). It is all the more curious that of all the biblical kisses that Jones enumerates, the kiss of the Song of Songs is not mentioned; and that is surely the kiss which, while it is not enough to "explain" the passionate kisses of medieval literature, certainly had the greatest single influence on them.

5. See L. Alfonsi, "L'amore-amicizia negli elegiaci latini," in *Aevum*, XIII, No. 3–4 (July–December 1945), 372–378.

6. *The Catullan Revolution* (London and New York, 1959), p. 81.

7. Nelli does, however, make much of the kiss episode in the *Flamenca* but chiefly for the exposition of the motif of the exchange of hearts.

8. Robert Harlan Gere, "The Troubadours, Heresy, and the Albigensian Crusade" (Unpublished dissertation, Columbia University, 1956), p. 129.

A Selective Bibliography

The nature of this study is such that a complete bibliography in the sense of one including all works consulted or even simply those quoted by me would be unwieldy and repetitious. The notes to the text give all necessary references to the authors and works I have cited. What follows then is a list of items known to me that deal to some degree specifically with the kiss. But I must qualify this by saying that although I have allowed some titles of little or no value to appear here, I have omitted, with the exception of Martin von Kempen, a number of seventeenth and early eighteenth century Latin writings on the kiss. The reader can find these older items listed in the articles on the kiss by F. Cabrol and B. Karle.

Anonymous [Docteur ———]. *Le baiser: étude littéraire et historique.* Nancy, 188?. (300 copies printed.)

Anonymous. "The Theory and Practice of Osculation," *North American Review*, CLXXXVI (October, 1907), 315–320.

Bombough, Charles Carrol. *The Literature of Kissing.* Philadelphia, 1876.

Burton, Robert. *The Anatomy of Melancholy*, Third Partition [*Love-Melancholy*], Section Two, Member III, Subsection IV. In the London, 1826, edition, II, 265–268.

Cabrol, F. "Baiser," *Dictionnaire d'archéologie chrétienne et de liturgie*, ed. F. Cabrol and H. Leclercq, Vol. II, Part 1 (Paris, 1925), cols. 117–130. (First in 1907 edition, Vol. II, cols. 117–130.)

Conybeare, F. C. "New Testament Notes," *The Expositor*, 4th series, IX (London, 1894), 460–462.

Crawley, A. E. "Kissing," *Encyclopaedia of Religion and Ethics*, ed. James Hastings, VII (New York, 1928), 739–744. Also in Crawley's *The Mystic Rose*, new edition, revised by Theodore Besterman, I (London, 1927), 338–359.

Crescini, Vincenzo. "Il bacio di Ginevra e il bacio di Paolo," *Studi danteschi*, III (1921), 5–57.

Dix, Gregory. *The Shape of the Liturgy* (Glasgow, 1945), pp. 105–110 ("The Greeting and Kiss of Peace").

d'Enjoy, Paul. "Le baiser en Europe et en Chine," *Bulletin de la Société d'Anthropologie*, IVᵉ Série, VIII (1897), 181–185.

Donne, John. "Sermon Preached upon Trinity Sunday" (c. 1620), *The Sermons of John Donne*, III, ed. G. R. Potter and E. M. Simpson (Berkeley and Los Angeles, 1962), pp. 313–331.

Du Cange. "Osculum," *Glossarium mediae et infimae latinitatis*, editio nova (L. Favre), VI (Paris, 1938), 72–74.

Dyer, T. F. Thiselton. "The History of Kissing," *Belgravia, an Illustrated London Magazine*, XLVIII (July–October, 1882), 200–208.

Ellis, Havelock. *Studies in the Psychology of Sex, IV, Sexual Selection in Man*, Appendix A (Philadelphia, 1914), pp. 215–222 ("The Origins of the Kiss").

Encyclopedic Dictionary of the Bible, A Translation and Adaptation of A. van den Born's Bijbels Woordenboek, 2nd rev. ed. 1954–1957, Louis F. Hartman (New York, Toronto, London, 1963), pp. 1286–1287.

Flauti, Benedetto. *Monografia su l'uso del bacio*. Naples, 1889. Pp. 34.

Frank, Emma. *Der Schlangenkuss. Die Geschichte eines Erlösungsmotivs in deutscher Volksdichtung*. Leipzig, 1928.

Gaselee, Stephen. "The Soul in the Kiss," *Criterion*, II (April, 1924), 349–359.

Hofmann, Karl-Martin. *Philema Hagion*. Beiträge zur Förderung christlicher Theologie, 2 Reihe, 38 Band, Gütersloh, 1938.

Hopkins, E. Washburn. "The Sniff-kiss in Ancient India," *Journal of the American Oriental Society*, XXVIII (1907), 120–134.

Jacobs, Joseph. "Kiss and Kissing," *The Jewish Encyclopedia*, VII, ed. I. Singer (New York, 1904), pp. 515–516.

Jones, George Fenwick. "The Kiss in Middle High German Literature," *Studia Neophilologica*, XXXVIII, 2 (1966), 195–210.

Jungmann, Joseph A. *The Mass of the Roman Rite: Its Origins and Development*, trans. Francis A. Brunner, II (New York, 1955), pp. 321–332 ("*Pax Domini* and the Kiss of Peace").

Kahle, Alb. *De osculo sancto*. Regiomonti, 1867.

Karle, B. "Kuss, küssen," *Handwörterbuch des deutschen Aberglaubens*, herausgegeben . . . von E. Hoffmann-Krayer und . . . von Hanns Bächtold-Stäubli, V (Berlin-Leipzig, 1933), cols. 841–863.

Kempen, Martin von [Kempius]. *Dissertatio Historico-Philologica gemina: prior de Osculo in genere ejusque variis speciebus, posterior de Osculo Judae*. Lipsiae, 1665.

——. *Opus Polyhistoricum, dissertationibus XXV de osculis, subnexisque de Judae ingenio, vita et fine, sacris epiphyllidibus, absolutum*, etc. Francofurti, 1680.

Kroll, Wilhelm. "Kuss," in Pauly-Wissowa, *Real-Encyclopädie der classischen altertumswissenschaft*, Supplementband V (Stuttgart, 1931), cols. 511–520.

Lejeune, Charles. "Le baiser," *Revue anthropologique*, XXVI (January, 1916), 478–482.

Lombroso, Cesare. "L'origine du baiser," *La Nouvelle Revue*, LXXXIII (1893), 673–680.

——. "An Epidemic of Kisses in America," *Pall Mall Magazine*, XVIII (May–August, 1899), 544–547.

Malespine, Emile. "The Kiss," *Forum*, LXVI (July, 1921), 13–22.

——. "Le baiser, essai de psycho-physiologie," *Mercure de France*, CXLIII (November, 1920), 660–693.

Matthews, J. Brander. "The Curiosities of Kissing," *Galaxy*, XVI (July–December, 1873), 280–283.

Moroni, Gaetano. "Bacio," *Dizionario di erudizione storico-ecclesiastica*, IV (Venice, 1840), 11–18.

A New English Dictionary, ed. Sir James Murray, V, Part 2 (Oxford, 1901), pp. 714–715 ("Kiss").

Nyrop, Christopher. *The Kiss and its History*, trans. Wm. F. Harvey. London, 1901.

Pearson, Norman. "The Kiss Poetical," *Fortnightly Review*, LXXXII (August, 1904), 291–306.

Pharr, Mary Brown. "The Kiss in Roman Law," *Classical Journal*, XLII (April, 1947), 393–397.

Scerbo, Ercole. *Il bacio nel costume e nei secoli*. Rome, 1963.

Snodgrass, A. E. "The Kiss," *Cornhill Magazine*, LXI (October, 1926), 459–463.

Steinlauf, Nathan T. "The Kiss in Roman Law," *Classical Journal*, XLI (October, 1945), 24.

Tamassia, G. "Osculum interveniens: Contributo alla storia dei riti nuziali," *Rivista storica italiana*, II (1885), 241–264.

Thurston, Herbert. "Kiss," *Catholic Encyclopedia*, VIII (New York, 1910), 663–665.

Van de Velde, Th. H. *Ideal Marriage, Its Physiology and Technique*, trans. Stella Browne (New York, 1957 [1962]), pp. 152–161 (on the kiss and love-bite as erotic foreplay).

Weber, Henri. *La création poétique au XVIe siècle en France*, I (Paris, 1956), pp. 369–391.

Wünsche, Auguste. *Der Kuss in Bibel, Talmud und Midrasch*. Breslau, 1911.

Index

Abélard and Héloïse: in Pope's poem, 224–245; in one tomb, 314–315
Acts of Perpetua, 17, 32
Agathon. *See* Plato, distich on
Alexander the Charlatan, 22
Alfonsi, Luigi, 265, 305n12
Allegory, Christian, and pagan myths, 32–33, 281n5. *See also* Song of Songs, Christian interpretations of
Amadeus, Bishop of Lausanne, 72
Amor-amicitia, 100; in *Carmina Burana*, 109; in medieval love poetry, 266–267. *See also* Friendship
Andreas Capellanus, 100–102, 111, 125, 177
Androgyne myth, 182–183, 184, 282n55. *See also* Hermaphrodite
Aquilano, Serafino, 196–198, 228
Aretino, Pietro, 202–203, 206
Ariosto, soul-kiss in *Orlando Furioso*, 198–199
Arnaut, Daniel, 94, 113
Arnaut de Mareuil, 96
Art: Indian, 4; Mexican, 6; medieval, 74–75, 130. *See also* Iconography
Athenagoras, *Plea Regarding Christians*, 29
Aulus Gellius, version of Plato's epigram, 159–160, 164, 198
Avicenna, 263
Aytoun, Sir Robert, 196

Baïf, Jean-Antoine, 220–221
Baiser âcre, in Rousseau, 245–246
Baptism, 18, 294n42
Basium (literary genre), 189
Beatrice: contrasted with Francesca and Guinevere, 156; Dante's desire for B.'s mouth, 156–157, 311n9
Beaumont, Joseph, 338n55
Beauty, ideal: in Ficino, 164; in Castiglione, 176; and *amor casto*, 183
Belleau, Rémy, 220–222
Bembo, Pietro, *Asolani*, 168; as character in *Il Cortegiano*, 176–177
Bernart de Ventadorn, 96, 102, 109n, 113

Bernart Marti, 93, 113
Bernini: sculpture of Saint Theresa, 111, 296n52
Betrayal, kiss of, 275n2, 338n55. *See also* Judas, kiss of
Bethrothal, kiss of, 40, 41
Binsica. See mors osculi
Bion: *Lament for Adonis*, 7, 199
Biondo, Michelangelo, 182
Blake, William, 148
Bliss-kiss rhyme, 229
Boccaccio, on Pyramus and Thisbe, 316n22
Boiardo, *Orlando Innamorato*, 198
Bölsche, Wilhelm, *Love-Life in Nature*, 10
Bonnefon, Jean, 331n8
Bossuet, Jacques Bénigne (Bishop of Meaux), 3, 287n84
Brancusi, Constantin, *Kiss*, 250, 341n9
Breath: concepts of, 4–6, 276n16; as soul or spirit, 15, 45, 57–58, 81, 177, 178, 182, 198, 230, 266, 272–273n12; as divine kiss, 54, 167, 299; as Dove, 257–259. *See also* Holy Spirit
Briffault, Robert, 2, 272n6
Brotherhood, kiss ritual of, 6, 130, 310n6, 343n4. *See also* Friendship
Browning, Robert, 211n
Burton, Robert, *The Anatomy of Melancholy*, 8, 274n21
Byron, George Gordon, Lord, 339n2, 340n4

Camillo, Giulio, 181
Capellanus, Andreas. *See* Andreas Capellanus
Carew, Thomas, 239; and breath, 336n36
Caritas-cupiditas, 143, 156, 260, 261, 262. *See also* Luxury
Carmina Burana, 104–109
Cartwright, William, 240, 337
Castiglione, Baldassare, 8, 175, 184, 199, 227, 274n21
Catharist heresy, 268
Cato, 159